Impact of International Business

The Academy of International Business
Published in Association with the UK & Ireland Chapter of the Academy of International Business

Impact of International Business

Challenges and Solutions for Policy and Practice

Edited by

Heinz Tüselmann, Stephen Buzdugan, Qi Cao, David Freund and Sougand Golesorkhi

Manchester Metropolitan University Business School, UK

IMPACT OF INTERNATIONAL BUSINESS: CHALLENGES AND SOLUTIONS FOR POLICY AND PRACTICE
Introduction, selection and editorial content © Heinz Tüselmann, Stephen Buzdugan, Qi Cao, David Freund and Sougand Golesorkhi 2016
Individual chapters © their respective authors 2016

First published 2016 by
PALGRAVE MACMILLAN

The authors have asserted their rights to be identified as the authors of this work in accordance with the Copyright, Designs and Patents Act 1988.

Palgrave Macmillan in the UK is an imprint of Macmillan Publishers Limited, registered in England, company number 785998, of Houndmills, Basingstoke, Hampshire RG21 6XS.

Palgrave Macmillan in the US is a division of Nature America, Inc., One New York Plaza, Suite 4500 New York, NY 10004–1562.

Palgrave Macmillan is the global academic imprint of the above companies and has companies and representatives throughout the world.

Hardback ISBN: 978–1–137–56945–5
E-PUB ISBN: 978–1–137–56947–9
E-PDF ISBN: 978–1–137–56946–2
DOI: 10.1057/9781137569462

Distribution in the UK, Europe and the rest of the world is by Palgrave Macmillan®, a division of Macmillan Publishers Limited, registered in England, company number 785998, of Houndmills, Basingstoke, Hampshire RG21 6XS.

Library of Congress Cataloging-in-Publication Data

Names: Tüselmann, Heinz-Josef, editor.

Title: Impact of international business : challenges and solutions for policy and practice / Heinz Tüselmann, Stephen Buzdugan, Qi Cao, David Freund, Sougand Golesorkhi, [editors].

Description: Houndmills, Basingstoke, Hampshire ; New York, NY : Palgrave Macmillan, 2016. | Includes bibliographical references and index.

Identifiers: LCCN 2015033230 | ISBN 9781137569455 (hardback)

Subjects: LCSH: International business enterprises. | International trade. | International economic relations.

Classification: LCC HD2755.5 .I457 2016 | DDC 338.8/8—dc23

LC record available at http://lccn.loc.gov/2015033230

A catalog record for this book is available from the Library of Congress

A catalogue record for this book is available from the British Library.

In Memory of Professor James Taggart

This book is dedicated to the memory of Professor James Taggart, who sadly died in 2014. He was a leading international business academic, businessman and lifetime believer in Scottish independence. His main contributions to the international business field relate to the strategies and strategy shifts of multinational subsidiaries and headquarters/subsidiary relationships, and the international management of technology. James was also a previous Chair of the Academy of International Business UK Chapter.

Contents

List of Figures

List of Tables

Preface

The Centre for International Business & Innovation (CIBI) at Manchester Metropolitan University hosted the 42nd Annual Conference of the Academy of International Business (AIB) UK & Ireland Chapter on 16–18 April 2015. This conference met at an opportune time to consider the relevance and impact of international business (IB) research for policy and practice, in light of recent challenges faced by the international economy, international organisations, governments and firms. This book contains a selection of the best papers presented at the conference under its theme, 'International Business Research: For the Bookshelf or the Boardroom and Corridors of Power?'

The conference location was an ideal backdrop to the theme of the conference. Manchester is the birthplace of the industrial revolution, free trade, the computer and the women's suffrage. Karl Marx and Friedrich Engels began to write the Communist Manifesto at Chetham's Library, the oldest public library in the English-speaking world. Manchester is also a prime example of a major international city that has transformed itself from an industrial city dependent on manufacturing to a thriving and diverse multicultural, modern, knowledge-based city, which is among the top ten European locations for academia, science and business, and the home of regional and national headquarters of major multinational companies.

Reflecting the theme of the conference, high-profile keynote speakers from the research user communities addressed the relevance of international business research for their work, programmes and policies, and highlighted topics and challenges that require answers and solutions by the IB community. This opened up subsequent avenues for IB research to better inform and support their policy responses and initiatives. Keynote speakers included Dr Ulrich Hoppe, Director General of the German–British Chamber of Industry & Commerce; Ms Penny Fowler, Head of the Private Sector Team at Oxfam GB; and Dr Michael Gestrin, Senior Economist at the OECD.

In light of the untimely passing of Professor Alan Rugman, there was a special panel session to honour his contributions to the field of IB. Professor Rugman was one of the 'founding fathers' of the field of IB, a worldwide renowned leading IB scholar, a dedicated mentor to early career researchers and doctoral students and a strong supporter of the AIB UK & Ireland annual conferences. The Alan Rugman Memorial Session Panelists were Professor Peter J. Buckley OBE, University of Leeds, Professor Mark Casson, University of Reading, Professor Alain Verbeke, University of Calgary, Dr Michael Gestrin, OECD and Dr Jing Li, Simon Fraser University.

The AIB UK & Ireland Chapter was delighted to award the inaugural John Dunning Award for Lifetime Achievement to Professor Stephen Young, Emeritus Professor of International Business at Glasgow University. The prize, presented during the conference gala dinner, was awarded in recognition of his contributions to the field of IB, to the growth of the next generation of IB researchers and to the AIB UK & Ireland Chapter. His passion for, and support and guidance of, doctoral students and early career researchers has made a major contribution to the development of the next generation of IB researchers and thus to safeguarding the long-term well-being of IB as a subject area. He is a founder and previous chair of the AIB UK Chapter and has remained a strong supporter and friend of the Chapter.

The 42nd Annual Conference attracted over 200 delegates from over 20 countries, including countries in Europe, South America, the Middle East, Africa, North America, Australia, China, India and beyond. The exploration of the relevance and impact of IB research in the research user communities, together with the high standards of papers and discussions in the doctoral colloquium, plenary and paper sessions, provided much stimulating food for thought – as did the special tracks that linked IB research with economic geography, comparative institutionalism and international marketing strategies of emerging country firms.

The work at the annual conference, which is reflected in the chapters in this book, signifies the commitment of the Chapter to promote and develop IB research and its application in the United Kingdom, Ireland and beyond. The AIB UK & Ireland Chapter is the main forum and leading association of scholars and specialists in the field of international business and international management in the United Kingdom and Ireland, and its federated position within the wider Academy of International Business links to work advancing IB worldwide. The Chapter organises annual conferences, special seminars and events and provides resources and information to advance the quantity and quality of IB research. Please visit our website (http://www.aib-uki.org) to explore the work of the Chapter and find out how to become involved in its work.

Heinz Tüselmann
Chair, Academy of International Business
UK and Ireland Chapter

Acknowledgements

Many thanks to the Centre for International Business & Innovation (CIBI) and the Manchester Metropolitan University Business School for hosting the 42nd Annual Conference of the Academy of International Business UK & Ireland Chapter. Thank you to Kirti Mistry, Gary Lindsay, Emma Mawby, Gary Shaw and Emily Gilhooley for their sterling organisational and administrative support of the conference, as well as to the doctoral students of Manchester Metropolitan University, Chris Kramer, Kate McLoughlin and Ahmad Abu-Arja for their help and support during the conference. Thanks to the doctoral convenor, Dr Margaret Fletcher, University of Glasgow, and Jane Brittin, for organising the doctoral colloquium. A special thanks to the reviewers, panelists and session chairs.

Notes on Contributors

Erkko Autio is Professor of Entrepreneurship and Chair of Technology Venturing at Imperial College London Business School, UK. He is also co-founder of the Global Entrepreneurship and Development Institute and co-author of the *Global Entrepreneurship and Development Index*. His current research interests are in entrepreneurship and entrepreneurship policy, innovation ecosystems, innovation momentum strategies, business model innovation and innovation from Big Science. Following his doctorate at Helsinki University of Technology (HUT), he held a number of academic roles, including director of the Institute of Strategy and International Business at HUT in 1999, visiting professor at CERN in 2001 and professor at HEC Université de Lausanne in 2003, before taking up his current position at Imperial College in 2006.

Kristin Brandl is Lecturer in International Business at Henley Business School, the University of Reading, UK. She holds an MSc in International Business and Trade from the School of Business, Economics and Law, the University of Gothenburg, and a PhD from Copenhagen Business School, Denmark. She was a visiting researcher at the Fox School of Business, Temple University and Said Business School, the University of Oxford. Her research has been nominated for awards at AIB and AOM and focuses on knowledge-intensive and value-adding services in an international and especially emerging market context.

Stephen Buzdugan is Senior Lecturer in International Political Economy in the Department of Management at the Manchester Metropolitan University Business School, UK. He holds an MA in Development Studies and a PhD in International Politics from the University of Manchester and leads undergraduate and postgraduate teaching modules that combine the fields of international business and international political economy. His current research and writings are in the areas of the politics of development, the global governance of foreign direct investment and the political origins of the current stalemate in the multilateral system.

Qi Cao is a research associate in the Management Department, Manchester Metropolitan University (MMU), UK. Before joining MMU, Qi completed his PhD at Innovation and Entrepreneurship Group, Imperial College Business School. His PhD research explores empirical evidence of entrepreneurial firm internationalisation antecedent and outcomes. His main research areas are internationalisation of small- and medium-sized companies, employment relations and HRM in foreign-owned firms, and EU SME market exploration strategy. He also holds an MSc from the Imperial College and a BSc in Economics from the University of International Business and Economics in Beijing.

Stephen Chen is Professor of International Business, University of Newcastle, Australia. He holds a BSc from King's College, London, an MBA from Cranfield School of Management and a PhD in Management from Imperial College, London. Previously he has also held academic positions at City University Business School (now Cass Business School), Manchester Business School, Henley Management College, Open University (UK), UCLA, Australian National University and Macquarie University. His research interests include the performance benefits of internationalisation by firms, international alliances and offshoring by firms.

Paola Criscuolo is Associate Professor of Innovation Management at Imperial College Business School, UK. She holds a PhD in the economics of innovation and technological change from Maastricht University. Her research interests include knowledge transfer and innovation at the firm and individual levels.

Izzet Darendeli is an assistant professor in the College of Business and Economics, California State University, East Bay (CSUEB). He holds a BA in Management, an MSc in International Affairs and Public Policy Management from Bilkent University, Turkey, and a PhD in Strategic Management from Fox School of Business, Temple University. Before pursuing his PhD, he worked for TTNET/Turk Telekom Turkey as project specialist and the Turkish Ministry of Transportation as assistant European Union expert. His research interests are institutional change, innovation and ownership with a focus on emerging country multinationals.

William Y. Degbey is a researcher and doctoral candidate in International Business at the Turku School of Economics, Finland. He works in the 'Value Creation in International Growth' M&A project, funded by the Academy of Finland. His research interest is in mergers and acquisitions and their effect on B2B relationships and networks. His articles have been published in the *Industrial Marketing Management, The International Journal of Human Resource Management* (forthcoming), *Management Research Review* (forthcoming), *Journal of Business and Industrial Marketing* and other journals. He serves as a reviewer for *Management Research Review,* and was also recently invited to be a reviewer for *Industrial Marketing Management.*

Pavlos Dimitratos is Professor of International Business at the Adam Smith Business School of the University of Glasgow, UK. His research interests include MNE subsidiary activities, SME internationalisation and international entrepreneurship. His articles have appeared in journals such as the *British Journal of Management, Business History, Entrepreneurship and Regional Development,*

Entrepreneurship Theory and Practice, Environment and Planning, International Business Review, International Journal of Human Resource Management, International Small Business Journal, Journal of Business Ethics, Journal of Business Research, Journal of Management Studies, Journal of Small Business Management, Journal of World Business, Long Range Planning, Management International Review and *Strategic Entrepreneurship Journal.*

Margaret Fletcher is a lecturer at the Adam Smith Business School, University of Glasgow, UK. Her research interests include small-firm internationalisation, international entrepreneurship, small-firm policy, financing of small firms and longitudinal study of internationalising firms in Scotland. Her articles have appeared in the *International Business Review, International Small Business Journal, Journal of International Marketing, International Journal of Entrepreneurial Behaviour and Research, Journal of Small Business and Enterprise Development, Journal of European Industrial Training* and *Venture Capital.*

David Freund is Senior Lecturer in Strategy and International Business at Manchester Metropolitan University Business School, UK. He holds a PhD from Manchester Metropolitan University. He was a visiting researcher at the European University Viadrina, Frankfurt (Oder), Germany. His research interests include the internationalisation and foreign market entry strategies of high-tech SMEs, the asset-exploiting and asset-augmenting properties of FDI undertaken by high-tech SMEs and related location factors in home and host countries. His current work focuses on innovation and policy initiatives in the context of high-tech SME internationalisation.

Sougand Golesorkhi is Senior Lecturer in International Business at the Manchester Metropolitan University Business School, UK. Her academic research includes determinants of entry-mode strategy of multinational enterprises and impact of internationalisation on performance of microfinance institutions. Her articles have appeared in *International Business Review and Long Range Planning, Research in International Business* and *Finance and Strategic Change.* She holds a PhD in International Business and Finance from the University of Manchester.

Yoo Jung Ha is Lecturer in International Business at the York Management School, University of York, UK. She holds a PhD from the University of Manchester and an MPhil from the University of Oxford. Her research interests include technology spillovers, the impact of activities by multinational enterprises on host countries and innovation strategy at the subsidiary level. Her articles have appeared in *International Business Review* and *Asian Business & Management.*

Robert D. Hamilton III is Professor of Strategic Management at the Fox School of Business at Temple University, US. His academic research has focused on firm capabilities, industry competitive interaction and the control of multi-national enterprises. He is the author of more than 30 articles in management journals and has presented more than 35 conference papers. He serves on the editorial board of *Journal of International Management*. Rob's academic training includes a Bachelor's from Cornell University, an MBA from the Darden School of Business at the University of Virginia and a PhD from the Kellogg School of Management at Northwestern University.

Melanie E. Hassett (DSc) is a post-doc researcher in International Business at the Turku School of Economics, Finland. She is working in two mergers and acquisitions (M&A)–related research projects: one is funded by the Academy of Finland and titled 'Value Creation in International Growth', and another is funded by the Finnish Funding Agency for Innovation and titled 'Emotions in Mergers and Acquisitions'. Her research interest lies in the cross-border M&A, particularly the sociocultural integration. She has written a number articles on M&As, and she has also co-edited the *Handbook on Longitudinal Research Methods in Organization and Business Studies*.

Igor Kalinic is a policy officer, European Commission. Previously he was an assistant professor at the University of Groningen, the Netherlands. He holds a PhD in Industrial Engineering and Management from the University of Padova, Italy with a focus on International Entrepreneurship. He has been a visiting scholar at King's College London, UK, at Darden School of Business, University of Virginia, US and more recently at the University of Uppsala, Sweden and Turku School of Economics, Finland. Before moving to the Netherlands, he also has been active in industry. His latest research interests are related to the SMEs' internationalisation, entrepreneurial decision-making and the impact of industrial policies.

Mari Ketolainen is a researcher at the Turku School of Economics, University of Turku, Finland. She holds an MSc in International Business and Global Innovation Management from Turku School of Economics. Her major research interests are capability development, knowledge-intensive firms and entrepreneurial internationalisation.

Olli Kuivalainen is Professor of International Marketing and Entrepreneurship in the School of Business at Lappeenranta University of Technology (LUT), Finland. He holds a DSc in Economics. His expertise covers broad areas of international business, marketing, entrepreneurship and technology management and their interfaces. His articles have appeared in journals such as *Journal of World Business, Journal of International Marketing, Technovation, International Marketing Review, International Business Review, International Journal of Production Economics* and *Journal of International Entrepreneurship*, among others.

Yusuf Kurt is a PhD candidate in International Business and member of the Centre for Comparative and International Business Research (CIBER) group at Manchester Business School, UK. He holds an MSc in Management from Leeds University Business School. His current research interests include investigating the role of spiritually based networks in firm internationalisation, social network analysis and emerging markets.

Jorma Larimo is Professor of International Marketing at the Faculty of Business Studies, University of Vaasa, Finland. He is also Director of the Finnish Doctoral Program in International Business. His main research areas include internationalisation of small- and medium-sized firms, firms' foreign direct investment strategies and performance, as well as entry and marketing strategies in emerging markets. He is an active member of several associations and his research has appeared, for example, in *Journal of Business Research, Journal of International Business Studies, International Business Research* and *Management International Review.*

Dimitris Manolopoulos is Assistant Professor of International Business in the Department of Business Administration, Athens University of Economics and Business, Greece. His research interests include international business, management and strategy, as well as human resources and technology management. His research has appeared in several international peer-reviewed journals, including *Management International Review, International Business Review, Journal of International Management, Employee Relations* and *International Journal of Human Resource Management*, among others.

Ram Mudambi is the Frank M. Speakman Professor of Strategy and Perelman Senior Research Fellow at the Fox School of Business, Temple University, US. He holds an MSc in Economics from the London School of Economics and a PhD from Cornell University. He is a fellow of the AIB, has served as an associate editor of the *GSJ* (2010–2013) and is an area editor at *JIBS* (2013–2016). His work has appeared in the *Journal of Political Economy*, the *Journal of Economic Geography*, the *Strategic Management Journal* and *JIBS*, among others. He serves on the editorial boards of numerous journals.

Huu Le Nguyen is an sssistant professor in the Department of Marketing, University of Vaasa, Finland, and a visiting lecturer at Hanken School of Economics. His research interests are international joint venture strategies, psychological traits of entrepreneurs and their international strategies, entry mode choice and strategies and performance of firms in recession. He has written articles that have appeared in *Journal of General Management, Baltic Journal of Management, Transnational Management Journal* and chapters in several international books. He has also served as ad hoc reviewer for different international journals.

Quyen T.K. Nguyen is Lecturer in International Business and Strategy at Henley Business School, International Business and Strategy, the University of Reading, UK. Her research focuses on multinational subsidiary strategy and subsidiary performance, assessing foreign subsidiary performance, and multinational subsidiary and development. She holds a PhD from the University of Reading in July. Her articles have appeared in leading peer-reviewed journals; she has also contributed chapters to edited volumes. Before joining academia, she had 13 years of professional and managerial experience in accounting, finance, and business administration. She worked for German, US, and New Zealand multinational subsidiaries in the ASEAN region, and in Canada.

Niina Nummela is Professor of International Business in the Turku School of Economics at the University of Turku, Finland. Her areas of expertise include international entrepreneurship, cross-border acquisitions, and research methods. She has written widely in academic journals, including the *International Business Review, Journal of World Business, Management International Review, Industrial Marketing Management, European Journal of Marketing*, and *International Small Business Journal*, among others. She has also contributed to several internationally published books, and edited a book for Routledge (Taylor & Francis Group), *International Growth of Small and Medium Enterprises*.

Kaisu Puumalainen is Professor of Technology Research in the School of Business at Lappeenranta University of Technology, Finland. Her areas of research interest include entrepreneurship, innovation, strategic orientations, sustainability and internationalisation. She has written more than 50 articles on these issues in *Journal of the Academy of Marketing Science, International Journal of Research in Marketing, International Business Review, European Journal of Marketing*, and *Technovation*, among others.

Sami Saarenketo is Professor of International Marketing in the School of Business, Lappeenranta University of Technology, Finland. His primary areas of research interest are international marketing and entrepreneurship in technology-based small firms. He has written on these issues in *Journal of World Business, International Business Review, Management International Review, European Business Review, European Journal of Marketing*, and *Journal of International Entrepreneurship*, among others.

Natalya Victor Smith is a freelance researcher and a visiting scholar at the University of Essex, UK. She holds a BSc in Economics from Moscow State University, Russia; an MSc in International Business and a PhD in Management from Aston University, UK. She worked at Aston, Liverpool and Leicester universities in the United Kingdom. Her research is in international business (political) economics and innovation with a focus on institutions. She has worked on various economic issues in Russia. She is co-author of chapters in books and articles in academic journals, including *Europe–Asia Studies* and the *Journal of East–West Business* and has presented in AIB and AIB-UKI conferences.

Emmanouil Sofikitis is a doctoral candidate in the Department of Management Science and Technology (DMST) at the Athens University of Business and Economics, Greece. His doctoral thesis focuses on the foreign operation modes of small- and medium-sized enterprises. His research interests include international business, management and strategy. His work has been presented in several international business conferences and has been published in the *Personnel Review*, an ABS-listed business journal.

Lasse Torkkeli is a post-doctoral researcher in the School of Business, Lappeenranta University of Technology, Finland. His PhD dissertation, completed in 2013, examined the concept of network competence in internationally operating small- and medium-sized enterprises (SMEs), in particular its development and influence on internationalisation outcomes of Finnish and Russian SMEs. His current research interests relate to SME internationalisation, dynamic capabilities in the context of international business, business networks and networking, and cultural aspects in international business, particularly in business-to-business interaction. His articles have appeared in journals, including the *Journal of International Entrepreneurship* and in the *European Management Journal*.

Heinz Tüselmann is Professor of International Business and Director of the Centre for International Business and Innovation (CIBI) at Manchester Metropolitan University, UK. He is Chair of the Academy of International Business UK & Ireland Chapter, and Chair of the Scientific Committee of the Academic Journal Guide of the Association of Business Schools (ABS). He was a member of the international advisory committee to the Economic and Social Research Council (ESRC). His research interests include labour relations in MNCs, investment for sustainable development and subsidiary development and performance. His research has appeared in, among others, *Journal of World Business, Regional Studies* and *Environment and Planning C: Government and Policy*.

Yi Wang is Assistant Professor of International Marketing in the Department of Marketing, University of Vaasa, Finland. His research interests focus on FDI entry strategies and survival/performance of foreign subsidiaries operating in transition economies. He has presented his research papers several times in conferences such as the Academy of International Business, the European International Business Academy, and the World Business Congress. His research articles have appeared in *Journal of Global Marketing* and in several international books as book chapters.

Mo Yamin is Professor of International Business at Manchester Business School, UK. His research focuses on the organisational and managerial aspects of the multinational enterprise. He holds a PhD in Economics from the University of Manchester. His articles have appeared in international business and international marketing journals such as *International Business Review, Journal of International Management, International Marketing Review, Journal of World Business, Critical Perspectives of International Business* and *Advances in Consumer Research*.

Stephen Young is Emeritus Professor at the University of Glasgow, UK. His research and consulting expertise concerns the internationalisation of the firm, and the management, economic development and public policy dimensions of MNE subsidiaries. Beginning his career as an economist with the government of Tanzania, he then became head of international economics with a UK food organisation. Besides UK academic posts, he has held visiting positions at three universities in the United States, and has his work published widely, with 160 outputs. In 2015 he received the inaugural John Dunning Lifetime Achievement Award at the AIB UKI Conference at Manchester Metropolitan University.

Introduction: Impact of International Business: Challenges and Solutions for Policy and Practice

Heinz Tüselmann, Stephen Buzdugan, Qi Cao, David Freund and Sougand Golesorkhi

Over the last several decades the international operations and activities of firms have evolved immeasurably in scale, scope, reach and form. In addition to, inter alia, the heightening of complex international interconnectivity between firms, institutions and economies at national and sub-national levels, new or nontraditional sources of international investment and trade, such as state-owned multinational enterprises (MNEs) and small and medium-sized enterprises (SMEs), are becoming increasingly important. At the same time, the international community is confronted with a new set of challenges, the scale and complexity of which are virtually unprecedented, such as ongoing economic crisis with prolonged and lacklustre return to growth and profitability in the aftermath of the worst financial crisis since the Great Depression; unsustainable economic and social developments; and heightened security threats. The impact of these challenges on firms, governments, international organisations and civil society, invites the research community to intensify its efforts to supply useful insights, answers and innovative ideas.

Research in the field of international business (IB) over the past decade or so would appear to offer a wealth of guidance on these issues. Questions nevertheless remain. Notably, how relevant has IB research been to decision makers in the 'boardroom' and 'corridors of power'? Has research in this discipline been overly isolated from practical applications, and, if so, how can it be orientated towards greater use outside the 'ivory tower' to offer solutions for 'real world' problems? Indeed, the question of relevance has become a general concern in business and management research, reflected inter alia by the current international demand of research-funding councils, national research assessment exercises and business school accreditation bodies to assess the impact and benefit of research beyond academia.

These issues relate directly to the wider controversy on the 'rigour–relevance gap' in management research. On the one hand, there is the assertion that the

1

twin requirement for academic rigour and practical relevance is fundamentally unbridgeable because researchers and research users inhabit separate social systems (Kieser and Leiner, 2009). On the other hand, there are numerous counter-illustrations where current management and business research generates knowledge that is both socially useful and academically rigorous, as well as being of practical relevance to managers of firms and organisations and/or policymakers in government (Hodgkinson and Rousseau, 2009). Notwithstanding, there are heightened demands for IB research to provide guidance to decision makers on how to solve actual problems faced by the international business community.

Current IB research has been criticised for not addressing sufficiently those issues that are relevant and interesting for practitioners today, and despite being theoretically and empirically relevant, not explaining properly the practical relevance for managers and government officials (Cuervo-Cazurra et al., 2013; Oesterle and Wolf, 2011). For IB research to provide answers to current challenges and problems faced by the international community and to bridge the gap between academic rigour and relevance for the research user communities, this may require among other things: (1) stronger links between academic research and practice and policy, and involvement of stakeholders in the conceptual phase of research projects; (2) stronger links to major international and national policy programmes and initiatives (e.g. *EU 2020 Entrepreneurship Action Plan* [European Commission, 2013], *New High-Tech Strategy – Innovations for Germany* [Federal Ministry for Economic Affairs, 2014], *Investment for Development* [UNCTAD, 2014]); (3) questioning of conventional wisdom and re-consideration of classical IB issues; (4) a greater emphasis of variables that can be influenced by practitioners; (5) locating the focus on particular questions within the context of the 'bigger picture'; (6) a greater willingness of IB researchers to take a stance on bigger politically sensitive issues (e.g. discrimination, ethics, human rights, poverty alleviation issues); (7) more systematic multidisciplinary approaches to offer solutions that reflect the multi-faceted and complex issues we face at sub-national, national, regional, bilateral and multilateral levels, necessitating among other things that IB research draw upon and incorporate related disciplines (e.g. economic geography, institutionalism, entrepreneurship, and international political economy). For a detailed discussion see e.g. Oesterle and Wolf, 2011; Schmid 2010; UNCTAD, 2014. Importantly, IB research needs to move beyond operating in 'response mode' in order to inform and provide guidance to management and policymakers on current issues and problems, to also drive the future agendas in the research user communities.

The aim of this book is to address the issues and challenges raised above and to provide both academically rigorous as well as practical relevant contributions on a number of important IB issues. This volume contains selected papers with particular relevance to the theme *International Business Research: For the bookshelf or the boardroom and corridors of power?* of the 42nd Academy of International Business (UK & Ireland Chapter) Conference, held at Manchester Metropolitan University in April 2015. As well as advancing IB research and providing fresh empirical and conceptual insights, a unifying attribute of all chapters in this book is their relevance for policy and practice. This book provides exemplars of successful collaborative research between academia and research users that bridge the rigour–relevance gap. It contains chapters that revisit classical IB issues in light of new realities, advance theoretical and conceptual issues of importance for both academia and practice, tackle current issues and problems faced by firms and organisations, and incorporate insights of other related disciplines into IB research in search of solutions in a complex and multi-faceted contemporary IB context.

Part 1: Impact of locations, institutions and governments

Papers in this part focus on the importance and impact of national and regional location aspects, institutional developments and governance structures on IB activities.

In Chapter 1, Chen examines the effects of geographic, institutional and linguistic regions on return on investment in foreign subsidiaries of UK multinational enterprises (MNEs) using a large panel dataset consisting of 55,726 subsidiaries over the period 1996–2005. The results show significant regional differences in the profitability of foreign direct investment (FDI) locations. For UK firms, FDI into EU member countries is likely to be more profitable compared to FDI into other countries. Secondly, FDI in the United States, Canada, Australia and New Zealand is more profitable compared with the rest of the world, excluding Europe. Thirdly, the effect of EU membership on subsidiary performance is greater than the effect of geographic distance, which in turn is greater than the effect of English language.

In Chapter 2, Smith examines the regional level impact of corruption and crime on multinational and domestic firms. She investigates the assumptions that investment should be unprofitable in the environments with 'bad institutions': foreign firms are likely to avoid places where negative growth of domestic firms is also expected. Using data of regions in Russia in 1995–2011, this chapter investigates these assumptions by quantifying the relationship between MNEs and domestic firms SMEs on the one hand, and corruption and crime on the other. While a significantly negative impact of corruption on MNEs is detected, such an impact is positive in the case of SMEs. When it comes to crime, however, despite the adverse effect of the current levels on foreign and domestic businesses, the (one year) lagged effect is positive. Smith suggests that there may be 'an adjustment' mechanism that kicks in as businesses 'settle' across the country – that is, as they get familiar with the environment they begin to take advantage of 'bad institutions'.

In Chapter 3 Nguyen examines the determinants of reinvested earnings of the multinational subsidiary. This chapter draws upon internalisation theory to develop hypotheses and empirically test them using original primary survey data from British multinational subsidiaries in six emerging economies in the ASEAN region. This study provides three new findings that have important implications for subsidiary managers and policymakers. First, reinvested earnings are a type of firm-specific advantage (FSA) in financial management of the subsidiary. Second, the perceptions and assessment on host country location factors by subsidiary managers influence reinvestment decisions. The two most important location variables are access to customers and the reliability and quality of local infrastructures. Third, the duration of operation of the subsidiary has a significant positive effect on reinvested earnings.

In Chapter 4 Brandl, Darendeli, Hamilton and Mudambi investigate the impact of actors, such as foreign MNEs and local firms, and the influence of time on global intellectual property (IP) protection standards exhibiting institutional change processes in developing country contexts. As such, 60 developing countries that became part of the Trade Related Intellectual Property Standards (TRIPS) agreement by the World Trade Organization (WTO) and their compliance with IP protection standards are studied. The authors argue and show that pressures by foreign MNEs and domestic firms influence institutional change processes and the pace of these processes. Countries with a high composition of foreign MNEs comply much faster to TRIPS than countries with a high composition of domestic firms. This study highlights the benefits for policy and practice from detailed insights on actors that impact policies and how their pressures impact institutional changes.

Part 2: International entrepreneurship and innovation: contexts and outcomes

Papers in this part examine important international entrepreneurship issues and outcomes in the context of high-tech industries and business strategies, as well as the impact of FDI on innovation in domestic firms, including SMEs.

In Chapter 5 Ketolainen, Nummela and Kalinic develop the concept of affordable loss in the context of decision-making in entrepreneurial internationalisation and offer both an in-depth conceptual analysis and practical application in the biotechnology sector. Their findings highlight that affordable loss seems to be connected to short-term, operative decisions, but is less applicable for long-term, strategic decisions. Furthermore, the use of the affordable loss principle appears to be more common in decisions involving a single decision maker than in shared decision-making. However, their findings challenge the premise of effectuation theory, as affordable loss and expected reward do not seem to present alternative elements when viewing decision-making in the context of entrepreneurial internationalisation. Instead, they are used in parallel, indicating that making a single decision may include the use of both causation and effectuation-based logic.

In Chapter 6 Torkkeli, Saarenketo, Kuivalainen and Puumalainen examine the influence of business strategies in internationalisation outcomes of SMEs. They highlight that business strategies focused on unique products development and quality have been found to determine the international success of rapidly internationalising firms known as 'born-globals'. However, it remains unclear if these strategies are also applicable in the context of internationalising SMEs in general. They apply a cross-sectional sample of 119 Finnish SMEs and examine how the two business strategies determine internationalisation outcomes among SMEs. The main findings are: (1) unique products development is a differentiating factor between born-globals and other SMEs, and is linked to increased turnover growth at the start of internationalisation; (2) the quality focus has no such effects; and (3) neither of the focal strategies is linked to increased international performance.

In Chapter 7 Ha examines the extent to which the impact of FDI on indigenous firms' innovation varies according to environmental features such as levels of dynamism. The study explores unobserved contingency factors in terms of indigenous firms' task environments to propose the specific conditions under which the impact of FDI on indigenous firms is likely to be positive. It focusses on the influence of environmental dynamism. Based on Korean Innovation Survey data, Ha shows that indigenous firms' innovation performance is likely to be affected positively by horizontal FDI spillovers in a stable environment and by backward FDI spillovers in a dynamic environment. This study extends recent research by showing how the impact of FDI depends on dynamic features of the environmental setting in the host country.

Part 3: Strategy and management: ownership modes, networks and people

The papers in this part consider strategy and management issues at country, industry and firm level with particular reference to modes of ownership, value creation and networks and human resource management issues.

In Chapter 8 Wang, Larimo and Nguyen analyse the determinants of the ownership mode strategies of multinationals in China at three levels: country, industry and firm levels. Their study is based on a sample of 402 manufacturing investments made by Nordic firms in China from 1987 to 2012. The findings indicate that the ownership mode strategy of Nordic firms is determined by factors at multiple levels. Furthermore, country-specific determinants (regional institutional advancement) significantly interact with firm-level variables (international experience and degree of product diversification). They highlight the implications of their findings for managers of firms originating from small open economies.

In Chapter 9 Degbey and Hassett examine the issue of creating value in cross-border merger and acquisitions (M&As) through strategic networks. Their study views M&As in their context, that is, the network in which the focal firms are embedded. The purpose of this chapter is: first, to study a focal firm's network position in the external environment of the industry; and, second, to analyse how the dissolution of acquired firm customers' network may influence a focal actor's ability to reduce its excess capacity. The empirical research is based on a case study of a European stainless steel company. The main findings suggest that the embeddedness of a focal actor in networks of external relationships with other actors may help shape its network position and network structure for superior value creation. Degbey and Hassett suggest that business relations are a strong antecedent for gaining preferred network position, and that the dissolution of acquired firm's customer networks may impact the acquirer's ability to reduce its excess capacity.

In Chapter 10 Sofikitis, Manolopoulos and Dimitratos shed light on determinants of professional career paths in MNC subsidiaries. Contemporary theoretical approaches on career choice have gained extensive credence in the career research stream. However, earlier contributions that favour more traditional career shapes have lately been revisited. Their study considers this career choice theme in the context of knowledge professionals' career preferences over a single or a hybrid career path. Research evidence based on a large-scale study of 921 professionals employed in 70 R&D units of MNC subsidiaries in Greece suggests that the type of R&D unit, employee age and marital status stand out as significant predictors of knowledge professionals' career choice over either a single or a hybrid path.

Part 4: Rigour and relevance: some roadmaps for internationalisation research

Papers in this part provide exemplars of successful engaged scholarship research in bridging rigour and relevance in IB research as well as conceptual papers addressing future avenues for academic research that addresses issues that are relevant and useful for practitioners.

In Chapter 11 Fletcher, Young and Dimitratos address calls for more policy-relevant academic research. They utilise an engaged scholarship approach to study an innovative evaluation and research (E&R) study of the Scottish Enterprise Global Companies Development Programme (GCDP). The latter was a public policy initiative to support the internationalisation of small- and medium-sized enterprises (SMEs) in Scotland. The study was undertaken by academics and included a combined formal evaluation and research study; a follow-up workshop and group interviews; and policy-maker reflections. The findings suggest that researchers and policymakers produced excellent results when they worked cooperatively over a longtime period, so that stakeholder groups acquired ownership of the outputs of their cooperation.

In Chapter 12 Cao, Criscuolo and Erkko develop a roadmap of future research areas for the exploration of the mechanisms that influence the SME internationalisation process and subsequent firm performance. They argue that small and medium-sized enterprises (SMEs) internationalisation is an entrepreneurial strategy that shapes these companies' future business development. The process of internalisation allows SMEs to survive and thrive through deployment of unique resources and the building of local capabilities. Resource elements, strategic dispositions and firm growth strategy constitute important determinants of the SME internationalisation process and subsequent firm performance. This chapter provides a comprehensive examination of the research in this stream and, more importantly, identifies the inadequate theoretical arguments and empirical evidences that need to be addressed to advance the understanding of the field. Based on their findings, they develop a roadmap of future research in this area.

In Chapter 13 Yamin and Kurt demonstrate how specific features of social network analysis (SNA) can enhance our understanding on firm internationalisation, particularly in the context of the liability of outsidership (LOO) perspective. The arguments are developed with specific reference to the revised Uppsala model in which internationalisation is regarded as overcoming LOO and building insidership in relevant networks. SNA is proposed as an analytical research tool through which structural and positional attributes of networks, which affect the process of overcoming LOO, can be deeply and systematically investigated. The chapter contributes to the greater appreciation of the value of SNA in deepening our knowledge on the process of overcoming LOO in internationalisation research.

Conclusions

While certainly not exhaustive, this book examines various contemporary IB issues from various viewpoints, draws on research conducted in different countries, examines IB issues in both developed and emerging country contexts, offers various theoretical perspectives and different methodologies. It provides both rigorous empirical and conceptual advances and insights that are useful and relevant for managers and policymakers in their search for solutions in face of current challenges posed by the international environment.

References

Cuervo-Cazzura, A., Caligiuri, P., Andersson, U. and Brannen, Y.M. (2013). 'From the editors: How to write articles that are relevant to practice', *Journal of International Business Studies*, 44(3), 285–289.

European Commission (2013). 'Entrepreneurship 2020 Action Plan', http://ec.europa.eu/enterprise/policies/sme/entrepreneurship-2020/index_en.htm.

Federal Ministry for Economic Affairs (2014). 'New High Tech Strategy: Innovation for Germany', http://www.bmwi.de/EN/Topics/Technology/hightech-strategy.html.

Hodgkinson, G.P., and Rousseau, D.M. (2009). 'Bridging the rigour-relevance gap in management research: It's already happening', *Journal of Management Studies*, 46(3), 534–546.

Kieser, A. and Leiner, L. (2009). 'Why the rigour-relevance gap in management research is unbridgeable', *Journal of Management Studies*, 46(3), 516–531.

Oesterle, M.J. and Wolf, J. (2011). '50 years of Management International Review and IB/IM research: An inventory and some suggestions for the field's development', *Management International Review*, 51, 735–754.

Schmid, S. (2010). 'Do we care about relevance in the international business field? On major problems of transferring our research to practice', *ESPC Europe Working Paper 52/2010.*

UNCTAD (2014). *The Global Academic Policy Research Work on Investment for Development*, Geneva: United Nations.

Part I

The Impact of Locations, Institutions and Governments

1
Effects of Geographic, Institutional and Linguistic Regions on FDI Performance

Stephen Chen

Introduction

Whether or not internationalisation benefits firms has been a key question in international business for at least the last 30 or so years (Gomes and Ramaswamy, 1999; Hitt et al., 1997). However, despite the extensive research and attempts to develop a general model explaining the link between internationalisation and performance (e.g. Contractor et al., 2003; Lu and Beamish, 2004), findings between studies are often conflicting. One reason that has been suggested for the conflicting findings is that the performance benefits of internationalisation vary according to the region where the firm internationalises. In several studies, Rugman et al. (Rugman and Oh, 2013; Rugman, 2007; Rugman and Verbeke, 2004; Rugman and Collinson, 2004; Oh and Rugman, 2006; Collinson and Rugman, 2008) have extensively documented how the world's leading MNEs have strong home-regional preferences in their internationalisation strategies. Other researchers (e.g. Oh and Contractor, 2014; Nguyen, 2014; Chen and Tan, 2012; Qian et al., 2008) have shown how the host countries and regions into which firms internationalise may affect the performance benefits firms obtain from internationalising.

However, there are a number of limitations with previous studies. First, some researchers have suggested that the findings of home-region preference are an artefact of how regions have been defined in the study. Different researchers have used different definitions of regions and different ways of classifying firms according to their regional preferences.

Another reason for the conflicting findings is that different studies have used different performance measures. These include a ratio of profits to total assets, to give return on total assets (ROA), or a ratio of profit to total sales, to give return on sales (ROS). Other studies have used market-based measures such as return on equity (Rugman et al., 1985) or Tobin's Q (Lu and Beamish, 2004). A problem with these measures is that they only measure performance at the aggregate firm level. They do not measure performance at the subsidiary level, so it is difficult to distinguish the impact on performance of a particular subsidiary. The aims of this chapter are to address the limitations above. First, it tests the effects of different regions defined according to different criteria. Second, it examines the effects of profitability at subsidiary level rather than firm level.

The remainder of the chapter is organised as follows: first, I provide a review of the theoretical background and literature on FDI and firm performance; second, I describe the data collection, analysis and results of the study; third, I discuss the implications of the results, limitations of the study and possible future directions for research.

Theoretical background

The relationship between internationalisation of firms and firm performance has long been a topic of interest to international business researchers (e.g. Hymer, 1976; Rugman, 1979; Caves, 1982; Gomes and Ramaswamy, 1999). However, despite many years of research, there is no clear consensus about the relationship between internationalisation and performance. Two of the problems that have been highlighted in previous studies are the measures used and the possible effect of additional contingency factors such as the economic, institutional and cultural characteristics of the host country and region.

Host region factors

There are good reasons to believe that subsidiary performance may vary with the regions that the firm enters when internationalising. As shown by Rugman (2000), even among the world's most internationalised companies, most still derive the bulk of their sales in their home region. Other studies have since confirmed the preference of firms to internationalise to countries in their home region (Rugman, 2007; Rugman and Verbeke, 2004; Rugman and Collinson, 2004; Oh and Rugman, 2006; Qian et al., 2008). By definition, home regional markets are geographically closer. This reduces transportation costs. As they are in the same time zone, it is also easier to coordinate activities. Rugman and Verbeke (2004: 13) assert that 'adaptation costs are simply higher in host-region markets than in home-region markets'. Another explanation is suggested by the internationalisation process model (Johanson and Vahlne, 1977) which indicates that firms seek regional markets that are proximate to their current markets because the degree of learning to operate in such markets is lower. Elango and Sethi (2007) proposed that firms face lower risks and incur reduced operational and coordination costs when operations are conducted regionally.

A number of studies have also examined the relationship between regionalisation strategies and performance (Rugman and Oh, 2010; Qian, Peng and Qian, 2008; Banalieva et al., 2012), but results are inconsistent. One criticism that has been levelled against previous studies by some researchers is that there is no consensus on how a region is defined and so the results could simply be an artefact of how different researchers have chosen to define regions and how they classified firms' regional strategies. For instance, in commenting on Rugman's (2000) classification of firms as home-regional, host-regional, bi-regional or global, Oswegowitsch and Sammartino (2008) commented that the classification was very sensitive to the threshold criteria set for different categories and that a minor shift in sales distribution would pull some firms into a different category. Furthermore, they noted that home-regional sales in Rugman's (2000) classification include domestic sales so the results may be distorted by firms that are primarily domestic. Consequently, they suggested that studies of firm-specific internationalisation advantages should exclude domestic sales in order to exclude the effect of advantages in the home country. This was confirmed by Asmussen (2009) who found that much of the regional effect reported by Rugman and Verbeke (2004) is due to a home country effect. There is, therefore, some question in the extant literature about both the most appropriate way to measure regional effect in strategies of firms and the size of the region effect on firm performance. The next section discusses three ways that have been suggested to define regions and the following section explains how the effects due to different definitions of regions were compared in this study.

Geographically defined region

The most common method of defining regions is according to geography. Geographic distance has been long regarded as a barrier of international trade (Deardorff, 1998; Harrigan, 2005). Anderson and Van Wincoop (2004) have comprehensively reviewed trade costs estimated in the literature, and, according to them, the total transport cost for the United States, for example, is estimated to be 21 per cent of the free-on-board (f.o.b) price. In US–Canada trade, the trade cost due to geographic distance is estimated to be 16 per cent of the f.o.b. price. Korinek and Sourdin (2009), using a newly available dataset on maritime transport rates, estimated that trade declines by 6 to 8 per cent with every 10 per cent increase in maritime transport costs (Korinek and Sourdin, 2009). While evidence for effects of geographic distance on internationalisation performance of individual firms is limited (Ellis, 2007), it seems likely that investments in geographically close regions incur the least costs and so, all else being equal, would be expected to generate the greatest profits. Therefore, the first hypothesis tested was as follows:

> *Hypothesis 1:* Internationalisation by UK firms within the geographic region of Europe should lead to greater performance compared with internationalisation outside Europe.

Institutionally defined region

Other researchers have argued in favour of regions based on trading blocs on the basis that firms in the same trading bloc benefit from reduced market entry barriers. Banalieva et al.'s (2012) findings indicate the need for alignment of firm regionalisation strategies with the degree of market integration to explain performance. In the case of the United Kingdom, by virtue of the United Kingdom being a Member State of the European Union (EU), firms from the United Kingdom have access to the world's largest single market of 500 million people. In addition to the benefits from the single market, UK firms benefit more directly in other ways, such as reduced costs of employment, communications, energy, transport and trade. The right of free movement for EU citizens enables UK firms to recruit from a far wider pool. EU competition rules have also kept costs of telecommunications and energy down. A significant benefit for UK exporters is that businesses only have to deal with one set of rules rather than 27 different sets of rules when exporting to or operating in more than one EU Member State. For all the above reasons, membership in the EU should reduce the costs of doing business in the EU for UK firms and make internationalisation within the EU more profitable compared with internationalisation to countries outside the EU. Therefore, the second hypothesis tested was as follows:

> *Hypothesis 2:* Internationalisation by UK firms within the European Union should lead to greater performance compared with internationalisation outside the EU.

Linguistically defined region

In addition to the geographic and institutional factors above, a third factor that has been examined in the literature on firm internationalisation is cultural similarity between the home and host countries. The Uppsala model of internationalisation (Johanson and Vahlne, 1977) proposed that firms internationalise incrementally from 'psychically close' countries to 'psychically distant' countries. This would predict a pattern of internationalisation in which one would find more internationalisation in familiar countries in the first stage and more internationalisation in less familiar countries in the latter stages. There are many dimensions of culture that may influence the ease of internationalisation of firms. However, one dimension that has been highlighted by a number of international business researchers is linguistic similarity. West and Graham (2004) showed that linguistic distance is highly correlated with values-based measures of cultural distance, while Hutchinson (2006) showed that linguistic distance affects trade flows at the country level. For example, Ghemawat (2001: 3) has found that '[all] other things being equal, trade between countries that share a language...will be 3 times greater than between countries without a common language'. Ashkanasy et al. (2002) found that countries in the 'Anglo Cluster' comprising Australia, Canada, England, Ireland, New Zealand, South

Africa, and the United States share many cultural characteristics, such as an individualistic performance orientation, a preference for charismatic inspiration, a participative leadership style and predominantly male orientation, although valuing gender equality. Therefore, based on these studies, the third hypothesis tested was the following:

> *Hypothesis 3:* Internationalisation by UK firms within the English-speaking countries (USA, Canada, Australia and New Zealand) should lead to greater performance compared with internationalisation outside these countries.

Methodology

Sample and data collection

The hypotheses were tested with a sample of UK companies drawn from the Annual Foreign Direct Investment (AFDI) Survey from the UK Office of National Statistics (ONS). The purpose of the annual foreign direct investment (FDI) surveys is to collect financial information on the relationship between UK companies and foreign parents and associates (inward FDI) and between UK companies and foreign subsidiaries, affiliates and branches (outward FDI). The information is primarily required for measuring the UK's balance of payments and international investment position. It covers the investment flows into and out of the direct investment enterprises, the earnings attributable to investors, current remittances (dividends and interest) to and from investors and the overall stock of direct investment at the end of the inquiry period. Data for the banking sector are collected by the Bank of England; data for other sectors are collected by the Office of National Statistics via sample surveys (Gilhooley, 2009).

The AFDI is conducted in two parts: an inward inquiry and an outward inquiry. The inward inquiry concerns the subsidiaries/associates of foreign firms operating in the United Kingdom, while the outward inquiry covers the investment made by UK firms in their overseas operations. This study only examined outward FDI by UK firms. UK firms are asked to provide information on a variety of aspects of their subsidiaries and branches in foreign countries. Notable areas include: country of ownership/investment, profit and loss, earnings, tax credits, sales/purchases of shares/loans, and gains/losses resulting from movements in exchange rates.

The outward AFDI survey includes observations on between 2,388 and 3,302 enterprise groups and between 11,168 and 13,393 subsidiaries per year over the period 1996–2005. However, many firms had to be excluded owing to incomplete information on some items. The final sample amounted to a total of 39,126 subsidiaries and 55,726 subsidiary-year observations over the period 1996–2005. Table 1.1 shows the breakdown of firms and observations in the sample by region and Table 1.2 shows the breakdown by industry.

Table 1.1   Sample by region

Region	No. of firms
Western Europe	17,506
Asia	6,884
North America	4,570
Africa	2,221
Pacific	2,110
South America	1,707
Eastern Europe	1,657
Central America	1,317
Middle East	1,189
Total	39,161

Table 1.2   Sample by industry

Industry	No. of firms	Industry	No. of firms
1 Agriculture	5,118	5 Wholesale	5,531
2 Mining	9,371	6 Transport	5,913
3 Manufacturing	3,946	7 Business Services	6,591
4 Utilities	1,873	8 Other	818
		Total	39,161

Multilevel model

A multilevel, crossed random effects model (Rabe-Hesketh and Skrondal, 2008) was used to test the hypotheses. Multilevel or hierarchical linear models have found widespread application when the data have a nested structure. In our case the subsidiaries are nested both within enterprise groups and host regions/countries; however, an enterprise group can be present in many host countries/regions and subsidiaries within a host region/country can belong to multiple firms. In such a case, a crossed random effects model is required in order to distinguish the region, firm and subsidiary effects (Zaccarin and Rivellini, 2002).

This is represented by the following regression equation:

$$y = \beta_1 + \beta_2 X_1 + \beta_3 X_2 + \beta_4 X_{3\ldots} + \beta_n X_{n-1} + \zeta_{1i} + \zeta_{2j} + \zeta_{3k} + \varepsilon_{ijk}$$

where y is subsidiary/branch performance, β_1 is the intercept, $\beta_{2\ldots n} X_{1\ldots n-1}$ represent the effect of the variables X_1-X_{n-1}, ζ_{1i} is the region effect, ζ_{2j} is the firm effect, ζ_{3k} is the subsidiary effect and ε is the residual.

Variables and measures

Dependent variable

Subsidiary/branch performance was measured by subsidiary/branch profit divided by net book value of the subsidiary/branch. As mentioned above, a common problem in many studies of FDI performance is that they measure performance at the aggregate firm level and they do not measure performance at the subsidiary/branch level so it is difficult to distinguish the specific impacts of foreign investments. As shown by Rugman, Yip and Jayaratne (2008), return on foreign assets (ROFA) provides a much better measure of the strategic performance of foreign subsidiaries in comparison to the traditional metrics of return on total assets (ROA) and the ratio of foreign to total sales or assets (F/T), as it directly measures the return a firm obtains from international investments. This paper makes use of performance data from individual subsidiaries/branches and so enables a more direct measure of returns on a particular foreign investment.

Independent variables

Since the definition of geographic region can vary, the effect of a number of different host regions was tested by including a number of dummy variables, coded as follows:

EU: 1 if the subsidiary located in the European Union; 0 otherwise
EU_NA: 1 if the subsidiary located in Europe or North America; 0 otherwise
EU_NA_PA: 1 if the subsidiary located in Europe, North America or Pacific (Australia or New Zealand); 0 otherwise.
Geographic-Europe: 1 if the subsidiary/branch is located in a country within the geographic continent of Europe; 0 otherwise.
English-speaking: 1 if the subsidiary/branch is located in a country where English is an official language; 0 otherwise.

Control variables

I also controlled for the following factors:

SIZE OF INVESTMENT (LNINVEST): This was measured by the natural logarithm of the net book value of the subsidiary and was used to control for the potential effect of scale economy differences. Logarithmic transformation not only makes the results easy to interpret, because the changes in the logarithm domain represent relative (percentage) changes in the original metric and also makes the distribution of data closer to normality.

INDUSTRY: To control for differences in profitability across industry sectors, I used dummy variables coded according to the industry of the subsidiary.

YEAR: To control for differences in profitability across years, I used dummy variables coded for the year of the observation.

BRANCH: The AFDI survey distinguishes between subsidiaries and branches. This was coded as 1 if it was branch, 0 otherwise.

DIVERSIFICATION: Some subsidiaries operate in a different industry sector from the parent company and this might lead to performance differences, so to control for this I included a dummy variable coded as follows: 1 if the first digit SIC of the industry of the parent company is different from that of the subsidiary; 0 otherwise.

Results

The results show clearly that the performance gains from FDI vary significantly depending on whether internationalisation takes place within the home region or outside the region.

Table 1.3 shows the effect of subsidiary/branch location in the European Union. This confirms that subsidiaries and branches of UK firms which are located in the EU earned significantly higher earnings on investment compared to subsidiaries and branches outside the EU, after controlling for the size of the investment, industry, year, diversification and branch. Earnings in industry seven (business services) and year one (1996) also showed up as significantly higher compared to the rest. Diversification and branch were not significant.

Table 1.4 shows the effect of subsidiary/branch location in Europe or North America. This confirms that subsidiaries that are located in the combined EU–North America region earned significantly higher earnings on investment after controlling for the size of the investment, industry, year, diversification and branch/subsidiary. Earnings in industry seven (business services) and

Table 1.3   Cross effect multilevel regression of return on foreign investment: Europe

	Coef.	Sig.		Coef.	Sig.
EU	0.27318	*	year_1	−0.527	**
lninvestment	−0.1804	****	year_2	−0.3384	
Industry_1	−0.1295		year_3	−0.1387	
Industry_2	−0.6153		year_4	−0.1672	
Industry_3	−0.9141		year_5	−0.1836	
industry_4	−0.9645		Branch	−0.102	
industry_5	−0.8091		Random-effects	Estimate	S.E.
industry_6	−0.502		Geographic Region	.0000386	.0000853
industry_7	−1.0486	*	Firm	.6155782	.1075213
industry_8	−0.8504		Subsidiary	1.873956	.259548
Diversify	−0.0476		Residual	10.65904	.0690627

Notes: * indicates < 0.1, ** indicates < 0.05, *** indicates < 0.01, **** indicates < 0.005.

Table 1.4 Cross effect multilevel regression of return on foreign investment: Europe and North America

	Coef.	Sig.		Coef.	Sig.
EU_NA	0.33573	**	year_1	−0.5294	**
Lninvestment	−0.1889	****	year_2	−0.3383	
industry_1	−0.1		year_3	−0.1378	
industry_2	−0.6105		year_4	−0.166	
industry_3	−0.9149		year_5	−0.1806	
industry_4	−0.9573		Branch	−0.0882	
industry_5	−0.802		Constant	1.67695	***
industry_6	−0.4823		Random-effects	Estimate	S.E.
industry_7	−1.0489	*	Geographic Region	9.35e-07	.0000802
industry_8	−0.8557		Firm	.6234491	.1068631
Diversify	−0.0556		Subsidiary	1.869732	.2601175
			Residual	10.65903	.0690649

Notes: * indicates < 0.1, ** indicates < 0.05, *** indicates < 0.01, **** indicates < 0.005.

Table 1.5 Cross effect multilevel regression of return on foreign investment: Europe, North America, Pacific

	Coef.	Sig.		Coef.	Sig.
EU_NA_PA	0.40725	**	year_1	−0.5311	**
lninvestment	−0.1911	****	year_2	−0.3398	
industry_1	−0.0728		year_3	−0.1388	
industry_2	−0.5965		year_4	−0.1691	
industry_3	−0.9033		year_5	−0.1829	
industry_4	−0.9388		branch	−0.0766	
industry_5	−0.7929		constant	1.60017	**
industry_6	−0.4666		Random-effects	Estimate	S.E.
industry_7	−1.0408	*	Geographic Region	4.12e-06	9.86e-06
industry_8	−0.8303		Firm	.627233	.1064929
diversify	−0.0563		Subsidiary	1.866511	.2604928
			Residual	10.65893	.0690607

Notes: * indicates < 0.1, ** indicates < 0.05, *** indicates < 0.01, **** indicates < 0.005.

year one (1996) also showed up as significantly higher compared to the rest. Diversification and branch/subsidiary were not significant.

Table 1.5 shows the effect of subsidiary/branch location in Europe, North America or the Pacific (Australia and New Zealand). This confirms that subsidiaries that are located in the combined Europe, North America and Pacific region earned significantly higher earnings on investment after controlling for the size of the investment, industry, year, diversification and branch/subsidiary. Earnings in industry seven (business services) and year one (1996) also showed up as significantly higher compared to the rest. Diversification and branch/subsidiary were not significant.

The above results confirm that geographic distance, EU membership and English language are all significant factors which affect the profitability of UK FDI. However, in order to more directly compare the relative contributions of regions defined according to each of these factors, a further analysis was conducted using industry and regions as random factors. This showed that the industry effect was much larger than the region effect. However, there were also significant differences in the size of the region effect depending on how the region is defined. Tables 1.6 and 1.7 show the relative effects of geographically

Table 1.6   Relative impacts of EU membership versus geographic region

	Coef.	Sig.
lninvest	−0.13798	***
diversification	−0.13589	
year_1	0.16915	
year_2	0.367619	
year_3	0.354308	
year_4	0.326287	
year_5	0.531316	*
constant	0.781659	***
Random-effects Parameters	Estimate	Std. Err.
EU member country	1.11E-12	5.12E-10
Geographic region	2.90E-14	1.41E-13
Industry	0.080111	0.074542
Residual	117.6847	1.187961

Notes: * indicates < 0.1, ** indicates < 0.05, *** indicates < 0.01, **** indicates < 0.005.

Table 1.7   Relative impacts of English-language versus geographic region

	Coef.	Sig.
Lninvest	−0.13889	***
diversification	−0.13562	
year_1	0.168429	
year_2	0.367219	
year_3	0.350493	
year_4	0.319004	
year_5	0.527512	*
constant	0.784281	***
Random-effects Parameters	Estimate	Std. Err.
English-speaking country	1.05E-13	3.66E-12
Geographic region	1.81E-08	7.28E-08
Industry	0.098304	0.092644
Residual	117.6744	1.207235

Notes: * indicates < 0.1, ** indicates < 0.05, *** indicates < 0.01, **** indicates < 0.005.

defined region versus EU membership and English-language country respectively (shown as random effects in the table). Table 1.6 shows that EU membership explains a much larger proportion of the variance in profitability compared with just taking geographic region into account (approximately 50 times). Table 1.7 shows that the English language of the country explains only a small proportion of the variance in comparison with the geographic region (by a factor of approximately 100,000 times).

Discussion and conclusions

The findings from this study confirm the findings of Rugman and others (Rugman, 2007; Rugman and Verbeke, 2004; Rugman and Collinson, 2004; Oh and Rugman, 2006; Qian et al., 2008) who found a strong preference for the home region in the internationalisation of MNEs based on foreign sales at the corporate level. However, our results show that there are regional effects on profitability of foreign subsidiaries as well as sales.

Foreign subsidiaries and branches in Europe are shown to be significantly more profitable compared with foreign subsidiaries in other regions whether the region is defined according to geography or EU membership. However, EU membership is shown to be a much more significant factor than the region defined according to geographic criteria. This confirms the importance of institutional arrangements such as the European Union on the profitability of foreign investments compared with simple geography. The results from the variance decomposition show that the effect of EU membership is estimated to be some 50 times greater compared with the geographically defined Europe region.

The results also show that in the case of UK firms, FDI into English-speaking countries such as the United States, Canada, Australia and New Zealand also contributes positively to profitability of investments compared with investments in other countries. This can be attributed to the long cultural associations between the UK and these former colonies. This is also reflected in the relatively large number of investments in these countries. After Europe, North America is the most popular destination for FDI by UK firms (Table 1.1).

Implications for management/policy

The findings have a number of implications for research on the relationship between internationalisation and firm performance. First, the results show that it is not just total foreign investment that matters but, more importantly, in which region the foreign investments are made. Second, the results show that how a region is defined makes a significant difference when assessing the effect on profitability. The study shows clearly that the effect of region defined according to trading blocs far outweighs the effect of region defined geographically and shows that even within a geographically defined region the institutional trading arrangements have a significant effect.

The study also shows that the effect of linguistic similarity may extend beyond the geographically defined region. In the case of UK firms the effects on profitability extend beyond the home geographic region to include the Anglophone countries in North America (United States and Canada) and Asia Pacific (Australia and New Zealand). This is consistent with research by Dow and Karuratna (2006), among others, who have highlighted the importance of linguistic similarity between home and host countries on the performance of internationalising firms.

The findings also have some implications for managers of firms considering FDI. The findings suggest that, for UK firms, FDI into EU member countries is likely to be more profitable compared to FDI into other countries. This is perhaps not surprising but it highlights the importance of trade agreements and trading blocs compared with geographic distance of countries. Even where countries are geographically close, trade agreements such as the European Union treaty play a much more significant role in determining profitability of FDI. The findings also show that in the case of UK firms, FDI into English-language-speaking countries is more profitable compared to FDI in non-English-speaking countries, although the difference is less compared with the effect of EU membership.

Limitations and further research

Clearly this study has limitations and there are several opportunities for further research. First, the sample may be biased as it only includes firms that provided the required financial data. Results may be different for firms that were excluded because they did not provide the necessary data. Secondly, although the results strongly suggest that geographic distance, trading blocs and cultural factors play a role in determining the choice of country and resulting performance of subsidiaries, there is no data on what actually motivated these firms to internationalise in the first place and what factors contributed to their choice of location. Further research might attempt to examine this question.

Acknowledgements

I am grateful to the UK Office of National Statistics for providing access to the data. The following advice should be noted: 'This work contains statistical data from ONS which is Crown Copyright. The use of the ONS statistical data in this work does not imply the endorsement of the ONS in relation to the interpretation or analysis of the statistical data. This work uses research datasets which may not exactly reproduce National Statistics aggregates.'

This chapter is dedicated to the memory of the late Professor Alan Rugman whose work on regional strategies inspired this research and who facilitated my gaining access to the ONS data. Sadly Professor Rugman passed away before he could see the results. Any errors in the chapter are entirely my own.

References

Almodovar, P. and Rugman, A.M. (2014). 'The M curve and the performance of Spanish international new ventures', *British Journal of Management*, 25(1), 6–23.

Anderson, J. and Van Wincoop, E. (2004). 'Trade costs', *Journal of Economic Literature*, 42(3), 691–751.

Ashkanasy, N.M., Trevor-Roberts, E. and Earnshaw, L. (2002). 'The Anglo Cluster: legacy of the British Empire', *Journal of World Business*, 37(1), 28–39.

Asmussen, C.G. (2009). 'Local, regional, or global? Quantifying MNE geographic scope', *Journal of International Business Studies*, 40(1), 1192–1205.

Banalieva, E., Santoro, M. and Jiang, J.R. (2012). 'Home region focus and technical efficiency of multinational enterprises: the moderating role of regional integration', *Management International Review*, 52(4), 493–518.

Caves, R.E. (1982). *Multinational Enterprise and Economic Analysis*. Cambridge: Cambridge University Press.

Chen, S. and Tan, H. (2012). 'Region effects in the internationalisation–performance relationship in Chinese firms', *Journal of World Business*, 47(1), 73–80.

Collinson, S. and Rugman, A.M. (2008). 'The regional nature of Japanese multinational business', *Journal of International Business Studies*, 39(1), 215–230.

Contractor, F.J., Kundu, S.K. and Hsu, C.C. (2003). 'A three-stage theory of expansion of international expansion: the link between multinationality and performance in the service sector', *Journal of International Business Studies*, 34(1), 5–18.

Deardorff, A. (1998). 'Determinants of bilateral trade: does gravity work in a neoclassical world?', In Frankel, J.F. (ed.), *The Regionalisation of the World Economy*, 7–32. Chicago: University of Chicago Press.

Dow, D. and Karuratna, A. (2006). 'Developing a multidimensional instrument to measure psychic distance stimuli', *Journal of International Business Studies*, 37(1), 578–602.

Elango, B. and Sethi, S.P. (2007). 'An exploration of the relationship between country of origin (COE) and the internationalisation–performance paradigm', *Management International Review*, 47(1), 369–392.

Ellis, P.D. (2007). 'Paths to foreign markets', *International Business Review*, 16(1), 573–593.

Ghemawat, P. (2001). 'Distance still matters', *Harvard Business Review*, 79(8), 137–147.

Gilhooley, B. (2009). 'Firm-level estimates of capital stock and productivity', *Economic & Labour Market Review*, 3(5), 36–41.

Gomes, L. and Ramaswamy, K. (1999). 'An empirical examination of the form of the relationship between internationalisation and performance', *Journal of International Business Studies*, 30(1), 173–188.

Harrigan, J. (2005). 'Specialization and the volume of trade: do the data obey the laws?', In Harrigan, J., Choi, K. (eds), *The Handbook of International Trade*. Malden, MA: Blackwell Publishing.

Hitt, M.A., Hoskisson, R.E. and Kim, H. (1997). 'International diversification: effects on innovation and firm performance in product diversified firms', *Academy of Management Journal*, 40(1), 767–798.

Hutchinson, W. (2006). 'Linguistic distance as a determinant of US bilateral trade', *Southern Economic Journal*, 72(1), 1–15.

Hymer, S.H. (1976). *A Study of Direct Foreign Investment*, Cambridge, MA: MIT Press.

Johanson, J. and Vahlne, J. (1977). 'The internationalisation process of the firm: a model of knowledge development and increasing foreign commitments', *Journal of International Business Studies*, 8(1), 23–32.

Korinek, J. and Sourdin, P. (2009). 'Maritime transport costs and their impact on trade', *OECD working paper TAD/TC/WP(2009)7*, Paris: OECD.

Lu, J. E. and Beamish, P. W. (2004). 'International diversification and firm performance: the S-curve hypothesis', *Academy of Management Journal*, 47(4), 598–609.

Nguyen, Q. (2014). 'The regional strategies of British multinational subsidiaries in South East Asia', *British Journal of Management*, 25(Special Issue), 60–76.

Oh, C. H. and F. Contractor (2014). 'A regional perspective on multinational expansion strategies: reconsidering the three stage paradigm', *British Journal of Management*, 25(1), 42–59.

—— and Rugman, A.M. (2006). 'Regional sales of multinationals in the world cosmetics industry', *European Management Journal*, 24(2–3), 163–173.

Osegowitsch, T. and Sammartino, A. (2008). 'Reassessing (home-) regionalisation', *Journal of International Business Studies*, 39(2), 184–196.

Qian, G., Li, L., Li, J. and Qian, Z. (2008). 'Regional diversification and firm performance', *Journal of International Business Studies*, 39(1), 197–214.

Rabe-Hesketh, S. and Skrondal, A. (2008). *Multilevel and Longitudinal Modeling using Stata*. College Station, TX: STATA press.

Rugman, A.M. (1979). *International Diversification and the Multinational Enterprise*. Lexington, MA: Heath.

—— (2000). *The End of Globalization: Why Global Strategy Is a Myth and How to Profit from the Realities of Regional Markets*. New York: Amacom.

—— (ed.) (2007). *Research on Global Strategic Management: Regional Aspects of Multinationality and Performance*. Amsterdam: Elsevier.

—— and Collinson, S. (2004). 'The regional nature of the world's automotive sector', *European Management Journal*, 22(5), 471–482.

—— and Oh, C.H. (2010). 'Does the regional nature of multinationals affect the multinationality and performance relationship?', *International Business Review*, 19(5), 479–488.

—— and —— (2013). 'Why the home region matters: location and regional multinationals', *British Journal of Management*, 23(4), 463–479.

—— and Verbeke, A. (2004). 'A perspective on regional and global strategies of multinational enterprises', *Journal of International Business Studies*, 35(1), 3–18.

——, Yip, G., and Jayaratne, S. (2008). 'A note on return on foreign assets and foreign presence for UK multinationals', *British Journal of Management*, 19(2), 162–170.

West, J. and Graham, J.L. (2004). 'A linguistic-based measure of cultural distance and its relationship to managerial values', *Management International Review*, 44(1), 239–260.

Zaccarin, S., Rivellini, G. (2002). 'Multilevel analysis in social research: an application of a cross-classified model', *Journal of Statistical Methods and Applications*, 11(1), 95–108.

2
Exploring Regional-Level Impact of Corruption and Crime on Multinational and Domestic Firms: The Evidence from Russia

Natalya Victor Smith

Introduction

It is now common knowledge that foreign direct investment (FDI) can be one of the key catalysts for technological development of a country. Indeed, to the extent it entails a transfer of technological, managerial and organisational skills, or provides access to other resources unavailable to certain economies, FDI can have a marked impact on the productivity spillovers, resulting in economic growth as technology transferred by multinationals enterprises (MNEs) stimulates domestic investment (Blomström et al., 2001) and facilitates improvements in institutions (Smith and Thomas, 2015b). Since FDI constitutes a very large share of capital formation in transition countries (UNCTAD, 2015), the FDI-promoting effect of good institutions should be the key channel in the overall growth and development for these economies.

That said, because the role of FDI in a number of developing countries has been limited, the resources needed to finance investments have to be generated locally (Ghura and Goodwin, 2000, p. 1820). This calls for domestic policies that should be directed at establishing an environment conducive to the development of the domestic private sector. A business environment with 'good institutions' (for example, with a sound domestic institutional framework) is a necessary condition for attracting FDI; it is also vital, however, for promoting domestic firms' investment (World Bank, 2003, p. 2). Hence, in implementing policies to improve the investment climate, both foreign and domestic investments should be taken into account.

The surge in FDI has motivated a host of empirical studies of its determinants and identified various factors that either attract or deter foreign investment.

One stream of this research has focused on institutions proxied by various indices of socio-political instability (Daude and Stein, 2007; Buchanan et al., 2012) and political freedom and democracy (Feng, 2001; Mathur and Singh, 2013) with the basic theoretical rationale that instability (in the form of social unrest, for example) can increase investment risks. The main conclusion these studies make is that institutional quality can affect the costs and/or risks of doing business in the country in question. For example, political freedom and democracy might reflect an increased stability and property rights might be more secure in countries ruled by good institutions.

The study adds to this literature by providing a more detailed understanding of the impact of institutions on investments. It expands on previous studies by estimating the impact of institutions on foreign and domestic investments simultaneously. Indeed, although within a country foreign and domestic investors can be similarly motivated (for example, expecting the highest possible return for the least amount of risk), they differ in many ways: they have different alternative investment opportunities, different perceptions of risks and face a different set of regulations.

The study performs an econometric analysis of the effect of 'bad institutions' (that is, corruption and crime) on the accumulation of multinational (MNEs) and domestic small and medium-sized firms (SMEs) across Russia, controlling for the host market potential in the model (these variables are specified from vast FDI literature). Russia is an interesting country in which to study institutions. First, it is the largest post-communist country with significant geographical, economic and ethnic diversity. Second, as a transition economy, it provides an interesting context to explore the impact of institutions on economic outcomes 'as the entire set of formal institutions has been remodelled in the 1990s' (Bevan and Estrin, 2004, p. 44) and a distinct yet diverse business environment has evolved in the process of transition from socialist planning to the market economy (Meyer, 2001).

The idea of this study resides in the perception of bad institutions in Russia by both foreign and domestic investors (FIAC, 2012): various data indicate corruption in Russia is widespread and crime rates have been sharply increasing. This can have a significant effect on MNEs' decision on whether or not to invest in the country. Likewise, it can have a significant effect on the potential owners of SMEs' decision on whether to start a business in Russia. Indeed, for a country like Russia it is important to have a complete understanding of the role that bad institutions play in affecting the investment environment, since the former may produce uncertainty affecting the domestic economy as a result. To the best of the author's knowledge, this is the very first study that provides comparable results of such an impact.

The approach to the estimation is simple. Econometrically, a model that includes bad institutions as a predictor of MNEs/SMEs (along with other potential determinants) is estimated, using the approach that controls for endogeneity of crime and corruption. An aggregate measure of crime along with corruption is used to understand the association between crime and MNEs/ SMEs. All crimes are then disaggregated into two types (property and violent) and the effect of each type of crime is examined. Such an approach gives an opportunity to understand if different types of crime have different impacts on MNEs versus SMEs.

The study finds a significant effect of corruption: negative in the case of MNEs but positive in the case of SMEs. Despite the adverse effect of the current levels of aggregated and disaggregated crimes on foreign and domestic businesses, their (one year) lagged effects are positive. Interestingly, higher stocks of MNEs are found in regions with higher current level of violent crimes. Overall, the results suggest there may be a sort of 'adjustment' mechanism that kicks in as businesses 'settle' across the country: as they get familiar with the environment they begin to take advantage of bad institutions.

Finally, and rather importantly, the process of MNE and SME accumulation in Russia has been dynamic: previous values of stocks (and flows) of MNEs and SMEs across the country had a significantly positive impact on their present values. The regions with more economically developed markets, with more power given to their regional governments in economic matters, and those that have generated more corporate tax, have attracted more MNEs and developed more SMEs. While natural resource abundance has deterred foreign investors, it did not stop the SME accumulation. The impact of (transport) infrastructure has also varied: it was important for SMEs' growth but there were more MNEs attracted to regions with poorer infrastructure.

The study is structured as follows. The next section sets out a conceptual framework. The study then presents the model, data and describes the variables used in the study. The results are discussed afterwards. The final section concludes, suggesting some potential areas for further research. It also discusses the relevance of this study for policymakers.

Conceptual framework

Institutions and business

The main function of institutions is to reduce the transaction costs (of negotiation, search, surveillance and enforcement) in the economy that arise due to the exchange of goods (North, 1990; Smith and Thomas, 2015a). Institutions put constraints on the behaviour of economic agents (Kostova et al., 2008) and their strategic choice through transaction costs (Hitt et al., 2011), and reduce the risk of opportunistic behaviour (North, 1990). Institutional theory has provided a rich theoretical foundation in MNE research (e.g. Dacin et al., 2002; Djelic and Quack, 2003). Recent developments in the literature have, however, questioned the nature of the relationship between MNEs and their institutional environments (Kostova et al., 2008). Emerging views suggest that MNEs have a lot of discretion and freedom in responding to their environments (Hoffman and Ventresca, 2002).

Institutional quality is one of the many aspects of business environment that can provide a framework for discussing firms' activities (Meyer and Peng, 2005). For example, North (1990) highlights that, to reduce uncertainty experienced by firms, an environment that increases information flow among the actors is imperative. Indeed, firms can be either constrained or empowered by institutions (Scott, 2008; Gohmann, 2012; Gupta et al., 2012; Stenholm et al., 2013; Smith and Thomas, 2015a) and entrepreneurs channel their efforts in different directions depending on institutional quality (Baumol, 1990).

The institutional structure determines the relative reward to investing entrepreneurial activities into productive market activities versus unproductive political and legal activities (for example, lobbying and lawsuits) (Baumol, 1990). SMEs can grow strong in a supporting institutional environment because they can benefit, for example, from well-organised and smoothly operating markets and from the opportunities for financing their activities (venture capital, business angels, crown funding).

Various risks (driven by the institutional forces that impact stability) have been linked to the nature and extent of firms' transactional interactions (Ghoshal, 1987). Indeed, as risk must be compensated for by higher expected gains, its perceived level has been significant in attracting FDI. For example, the risky environments have been shown to limit the ability of SMEs to form alliances (Dickson and Weaver, 2011) and deter FDI (Oxley, 1999; Henisz, 2000), particularly in the settings in which there is a history of government expropriation of foreign-held assets.

Equally, volatility of regime change can increase uncertainty of investors about the host country's future economic policies but stable domestic political institutions reduce the risk for foreign capital (Li and Resnick, 2003). Government stability, law and order and quality of bureaucracy can be key in attracting FDI (Busse and Hefeker, 2007). In transition economies, for example, political and macroeconomic stability and transparent legal regulations have been important factors attracting potential investors (Resmini, 2000) and good institutions have helped innovation (Smith and Thomas, 2014; Smith et al., 2014; Smith and Thomas, 2015a, b).

Aidis et al. (2008), for example, show that Russia's institutional environment is important in explaining its relatively low levels of entrepreneurship development (measured by a number of start-ups). Smith and Thomas (2015a) reveal that SMEs in Russia prefer to operate in the informal economy because of corruption (possibly because they do not want to get involved with the public sector). One reason for this is the financial cost of regulatory compliance and of dealing with bureaucratic obstacles. These costs are usually the same whatever the size of the business, and therefore regulation at the federal, regional and municipal levels affects SMEs disproportionately. In other words, for SMEs these costs represent a higher percentage of their profits than that paid by MNEs.

Moreover, poor quality of bureaucracy can deter investors as they conceive it as a high transaction cost which directly affects profitability of their investment projects (Kinoshita and Campos, 2003; Smith and Thomas, 2015a). Thus, institutions are important determinants of FDI location and SME operations. However, recent surges of political instability and domestic conflict have demanded new research on true correlation between investments and institutions. For example, the very strategies that are promoted by MNEs (as means for achieving their own growth) may lead to different types of domestic conflict in host countries if these countries stop receiving the investments they expect (Habib and Zurawicki, 2002). In particular, domestic stability and absence of violence can be significant in affecting the economic activity (Lederman et al., 2002).

Corruption and business

One measure of institutional quality often used in the studies is the prevalence of corruption (defined as an act of using the power for personal gain by public officials breaching the rules of 'the game'; see Jain, 2001; Aidt, 2003) due to its particularly damaging economic effect relative to the other indicators of institutional quality. For example, Schleifer and Vishny (1993) underline the distortionary effect of corruption in relation to regular taxation and consider the bribes' expenses to be inefficiently allocated resources and, thus, more costly than taxation.

The literature emphasises a disincentive effect of corruption (by amplifying the risk and uncertainty a business might face) (e.g. Getz and Volkema, 2001). For FDI, the role of 'the grabbing hand' of corruption has been empirically detected (Habib and Zurawicki, 2002; Lambsdorff, 2003; Voyer and Beamish, 2004): by extracting rents from foreign investors, bureaucrats in host countries can increase the cost of doing business (Smith et al., 2014; Smith and Thomas, 2015b).

However, the role of corruption in raising efficiency through, for example, contract enforcement has also been emphasised (Shleifer and Vishny, 1993; Boycko et al., 1996). Empirically, 'the helping hand' of corruption for FDI has been confirmed (Smith et al., 2014; Smith and Thomas, 2015b): it can speed up business processes in overcoming bureaucratic issues or gaining favourable treatment regarding public-funded projects (Tanzi and Davoodi, 2000). When the governmental and regulatory situation allows corrupt practices, it may increase business profits, enhance their efficiency and eventually raise FDI levels (Leff, 1964; Smith and Thomas, 2015b).

Crime and business

In its adverse impact on investment climate, crime can deter or delay investments. It can divert investment away from business expansion and productivity improvement. It can lead to a less than optimal operating strategy and to business losses (arising from theft, extortion and fraud), as well as to loss of output (due to reduced hours of operation) or loss of workdays arising from outbreaks of violence and avoidance of some types of economic activity.

During the past decades, crime rates have risen considerably. Since the late 1960s, crime rates in industrialised countries have increased by 300–400 per cent (Fajnzylber et al., 2000): from the early 1980s to mid-1990s murder rates in Eastern Europe and Central Asia increased by more than 100 per cent, where in 2005–2009 about 20 per cent of domestic and foreign firms were victims of a crime (World Bank Group, 2010).

As indicated in Table 2.1, between 2002–2009 there were over 28 per cent of domestic and 20 per cent of foreign firms in Russia that reported corruption as the key obstacle for their business operations (World Bank Group, 2010). Similarly, crime was the major obstacle for about 20 per cent of domestic and 24 per cent of foreign firms. Of foreign firms, 56.8 per cent were affected by crime and 37.3 per cent by corruption, while there were more than 50 per cent of Russian domestic firms affected by corruption (World Bank Group, 2010).

For various reasons the literature examining the impact of crime on businesses is scarce. Data on murders have been of special interest in the studies. In cross-national and regional studies, the justification for the use of data on murders is given by the fact that it is less sensitive to changing definitions across legal systems. It can suffer the least from the problems of underreporting that afflict official crime statistics (Fajnzylber et al., 2000), it is 'a fairly reliable barometer of all violent crimes' and 'no other crime is measured as accurately and precisely' (Fox and Zawitz, 2000, p. 1).

Table 2.1 Percentage of domestic and foreign firms reporting corruption and crime as major obstacles to operations in Russia, 2002–2009

	Ownership	2002 (%)	2005 (%)	2009 (%)
Corruption	*Domestic*	15.2	17.7	50.1
	Foreign	9.9	13.5	37.3
All crimes (including thefts and disorders)	*Domestic*	15.7	7.6	37.3
	Foreign	4.2	11.1	56.8
Observations	Total	886	473	1004

Note: These firms reported crime and corruption to be the major obstacle for their business conduct in Russia.

Source: www.doingbusiness.org

Although official statistics on crimes might not give an accurate represen-tation of the extent of actual criminal activity, it can be a useful indicator of socio-economic environment (Lotspeich, 1995). As Donohue (1998, p. 1425) has put it, 'while homicide data may not be perfectly reflective of the time trend in all crimes, it does seem to follow the pattern of most other crimes fairly well ... while murder may not be a perfect proxy for crime, it is simply the best available'.

Empirically, Daniele and Marani (2010) examined and found that organised crime (the sum of extortion, bomb attacks, arson and crimes of criminal asso-ciation) deterred FDI inflows in Italy. Brock (1998) concluded that crime rates should be decreased to attract more FDI in Russia. Despite the limited attempts, however, the exact effect of crime on foreign and domestic investment in tran-sition economies and Russia alike is understudied. The impact of crime along with corruption on the international flows of investment at the intra-country level of foreign and domestic investors has been a neglected area.

To sum up, the quality of institutions should matter for both domestic and foreign investments in the following ways. Good institutions may attract foreign and help domestic investors by raising productivity prospects. Bad institutions can bring additional costs to investors (for example, in the case of corruption, see Aidis et al., 2008; Anokhin and Schulze, 2009). Investors (especially foreign) can be vulnerable to any form of uncertainty (including uncertainty stemming from poor government efficiency, policy reversals, graft or weak enforcement of property rights and of the legal system) due to high sunk costs.

Therefore, institutional quality of a country should have a significant effect on its economic outcomes since it is expected that investors are likely to invest in places with good institutions. On the other hand, they might disinvest or not invest at all if the government or other parties in the economy (with bad institutions) are likely to take over the investment efforts (Acemoglu et al., 2002).

Model specification and methodology

Model

Based on the discussion above, the study builds and estimates the following equation:

$$Yit = \alpha + \beta1Yt{-}1 + \beta2CORRit + \beta3CORRit{-}1 + \beta4CRIMEit + \beta5CRIMEit{-}1 + \beta Xit + dt + \eta i + \varepsilon it \tag{2.1}$$

where Y is the dependent variable, either (stock of) MNEs, namely *MNEST* or (stock of) SMEs, namely *SMEST*. The two key variables of interest are corruption, namely *CORR* (measured by the number of economic crimes registered) and crime, namely *CRIME* (measured by the number of all crimes registered by the police); *MURD* (or violent crimes) is measured by the number of murders and murder attempts and *PROP* (or property crimes) is measured by the number of thefts and burglaries. To account for the population differences across the country, the crime data used are per 100,000 people.

Vector of control variables *βXit* (specified from vast FDI literature) includes: *POWER* (measured by the volume of regional expenditures) that controls for the role of local (or regional) governments and semi-national bodies in attracting MNEs and in development of SME sector; *CORPTAX* (measured by the volumes of regional revenues from corporation tax) controls for laws regarding corporate tax; *HUMCAP* (measured by the number of people with secondary and higher education qualifications per capita) controls for human capital or skilled labour.

In addition, *INFRA* (measured by the total length of paved roads per square kilometre) controls for regional transport infrastructure; *MARKET* (measured by gross domestic product per capita) controls for market size and *NATRES* (a dummy that takes value 1 for any positive volumes of oil, gas and gas condensate extracted in a region) controls for natural resources abundance.

Time dummies were added to account for the unobserved economic shocks. All variables (except the dummy) are used in the logarithm form. The data source is Rosstat (Russia's National Bureau of Statistics). The crime data consist of a balanced panel covering the period 1995–2011. The data on property and violent crimes consist of a balanced panel covering the period 2000–2011. Descriptive statistics of the variables is in Table 2.2.

Methodology

The process of attracting MNEs and of SME sector development in a region may be dynamic (with current realisations of the dependent variables influenced by their past values). To account for this possibility, the dynamic panel data model was utilised. Estimating Equation (2.1), however, may yield biased and inefficient coefficient estimators due to a number of issues. First, as causality may run from corruption and crime to FDI and SMEs (respectively) and (vice versa), this can lead to endogeneity. Second, there might be some time-invariant regional characteristics correlated with the explanatory variables, resulting in autocorrelation (the past values of corruption and crime can have a significant effect on their current values).

To deal with these possible problems, the system generalised two-step method of moments (as more efficient in this case, see Roodman, 2009) with corrected standard errors (Windmeijer, 2005) was applied (see Arellano and Bond, 1991; Arellano and Bover, 1995; Blundell and Bond, 2000). To obtain robust results, the specification was tested using Arellano-Bond test (for serial autocorrelation in the residuals) and the Sargan-Hansen test (of over-identification).

Table 2.2 Descriptive statistics

Variables	Observations	Mean	Standard Deviation	Min	Max
MNEST	1135	602.0141	2731.412	0	35952
MNE	1135	85.72159	316.4443	0	3361
SMEST	1391	103833.3	253459.4	100	3444500
SME	1392	13422.86	26496.39	100	279000
CORR	1245	192.8167	270.2491	13.97849	3272.464
RCORR	1245	1	1.381757	0.11651	20.72853
CRIME	1411	2006.699	732.0106	58	6249
RCRIME	1338	1	0.3384805	0.031777	2.991935
PROP	996	1074.991	494.9737	38.89515	6551.613
RPROP	913	1	0.3887826	0.0364942	2.456806
MURD	996	60.69397	41.48094	7.680491	441.9355
RMURD	996	1	0.6825742	0.1579492	9.088399
POWER	1399	0.0121515	0.0206243	0.0006081	0.2256699
HUMCAP	1397	0.004277	0.0018168	0.0001761	0.0451613
INFRA	1454	118.5627	99.03367	0.8	672
CORPTAX	914	16.67112	10.94546	0.3	95.7
MARKET	1386	0.0011111	0.0023891	7.38E-06	0.037904
NATRES	1493	0.422639	0.4941445	0	1

To further check for robustness, Equation (2.1) was (1) re-estimated by using alternative measures of (i) dependent variables (measured by the number of MNEs and SMEs) and (ii) corruption and crimes (measured by the number of crime cases registered as a share to Russia's average). The results held (these are not presented but available on request).

Results and discussion

The main results are summarised in Table 2.3.

The study confirms that institutions, indeed, matter for businesses: both corruption and crimes have been the key predictor of how much (or little) of MNEs a region attracts and of its SME sector development. There is evidence of 'the helping hand' of corruption for SMEs but not for MNEs and of the 'grabbing hand' of the current level of crimes for all firms (except for violent crimes in the case of MNEs that were found to have a positive effect on MNEs).

It seems there might be a sort of 'adjustment' mechanism that has developed that kicks in (within a year) as businesses 'settle' across the country: as firms get familiar with the environment and, most importantly, with the institutions, they begin to learn how to take advantage of institutional weaknesses, possibly by adjusting their strategies. That is, contrary to the expectation based

Table 2.3 Main results: the impact of corruption and crime on (current and one year lagged stock of) MNEs and SMEs across Russia

Variables	Model 1	Model 2	Model 3	Model 4	Model 5	Model 6	Model 7	Model 8
$MNEST_{t-1}$	0.827***							
	(0.007)							
$SMEST_{t-1}$		0.886***	0.887***	0.808***	0.890***	0.845***	0.906***	0.890***
		(0.009)	(0.003)	(0.006)	(0.007)	(0.012)	(0.005)	(0.005)
$CORR_t$	−0.083***				0.005**			
	(0.008)				(0.002)			
$CORR_{t-1}$	0.004*				0.014***			
	(0.010)				(0.0043)			
$CRIME_t$		−0.129***				−0.020***		
		(0.014)				(0.003)		
$CRIME_{t-1}$		0.079***				0.055***		
		(0.017)				(0.005)		
$PROP_t$			−0.200***				−0.024***	
			(0.014)				(0.002)	
$PROP_{t-1}$			0.183***				0.005**	
			(0.014)				(0.002)	
$MURD_t$				0.286***				−0.049***
				(0.008)				(0.002)
$MURD_{t-1}$				0.025**				0.036***
				(0.012)				(0.003)
$POWER_t$	0.020***	0.027***	0.036***	0.008***	0.011***	0.014***	0.004***	0.003***
	(0.004)	(0.005)	(0.004)	(0.003)	(0.001)	(0.002)	(0.001)	(0.001)

	(1)	(2)	(3)	(4)	(5)	(6)	(7)	(8)
$HUMCAP_t$	0.020***	−0.030***	0.016***	0.053***	0.008***	0.018***	0.009***	−0.002*
	(0.005)	(0.010)	(0.005)	(0.008)	(0.002)	(0.003)	(0.002)	(0.001)
$INFRA_t$	0.023***	0.0967***	0.042***	0.061***	0.053***	0.069***	0.036***	0.079***
	(0.006)	(0.011)	(0.005)	(0.009)	(0.005)	(0.007)	(0.002)	(0.006)
$CORPTAX_t$	0.085***	0.064***	0.076***	0.059***	0.006***	0.004***	0.009***	0.004***
	(0.008)	(0.005)	(0.004)	(0.004)	(0.001)	(0.001)	(0.001)	(0.001)
$MARKET_t$	−0.016**	−0.018**	−0.058***	−0.083***	0.010**	0.007	−0.004*	−0.001
	(0.007)	(0.008)	(0.013)	(0.010)	(0.004)	(0.005)	(0.002)	(0.002)
$NATRES_t$	−0.182***	−0.397***	−0.109***	0.057**	0.158***	0.153***	0.295***	0.091***
	(0.024)	(0.039)	(0.014)	(0.026)	(0.013)	(0.025)	(0.022)	(0.021)
Constant	1.441***	1.437***	0.351**	0.982***	1.205***	1.439***	1.029***	0.960***
	(0.074)	(0.212)	(0.169)	(0.093)	(0.051)	(0.121)	(0.050)	(0.043)
Observations	819	819	676	676	879	879	720	720
Number of regions	77	77	77	77	81	81	81	81
Number of instruments	146	167	110	110	179	200	134	134
AR1	−1.736*	−1.740*	−1.766*	−1.705*	−2.843***	−1.483**	−1.646**	−1.953**
	(0.082)	(0.082)	(0.077)	(0.088)	(0.004)	(0.038)	(0.051)	(0.051)
AR2	−0.934	−0.226	−1.297	−0.409	−0.991	−1.182	−1.575	−1.313
	(0.350)	(0.821)	(0.194)	(0.683)	(0.322)	(0.237)	(0.115)	(0.189)
Sargan-Hansen	56.288***	63.199***	62.943***	58.477***	65.835***	64.467***	67.510***	62.036***

Note: Robust standard errors (clustered by region) are reported. ***, **, and * indicate that the coefficient is significantly different from zero at the 1 per cent, 5 per cent and 10 per cent levels, respectively.

Source: See paper for the variables' abbreviations.

on the literature reviewed, it is the environments with poor institutions that have attracted more MNEs and accumulated a higher level of SMEs.

One likely explanation for this central finding is that MNEs and SMEs may have learned to deal with corruption and crimes using this ability to their advantage: to capture the market and fill in the void left by the displaced, or the non-materialised (possibly due to inefficiency of institutions) domestic private sector. One typical example is the protection offered by criminal gangs to businesses. In this case, one would expect that SMEs should be more flexible in dealing with such a situation, whereas MNEs may consider any such inter-action as too risky, costly and, hence, prohibitive. This study confirms this is not always the case.

It seems that, first, firms may have learned how to benefit from dealing with corruption and violence (hence, have expanded possibly by support offered by the patronage of criminals) and may have considered this as a (somewhat fixed) cost. Second, however, the current levels of crime and corruption (for MNEs) may have been far too unpredictable (hence, an overhead) for them, so no value could be attached to them, and, by consequence, markets with high criminal activity have not been entered at all, or have been possibly exited once such activity was detected.

Economic dynamism is usually premised on the more economically developed areas (perhaps due to extracting enterprises operating in such places): indeed, corruption and crime have been correlated with foreign and domestic firms conditional on the regional market potential. It is also likely that the regional authorities in these places may have been involved in the crime through rent seeking (which could potentially be higher in more decentralised places) due to higher rents they can gain from the dynamism of such places. Indeed, the sig-nificance of positive effects of corruption and of a control for the role of local (or regional) governments and semi-national bodies in attracting MNEs and in development of SME sector confirms this can, indeed, be the case.

Besides, the fact that higher stock of MNEs is found in the regions with poorer transportation infrastructure (and SMEs – in places where infrastructure is better) may be due to the possibility that these regions have also been among the most corrupt (as corruption goes hand in hand with infrastructure projects). It equally possible that such 'dynamic' regions have been picked up as 'likely targets' for MNE/SME activities in their early stages of economic development (when it is the informal institutions that mostly prevail).

That said, it is expected that, as institutional importance becomes more obvious in these places, MNEs and SMEs may put (more) pressure on the local communities to introduce 'better' formal institutions or to improve the formal institutions that already exist. The gradual introduction of the formal institu-tions (or their improvement) may then identify as crimes activities that were not considered as such in the context of the informal institutional context, or may offer legitimacy to now reported crimes (that would not have been previously reported due to either lack of appropriate legislation or perhaps because reporting them would have been 'socially unacceptable'). If this stands, the increase in crimes in economically dynamic regions would only be a by-product of redefining what actually constitutes a crime in newly introduced formal institutional environments, coupled with a more effective framework for tackling committed crimes that makes it worth reporting them.

Conclusion

Using dynamic panel data for regions in Russia from 1995 to 2011 and controlling for endogeneity of institutional factors (corruption and crime), this chapter examined the link between corruption and crime (on the one hand) and the growth of MNEs and SMEs (on the other) across Russia. To the best of the author's knowledge, this is the very first study that accomplished such investigation at the intra-country level. Its contribution is, therefore, twofold.

First, it added value to the FDI literature: there is still not much known as to the effect of crime on FDI. Secondly, it added value to the literature on international entrepreneurship which shed only little light on the impact of crime (and corruption) on domestic firms' start-ups. It estimated the impact of corruption and crime per se and of two different types of crime (violent and property) on the growth of FDI and SMEs across the large and heterogeneous transition economy of Russia. This is something that has not yet been accomplished.

This chapter yields a central result: higher levels of crime and corruption have been associated with higher stock of FDI and SMEs in a region. That is, in Russia, domestic and foreign businesses have been expanding in places with bad institutions. The most plausible explanation of this finding is that investing in such environments is advantageous to investors: MNEs that have invested in Russia and domestic SMEs may have already been or become prone to navigating in such a business environment.

As such environments are usually more corrupt due to institutional inefficiency, it is also possible that MNEs may have, indeed, been tempted to go to the places where they can bribe government officials (possibly to avoid costly government regulation, to obtain some preferential treatments and to win permissions to execute public capital projects). That said, equally possible in this case since crime rates are usually high in more economically dynamic regions, if SMEs and FDI were to 'relocate' to places with better institutions (providing such a place can be found) crime would follow them.

Implications and relevance for policymakers

The results of this investigation have vital policy implications. If anything, policymakers and business practitioners should have a better understanding of how economic and socio-economic factors are related to FDI/SMEs. This understanding may, for example, reduce the willingness of policymakers to attract MNEs in the absence of a strong and transparent legal framework that could prevent foreign firms from participating in the criminal activities and gaining from institutional inefficiencies.

Bad institutions result in immense costs for businesses. Corruption, in particular, is a crime that increases these costs. Crime can increase cost through racketeering and retail market limitations and/or through distortions to the goods and correct functioning of the market and institutions (Dawid et al., 2002). For example, especially in the 1990s, this has been the case in transition economies (in general) and Russia (in particular) through crime's traditional methods of discouraging competition with illegal tactics ranging from threats to murder (Lotspeich, 1995).

Crime poses a significant cost to businesses but also to individuals and society. Indeed, vast resources are wasted as governments spend public funds for police departments, prisons and jails, courts and treatment programs. The amount of time spent during court trials also takes away from productivity. Economic productivity can be affected through loss in developmental opportunities, and domestic and foreign investments.

With all that, crime as an aspect of an unfavourable business climate could be a disincentive for the growth of domestic and foreign firms. And, indeed, this is how it should be seen by policymakers in Russia (and other countries as well) where, according to numerous economic surveys, the increased costs of crime have made its already complex process of starting and opening a business even more difficult, scaring off would-be entrepreneurs and inhibiting the development of a market economy.

Specific strategies must be developed to jointly combat corruption and crime. For example, lending institutions (the World Bank, the IMF) may want to consider withholding their investments to 'criminal countries'. Among other things, there is a need to include focused efforts by police, making the punishment (if caught) more severe and eliminating all plea bargaining. Moreover, policymakers should (through legislation) make foreign firms combat crime by, for example, making them avoid places with high crime.

That said, if all MNEs were to take concerted action and simultaneously relocate to such 'non-corrupt and non-crime' regions as a political gesture (and to ensure they are more effective as a result of collective action), criminals and corruptors may follow them. Therefore, this zero-sum game is likely what keeps MNEs located in areas with some level of crime. This is not to say that MNEs do not prefer more crime-free (and less corrupt) environments; they, however, often are more pragmatic towards sacrifices that they have to accept to obtain the final goal they seek in those environments (for instance, increased market share, profit maximisation).

Several limitations of this study must be considered. Reliance on crime data is problematic. A longitudinal analysis of more objective data (whenever such data become available) may be considered in future research. It is important to remember that correlations and causal connections are not the same. Indeed, the causal connections can rarely be proven. Therefore, given a sustained record of FDI influx into the Russian areas, presumption must be that crime in any given country is likely to be decisive for that country's ability to sustain its FDI-led economic development.

This is equally relevant to the development of SMEs: given higher stocks of SMEs accumulating in places with bad institutions, presumption must be that it is but good institutions that are likely to be decisive for that country's sustainable economic development. It is possible that 'regular' crime may not have any impact on FDI if this crime is committed against domestic firms rather than MNEs. In this case, the discussion has to be based on the crimes that affect MNEs and their subsidiaries directly. However, to investigate this hypothesis, a different type of data (currently unavailable) is needed.

Overall, the literature on the impact of institutions does not provide sufficient evidence as to the effect of crime on business (neither foreign or domestic). This chapter calls for such research. The international business field will also benefit from research that will further examine the reasons behind the willingness of MNEs to locate and for SMEs to start up their business, in places that are not 'crime-prone', and the impact of MNEs and SMEs on crime. For all that, it is hoped that this study is a good starting point.

References

Acemoglu, Daron, Simon Johnson, and James A. Robinson (2002), 'Reversal of Fortune: Geography and Institutions in Making of the Modern World Income Distribution'. *Quarterly Journal of Economics*, 118, 1231–1294.

Aidis, Ruta, Saul Estrin, and Tomasz Michiewicz (2008), 'Institutions and Entrepreneurship Development in Russia: A Comparative Perspective.' *Journal of Business Venturing*, 23, 656–672.

Aidt, S. Toke (2003), 'Economic Analysis of Corruption: A Survey.' *Economic Journal*, 113 (491), 632–652.

Anokhin, Sergey and William S. Schulze (2009), 'Entrepreneurship, Innovation, and Corruption'. *Journal of Business Venturing*, 24 (5), 465–476.

Arellano, Manuel and Stephen Bond (1991), 'Some Tests of Specification for Panel Data: Monte Carlo Evidence and an Application to Employment Equations'. *Review of Economic Studies*, 58, 277–297.

Arellano, Manuel and Olympia Bover (1995), 'Another Look at the Instrumental Variable Estimation of Error Component Models'. *Journal of Econometrics*, 68, 29–51.

Baumol, William J. (1990), 'Entrepreneurship: Productive, Unproductive, and Destructive.' *Journal of Political Economy*, 98 (5), 893–921.

Bevan, Alan and Saul Estrin (2004), 'The Determinants of Foreign Direct Investment into European Transition Economies'. *Journal of Comparative Economics*, 32 (4), 775–787.

Blomström, Magnus, Ari Kokko, and Steven Globerman (2001), 'The Determinants of Host Country Spillovers from Foreign Direct Investment: A Review and Synthesis of the Literature', in Nigel Pain (ed.), *Inward Investment, Technological Change and Growth: The Impact of Multinational Corporations on the UK Economy*, Basingstoke: Palgrave, 34–65.

Blundell, Richard and Steve Bond (2000), 'GMM Estimation with Persistent Panel Data: An Application to Production Functions'. *Econometric Reviews*, 19 (3), 321–340.

Boycko, Maxim, Andrei Shleifer, and Robert W. Vishny (1996), 'A Theory of Privatisation.' *Economic Journal*, 106 (435), 309–319.

Brock, Gregory J. (1998), 'Foreign Direct Investment in Russia's Regions 1993–95. Why So Little and Where Has It Gone?' *Economics of Transition*, 6 (2), 349–360.

Buchanan, Bonnie G., Quan V. Le, and Meenakshi Rishi (2012), 'Foreign Direct Investment and Institutional Quality: Some Empirical Evidence'. *International Review of Financial Analysis*, 21, 81–89.

Busse, Matthias and Carsten Hefeker (2007), 'Political Risk, Institutions and Foreign Direct Investment'. *European Journal of Political Economy*, 23 (2), 397–415.

Dacin, Tina M., Gerry Goodstein, and Richard W. Scott (2002), 'Institutional Theory and Institutional Change: Introduction to the Special Research Forum'. *Academy of Management Journal*, 45 (1), 45–57.

Daniele, Vittorio and Ugo Marani (2010), 'Organised Crime, the Quality of Local Institutions and FDI in Italy: A Panel Data Analysis'. *European Journal of Political Economy*, 27 (1), 132–142.

Daude, Christian and Ernesto Stein (2007), 'The Quality of Institutions and Foreign Direct Investment'. *Economics and Politics*, 19 (3), 317–344.

Dawid, Herbert, Gustav Feichtinger, and Andreas Novak (2002), 'Extortion as an Obstacle to Economic Growth: A Dynamic Game Analysis'. *European Journal of Political Economy*, 18, 499–516.

Dickson, Pat H. and Mark K. Weaver (2011), 'Institutional Readiness and Small to Medium-Sized Enterprise Alliance Formation'. *Journal of Small Business Management*, 49 (1), 126–148.

Djelic, Marie L. and Sigrid Quack (2003), 'Governing Globalisation – Bringing Institutions Back In', in Djelic L. Marie and Sigrid Quack (eds), *Globalisation and Institutions: Redefining the Rules of the Economic Game*, Cheltenham: Edward Elgar, 1–14.

Donohue, Joan J. (1998), 'Understanding the Time Path of Crime'. *The Journal of Criminal Law or Criminology*, 88 (4), 1423–1452.

Fajnzylber, Pablo, Daniel Lederman, and Norman Loayza (2000), 'Crime and Victimisation: An Economic Perspective'. *Economia*, 1, 219–302.

Feng, Yi (2001), 'Political Freedom, Political Instability, and Policy Uncertainty: A Study of Political Institutions and Private Investment in Developing Countries.' *International Studies Quarterly*, 45 (2), 271–294.

Foreign Investment Advisory Council (2012), *Russia's Investment Climate 2012*, available at: www.fiac.ru [accessed 25 January 2013].

Fox, James A. and Marianne W. Zawitz (2000), *Homicide Trends in the United States: 1998 Update*, Washington, DC: US Department of Justice.

Getz, Kathleen A. and Roger J. Volkema (2002), 'Culture, Perceived Corruption, and Economics: A Model of Predictors and Outcomes'. *Business and Society*, 40 (1), 7–30.

Ghoshal, Sumantra (1987), 'Global Strategy: An Organising Framework'. *Strategic Management Journal*, 8 (5), 425–440.

Ghura, Dhaneshwar and Barry Goodwin (2000), 'Determinants of Private Investment: A Cross-Regional Empirical Investigation.' *Applied Economics*, 32 (14), 1819–1829.

Gohmann, Stephan F. (2012), 'Institutions, Latent Entrepreneurship, and Self-Employment: An International Comparison'. *Entrepreneurial Theory and Practice*, 36 (2), 295–321.

Gupta, Vishal K., Chun Guo, Mario Canever, Hyung R. Yim, Gaganjeet K. Sraw, and Ming Liu (2012), 'Institutional Environment for Entrepreneurship in Rapidly Emerging Major Economies: The Case of Brazil, China, India, and Korea'. *International Entrepreneurship Management Journal*, 10 (2), 376–384.

Habib, Mohsin and Leon Zurawicki (2002), 'Corruption and Foreign Direct Investment'. *Journal of International Business Studies*, 33 (2), 291–307.

Henisz, Witold J. (2000), 'The Institutional Environment for Multinational Investment'. *Journal of Law, Economics and Organisation*, 16 (2), 334–364.

Hitt, Michael A., Duane R. Ireland, David G. Sirmon, and Cheryl A. Trahms (2011), 'Strategic Entrepreneurship: Creating Value for Individuals, Organisations, and Society'. *The Academy of Management Perspectives*, 25 (2), 57–76.

Hoffman, Andrew J. and Mark J. Ventresca (2002), *Organisations, Policy and the Natural Environment*. Stanford: Stanford University Press.

Jain, Arvind K. (2001), 'Corruption: A Review'. *Journal of Economic Surveys*, 15 (1), 71–121.

Kinoshita, Yuko and Nauro Campos (2003), 'Why Does FDI Go Where it Goes? New Evidence from the Transition Economies'. *IMF Working Papers*, 03 (228).

Kostova, Tatiana, Kendall Roth, and Tina M. Dacin (2008), 'Institutional Theory in the Study of Multinational Corporations: A Critique and New Directions'. *Academy of Management Review*, 33 (4), 994–1006.

Lambsdorff, Johann G. (2003), 'How Corruption Affects Productivity'. *Kyklos*, 56 (4), 457–474.

Lederman, Daniel, Norman Loayza, and Ana María Menéndez (2002), 'Violent Crime: Social Capital Matter?' *Economic Development and Cultural Change*, 50 (3), 509–539.

Leff, Nathaniel H. (1964), 'Economic Development through Bureaucratic Corruption'. *American Behavioural Scientist*, 8 (3), 8–14.

Li, Quan and Adam Resnick (2003), 'Reversal of Fortunes: Democratic Institutions and Foreign Direct Investment Inflows to Developing Countries'. *International Organisation*, 57 (1), 175–211.

Lotspeich, Richard (1995), 'Crime in the Transition Economies'. *Europe–Asia Studies*, 47 (4), 555–589.

Mathur, Aparna and Katikeya Singh (2013), 'Foreign Direct Investment, Corruption and Democracy'. *Applied Economics*, 45 (8), 991–1002.

Meyer, Klaus E. (2001), 'Institutions, Transaction Costs, and Entry Mode Choice in Eastern Europe'. *Journal of International Business Studies*, 32 (2), 357–367.

Meyer, Klaus E. and Michael W. Peng (2005), 'Probing Theoretically into Central and Eastern Europe: Transactions, Resources, and Institutions'. *Journal of International Business Studies*, 36, 600–621.

North, Douglass C. (1990), *Institutional Change and Economic Performance*. Cambridge: Cambridge University Press.

Oxley, Joanne E. (1999), 'Institutional Environment and the Mechanisms of Governance: The Impact of Intellectual Property Protection on the Structure of Inter-Firm Alliances'. *Journal of Economic Behaviour and Organisation*, 38 (3), 283–309.

Resmini, Laura (2000), 'The Determinants of Foreign Direct Investment in the CEECs: New Evidence from Sectoral Patterns'. *Economics of Transition*, 8 (3), 665–689.

Roodman, David M. (2009), 'A Note on the Theme of Too Many Instruments'. *Oxford Bulletin of Economics and Statistics*, 71 (1), 135–158.

Scott, Richard W. (2008), *Institutions and Organisations: Ideas and Interests*. Thousand Oaks, CA: Sage Publications.

Shleifer, Andrei and Robert W. Vishny (1993), 'Corruption'. *The Quarterly Journal of Economics*, 109 (3), 599–617.

Smith, Natalya V. and Ekaterina Thomas (2014), 'Innovation in Emerging Economies: The Spillover Effects of Foreign Direct Investment and Institutions in Russia', in Svetla Marinova (ed.), *Institutional Impacts on Firm Internalisation*, London: Palgrave McMillan, 146–172.

Smith, Natalya V., Ekaterina Thomas and Christos Antoniou (2014), 'Multi-National Firms, Corruption and Innovation in Russia', in Alan Verbeke, Rob Van Tulder, and Sarianna Lundan (eds), *Multinational Enterprises, Markets and Institutional Diversity*, Bingley, UK: Emerald Group Publishing Limited, 9, 347–371.

Smith, Natalya V., Ekaterina Thomas and Christos Antoniou (2015a), 'Determinants of Russia's Informal Economy: The Impact of Corruption and Multinational Firms'. *Journal of East–West Business*, 21 (2), 102–128.

Smith, Natalya V., Ekaterina Thomas and Christos Antoniou (2015b), 'The Role of FDI and State Capture in Shaping Innovation Outcome in Russia'. *Europe–Asia Studies*, 67 (5), 777–808.

Stenholm, Pekka, Zoltan J. Acs, and Robert Wuebker (2013), 'Exploring Country-Level Institutional Arrangements on the Rate and Type of the Entrepreneurial Activity'. *Journal of Business Venturing*, 28 (1), 176–193.

Tanzi, Vito and Hamid R. Davoodi (2000), 'Corruption, Growth, and Public Finances'. IMF Working Papers, 1–27.

United Nations Conference on Trade and Development (UNCTAD) (2015), *United Nations Statistical Databases*, United Nations Statistics Division, available at: http://unstats.un.org/unsd/databases.htm, [accessed 25 June 2015].

Voyer, Peter A. and Paul W. Beamish (2004), 'The Effect of Corruption on Japanese Foreign Direct Investment'. *Journal of Business Ethics*, 50 (3), 211–224.

Windmeijer, Frank (2005), 'A Finite Sample Correction for the Variance of Linear Efficient Two-Step GMM Estimators'. *Journal of Econometrics*, 126 (1), 25–51.

World Bank (2003), *World Development Indicators 2003. Sustainable Development in a Dynamic World*. Washington: The World Bank.

World Bank Group (2010), *Doing Business: Measuring Business Regulations*, available at: http://www.doingbusiness.org/, [accessed 24 June 2015].

3

Determinants of Reinvested Earnings of Multinational Subsidiaries in Emerging Economies

Quyen T.K. Nguyen

Introduction

Reinvested earnings (profit reinvestments) of multinational subsidiaries refers to subsidiaries reinvesting their own retained earnings into the existing operations. Retained earnings are a type of internal equity financing, that is, internally generated financing sources (Nguyen and Rugman, 2015). They are important resources to finance incremental investments for continuing expansion and growth of foreign subsidiaries of multinational enterprises (MNEs) from advanced economies operating in emerging economies, as financial markets in host countries are underdeveloped compared to home countries.

Reinvested earnings are a major component of global foreign direct investment (FDI) flows. One third of inward FDI income is retained within host countries as reinvested earnings (UNCTAD, 2013). An important feature of reinvested earnings is that they come from within host countries and do not involve cross-border fund transfer compared to two other components of FDI, equity investments and intra-firm loans, which give rise to cross-border transactions (UNCTAD website, 2015). In terms of absolute value, the world's reinvested earnings have increased from 258 billions of dollars in 2005 to 499 billions of dollars in 2011 (UNCTAD, 2013).

However, reinvested earnings have been largely under-researched in the international business (IB) literature, despite important implications for managers and policymakers (Lundan, 2006; Dunning and Lundan, 2008). There are very few studies that examine reinvested earnings using subsidiary-level data (Mudambi, 1998; Song, 2002; Nguyen and Rugman, 2015; Demirbag et al., 2015). This topic has received some attention in the financial economics literature in the context of domestic businesses and small enterprises in developing countries (Johnson et al., 2002; Cull and Xu, 2005; Chakravarty and

Xiang, 2011). However, the insights of these studies might be difficult to transfer to multinational subsidiaries, which are influenced by their parent firms with operations in diverse international environments. Thus, this literature warrants further research.

The focus of our study is to examine the determinants of reinvested earnings of multinational subsidiaries in emerging economies. Specifically, we address two research questions:

1. To what extent do the perceptions and assessment on host country location factors by subsidiary managers affect reinvested earnings decisions? Do all location variables have the same effects?
2. How does the duration of operations of subsidiaries influence reinvested earnings?

We make three significant theoretical and empirical contributions to the literature. First, we establish that reinvested earnings is a type of firm-specific advantage (FSA), as this reflects the development of new capabilities and decision-making in financial management of the subsidiary in response to deficiencies in financial infrastructures in emerging countries in general and in the ASEAN region (except Singapore). Second, we provide a compelling theory-driven explanation on reinvestment decisions of subsidiaries, in which the most notable factors are duration of operations, access to customers, and the quality and reliability of local infrastructures. Third, we use a new primary dataset of British multinational subsidiaries in six countries (Malaysia, Indonesia, the Philippines, Singapore, Thailand and Vietnam) in the ASEAN region (Association of South East Asian Nations).

Theoretical synthesis and hypotheses development

Internalisation theory

Internalisation theory (Buckley and Casson, 1976; Hennart, 1982; Rugman, 1981) postulates that the MNE expands internationally by transferring its tacit knowledge in intermediate products by establishing a network of foreign subsidiaries rather than exporting or licensing. The MNE creates an internal market within its hierarchical structure to substitute for the missing market for the sale of knowledge. This is an example of the firm overcoming an externality. There are many such imperfections in the goods and factor markets which have led to the need for internalisation of markets within the structure of the MNE.

Rugman (1981) popularises internalisation theory with the matrix of country-specific advantages (CSAs) and firm-specific advantages (FSAs). CSAs are strengths and benefits to a country which results from its competitive environment, labour force, geographic location, government policies, industrial clusters, and so forth. FSAs are strengths and benefits to a firm and a result of contributions which can be made by its product and process technology, brands, marketing or distribution skills (Rugman, 1981; Rugman and Collinson, 2012). FSAs can be created by both parent firms and by foreign subsidiaries.

Development of sustainable financial management strategies by multinational subsidiaries in emerging economies

Emerging economies offer prospects for business growth, and opportunities for sourcing and production advantages (Rugman and Collinson, 2012). However, emerging economies present challenges for MNEs due to institutional voids (Khanna and Palepu, 2010). Institutional voids refer to the absence of inter-mediaries, and the deficiency in market institutions and regulatory systems which facilitate the effective functioning of markets.

Subsidiary managers in emerging economies have in-depth knowledge and insights into these institutional voids. With their cumulative experience they develop necessary capabilities to overcome such challenges. We establish that reinvested earnings are a type of FSAs in financial management, along with other traditional knowledge-based intangible FSAs. Reinvested earnings are related to the three most important decisions, namely, investment, financing and dividend in the parent-subsidiary relationships in financial management. The subsidiary must balance its needs for financial resources (retained earnings), and the requirements of profit repatriation to the parent firm through dividend distribution, interest and royalty payments (Nguyen, 2013; Desai et al., 2007), as the parent firm can claim profits from the subsidiary.

To establish the nature of reinvested earnings as an FSA, it is necessary to rec-ognise that external capital markets in emerging economies in general and in the ASEAN region in particular (except Singapore) are imperfect due to different types of institutional voids. There might be deficiency in credit availability, the costs and interests of borrowing are high, and access to finance may be challenging (Nguyen and Rugman, 2015). Subsidiary managers make strategic decisions to use their own retained earnings to finance new investment oppor-tunities. These projects are reviewed, assessed and approved by the headquarters in the annual budgeting in accordance with required reinvestment rates, as the corporate finance function tends to be centralised in the MNE (Rugman, 1980). This is in line with the pecking-order theory (Myers and Majluf, 1984). Due to adverse selection and information asymmetries, firms prioritise their sources of financing, in which internal funds (retained earnings) are used first, and when that is exhausted, debt is issued, and when it is not sensible to issue any more debt, equity is issued. In short, subsidiary managers have developed FSAs in financial management in response to challenges of underdeveloped financial markets in the host countries. Our empirical findings on the major financing sources of subsidiaries support theoretical propositions here.

Hypotheses development

Subsidiary managers' perceptions and assessment on host country location factors and reinvested earnings

We draw upon the literature on determinants of inward FDI and profit reinvestments to develop our hypothesis. Dunning and Lundan (2008), and Flores and Aguilera (2007) provide lists of host CSAs which influence inward FDI. Enright (2009) suggests that location factors can be broadly grouped into demand, supply and institutional features. Demand features include the size, the growth and the affluence level of the market. Host economy market size (Flores and Aguilera, 2007; Sethi et al., 2003), growth (Loree and Guisinger, 1995; Sethi et al., 2003) and affluence (Root and Ahmed, 1978) are found to have positive relationships with inward FDI. Supply-side features focus on the quality of infrastructure and capabilities in a nation, and prevailing costs (Enright, 2009). These include the quality of infrastructure (Wells, 1993), technological capabilities (Kuemmerle, 1999), managerial experiences (Caves, 1998) and wage rates (Woodward and Rolfe, 1993). Apart from legal features, there are various institutional features that advance firm's operation in an economy. These include political stability (Krobin, 1976), economic openness (Root, 1987) and tax rates (Desai et al., 2002; Grubert and Mutti, 1991). Flores and Aguilera (2007) use measure of political and legal institutions to represent host nation institutions. Defever (2006) uses a measure of quality of judicial system as a proxy for institutional environment.

Similarly, the literature on the determinants of profit reinvestments has identified institutional and contextual factors as significant variables for a firm's reinvestment decisions. These include the security of property rights (Johnson et al., 2002; Cull and Xu, 2005), access to external financing (Chakravarty and Xiang, 2011; Cull and Xu, 2005), corruption and quality of judicial system (Demirbag et al., 2015). Our study draws upon the insights of subsidiary managers with whom we interact during the data collection process. We understand that they examine the economic and competitive environments of the host countries to identify opportunities for expansion and growth, and to use their own retained earnings to finance. Thus, we predict that

> *Hypothesis 1:* The perceptions and assessment on host country location factors by subsidiary managers are positively related to reinvested earnings by the subsidiary into the existing locations.

Duration of operations and reinvested earnings

Subsidiaries accumulate experience and knowledge of cultures and institutions of the host countries from their operations (Butler, 1995; Gao et al., 2008; Luo and Peng, 1999; Makino and Delios, 1996; Mudambi, 1998).

Cumulative experience and learning comes from different sources, including from direct experience, from previous decision outcomes, and from observing experiences of other firms (Gao et al., 2008). The accumulation of knowledge enables subsidiaries to deal with challenges in emerging economies, and to reduce their liabilities of foreignness. Subsidiary managers' perceptions on host countries' uncertainty and risks likely decrease, and they face less operational difficulties (Delios and Beamish, 2001). They develop experience-based capabilities, refined routines, and the ability to adapt, which is a type of FSA (Henderson, 1999; Baum and Shipilov, 2006). Over time, they are able to manage their business more effectively (Gao et al., 2008), and the performance of subsidiaries is likely better (Slangen and Hennart, 2008). Better performance in turn encourages profit reinvestments (Lundan, 2006; Nguyen and Rugman, 2015).

Furthermore, compared to headquarters managers, subsidiary managers are in better positions to identify incremental investment opportunities which can be traced to their experience and insightful knowledge of local markets (Nguyen and Rugman, 2015). Mudambi (1998) finds that a subsidiary with a greater experience of a particular known location is more likely to reinvest there than a firm with less experience. Thus, we predict

Hypothesis 2: The duration of operation of a subsidiary is positively related to its reinvestment into the same host country.

Methodology

Research context, data sources, samples and questionnaire survey

We used OneSource Database by Thomson Reuters, Reuters Research Inc. to compile a list of the largest British firms by total sales (Yip et al., 2006). We identified a total of 91 parent firms having operations in the ASEAN region after we manually consulted their annual reports and websites. Among these firms, 78 firms were publicly listed, and 13 firms were private. From the list of 91 parent firms, and from the websites of British, US and European chambers of commerce, we identified a total of 504 British MNE subsidiaries in six countries (Malaysia, Indonesia, the Philippines, Singapore and Thailand) out of ten member countries of the ASEAN.

We used a 40-question questionnaire to collect data for a number of research projects. We carefully designed our questions based on theories of international business, finance and accounting standards. We documented our survey in English, using simple and concise language. We avoided ambiguous and unfamiliar terms, academic jargon, and double questions. We pre-tested our questionnaire with five experienced subsidiary managers. All these procedures ensured that all questions were easy to understand.

We invited managers of British multinational subsidiaries to participate in the survey by email. This method allowed us to interact and to exchange with subsidiary managers, to ask follow-up questions, to collect additional information, and to obtain their insights which were not in the original survey. However, the process was very challenging and time-consuming (between July 2010 and February 2011). Participating subsidiaries provided data for the period 2003–2007 (due to commercially confidential reasons, they provided recent data only).

We achieved a good response rate of 20 per cent, which compared favourably to previous studies using surveys with managers (for response rate in mail surveys, see Harzing, 2000). A total of 101 replies were returned with no missing values for the analysis. Ninety per cent was responded to by the top management team. The respondents have approximately eight years of working experience in the ASEAN region.

All 101 subsidiaries are private, that is, their shares are not listed on the stock exchanges in the host countries. They belong to 78 parent firms, of which 44 are public and 13 are private. We collected data of public parent firms; however, information for 13 private parent firms was not available. From the annual reports of 44 public parent firms, we found that, as of the end of the year 2008, they had average revenues of GBP 23,906 million, and average assets of GBP 167,101 million.

We found that the average invested capital of the participating subsidiaries was US$78 million in 2007 (subsidiaries were asked to report financial data in US$ currency in the survey). The average age of the subsidiaries at the time of data collection was 26 years. They generated 77 per cent of their total sales from domestic sales, and 23 per cent from exports. They operated in a wide range of industries which are classified into service sector at 56 per cent and manufacturing/processing sector (including energy, petroleum and refining) at 44 per cent.

Non-response bias test

To check whether the potential non-response bias exists, we compared key characteristics (sales, assets and employee data for 2008) of the publicly listed parent MNEs of the respondent and non-respondent subsidiaries. The results of t-tests showed no significant differences at a 5 per cent significance level (two-tailed test) between two groups. Armstrong and Overton (1977) argue that late respondents represent non-respondents. We compared data characteristics of early and late respondents, and there were no significant differences between the two groups.

Common method variance

To mitigate the risks of potential common method variance, we implemented a number of ex-ante and ex-post procedures (Chang et al., 2010; Podsakoff et al., 2003). The ex-ante procedures were included to assure respondents of complete confidentiality and anonymity. A number of questions were fact-based; subsidiary managers could obtain these data from their accounting and reporting systems. Furthermore, we used multi-item constructs, and we varied scale formats to minimise potential consistency. Scale items of interest were spread throughout the questionnaire and they were separated as far apart from one another as practically possible.

The ex-post procedures included a Harman's one-factor test which was used to check the presence of common method effects. The test results did not reveal one overarching factor, and thus suggested that common method variance was not present. Additionally, we adopted data triangulation by using archival sources and we used complex regression models. All these careful procedures confirmed that common method variance was not a serious problem in this dataset.

Dependent, independent and control variables

Dependent variable

Subsidiary reinvested earnings: This construct was developed on the basis of the pecking-order theory (Myers and Majluf, 1984). Subsidiary managers were asked to self-report the percentages of major financing sources of the subsidiary's capital (retained earnings; capital investment by parent firms; intra-firm borrowing, i.e. intra-firm loans from parent firms and/or sister affiliates; borrowing/loans from bank(s), and/or venture capital(s) within the host country, and borrowing from international bank(s) outside the host country). Reinvested earnings are measured by the percentage of profits that were reinvested in the subsidiary.

Independent variables

Subsidiary managers' perceptions and assessment on host country location factors: This construct was developed from the insights of Rugman's FSA/CSA matrix (Rugman, 1981), and Dunning's eclectic paradigm and four FDI motives of market-seeking, efficiency-seeking, resource-seeking and strategic-asset-seeking (Dunning, 1998; Dunning and Lundan, 2008, Box 10.1, pp. 325–326). Subsidiary managers were asked 'to think about when you were selecting the host country location where it currently operates and/or when you were considering to expand the operation, how influential/ important would you say that each of the following was to your decision?' A Likert 7-point scale was used from 1=not very influential at all to 7=very influential. The ten-item location factors include: access to customers; access to suppliers; access to raw materials; stable economic, social and political environment; ease of doing business, legal regulations and law enforcement; availability of grants and incentives; taxes;

access to finance; labour (availability, quality and regulations); and the reliability and quality of infrastructure.

In the OLS regression analysis, this construct is first tested as a ten-item summated scale with a Cronbach alpha of 0.743. After that, all ten items are included one –after another in a series of regressions in the attempt to identify the most important location factors which influence subsidiary managers in their reinvestment decision into the existing known location.

Duration of operations of subsidiaries: is measured by the number of years that the subsidiaries have been in operation since the year of establishment (Luo and Peng, 1999; Gao et al., 2008; Makino and Delios, 1996). It is coded as 7=established since 1880; 1=established in the 2000s onward.

Control variables

We include a comprehensive set of control variables: parent firm characteristics, subsidiary characteristics, historical links with the United Kingdom, and sectors.

Parent firm characteristics

Parent firm size: is measured by the number of employees of parent firms, using data from OneSource database. It is coded as 1=10,000 employees and 7=70,000 employees or more.

Subsidiary characteristics

Subsidiary size: is measured by the number of employees (Demirbag et al., 2015), using survey data, and is coded as 1=below 500 employees; 7=2,000 employees or more.

Relatedness to parent firms' activities: We follow the procedures in Slangen and Hennart (2008) to measure the relatedness to parent MNEs' activities in which relatedness to parent firm's activities takes the value of 0, otherwise 1.

Subsidiary autonomy: Subsidiary autonomy is defined as the level of freedom of the subsidiary in decision-making rights relative to the parent firm and the role it has to fulfil (McDonald et al., 2008; Nobel and Birkinshaw, 1998). We follow previous studies to collect information on subsidiary autonomy by questionnaire (Birkinshaw and Hood, 1998; Roth and Morrison; 1992; Slangen and Hennart, 2008). Subsidiary managers were asked 'to indicate your subsidiary's level of freedom to make a range of decisions without reference from headquarters (HQ)/regional offices on different areas of decisions'. These include supply chains (key suppliers, production/service delivery process); sales, marketing and distribution (product/ service offerings, key customers, advertising, promotion and brands); human resources management (selection, recruitment, remuneration, training and development of employees); international financial management (investment, financing and dividend), and non-business infrastructure relations. A Likert 5-point scale was used: 1=decisions exclusively made by HQ; 2=decisions largely made by HQ; 3=shared decision; 4=decisions largely made by subsidiary; 5=decisions exclusively made by subsidiary. The result of scale reliability test showed a Cronbach alpha of 0.870.

Ownership forms: is a dummy variable which assumes the value of 1 if the equity of the affiliate is a WOFS, and 0 if it is a JV (Kim and Gray, 2008).

Foreign entry mode: We control for the potential effects of foreign entry mode, using a dummy variable 1=acquisitions, 0=greenfields (Slangen and Hennart, 2008).

Historical links with the United Kingdom: We use a dummy variable 1= having historical links with the UK (former British colonies), otherwise 0 (Ghemawat, 2001).

Sectors: A dummy control variable assumes the value of 1 for manufacturing, and 0 for service.

Results and discussions

We find that equity capital by parent firms accounts for 56 per cent of total funding in British subsidiaries. They have effectively utilised these financial resources, and they have operated at a profit. A proportion has been repatriated to their parent firms (dividend payments), and a proportion has been retained and reinvested. Retained earnings are important financing sources, accounting for 29 per cent of total funding. Intra-firm borrowing from parent firms and/or sister affiliates accounts for 8 per cent, and external debts for 7 per cent of total funding.

Our hypotheses are tested by OLS regressions. We report key descriptive statistics and correlations for all variables in Table 3.1. We have carefully examined our data to ensure that they comply with the requirements of regression analysis in terms of linearity, equality of variance and normality. The plotting of standardised residuals against standardised predicted values shows no major violations. There is sufficient variance of independent variables and low correlation of the zero order correlation matrix ($r<0.4$). This is consistent with Hair et al. (2010) who suggest that the correlation should be below the usual threshold of 0.50.

We examine the tolerance for individual variables in the model, and they all exceed 0.7. We also examine the variance inflation factor (VIF) values for individual variables across models. They do not exceed the value of 2 and they are below the commonly specified cut-off values of 10 (Hair et al., 2010). All these procedures confirm that multicollinearity is not a problem in our dataset.

Table 3.1 Descriptive statistics and Pearson correlations

Var.	Mean	SD	1	2	3	4	5	6	7	8	9	10	11	12	13	14	15	16	17	18	19	20
1.	29.07	4.01	1																			
2.	5.98	1.34	.21**	1																		
3.	3.88	1.82	.01	.23*	1																	
4.	3.04	2.09	-.03	-.02	.68**	1																
5.	5.35	1.18	.11	.10	.17	.16	1															
6.	5.19	1.29	.20*	.22*	.43**	.23*	.60**	1														
7.	3.39	1.84	.20*	.05	.29**	.44**	.29**	.40**	1													
8.	4.30	1.53	.10	-.03	.38**	.38**	.49**	.51**	.47**	1												
9.	3.52	1.91	.11	.17	.24*	.28**	.36**	.24*	.47**	.45**	1											
10.	4.78	1.38	.15	.27**	.38**	.19*	.35**	.41**	.34**	.29**	.32*	1										
11.	4.89	1.38	.23**	-.03	.33**	.28**	.49**	.51**	.36**	.49**	.34*	.30**	1									
12.	2.62	1.26	.02	.12	.06	.02	-.08	.03	.08	.06	-.04	-.02	.15	1								
13.	3.29	2.56	.02	.04	.06	.17	-.18	-.07	.04	.02	-.05	-.07	.08	.33**	1							
14.	1.62	1.14	.11	.13	-.12	.02	-.20*	-.12	.07	-.08	-.06	-.05	-.04	.26*	.37*	1						
15.	0.02	0.17	.12	.01	.01	-.032	.09	-.02	.28**	.11	.04	.11	-.15	-.04	-.02	-.04	1					
16.	3.36	0.79	-.04	.26***	.03	-.02	-.18	-.11	-.12	-.14	-.01	-.07	-.23*	.01	-.01	.07	-.08	1				
17.	0.79	0.40	.14	.15	.01	-.13	.01	.05	.05	.05	.01	.06	-.02	.13	.01	.02	.08	.009	1			
18.	0.28	0.45	-.06	.04	.04	-.02	.16	-.03	-.07	.03	-.02	.01	-.11	-.17	-.01	-.07	.14	-.044	-.217*	1		
19.	0.37	0.48	.31**	-.05	.02	-.13	.14	.30**	.12	.24*	.04	.09	.12	.21**	-.25**	-.16	-.10	-.120	.105	.053	1	
20.	0.43	0.49	-.012	-.10	.15	.44**	.01	-.01	.20*	.17	.09	-.09	.11	.08	.14	.09	-.036	.022	.239*	-.160	.081	1

Notes: 1. Reinvested earnings; 2. Access to customers; 3. Access to suppliers; 4. Access to raw materials; 5. Stable environment; 6. Ease of doing business ; 7. Availability of grants and incentives; 8. Taxes; 9. Access to finance; 10. Labour; 11. Local infrastructures; 12. Duration of operation; 13. Parent firm size; 14. Subsidiary size; 15. Relatedness to parent activities; 16. Subsidiary autonomy; 17. Ownership forms; 18. Foreign entry mode; 19. Historical links with the United Kingdom; 20.Sectors. n = 101, * p<0.1, ** p<0.05, *** p<0.01, 2-tail test.

We report our regression results in Table 3.2. Model 1 includes control variables. Model 2 contains independent variables only (summated scale of host country location factors, and duration of operation). Model 3 is a full model.

Our two hypotheses are empirically supported. Specifically, hypothesis 1 predicts that the perceptions and assessment on host country location factors by subsidiary managers are positively related to reinvested earnings by the subsidiary into the existing locations. The coefficients in the models are statistically significant. Thus, hypothesis 1 is fully supported. Hypothesis 2 predicts that the duration of operation of a subsidiary is positively related to its reinvestment in the same host country. The coefficients confirm statistically significant positive effects of this variable on reinvestment. Thus, hypothesis 2 is fully supported. Our finding is consistent with Mudami (1998) and Demirbag et al. (2015).

In order to obtain an in-depth understanding of which location factors are the most important in influencing perceptions and assessment of subsidiary managers, we include 10 location factors one –after another in a series of regressions. Due to space constraints, we report the final regression results in

Table 3.2   Multiple OLS regressions (models 1–3)

Variables	Model 1		Model 2		Model 3	
(Constant)	27.42***	(1.98)	21.62***		22.56***	(3.05)
Independent variables						
Subsidiary managers' perception and assessment of host country location factors (summated scale)			1.033***	(0.42)	0.77**	(0.43)
Duration of operation			0.84***	(0.29)	0.56**	(0.34)
Control variables						
Parent firm characteristics						
Parent firm size	0.08	(0.16)			−0.02	(0.17)
Subsidiary characteristics						
Subsidiary size	0.53	(0.36)			0.47	(0.36)
Relatedness to parent firms' activities	3.16	(2.27)			3.13	(2.23)
Subsidiary autonomy	−0.41	(0.48)			−0.25	(0.48)
Ownership forms	1.10	(0.99)			0.73	(0.98)
Foreign entry modes	−0.63	(0.88)			−0.38	(0.88)
Institution						
Historical links with the United Kingdom	2.83**	(0.83)			2.02**	(0.87)
Sectors	0.08	(0.81)			−0.09	(0.79)
R square	**0.16**		**0.13**		**0.23**	
F-change	**2.24****		**7.51*****		**2.50****	

Notes: n = 101. Variables are shown with unstandardised coefficients followed by standard errors in brackets. *$p<0.1$; **$p<0.05$; ***$p<0.01$.

Table 3.3. We carefully check the variance inflation factors (VIF) of these 10 location items and find no multicollinearity.

We find that only two location factors are the most influential in reinvestment decisions of subsidiaries: access to customers, and the reliability and quality of infrastructures. Access to customers reflects market-seeking FDI motives of multinational subsidiaries. This is consistent with Nguyen (2014), who finds that market-seeking is the predominant FDI motive of foreign subsidiaries in the ASEAN region (66 per cent for manufacturing subsidiaries and 71 per cent

Table 3.3   Multiple OLS regressions (models 1, 2)

Variables	Model 1		Model 2	
(Constant)	20.91***	(2.59)	21.69***	(3.24)
Independent variables				
Access to customers	0.53*	(0.33)	0.56*	(0.35)
Access to suppliers	−0.33	(0.35)	−0.41	(0.37)
Access to raw materials	−0.13	(0.29)	0.16	(0.33)
Stable economic, social, and political environment	−0.23	(0.46)	−0.35	(0.50)
Ease of doing business, legal regulations and law enforcement	0.34	(0.46)	0.27	(0.48)
Availability of grants and investment incentives	0.31	(0.28)	0.01	(0.31)
Taxes	−0.07	(0.35)	−0.36	(0.36)
Access to finance	0.03	(0.26)	0.13	(0.26)
Labour (availability, quality and regulations)	0.17	(0.34)	0.13	(0.34)
Reliability and quality of infrastructure	0.53*	(0.37)	0.79**	(0.39)
Duration of operation	0.71***	(0.32)	0.47**	(0.36)
Control variables				
Parent firm characteristics				
Parent firm size			−0.04	(0.18)
Subsidiary characteristics				
Subsidiary size			0.30	(0.39)
Relatedness to parent firms' activities			4.63*	(2.62)
Subsidiary autonomy			−0.33	(0.53)
Ownership forms (WOFS vs. JV)			0.63	(1.01)
Foreign entry modes (greenfields vs. acquisition)			0.07	(0.93)
Institution				
Historical links with the United Kingdom			2.32**	(0.95)
Sectors			0.13	(0.92)
R square	**0.19**		**0.28**	
F-change	**1.97***		**1.63***	

Notes: n = 101. Variables are shown with unstandardised coefficients followed by standard errors in brackets. *$p<0.1$; **$p<0.05$; ***$p<0.01$.

for service subsidiaries). The reliability and quality of local infrastructures, which facilitates business activities, is an important factor. Our finding is consistent with previous studies which find a positive relationship between local infrastructures and aggregate inward FDI (Cheng and Kwan, 2000; Loree and Guisinger, 1995; Wells, 1993). We find that access to suppliers, access to raw materials and labour (availability, quality and regulations) are not influential location factors. This is in line with Nguyen (2014) who finds that efficiency-seeking is not primary FDI motives of British subsidiaries in the ASEAN region (25 per cent for manufacturing subsidiaries and 26 per cent for service subsidiaries).

Other institutional factors, such as stable economic, social and political environment, ease of doing business, legal regulations and law enforcement, availability of grants and incentives, taxes, and access to finance have no significant effects on reinvested earnings of subsidiaries. Our findings differ from previous studies on reinvestments using data of small businesses in post-communist countries and in transitional and developing countries (Johnson et al., 2002; Cull and Xu, 2005; Chakravarty and Xiang, 2011; Demirbag et al., 2015). Johnson et al. (2002) find that weak property rights discourage firms in post-communist countries from reinvesting their profits, even when bank loans are available. Chakravarty and Xiang (2011) find that access to external financing plays an important role in a small firm's reinvestment decision in developing countries. We suggest that ASEAN subsidiary managers have developed necessary capabilities to deal with institutional challenges in the host countries and to operate successfully (Nguyen and Rugman, 2015).

We offer a plausible explanation why access to finance is not an influential location factor for multinational subsidiaries in their reinvestment decisions. British MNEs have access to their home country and international capital markets which help them lower costs of capital compared to domestic firms. They use these financial resources to make equity capital in their foreign subsidiaries. In other words, MNEs overcome imperfections in external capital markets by developing efficient internal capital markets within their own organisation structures to redistribute financial resources (Rugman, 1980; Mudambi, 1999; Aulakh and Mudambi, 2005; Desai et al., 2004; Nguyen and Rugman, 2015). Foreign subsidiaries can overcome constraints of local capital markets in emerging economies. This reflects finance-specific competitive advantages of MNEs (Oxelheim et al., 2001). Our findings on major financing sources confirm the importance of internal capital market for multinational subsidiaries in which internal financing sources account for 93 per cent of total funding, whereas external debt accounts for only 7 per cent.

The relationships between control variables and dependent variable also present interesting findings. We find that parent firm size has no effect on reinvested earnings of subsidiaries (Table 3.2), which is consistent with

Nguyen and Rugman (2015), and Slangen and Hennart (2008). We find that subsidiary size has no effect on reinvestment, which differs from Demirbag et al. (2015).

Subsidiary autonomy has an insignificant effect on reinvested earnings of subsidiaries, which is consistent with McDonald et al. (2008), and Nguyen and Rugman (2015). Subsidiaries might use autonomy to engage in rent-seeking behaviour (Mudambi and Navarra, 2004) and to gain bargaining power (Ciabuschi et al., 2012; Chen et al., 2012; Dorrenbacher and Gammelgaard, 2011). Autonomy might prompt subsidiaries to take peripheral positions in the multinational networks, which might result in less support from parent firms. Thus, Taggart and Hood (1999) maintain that autonomy should not be seen as an end in itself and it should be reduced in integrated MNEs.

We find that ownership forms and foreign entry modes have no significant impact on reinvested earnings of subsidiaries. Our findings are consistent with Tran (1977), Eckert and Rossmeissl (2007) and Williams (1998). Historical links (former colonies) with the United Kingdom have a significant positive effect on reinvested earnings of subsidiaries. Our finding is consistent with Ghemawat (2001), who uses country-level aggregate trade data and reports that colony-coloniser relationships have a positive significant relationship with trade. Finally, sectors do not have any explanatory power on reinvested earnings of subsidiaries. ASEAN countries do not protect specific industries and sectors, nor promote national championships and regionalism compared to a large emerging economy like China. The competitive environments that might influence the structure of these industries and sectors do not affect reinvested earnings of subsidiaries.

Robustness tests

We perform additional robustness tests to exclude alternative explanations. We replace our survey data of subsidiary managers' perceptions and assessment on host country location factors with public data of economic freedom of the world index (EFWI) published by Fraser Institute, Vancouver, Canada. The EFWI is a summated scale of five areas, including size of government (expenditures, taxes and enterprises); legal system and property rights (legal system and security of property rights); sound money (access to sound money); freedom to trade internationally; regulation (regulation of credit, labour and business). We use the average of the index for six ASEAN countries for the period 2003–2007. We find a positive significant relationship between economic freedom index and reinvested earnings of subsidiaries. However, we cannot include all sub-index components in a series of regressions due to high multicollinearity among them. Due to space constraints, the results are not reported here.

Managerial and public policy implications

Our findings provide important implications for managers and public poli-cymakers. Reinvested earnings are a proactive sustainable investment and financing strategy for subsidiaries. Retained earnings are low-risk means to finance reinvestment activities for continuing expansion and growth, which is in line with the pecking-order theory. This strategy benefits foreign subsid-iaries which ultimately contribute to the overall performance of parent firms.

We address the roles of multinational subsidiaries in economic development of the host countries (Hood and Young, 1976). We find that multinational subsidiaries in emerging economies use their own internal financing sources, and depend less on external debt financing from local financial institutions. They act as development agencies through their foreign subsidiaries to fund economic development of the host countries (Nguyen, 2013; Nguyen and Rugman, 2015). Thus, it is recommended that host governments develop pol-icies which encourage greater use of retained earnings for reinvestments of foreign subsidiaries.

We find that the most important factors influencing reinvestment decisions of subsidiary managers are access to customers, the reliability and quality of infrastructures, and the length of operations. It is recommended that host governments focus their scarce national resources on promoting free trade and developing high-quality and efficient infrastructures to facilitate firms to do business effectively. Investment agencies should devote effort to encourage investors with current operations to reinvest as they are likely to do so.

Conclusion

In this study we establish that subsidiary-level reinvested earnings are an important FSA, along with other traditional FSAs, as this reflects capabilities and decision-making in financial management of the subsidiary. We show that subsidiary managers have in-depth knowledge about challenges and opportun-ities of emerging economies, and they have developed sustainable strategies in financial management thanks to their cumulative experience. We find that British subsidiary managers act strategically to use their own retained earnings to finance reinvestments for continuing expansion and growth. We provide a compelling theory-driven explanation on the determinants of reinvested earn-ings of subsidiaries. We find that the most important variables influencing reinvestment decisions are access to customers and the reliability and quality of infrastructures, and the duration of operations.

Our study is subject to several limitations, some of which might provide avenues for future research. We use a dataset of British subsidiaries in the ASEAN region. Future research might examine subsidiaries of MNEs from other countries having active operations in the ASEAN region. It will be interesting to compare and to contrast with our findings. In addition, the context of subsidiaries in other emerging economies might be considered for future research.

References

Armstrong, S. and Overton, T.D. (1977). 'Estimating nonresponse bias in mail surveys'. *Journal of Marketing Research*, 14(1), 396–402.

Aulakh, P.S. and Mudambi, R. (2005). 'Financial resource flows in multinational enterprises: The role of external capital markets'. *Management International Review*, 45(3), 307–325.

Baum, J.A. and Shipilov, V. (2006). 'Ecological approaches to organisations'. In S.R. Clegg, C. Hardy, T. Lawrence and W. Nord (eds), *Handbook of Organisation Studies*. Thousand Oaks, CA: Sage Publishing.

Birkinshaw, J.M. and Hood, N. (1998). 'Multinational subsidiary evolution: Capability and charter change in foreign owned foreign subsidiary', *Academy of Management Review*, 23(4), 773–795.

Buckley, P. and Casson, M. (1976). *The Future of Multinational Enterprise*. Basingstoke and London: Macmillan.

Butler, R. (1995). 'Time in organisations: Its experience, explanations, and effects', *Organisation Studies*, 16(6), 925–950.

Caves, R.E. (1998). 'Research on international business: Problems and prospects', *Journal of International Business Studies*, 29(1), 5–19.

Chakravarty, S. and Xiang, M. (2011). 'Determinants of profit reinvestment by small businesses in emerging economies', *Financial Management*, 40(3), 553–590.

Chang, S.J., van Witteloostuijn and Eden, L. (2010). 'Common method variance in international business research', *Journal of International Business Studies*, 41(1), 178–181.

Chen, T-J., Chen, H. and Ku, Y-H. (2012). 'Resource dependency and parent-subsidiary capability transfers', *Journal of World Business*, 47(2), 259–266.

Cheng, L.K. and Kwan, Y.K. (2000). 'What are the determinants of the location of foreign direct investment? The Chinese experience', *Journal of International Economics*, 1(2), 379–400.

Ciabuschi, F., Dellestrand, H. and Kappen, P. (2012). The good, the bad, the ugly: Technology transfer competence, rent-seeking and bargaining power', *Journal of World Business*, 47(4), 664–674.

Cull, R. and Xu, L.C. (2005). 'Institutions, ownership, and finance: The determinants of profit reinvestment among Chinese firms', *Journal of Financial Economics*, 77(1), 117–146.

Defever, F. (2006). 'Functional fragmentation and the location of multinational firms in the enlarged Europe', *Regional Science and Urban Economics*, 36(5), 658–677.

Delios, A. and Beamish, P.W. (2001). 'Survival and profitability: The role of experience and intangible assets in foreign subsidiary performance', *Academy of Management Journal*, 44(5), 1028–1038.

Demirbag, M., McGuinness, M., Wood, G. and Bayyurt, N. (2015). 'Context, law, and reinvestment decisions: Why the transitional periphery differs from other post-state socialist economies', *International Business Review*, *forthcoming*. Available at http://dx.doi.org./10.1016/j.ibusrev.2015.03.003.

Desai, M.A., Foley, C.F. and Hines, J.R. Jr. (2002). 'Chains of ownership, regional tax competition, and foreign direct investment', Working paper No. 9224. National Bureau of Economic Research.

—— (2004). 'A multinational perspective on capital structure choice and internal capital markets', *Journal of Finance*, 59(6), 2451–2487.

—— (2007). 'Dividend policy inside the multinational firm', *Financial Management*, 36(1), 5–26.

Dorrenbacher, C. and Gammelgaard, J. (2011). 'Subsidiary power in multinational corporations: The subtle role of micro-political bargaining power', *Critical Perspectives on International Business*, 7(1), 30–47.

Dunning, J.H. (1998). 'Location and the multinational enterprise: A neglected factor?', *Journal of International Business Studies*, 29(1), 45–66.

Dunning, J.H. and Lundan, S.M. (2008). *Multinational Enterprises and the Global Economy*, 2nd Edition. Cheltenham, UK: Edward Elgar.

Eckert, S. and Rossmeissl, F. (2007). 'Local heroes, regional champions, or global mandates? Empirical evidence on the dynamics of German MNC subsidiary roles in Central Europe', *Journal of East West Business*, 13(2), 191–218.

Enright, M.J. (2009). 'The location of activities of manufacturing multinationals in the Asia-Pacific', *Journal of International Business Studies*, 40(1), 818–839.

Flores, R.G., and Aguilera, R.V. (2007). 'Globalisation and location choice: An analysis of US multinational firms in 1980 and 2000', *Journal of International Business Studies*, 38(6), 1187–1210.

Gao, G.Y., Pan, Y., Lu, J. and Tao, Z. (2008). 'Performance of multinational subsidiaries: Influences of cumulative experience', *Management International Review*, 48(6), 749–768.

Ghemawat, P. (2001). 'Distance still matters: The hard reality of global expansion', *Harvard Business Review*, 79(8), 1–12.

Grubert, H., and Mutti, J.H. (1991). 'Do taxes influence where US corporations invest?', *National Tax Journal*, 53(4), 825–839.

Hair, J.F., Black, W.C., Babin, B. and Anderson, R.E. (2010). *Multivariate Data Analysis*, 7th Edition. London: Pearson Prentice Hall.

Harzing, A.W. (1997). 'Response rates in international mail surveys: Results of 22-country study', *International Business Review*, 6(6), 641–665.

—— (2000). 'Cross national industrial mail surveys: Why do response rates differ between countries?', *Industrial Marketing Management*, 29(3), 243–254.

Henderson, A.D. (1999). 'Firm strategy and age dependence: A contingent view of the liabilities of newness, adolescence, and obsolescence', *Administrative Science Quarterly*, 44(1), 281–314.

Hennart, J.F. (1982). *A Theory of Multinational Enterprise*. Ann Arbor: University of Michigan Press.

Hood, N. and Young, S. (1976). 'US investments in Scotland: aspect of the branch factory syndrome'. In N. Hood (ed.) *Multinational Subsidiary: Management, Economic Development and Public Policy*, Basingstoke: Palgrave Macmillan.

Johnson, S., McMillan, J. and Woodruff, C. (2002). 'Property rights and finance', *The American Economic Review*, 92(5), 1335–1356.

Khanna, T. and Palepu, K.G. (2010). *Winning in Emerging Markets*. Cambridge, MA: Harvard Business Press.

Kim, Y. and Gray, S.J. (2008). 'The impact of entry mode choice on foreign affiliate performance: The case of foreign MNEs in South Korea', *Management International Review*, 48(2), 165–188.

Krobin, S.J. (1976). 'The environmental determinants of foreign direct manufacturing investment: An ex-post empirical analysis', *Journal of International Business Studies*, 7(2), 29–42.

Kuemmerle, W. (1999). 'The drivers of foreign direct investment into research and development: An empirical investigation', *Journal of International Business Studies*, 30(1), 1–24.

Loree, D. and Guisinger, S.E. (1995). 'Policy and non-policy determinants of US equity foreign direct investment', *Journal of International Business Studies*, 26(2), 281–299.

Lundan, S.M. (2006). 'Reinvested earnings as a component of FDI: An analytical review of the determinants of reinvestment', *Transnational Corporations*, 15(3), 35–66.

Luo, Y. and Peng, M.W. (1999). 'Learning to compete in a transitional economy: Experience, environment, and performance', *Journal of International Business Studies*, 30(2), 269–296.

Makino, S. and Delios, A. (1996). 'Local knowledge transfer: Implications for alliance formation in Asia', *Journal of International Business Studies*, 27(5), 905–928.

McDonald, F., Warhurst, S. and Allen, M. (2008). 'Autonomy, embeddedness and the performance of foreign owned subsidiaries', *Multinational Business Review*, 16(3), 73–92.

Mudambi, R. (1998). 'The role of duration in multinational investment strategies', *Journal of International Business Studies*, 29(2), 239–261.

——— (1999). 'MNE internal capital markets and subsidiary strategic independence', *International Business Review*, 8(1), 197–211.

Mudambi, R. and Navarra, P. (2004). 'Is knowledge power? Knowledge flows, subsidiary power and rent-seeking within MNCs', *Journal of International Business Studies*, 35(5), 385–406.

Myers, S.C. and Majluf, N.S. (1984). 'Corporate financing and investment decisions when firms have information that investors do not have', *Journal of Financial Economics*, 13(1), 187–222.

Nguyen, Q.T.K. (2013). 'Can British multinational enterprises finance economic development in South East Asia?', *Multinational Business Review*, 21(2), 122–147.

——— (2014). 'The regional strategies of British multinational subsidiaries in South East Asia', *British Journal of Management*, 25(S1), 60–76.

Nguyen, Q.T.K. and Rugman, A.M. (2015). 'Internal equity financing and the performance of multinational subsidiaries in emerging economies', *Journal of International Business Studies*, 46(4), 468–490.

Nobel, R. and Birkinshaw, J.M. (1998). 'Innovation in multinational corporations: Control and communication patterns in international R&D operations', *Strategic Management Journal*, 19(5), 479–496.

Oxelheim, L., Randoy, T., and Stonehill, A. (2001). 'On the treatment of finance-specific factors within the OLI paradigm', *International Business Review*, 10(4), 381–398.

Podsakoff, P.M., MacKenzie, S.B., Lee, J.Y., and Podsakoff, N.P. (2003). 'Common method biases in behavioral research: A critical review of the literature and recommended remedies', *Journal of Applied Psychology*, 88(5), 879–903.

Root, F.R. (1987). *Entry Strategies for International Markets*. Lexington, MA: D.C. Health.

Root, F.R. and Ahmed, A.A. (1978). 'The influence of policy instruments on manufacturing direct foreign investment in developing countries', *Journal of International Business Studies*, 9(3), 81–93.

Roth, K. and Morrison, A.J. (1992). 'Implementing global strategy: Characteristics of global subsidiary mandates', *Journal of International Business Studies*, 23(4), 715–735.

Rugman, A.M. (1980). 'Internalisation theory and corporate international finance', *California Management Review*, 23(2), 73–79.

—— (1981). *Inside the Multinationals: The Economics of Internal Markets*, New York: Columbia University Press.

Rugman, A.M. and Collinson, S. (2012). *International Business*, 6th Edition. Harlow, UK: Pearson.

Sethi, D., Guisinger, S.E., Phelan, S.E., and Berg, D.M. (2003). 'Trends in direct foreign investment flows: A theoretical and empirical analysis', *Journal of International Business Studies*, 34(4), 315–326.

Slangen, A. and Hennart, J-F. (2008). 'Do foreign Greenfields outperform foreign acquisitions or vice versa? An institutional perspective', *Journal of Management Studies*, 45(7), 1301–1328.

Song, J. (2002). 'Firm capabilities and technology ladders: Sequential foreign direct investment of Japanese electronic firms in East Asia', *Strategic Management Journal*, 23(3), 191–210.

Taggart, J.H. and Hood, N. (1999). 'Determinants of autonomy in multinational corporation subsidiaries', *European Management Journal*, 17(2), 226–236.

Tran, T.D. (1977). 'Ownership, control, and performance of the multinational corporation: A study of US wholly-owned subsidiaries and joint ventures in Philippines and Taiwan', PhD thesis, Los Angeles: University of California.

UNCTAD (2013). *World Investment Report*. Geneva: United Nations Conference on Trade and Development (UNCTAD).

UNCTAD (2015). http://unctad.org/en/Pages/DIAE/Reinvested-Earnings.aspx [accessed 5 June 2015].

Wells, L.T. Jr. (1993). 'Foreign direct investment'. In D.L. Lindauer and M. Roemer (eds), *Developments in Asia and Africa: Legacies and Opportunities*, Boston: Harvard Institute for International Development.

Williams, D. (1998). 'The development of foreign-owned manufacturing subsidiaries: Some empirical evidence', *European Business Review*, 98(5), 282–286.

Woodward, D.P., and Rolfe, R.J. (1993). 'The location of export-oriented foreign direct investment in the Caribbean Basin', *Journal of International Business Studies*, 24(1), 121–144.

Yip, G., Rugman, A.M. and Kudina, A. (2006). 'International success of British companies', *Long Range Planning*, 39(1), 241–264.

4

The Impact of Actors and the Aspect of Time in Institutional Change Processes in a Developing Country Context

Kristin Brandl, Izzet Darendeli, Robert D. Hamilton III and Ram Mudambi

Introduction

The rise of developing countries is undeniably evident in the global business arena. There is increasing evidence of innovative and highly intellectual business activities from these countries, for example in the form of new drug developments from India and technological innovation from China. These innovations often require searching for and utilising tacit knowledge (Asheim and Coenen, 2005) which is prone to asymmetric information problems and intellectual property (IP) abuse. Thus, a firm that operates in these environments emphasises either loose or stringent IP protection standards which then influences the firm's decision regarding the nature and location of innovative activities, in addition to capability endowments and cost calculations (Buckley and Casson, 1976; Dunning, 1988; Teece, 2006). As a result, governments are in continuous search for optimal levels of IP protection standards (varying from high to low levels) to ensure that there is a conducive environment for the advancement of local innovation systems (Chaminade et al., 2012; Jaffe et al., 1993). This is especially true in developing countries.

While high IP protection standards long have been introduced and enforced by institutions in developed countries, many developing countries transitioned to higher IP standards only after they became signatories to the World Trade Organization (WTO) and its Trade-Related Intellectual Property Standards (TRIPS) agreement in 1995 (Li, 2008; Waguespack et al., 2005). The TRIPS agreement set a minimum level of rules and regulations in order to secure consistent IP protection levels among WTO member states. Many developing countries were required to pass certain IP laws and implement innovation policies to reach these standards. In order to allow this transition, developing countries were given transition options such as a ten-year grace period or the possibility of amending the original TRIPS text, which either led to a fast or a slow change process. We are interested in these change processes of IP protection standards and why some developing countries adapted fast while others adapted slow changes to these processes.

Institutional theory suggests that IP protection standards are driven by government policies which are decided collectively through political strategies, actions, lobbying and connectedness of actors inside and outside of a country (Boddewyn and Brewer, 1994; Dolowitz and Marsh, 1996, 2002; Suchman, 1995; Bonardi et al., 2005). More specifically, change processes of institutional regulations are influenced by pressures inflicted through actors and time (North, 1990). Thus, our main argument is that different actors, such as domestic firms or foreign MNEs, differently impact local policy decisions of developing countries, which result in varying TRIPS implementation choices by local governments.

The existence of variation among ratification of TRIPS in developing countries and their rate of compliance to TRIPS suggest these changes do not always comply with national interests (Scholte, 2001). National interests can be based on various indicators or pressured by different actors that operate in the countries. The data on developing countries' TRIPS compliance process suggests that if foreign MNEs have a high presence in the local innovation system in a developing country, such countries comply to TRIPS faster and, conversely, developing countries with a high composition[1] of domestic firms transition into full compliance with TRIPS slowly. We will continue to elaborate on this statement with some empirical support in the following sections of this book chapter. We first elaborate on the background of TRIPS and this empirical support, then use the data to support our theoretically derived arguments. We discuss and conclude the chapter with implications for policy and practice as well as future research directions.

Trade-related intellectual property standards and developing countries

When the World Trade Organization designed the Trade-Related Intellectual Property Standards, the aim was to establish a minimum level of rules and regulations to secure consistent IP protection levels among member states. While these regulations were easy to meet for developed countries, developing countries commonly applied significantly lower levels of IP standards and were required to reach TRIPS standards through new IP laws and innovation policies. In order to ease this process, 60 developing countries were given various transition options at the time of signing the WTO agreement in 1995.

First, countries could use a ten-year grace period to decide when and how fast to ratify TRIPS in their domestic national assemblies and make the international treaty part of local jurisdiction (Kale, 2010; Li, 2008). Thus, some countries ratified TRIPS without delay while others gradually changed or delayed ratification to the end of the ten-year period (Hamdan-Livramente, 2009).

Second, beside the transition period, developing countries were given the flexibility to propose and introduce amendments to the original TRIPS text, designed by the WTO, during the enforcement of the protection laws in their domestic legal system (Li, 2008; WTO, 2012). Similar to the ten-year grace period, some developing countries made amendments (in a few cases even applied changes beyond TRIPS regulation minimum levels) or did not capitalise on this option at all (Yang and Sonmez, 2013). Accordingly, countries had four options: adopt or not adopt a ten-year grace period, and/or amend or not amend the original TRIPS text.

The impact of TRIPS is most significant in the development of a country's innovation system, especially for IP-intensive industries such as pharmaceutical, electronics, as well as computer and software industries. We use these IP-intensive industries as empirical support in this chapter (similar to Delgado et al., 2013), and combine data from the WTO (to outline TRIPS decisions) and the Harvard Patent Data Verse with its United States Patent and Trademark Office (USPTO) data (to outline a country's innovation system). Table 4.1

Table 4.1   TRIPS decisions and developing countries

TRIPS decision	# of countries	Country name
(1) no transition period and no amendment(s)	14	Argentina, Barbados, Belize, Botswana, Brazil, Colombia, Cyprus, Indonesia, South Korea, Malaysia, Mexico, Nicaragua, Trinidad and Tobago, Turkey
(2) use of transition period with early* ratification and no amendment(s)	10	Bahrain, Bolivia, Cameroon, Côte d'Ivoire, Dominica, El Salvador, Gabon, Grenada, Pakistan, Tunisia
(3) use of amendment(s) only	6	Estonia, Philippines, Poland, Singapore, Uruguay, Venezuela
(4) use of transition period with late* ratification and no amendment(s)	27	Brunei, Chile, Costa Rica, Egypt, Ghana, Guatemala, Guyana, Honduras, Israel, Jamaica, Kenya, Kuwait, Macau, Malta, Mauritius, Morocco, Namibia, Nigeria, Papua New Guinea, Paraguay, Peru, Saint Lucia, Sri Lanka, Surinam, Thailand, United Arab Emirates, Zimbabwe
(5) use of transition period and amendment(s)	3	China, Hong Kong, India
Total	60	

Note: * ratifications between 1995 and 1998 are early ratifications, from 1999 to 2005 are late ratifications.

Source: WTO (2012).

provides an outline of all 60 developing countries in the sample and their TRIPS decision.

Most of the 60 developing countries in the sample used either the ten-year grace period and/or amendments as intended by the WTO. Thus, these countries ratified the TRIPS agreement late in their national assemblies so the jurisdiction of the international agreement came into force later than in developed countries (TRIPS decision 2 and 4). To the contrary, 30 per cent of the developing countries did not use the ten-year grace period and did not introduce any amendments ratifying TRIPS immediately (TRIPS decision 1). Introducing amendments (TRIPS decision 3) and using the ten-year grace period and amendments (TRIPS decision 4) were less observed cases among the countries.

Actors within innovation systems and institutional change

Institutions are a collection of formal and informal rules that shape behaviour and human interaction. These rules are reflected in legal systems, regulations, habits and customs (Coriat and Weinstein, 2002; Scott, 2001). While there is an established literature on institutions, less attention was placed on the aspect of institutional change processes. We focus on the institutional change process which transforms established norms impacting the operations or conditions that provide legitimacy to organisations within the institutional environment (North, 1990). Dacin et al. (2002) argue that institutional change processes imply various indicators such as levels of change, approach and periods/time and different levels within organisations, macro-societal and even global, can impact these institutional changes. Transformations can be caused by functional, political and social sources (Oliver, 1992), that is, through internal or exogenous change; for example, external pressures are caused by professional associations or nongovernmental international organisations such as the WTO which is promulgating new standards, conceptions and practices (Boli and Thomas, 1999). Moreover, change can be both incremental in an evolutionary way or dramatic with sudden and abrupt changes with actors that often cannot predict the development and outcome of institutional transformations (Darendeli and Hill, forthcoming).

The existing literature has connected institutional changes with variations in either internal factors such as the development level of countries (Park, 1995), changing income levels (Jacobson and Weiss, 1998) and changing governments (Li and Resnick, 2003) or external factors such as trade activity and becoming a member of the WTO (Yang and Sonmez, 2013). However, as Waguespack et al. (2005) point out, we still have a limited understanding of how a country's innovation-related institutions develop.

What we know is that institutions impact economic change (North, 1990; Williamson, 1985) and that a country's government establishes these formal institutions that determine the domestic borders of the legal and regulatory environment (Peng et al., 2008), based on sole decision-making power and complete information, such as in the case of national innovation systems (Nill and Kemp, 2009). However, studies show that governments often have only limited and imperfect information (Coriat and Weinstein, 2002), and often lack an understanding of innovation (Paraskevopoulou, 2012).

We question if a single actor, such as the government, has complete information on creating institutions and policies and argue that additional actors such as firms influence institutions as much as institutions influence decisions of firms. For example, firms try to increase performance by shaping institutional contexts (Feinberg et al., 2015). Moreover, incentives and power dynamics of *different* actors within the institutional environment shape institutions (Greenwood and Suddaby, 2006).

Thus, the relationship between regulation and organisational innovation should not be considered as unidirectional and static, but rather is bi-directional and dynamic. Organisations seek to influence the direction of institutional change towards their motives and incentives, and in-turn the newly emerged institutional environment changes other organisations. Based on different selection processes in institutional environments, this change process can take different trajectories which then lead to institutions changing at different paces in different contexts (Carney and Gedajlovic, 2002). Along those lines, we argue that the level and complexity of interaction of different actors within the institutional environment is central in deciding the change trajectory in terms of pace of institutional change (see, similarly, Cantwell et al., 2010). Firms are among the most influential actors in the emergence of institutions (North, 1990), domestic or foreign.

The potential for institutional volatility in developing countries makes the relationship between institutions and organisations more salient (Makino et al., 2004). For developing countries, institutional change processes and implications of actors, as well as path dependency, is important as the countries imply more institutional complexity (Li et al., 2000). Next, we investigate TRIPS compliance processes from the perspective of foreign and domestic firms considering the pace of institutional change in developing countries.

Foreign firms' pressures

The literature on institutional voids argues that MNEs are often active in law-making processes in developing countries and thus also influence IP standards (Khanna et al., 2005). Since lower levels of IP protection in developing countries hinder firms engaging in competence-creating activities in such locations, multinational firms are often very protective of their IP and competitive assets (Cantwell and Mudambi, 2005). Moreover, the literature has argued that MNEs have the capabilities to develop organisational connections with leading figures and entities in the government as well as personal connections (Cuervo-Cazurra, 2006; Sun et al., 2010).

Especially in developing countries, relational political behaviour has been found to shape institutional change decisions (Hillman and Hitt, 1999). As a result of increasing pressures from foreign MNEs, developing-country governments raise IP standards to attract MNEs especially if they are seeking new innovation and R&D (Dunning and Lundan, 2008). For example, in the case of the pharmaceutical industry, MNEs and governments from mature market economies extensively lobbied towards a fast ratification of TRIPS during TRIPS talks (Kale and Wield, 2008). Thus, a high composition of foreign MNEs in an innovation system of developing countries results in no usage of a 10-year grace period. Moreover, amendments to original IP regulations are also implemented faster, as is the adaptation of a ten-year grace period, resulting in a faster transition to full TRIPS compliance.

Figure 4.1 supports this argument and shows assignee compositions of the 60 developing countries that did not use a ten-year grace period or introduced amendments. As seen in the figure, eight out of 13 of these developing countries reflect a national innovation system that is dominated by foreign MNEs. Out of these eight countries, six countries have a significantly higher composition of foreign MNEs than local firms. Moreover, the five remaining countries with no innovative activity showed no innovation policies prior to TRIPS and simply did not take advantage of the grace period or amendments, probably because there was no lobbying activity of any kind.

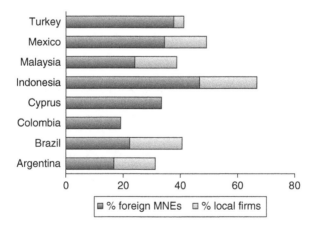

Figure 4.1   TRIPS decision 1 – composition of innovation systems in 1996

Note: Barbados, Belize, Botswana, Nicaragua, and Trinidad and Tobago had no active innovation system in 1996.

Similarly, Figure 4.2 shows the compositions of the national innovation system of developing countries that used the ten-year grace period but ratified TRIPS early (before 1998). As the figure indicates, only one of eight countries showed innovative activities by foreign MNEs. This suggests that the countries initially took advantage of the ten-year grace period, but since they did not have any firm lobbying one way or the other, they ended up ratifying the TRIPS agreement right away. Only Dominica had some innovative activities from foreign MNEs in 1996, during the TRIPS compliance decision process. The remaining actors in the national innovation system in these countries were either investors or foreign universities.

Figure 4.3 shows the compositions of innovation systems within developing countries that introduced amendments to the original TRIPS text, but did not use the ten-year grace period. As the figure shows, all of these countries already had some kind of innovative activity by local or foreign firms. Foreign firms dominated two of the countries' innovation systems, which explains why they did not use a ten-year grace period. However, Singapore's local firm composition was very high compared to countries in the prior cases and the local

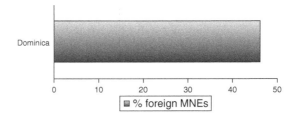

Figure 4.2   TRIPS decision 2 – composition of innovation systems in 1996

Note: Bahrain, Bolivia, Cameroon, Côte d'Ivoire, El Salvador, Gabon and Grenada had no active innovation system in 1996.

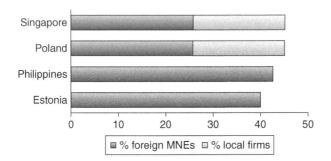

Figure 4.3   TRIPS decision 3 – composition of innovation systems in 1996

Note: Uruguay and Venezuela had no active innovation system in 1996.

firms and foreign firms make up most (44 per cent) of the total innovations in these countries, suggesting that maybe local institutions were influential in pushing the local governments to introduce amendments in cases where local firm assignees were missing.

Domestic firms' pressures

Domestic firms of a country are interested in the development of the domestic market and thus inform, train and engage with governments to influence decisions that change policies, laws and regulations (Fisman, 2001; Hillman and Hitt, 1999). In the case of intellectual property protection, the incentives of domestic firms are different from incentives of foreign firms. In a developing country, and especially in the early stages of development, most domestic firms will possess process capabilities which allow them to develop new process innovations rather capabilities that allow for the development of new innovations on the whole (Kumaraswamy et al., 2012). For instance, Brandl and Mudambi (2014) show that Indian firms were not able to compete with foreign firms in the national innovation system early on in the country's development but only over time were able to develop capabilities to compete.

Lower IP protection standards can help domestic firms, especially in developing countries, to learn how to source knowledge from other firms and form collaborations, allowing them to capitalise on imitation activities and knowledge spillovers (Kumaraswamy et al., 2012). The firms are then able to develop necessary absorptive capacities to move to the next stage of development (Awate et al., 2012). Thus, only with low IP protection regulations implemented and supported by local governments are these activities possible. Local governments are aware of domestic firms' innovative capabilities and maturity to compete with multinational firms (Li, 2008). Domestic firms can then collectively act with the objective of influencing government policies or, in our case, IP protection policies, in order to get them designed and implemented with their own interests in mind (Edquist, 2001). As found by Bonardi et al. (2005), firms lobby for their own interests and influence policies. These activities are evident in the innovation systems of developing countries. Consequently, high composition of domestic firms in innovation systems of developing countries results in the usage of a ten-year grace period and introduced amendments to original IP regulations, resulting in a slow transition to full TRIPS compliance – see Figures 4.4 and 4.5 for empirical support.

Figure 4.4 shows the composition of the innovation systems of developing countries which used the ten-year grace period entirely with ratification in 2005 or ratified TRIPS late (after 1999). Thus, TRIPS compliance process took longer and was slower than in the prior three TRIPS decisions. As the figure indicates, local firm composition was much higher in these countries, compared to prior decisions. In three of the 27 developing countries local firms dominated

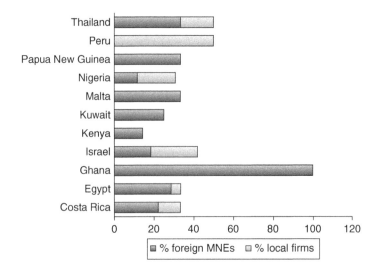

Figure 4.4   TRIPS decision 4 – composition of innovation systems in 1996

Note: Brunei, Chile, Guatemala, Guyana, Honduras, Jamaica, Macau, Mauritius, Morocco, Namibia, Paraguay, Saint Lucia, Sri Lanka, Surinam, United Arab Emirates, and Zimbabwe did not have an active innovation system in 1996.

innovative activities. Sixteen of the developing countries did not have an active innovation system in 1996, and in these countries either the local institutions could have been active in lobbying governments to slow down the TRIPS compliance process or governments intentionally wanted to slow down the process in order to start building up innovative capability slowly.

Lastly, Figure 4.5 shows the compositions of innovation systems of developing countries that used the ten-year grace period, ratified TRIPS late and introduced amendments to the original TRIPS text. As the figure indicates, all of the countries had at least some amount of local firms active in innovation processes, which was not the case in countries which decided to comply with TRIPS faster. Although Hong Kong's innovation system is well advanced (in terms of total number of patents), local firms dominated innovative activities. Strong local institutions lobbying for a slower compliance to TRIPS back up the low composition of local firms compared to foreign firms in India as also argued by Brandl and Mudambi (2014).

Concluding discussion and implications

This chapter set out to study the impact of actors and time on institutional change in a developing-country context. It aimed to shed light on the aspect of the pace of change and drivers as well as actors of change in a unique country

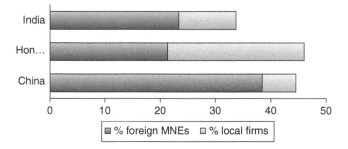

Figure 4.5   TRIPS decision 5 – composition of innovation systems in 1996

context studying TRIPS ratification processes. The above outlined discussion supported by tables and figures shows that countries with a high amount of patent output by local firms show a slow transition to TRIPS IP protection standards. This leads to the conclusion that local firms do hinder and influence the compliance to TRIPS. As argued above, local firms in a national innovation system of a developing country try to influence policies to hinder TRIPS compliance for as long as possible. In addition, the composition of foreign MNEs in the national innovation system of a developing country also has an impact on TRIPS compliance: the higher the composition of foreign MNEs, the faster TRIPS compliance is achieved. The pressure by multinational firms is impacting local governments to comply with TRIPS regulations faster. Or, put differently, the lower the composition of foreign MNEs in the national innovation system of the developing country the less pressure is on governments and the more impact domestic firms have slowing down TRIPS compliance.

These results show two main findings. First, change process of institutions and the differences in terms of time and pace of change. We can see that different countries apply changes differently. Depending on country contexts and decisions taken by the country, compliance to TRIPS regulations is either fast- or slow-paced similar to earlier discussions on institutional changes. Second, in line with this finding, we identify two major actors that influence these changes and the pace of institutional changes. We found that political activism and lobbying (Boddewyn and Brewer, 1994; Hillman and Hitt, 1999), as argued earlier, is responsible for these influences with varying impact on institutional change processes.

We combine these two findings to generate a contribution to the academic literature, to bring together the focus on actors of institutional change processes and aspects of time and pace in institutional change processes (Dacin et al., 2002) which has not been attempted thus far (Cantwell et al., 2010). We offer a contribution with an extension of institutional change theory that presents the different actors that influence institutions and their impact on the pace of change, especially extending North (1990, 2006) who argued that actors not only adapt to given institutions, but aim to shape institutions by providing a process mode of interactions.

Implications for policy and practice

Our findings strongly suggest that policymakers, especially from developing countries, need to be aware of competing and complementing actors within the institutional environment of their countries to ensure that governments develop an optimal set of rules and regulations that are conducive to their national innovation system and, as a result, the catch-up process of their countries in terms of innovation capabilities. If not considered satisfactorily, they can end up implementing suboptimal standards which might curtail further development of the developing country and slow or even hinder this catch-up. Moreover, it is important to know the different actors and their drive to influence and pressure policymakers. Knowing their intentions allows the government to take appropriate actions to both acknowledge and act upon or act against these pressures.

Moreover, findings related to the pace and change process of institutions, influenced by these actors, could allow policymakers and governments to make educated assumptions of further developments of their country and the impact policies in other fields or industries could have on institutional changes. However, this finding of time and pace needs to be considered with caution, as there is a strong country and situation context. TRIPS regulations and the need to reach a certain IP standard was forced through the WTO and can be considered as an exogenous shock and driver for change, also in relation to the pace of change. A natural process of institutional change might have different outcomes with different institutional change processes as well as pace. Moreover, these results suggest lessons for managers of domestic and foreign firms that are active in the innovation systems of developing countries. As variation among developing countries in their TRIPS compliance decisions indicate, if domestic firms increase their presence within the innovation system, they can slow down the institutional change towards higher IP standards so that they might have more time to transform their output capabilities to innovation capabilities. Conversely, if foreign MNEs increase their composition within innovation systems of developing countries, they can speed up the compliance to global standards, which will decrease uncertainties related to institutional voids in developing-country contexts.

Suggestions for future research

When we consider institutional change we mean the change of institutional rules and regulations regarding IP protection standards before TRIPS and after TRIPS ratification. We do not study the actual change that happens and do not consider institutional design in developing countries pre- and post-TRIPS. Moreover, TRIPS ratification implies institutional changes and changes of IP protection standards, especially in a developing country context with initial low protection levels that need to reach high protection levels according to TRIPS requirements. Thus, these changes are exogenously influenced and driven, and thus not a 'natural' occurrence. Institutional change in this study is forced and time-restricted to a maximum of ten years (the ten-year grace period). Future studies could see if our arguments hold in a non-restricted context where institutional change in developing countries is not influenced by exogenous pressures. Moreover, we only consider two actors as influencing factors for institutional change with regard to TRIPS. However, there are additional actors in- or outside of national innovation systems that might influence these change processes. We purposefully left out national or foreign institutions such as national laboratories or universities that are connected to governments making these institutional change decisions. The connection between these institutions and governments are strong and may skew the decision of institutional change. Additionally, the influence of supranational institutions such as the IMF might have an impact on institutional change processes as well, and future research could follow up on this aspect.

Note

1. The composition of a national innovation system is calculated as the proportion of specific actors (e.g. domestic firms, foreign firms, national institutions, individuals) in relation to all actors of an innovation system, using patent assignees as indicators.

References

Asheim, B.T. and Coenen, L. (2005), 'Knowledge bases and regional innovation systems: Comparing Nordic clusters', *Research Policy*, 34(8), 1173–1190.

Awate, S., Larsen, M.M., and Mudambi, R. (2012), 'EMNE catch up strategies in the wind turbine industry: Is there a tradeoff between output and innovation capabilities?' *Global Strategy Journal*, 2(3): 205–223.

Boddewyn, J.J. and Brewer, T.L. (1994), 'International-business political behavior: New theoretical directions', *Academy of Management Review*, 19(1), 119–143.

Boli, J. and Thomas, G.M. (1999), *Constructing World Culture: International Nongovernmental Organizations since 1875*, Stanford, CA: Stanford University Press.

Bonardi, J.P., Hillman, A.J. and Keim, G.D. (2005). 'The attractiveness of political markets: Implications for firm strategy', *Academy of Management Review*, 30(2), 397–413.

Brandl, K. and Mudambi, R. (2014), 'EMNCs and catch-up processes: The case of four Indian industries'. In Cuervo-Cazurra, A., and Ramamurti R. (eds) (2014), *Understanding Multinationals from Emerging Markets*. Cambridge: Cambridge University Press.

Buckley, P.J. and Casson, M. (1976), *The Future of the Multinational Enterprise* (vol. 1). London: Macmillan.

Cantwell, J. and Mudambi, R. (2005), 'MNE competence-creating subsidiary mandates', *Strategic Management Journal*, 26(12), 1109–1128.

Cantwell, J., Dunning, J.H., and Lundan, S.M. (2010), 'An evolutionary approach to understanding international business activity: The co-evolution of MNEs and the institutional environment', *Journal of International Business Studies*, 41(4), 567–586.

Carney, M. and Gedajlovic, E. (2002), 'The co-evolution of institutional environments and organizational strategies: The rise of family business groups in the ASEAN region', *Organization Studies*, 23(1), 1–29.

Chaminade, C., Intarakumnerd, P., and Sapprasert, K. (2012), 'Measuring systemic problems in national innovation systems. An application to Thailand', *Research Policy*, 41(8), 1476–1488.

Coriat, B. and Weinstein, O. (2002), 'Organizations, firms and institutions in the generation of innovation', *Research Policy*, 31(2), 273–290.

Cuervo-Cazurra, A. (2006), 'Who cares about corruption?' *Journal of International Business Studies*, 37(6), 807–822.

Dacin, M.T., Goodstein, J., and Scott, W.R. (2002), 'Institutional theory and institutional change: Introduction to the special research forum', *Academy of Management Journal*, 45(1), 45–56.

Darendeli, I.S. and Hill, T.L. (forthcoming), 'Uncovering the complex relationships between political risk and MNE firm legitimacy: Insights from Libya', *Journal of International Business Studies* forthcoming.

Delgado, M., Kyle, M., and McGahan, A.M. (2013), 'Intellectual property protection and the geography of trade', *The Journal of Industrial Economics*, 61(3), 733–762.

Dolowitz, D.P. and Marsh, D. (1996), 'Who learns what from whom: A review of the policy transfer literature', *Political Studies*, 44(2), 343–357.

——— (2000), 'Learning from abroad: The role of policy transfer in contemporary policy-making', *Governance*, 13(1), 5–23.

Dunning, J.H. (1988), 'The eclectic paradigm of international production: A restatement and some possible extensions', *Journal of International Business Studies*, 1–31.

Dunning, J.H. and Lundan, S.M. (2008), 'Institutions and the OLI paradigm of the multinational enterprise', *Asia Pacific Journal of Management*, 25(4), 573–593.

Edquist, C. (2001) 'The systems of innovation approach and innovation policy: An account of the state of the art'. In DRUID Conference, Aalborg, 12–15 June.

Feinberg, S., Hill, T.L., and Darendeli, I.S. (2015), 'An institutional perspective on nonmarket strategy for a world in flux'. In Lawton, T. (ed.) *Companion to Nonmarket Strategy*, London: Routledge.

Fisman, R. (2001), 'Estimating the value of political connections', *American Economic Review*, 1095–1102.

Greenwood, R. and Suddaby, R. (2006), 'Institutional entrepreneurship in mature fields: The big five accounting firms', *Academy of Management Journal*, 49(1), 27–48.

Hamdan-Livramento, I.M. (2009), 'How compliant are developing countries with their TRIPS obligations?' No. CEMI-WORKING PAPER-2009–001.

Hillman, A.J. and Hitt, M.A. (1999), 'Corporate political strategy formulation: A model of approach, participation, and strategy decision', *Academy of Management Review*, 24(4), 825–842.

Jacobson, H.K. and Weiss, E.B. (1998), 'Assessing the record and designing strategies to engage countries', *Engaging Countries: Strengthening Compliance with International Environmental Accords*, 511.

Jaffe, A.B.,Trajtenberg, M., and Henderson, R. (1993), 'Geographic localization of knowledge spillovers as evidenced by patent citations', *The Quarterly Journal of Economics*, 108(3), 577–598.

Kale, D. (2010), 'The Distinctive Patterns of Dynamic Learning and Inter-firm Differences in the Indian Pharmaceutical Industry', *British Journal of Management*, 21(1), 223–238.

Kale, D. and Wield, D. (2008), 'Exploitative and explorative learning as a response to the TRIPS agreement in Indian pharmaceutical firms', *Industry and Innovation*, 15(1), 93–114.

Keupp, A.P.M.M., Beckenbauer, P.C.A., and Gassmann, O. (2010), 'Enforcing intellectual property rights in weak appropriability regimes', *Management International Review*, 50(1), 109–130.

Khanna, T., Palepu, K.G., and Sinha, J. (2005), 'Strategies that fit emerging markets', *Harvard Business Review*, 83(6), 4–19.

Kumaraswamy, A., Mudambi, R., Saranga, H., and Tripathy, A. (2012), 'Catch-up strategies in the Indian auto components industry: Domestic firms' responses to market liberalization', *Journal of International Business Studies*, 43(4): 368–395.

Li, J.T., Tsui, A.S., and Weldon, E. (2000), *Management and Organizations in the Chinese Context*. London: Macmillan.

Li, Q. and Resnick, A. (2003), 'Reversal of fortunes: Democratic institutions and foreign direct investment inflows to developing countries', *International Organization*, 57(01), 175–211.

Li, X. (2008), 'The impact of higher standards in patent protection for pharmaceutical industries under the TRIPS agreement: A comparative study of China and India,' *The World Economy*, 31(10), 1367–1382.

Makino, S., Isobe, T., and Chan, C.M. (2004), 'Does country matter?' *Strategic Management Journal*, 25(10), 1027–1043.

Nill, J. and Kemp, R. (2009), 'Evolutionary approaches for sustainable innovation policies: From niche to paradigm?' *Research Policy*, 38(4), 668–680.

North, D.C. (1990), *Institutions, Institutional Change and Economic Performance*. Cambridge: Cambridge University Press.

——— (2006), *Understanding the Process of Economic Change*. New Delhi, India: Academic Foundation.

Oliver, C. (1992), 'The antecedents of deinstitutionalization', *Organization Studies*, 13(4), 563–588.

Paraskevopoulou, E. (2012), 'Non-technological regulatory effects: Implications for innovation and innovation policy', *Research Policy*, 41(6), 1058–1071.

Park, W.G. (1995), 'International R&D spillovers and OECD economic growth', *Economic Inquiry*, 33(4), 571–591.

Peng, M.W., Wang, D.Y.L., and Jiang, Y. (2008), 'An institution-based view of international business strategy: A focus on emerging economies', *Journal of International Business Studies*, 39(5), 920–936.

Qian, Y. (2007). 'Do national patent laws stimulate domestic innovation in a global patenting environment? A cross-country analysis of pharmaceutical patent protection', *The Review of Economics and Statistics*, 89(3), 436–453.

Scholte, J.A. (2001), 'Globalisation, governance and corporate citizenship', *Journal of Corporate Citizenship*, 2001(1), 15–23.

Scott, W.R. (2001), *Institutions and Organizations* (2nd ed.). Thousand Oaks, CA: Sage.

Suchman, M.C. (1995), 'Managing legitimacy: Strategic and institutional approaches', *Academy of Management Review*, 20(3), 571–610.

Sun, P., Mellahi, K., and Thun, E. (2010), 'The dynamic value of MNE political embeddedness: The case of the Chinese automobile industry', *Journal of International Business Studies*, 41(7), 1161–1182.

Teece, D.J. (2006), 'Reflections on profiting from innovation', *Research Policy*, 35(8), 1131–1146.

Waguespack, D.M., Birnir, J.K., and Schroeder, J. (2005), 'Technological development and political stability: Patenting in Latin America and the Caribbean', *Research Policy*, 34(10), 1570–1590.

Williamson, O.E. (1985), *The Economic Institutions of Capitalism*. New York: Simon and Schuster.

World Trade Organization [WTO] (2012), Country Documents, https://www.wto.org/english/tratop_e/trips_e/intel6_e.htm [accessed June 2015].

Yang, D. and Sonmez, M. (2013), 'Integration and divergence of patent systems across national and international institutions', *Journal of World Business*, 48(4), 527–538.

Part II

International Entrepreneurship and Innovation: Contexts and Outcomes

5

Affordable Loss in Entrepreneurial Internationalisation: A Focus on Finnish Biotechnology Firms

Mari Ketolainen, Niina Nummela and Igor Kalinic

Introduction

Despite the extensive amount of research on decision-making in the context of international business, some elementary themes have been almost neglected. In particular, criticism concerning the assumption of rational decision-making has been growing and there has been an explicit call for studies that place the decision-makers under exhaustive scrutiny (Aharoni et al., 2011). Furthermore, some key elements of the decision-making process have been ignored. Although earlier examples of international business research (e.g. Aharoni, 1966) highlight the importance of uncertainty as well as the cognitive constraints of the decision-maker, the number of studies that focus on these themes is surprisingly low.

This lack of interest is unexpected, particularly in the field of international entrepreneurship where processes typically involve the parallel execution of a variety of activities to exploit recognised opportunities (Mathews and Zander, 2007). This in turn generates a continuous flow of concurrent decisions. In international entrepreneurial firms these decisions are made under the condition of genuine uncertainty and so entrepreneurs adopt different strategies to cope with it. Entrepreneurial judgement is a cognitive process that is influenced by the person, the place and access to relevant knowledge (Mainela et al., 2014). In the context of entrepreneurial internationalisation, uncertainty is embedded in the cultural, political, economic and institutional environment (Ellis, 2011), and is highlighted here because of less rational approaches to decision-making, such as hunches, intuition, and incomplete or biased information. It is possible that if the perceived opportunity is evaluated too high, the decision-maker will refrain from taking action (Shane and Venkataraman, 2000). Entrepreneurs may try to reduce any uncertainties by gathering information over the course of time or they may exploit opportunities immediately, thereby anticipating that the instant returns and first-mover advantages will cover the costs of uncertainty (Choi and Shepherd, 2004). In practice, international entrepreneurial firms need to constantly balance the acceptable level of uncertainty with the time frame in which the industry operates.

Decision-making under the condition of uncertainty is steered by a number of criteria that determine the chosen action. In the recent literature on effectuation, it is suggested that decision-makers would either choose an opportunity to maximise their expected returns or, alternatively, keep the decision-related risks at an acceptable level, thus resulting in affordable loss (Sarasvathy, 2001). Of these two options, our knowledge of the former is fairly extensive and the possibilities for calculating the expected returns are numerous. Regarding the latter, research has previously explored the concept of affordable loss from a mainly theoretical point of view (e.g. Read et al., 2009). Nevertheless, the empirical evidence is limited and so far it has failed to provide indicators that force decision-makers to follow affordable loss principles rather than focusing on mechanisms for returns on investment.

This study advances our understanding of affordable loss in entrepreneurial internationalisation with the help of a conceptual analysis and three illustrative case studies from the Finnish biotechnology industry. In particular, this study focuses on the decisions made when the companies were expanding their operations abroad. Three key findings, each making a distinct contribution to the previous research, were derived. First, the empirical evidence suggests that the principle of affordable loss is typically used for short-term, operative decisions. On the other hand, when a decision is more long term and strategic in nature, affordable loss and risks are assessed but they are also compared with the expected rewards. In addition, contrary to what Sarasvathy (2001) suggests, our study showed that affordable loss and expected returns are used as complementary decision-making criteria since they can be applied simultaneously. Second, it seems that when only a single person is involved in the decision-making process, it is more likely that the decision-makers will base their decision on the affordable loss principle. Conversely, when the number of decision-makers increases, the decision-making process follows a more causation-based logic. Third, the concept of affordable loss seems to be closely related to the context. In rapidly developing industries, such as information technology, it is important to meet objectives in a timely fashion. However, due to the nature of the industry, entrepreneurial biotechnology companies appear to favour losing time over losing money.

This study looks at international entrepreneurship with a particular focus on the components of affordable loss principle, while also contributing to both the emerging theory of effectuation and adding to our understanding of entrepreneurial internationalisation. The prevailing assumptions are challenged and a critical view is taken, particularly on the applicability of previous research in the context of biotech firms.

Affordable loss in decision-making

For entrepreneurial firms it is typical that two central concepts, namely the firm and the market, are not given: the firms are new, the markets are new, or both (Dew et al., 2008). In the case of biotechnology firms, the latter is often true and thus the decision-maker faces the dilemma of not being able to predict or control the development of either the market or the firm. Decision-makers in these firms have to make decisions based on the knowledge and capabilities at hand (e.g. Kalinic et al., 2014). One could argue that they are operating under Knightian uncertainty since human creative action produces a non-existent and hard-to-predict future (cf. Wiltbank et al., 2006). In the turbulent and global environment of biotechnology firms, the application of effectual logic becomes lucrative because it is non-predictive, that is, it does not require clear goals, accurate predictions or an adaptive stance towards a largely exogenous environment (Dew et al., 2008). Furthermore, it has been argued that effectual logic is particularly suitable for environments with a high level of uncertainty (Sarasvathy, 2001), which is the case in the field of biotechnology.

Sarasvathy (2008), Dew et al. (2009a) and Sarasvathy et al. (2014) have discussed the principles of effectual logic. These principles have been referred to as *bird-in-hand, affordable loss, crazy quilt, lemonade* and *pilot-in-the-plane*. The first, *bird-in-hand*, refers to the means-oriented approach. Entrepreneurs are likely to make their decisions based on the given means instead of first setting the goals. They tend to focus on the question 'What can I do?' instead of 'What should I do?' (Dew et al., 2009a; Sarasvathy et al., 2014). Second, *affordable loss* refers to the situation where entrepreneurs base their decisions on what they can lose (affordable loss) instead of focusing on the expected returns (Dew et al., 2009a). Affordable loss is easily calculated when the entrepreneur knows what he/she has and can estimate what the affordable loss is (Sarasvathy et al., 2014).

Third, when following effectual logic, entrepreneurs prefer to commit key stakeholders instead of completing detailed competitive analyses. This is referred to as *crazy quilt* (Sarasvathy et al., 2014). The fourth principle, *lemonade*, refers to leveraging unexpected environmental contingencies instead of exploiting pre-existing knowledge. As Sarasvathy et al. (2014) have stated, the process of 'turning lemons into lemonade' by embracing contingency plays out through the effectual process, which is based on the evolving means, goals and stakeholders of the venture. *Pilot-in-the-plane*, the fifth principle, was added by Sarasvathy (2008). It is the *explicit rejection of inevitable trends* and refers to the logic itself (Sarasvathy et al., 2014).

From the viewpoint of this study, the interesting aspect of this classification is the suggestion that the decision-maker uses affordable loss as a decision-making criterion instead of expected returns (cf. Perry et al., 2011; Sarasvathy, 2001). Affordable loss as a concept refers to the *decision-maker's subjective perception of what he/she estimates to be able to put at risk and potentially lose as an outcome of the action* (Dew et al., 2009b). Particularly during the early phases of the venture, it is typical for the decision-maker to not have a clear view of the size of the market or the potential of the product; hence, the expected returns are impossible to calculate using traditional means. Instead, the decision-maker needs to judge the potential loss and make an explicit decision (Wiltbank et al., 2006). In order to make this decision, the decision-maker evaluates the resources at his/her disposal: who they are, what they know and who they know (Sarasvathy, 2001). Based on this preliminary information, he/she makes the decision.

Earlier research on effectual decision-making identified three main elements that, when combined, push the decision-makers to adopt effectual logic rather than causal logic and, in particular, the affordable loss principle versus the expected returns mechanism (Sarasvathy, 2008; Dew et al., 2009b). The first element is the *perception of uncertainty* (Sarasvathy, 2008). In conditions of high uncertainty, or when the entrepreneurs perceive a high level of uncertainty, they are not able to predict the future outcome or construct different scenarios and, therefore, cannot best identify the scenario with the highest returns and lowest risks. Therefore, the higher the perception of uncertainty, the more likely it is that the entrepreneur will adopt the affordable loss principle.

The second element is the *desire for control* (Wiltbank et al., 2006). The entrepreneurs can choose how much they try to control the external environment. On the one hand, they can try to move fast and adapt to a rapidly changing environment in order to identify good opportunities. In this case the emphasis on control is low. On the other hand, they can focus on the means of disposal; they can transform them, interact with potential stakeholders and create new and unexpected goals/opportunities. In this example, the emphasis on control is high, so the entrepreneurs do not try to estimate a potential for return in the future, but instead they downsize today's risk. Therefore, the higher the desire for control over resources, the more likely the entrepreneurs will adopt the affordable loss principle.

The third element is the *willingness to lose/invest* a certain amount (Dew et al., 2009b). Each entrepreneur estimates how much he/she or the firm is willing to invest and how much they can lose if the investment fails or does not reach its goals. In the ultimate analysis, if the decision-maker, that is, the entrepreneur, is not willing to commit and invest a certain amount, there will be hardly any financial gain.

These three elements are all rather general and vague. It is not easy to understand what actually influences the decision-makers and how they decide to follow effectual logic rather than causal logic. In their conceptual paper, Dew et al. (2009b) went into more detail, although they were not very explicit in their discussion. Although they discussed the consequences and influences of affordable loss, they did not explicitly state what they meant by affordable loss. In this chapter we intend to build on their thoughts and, based on empirical evidence, examine the conditions under which an entrepreneur is more likely to adopt the affordable loss principle rather than the maximisation of returns theory. Additionally, we intend to shed light on the indicators that might encourage or discourage decision-makers in applying the affordable loss principle.

Research design

In order to increase our understanding of the applicability and usefulness of the affordable loss concept in international entrepreneurship, a qualitative case study approach was chosen. We pursued the principles of data collection established by Eisenhardt (1989) and Yin (1994), and used multiple sources of evidence when gathering our data (interviews and company documentation). A qualitative approach was considered appropriate because it describes lifeworlds 'from the inside out' or, rather, from the point of view of the people who participate. By doing so it seeks to contribute to a better understanding of social realities and to draw attention to processes, meaning patterns and structural features (Flick et al., 2004). On the other hand, case study as a research strategy allows for the inductive, in-depth investigation of the research topic, analysis of the phenomenon in its contextual setting, and a more holistic coverage of the companies selected (cf. Ghauri, 2004). In order to minimise the effects of environmental and situational factors, we limited the number of cases to three Finnish biotechnology companies.

The choice of context is imperative, as the appropriateness of the internationalisation strategies depends on the industrial context in which the companies operate (Andersson, 2004). It can also be asserted that the decision-making logic of international entrepreneurial firms may be different across industries. The biotechnology industry is a science-led industry that can be described as entrepreneurial, knowledge-intensive and rapidly changing (Hine and Kapeleris, 2006; Brännback et al., 2007). Although there seems to be agreement as to what biotechnology is – the application of science and technology with living organisms, as well as parts, products and models thereof, to alter living or non-living materials for the production of knowledge, goods and services (OECD, 2014) – included in that definition are numerous heterogeneous subfields, such as healthcare biotechnology, agricultural biotechnology and industrial biotechnology (EuropaBio, 2015).

The present study is limited to healthcare biotechnology (also known as red biotechnology or life sciences), and the biotechnology industry refers to organisations conducting research and development (R&D) activities in order to develop healthcare-related products or technologies. This focus was chosen for several reasons. First, it is economically significant due to the applications used in product development in the pharmaceutical industry (Brännback et al., 2001; Pisano, 2006). Second, it has high growth potential due to the development of medical research (Burns, 2005). Third, the product development processes are long and expensive: biotechnology applications are expected to generate cost savings in the long run by shortening and improving these processes and thereby reducing risks or making time-consuming diagnostic methods more efficient (Hermans et al., 2005; Bains, 2006). This long product development process has made the industry very capital intensive and highly regulated, which means that capital needs to be raised continuously (Hine and Kapeleris, 2006). When looking at decision-making criteria, these characteristics are very interesting from the perspective of this study as the theories of expected return and affordable loss might be relevant here.

Healthcare biotechnology as an industry is characterised by two phenomena: convergence and consolidation. It is converging in order to create new, innovative healthcare solutions, and so the division between the core technologies (drugs, diagnostics and devices) is becoming blurred (Eselius et al., 2008). This requires a global business approach as the best partners and providers are located around the world. Second, a wave of consolidation has polarised the industry. On the one hand, the so-called Big Pharma (the largest pharmaceutical companies) dominate the market, yet their future success is increasingly dependent on collaboration with small, innovative biotechnology companies (Weintraub, 2008). Therefore, it is not surprising that in recent years we have witnessed the rise of international entrepreneurial biotechnology firms in all industrialised economies.

In order to shed light on the concept of affordable loss, we studied the decision-making of three new Finnish ventures in the biotech industry. The selection of cases is a crucial decision in the research process and theoretical sampling is recommended (Eisenhardt and Graebner, 2007). This involves choosing cases that are likely to replicate or extend the emergent theory (Eisenhardt, 1989). The theoretical qualifications of the case also have to be kept in mind; in other words, how well they comply with the conceptual categories and the extent of their explanatory power (Eisenhardt, 1989; Smith, 1991). Besides being Finnish biotechnology firms, the companies in this case study all share the following characteristics: they are small and medium-sized (SMEs), they operate in healthcare life sciences, they have a commercialised product and they are international. Key information regarding the case companies is summarised in Table 5.1.

Table 5.1 Key characteristics of the case companies

	Turnover (Euro)	Employees (5/2012)	Founded	Share of Exports	Start of Exports
A	131,000	10	2004	90%	2011
B	356,000	10	2009	75%	2009
C	879,000	10	2007	85%	2007

The cases can be described as instrumental (Stake, 1995) since they illustrate the phenomenon under study in real-life contexts. The empirical data for the study was collected in 2012 and the main source of data was face-to-face interviews with the case companies' management. The case companies chosen fulfilled the pre-set requirements and the persons interviewed were the key individuals behind each company's decision-making. In two of the companies the interviewees were CEOs or managing directors. In the third company, the key decision-maker, the managing director, was on parental leave and, therefore, three people (deputy managing director, production manager and head of marketing) were interviewed. We considered these people to be key sources of information because the international growth of their company reflects company strategy, which is based on their decisions. The persons involved in the process were willing to discuss their experiences, but in order to preserve the anonymity of the interviewees, the case companies were disguised.

In order to follow the decision-making logic of the interviewees, we adopted a semi-structured process that facilitated the free expression of the entrepreneur's ideas. This kind of 'think-aloud' method has been used in earlier studies of entrepreneurial effectuation (Sarasvathy et al., 1998). On the other hand, the themes studied in each interview allowed us to compare responses across subsequent interviews and secure for data equivalence during the data collection. Collecting data through interviews and observations is considered appropriate in the context of effectuation (Perry et al., 2011). The interviews were conducted by two or three individuals, thereby increasing our confidence in the reliability of interpretation. The interview questions dealt with several topics, such as the internationalisation of the company, the decision-making process and the evolution of the company. With the consent of the interviewees, the discussions were recorded and transcribed verbatim. All the interviews were conducted in English, although some of the interviewees added a few words and comments in Finnish during the interviews.

The data obtained was further analysed in several phases (cf. Yin, 2009). First, the interview recordings were transcribed and a within-case analysis of each company was conducted (Eisenhardt, 1989). Consequently, the information obtained from the interviews was reorganised to form descriptive narratives which helped us to identify the key events and the background of each case. We then augmented the interview data with some additional information available from databases, company websites and other secondary sources. The internationalisation of each case company was described using the critical-incident technique (cf. Butterfield et al., 2005) in terms of its international-isation activities and evaluated from the viewpoint of affordable loss. Finally, we included a cross-case comparison in order to reveal the similarities and differences among the companies.

Analysing affordable loss

Our analysis began with the aim of understanding the decision-making logic of the case companies, particularly when making decisions regarding inter-nationalisation and market expansion. In other words, we were interested in whether the entrepreneurs/key decision-makers framed their decisions using either causal or effectual thinking. In line with Perry et al. (2011) and Sarasvathy (2001), this classification was conducted according to the following dimensions: goal-setting versus given means as the driver for decision-making; expected returns versus affordable loss as a decision-making criterion; decisions based on environmental analysis versus strategic alliances and prior commit-ments; exploitation of existing knowledge versus leveraging opportunities; and predicting versus controlling the future.

All in all, the decision-making in the case companies was very entrepreneurial in nature. In fact, the interviewees often compared their decision-making with that of large multinationals and pointed out that in entrepreneurial firms like theirs, decision-making is often flexible and less bureaucratic:

> *I worked 12 years for big companies and I have to say that this is so much more fun. You are not leading like quarter to quarter to quarter to quarter, you are not spending your time filling totally meaningless papers. The amount of bureaucracy is so much lower. (Company C)*

> *Well, I've understood that when the headcount goes from 20 to 40 there are significant changes. ... There has to be more structured communication, more official meetings, so less talking in the corridor. You then have five that you have to report to and they again have five and so on, so you don't engage with the people so much. (Company B)*

The decision-making processes of these entrepreneurial firms were also experi-enced as being faster and shorter than those of multinationals, as the following quotes demonstrate:

> *And when the size of the organisation grows you have to have, make some defined decision-making routes, and they bring a certain kind of...inflexibility. Time*

consuming things. You lose the agility and flexibility ... everything has to be done in meetings or boards or whatever. We can make decisions just by shouting to the next room here. (Company A)

The difference between a small start-up and a multinational company is in the structure and decision-making processes. It's a lot quicker and you can move quicker when you're a small company. (Company B)

The interviewees also emphasised that even if, from the company's per-spective, it is all about balancing the investment, the viewpoint of the board may be different. In particular, the representatives of the venture capitalist often emphasise the expected returns and pay less attention to the short-term losses.

It is a balance between expected returns by the venture capitalist and the losses the company can afford – but all needs to be earned back. (Company A)

Next, in order to dig deeper into the construct, we continued by analysing it according to the dimensions of affordable loss (Dew et al., 2009b): acceptable risk, predetermined level of affordable loss, available internal means, amount of information needed for making a decision, and which resources are consid-ered 'losable' or 'patient'. In order to provide a contextualised explanation of the concept, we also investigated the context when the affordable loss principle was used (i.e. for what kind of decisions, in what kind of situations, when and by whom). The key findings are discussed in the following section.

Affordable loss – when, what and how?

The interviews indicated that the affordable loss principle was typically used when making *'smaller' decisions* that involved a *limited window of opportunity* and required a fast decision. These decisions were often related to the daily operations of the company, independently of the task or function that they were related to. The use of the affordable loss principle was spread throughout the company to all of its functions, such as marketing, purchasing, pricing, R&D and order processing. Commonly, as illustrated by the following quote, these decisions were made by a single decision-maker such as the managing director, CEO or marketing manager:

Basically, regarding pricing, I have the freedom to make decisions. Of course, we discuss it, different options, with the top management team. (Company C)

In the case of more significant decisions that have a long-term impact, the deci-sion-making was the responsibility of the whole management team and/or the board. In the latter case, the affordable loss principle was no longer applied in the decision-making, or at least not as the main or only criterion. On the contrary, external information was searched for, sometimes even extensively, and that information was utilised in decision-making in order to assess the related risks, investment required and *expected rewards*. This kind of decision-making was considered to be more 'safe', but also time consuming and, therefore, it could only be applied to the most important decisions.

> *As a group, you can make a better risk-assessment and it's more certain. ... (If there are many people involved in the decision-making process) you will need more information or more data and also it will take more time. (Company C)*

When more people are involved in the decision-making process, they need some common basis on which to build their decisions. This basis can be data from, for example, market surveys or competitor analysis, as the following quotation demonstrates:

> *... when we changed the direction (of the company), we went through a number of market reports, publications, all kind of news, everything, we just tried to collect as much information as we could. (Company A)*

The expected rewards were never used as the sole decision-making criterion, but they were always assessed in relative terms compared with affordable loss or acceptable risk. The evaluation of risk varied across interviewees, but two main types of risk were identified: risk of losing time and risk of losing money.

  Risk of losing time referred to delays in operations and delivery or loss of the interviewee's personal efforts. These were considered as something the company could afford to lose and so no financial value was calculated for them. This might be due to the nature of the business; for these companies, it is not about being the fastest to market but more about having the best product.

> *The only thing I'm investing in is plane tickets and then time. So what I stand to lose is perhaps one year in business if they are not performing because then we terminate the agreement and find another partner. So that's the largest risk: a delay in launching or implementing business in a certain country. (Company B)*

In the biotechnology industry, it is typical that the product development process takes years. Therefore, the speed of operations is also considerably slower than it is in many other fields and so companies do not purposefully target being the first ones in the market.

> *I will never be the first in the market, it is a very established market. ... We are playing in the niche; we have a niche strategy within the market. (Company B)*

In the biotechnology industry, it is also typical that market development and value creation are blurred and the estimation of future market development is very difficult to make. Therefore, it is not surprising that most of the interviewees preferred to estimate risk in terms of time instead of money. However, one informant from Company A was able to evaluate the affordable loss in financial terms:

> ... *say, a very rough number is 100,000 euros or something like that. So, it's not the world's biggest sum of money if you start to develop a test, go a little bit and stop it there. Maybe you have burned something like 10, 20, 30,000 euros. So it's not really a big thing to stop such a project. (Company A)*

Interestingly, the interviewees also stressed the fact that their personal investment in the business was often limited. As is usual in the biotechnology industry, the first years of business are seldom profitable. The business operations are run with venture capital and the financial risk is divided among the entrepreneur, business angels and investors. Additionally, some business models involve very little financial risk for the company, as they involve building a long-term relationship and getting the other party (partner) committed. This is demonstrated in the following quotations:

> *But to be able to estimate the risks. ... The risk I think is best to limit ... but it's something that you have to little bit jump into cold water and see how it goes. ... Well, the thing is, I don't have to invest (a lot) when I start with a partnership because it starts with them purchasing products from me. (Company B)*

> *I don't know if we are looking for fast income. ... At least I'm not thinking that way. We're looking for long-term relationships and we maybe have to start by putting in a little bit of money, giving some samples and so on, you know, starting slowly. (Company C)*

Besides the concept of risk or loss, whether it was affordable or acceptable also seemed to vary. Interestingly, the interviewees with considerable previous experience considered many issues to be acceptable just because they thought it was 'the name of the game'. In other words, it was an essential feature of the business and so out of their control.

> *We wouldn't have the company in place, basically. We would have run out of money, before we ... would have been in a situation where we have some initial sales. Because it's, this is, running a company like this, it's kind of a, game of, funding at the same time. (Company A)*

On the other hand, the less experienced interviewees reported spending considerable time discussing the issues with other team members and decision-makers in order to determine an acceptable level of risk.

And usually, when we make decisions, we really think about the risks and we are thinking 'Are we going to take this risk?' If we take it, then we took it.... Yeah, like basically our current cash flow doesn't allow us to take any huge risks. (Company C)

Our findings therefore challenge some earlier thoughts on affordable loss. For example, instead of treating the different types of risk as alternatives or opposites, time versus money (Dew et al., 2009a), our informants seemed to consider the two as complementary methods of mental accounting.[1] In addition, we were able to identify decisions where affordable loss and expected return logic did not just complement each other, but were actually used simultaneously. Finally, it seems that the level of experience and learning of the decision-maker has an impact on the interpretation of affordable loss. All this indicates that using a standardised tool, such as quantitative scales, for assessing affordable loss and the related decision-making may not provide an accurate picture of the concept.

Conclusions and implications

In this chapter we analysed decision-making regarding the internationalisation process of three Finish international ventures and achieved a deeper knowledge about affordable loss in the context of entrepreneurial internationalisation. We found that the nature of the decision and the number of decision-makers both seem to affect whether the affordable loss principle is used in decision-making. When a single person is making the operational decisions, the affordable loss principle is often used. However, when the number of individuals making the decision increases and, for example, the board becomes involved, the decision-making process becomes slower, longer and leans more towards additional information and calculations of expected returns. Hence, the gut feeling and previous experience of one particular individual are no longer important.

Affordable loss was conceptualised as loss of time, loss of financial resources and loss of independence. Entrepreneurial firms seem to consider time and the efforts of personnel to be losable resources which do not endanger the company. Accordingly, they were not included in calculations of any financial value. Considering time as an affordable loss can be seen as very much a context-related issue; companies in the biotechnology industry are used to long product development and patent processes and so for them it is not always crucial to be the first and fastest to the market. As the temporal context is so decisive when studying affordable loss, we may assume that the findings might be different if we were to study an industry with a faster pace of operations.

Estimating affordable loss in terms of finance was very demanding since all financial loss is taken extremely seriously in small companies with limited resources. Decision-makers following the affordable loss principle were also worried about the loss of independence. The managers of these entrepreneurial companies were not only worried about their personal loss of control but also about the risk of being acquired or merged with some other company due to being too dependent on the investors' money. Hence, the level of affordable loss is also evaluated on the basis of 'how much investment we need and how much external funding we should accept'. Additionally, the findings point out that a contextualised interpretation of the concept is recommended when studying the phenomenon.

The previous literature has suggested that, in the early phases of the venture, the decision-makers do not have a clear image of the market or the expected returns, and this drives the decision-makers to consider the affordable loss. The case companies' decision-makers considered both the affordable loss and expected returns when making their decisions. These two issues were present as complementary aspects of decision-making, although they were also considered simultaneously. This might be because the case companies studied here were not pure new ventures, but were more accurately in the transition phase from being a 'new' to being a 'more established' venture.

Implications and suggestions for future research

One important implication for entrepreneurs and management teams consists of showing that the type of decision-making adopted depends on the size of the company. In smaller and more dynamic companies, it is possible to make rapid decisions and so the decisions can be taken by one or few people. In this case the amount of necessary information on which the decision is based is lower and decision-makers can adopt the affordable loss principle. Affordable loss is often quantified in terms of time, individual efforts and money. Small companies can afford to lose plenty of time, but only a very limited amount of financial resources. However, it is important for decision-makers to recognise that in rapidly changing industries time should also be considered as a valuable resource, and losing it might ultimately lead to losses in financial terms.

The findings of this study propose several avenues for future research. For example, it might be interesting to expand on the earlier works regarding the composition of top management teams in international entrepreneurial firms. After all, prior research does indicate that the mindset of the entrepreneur (Nummela et al., 2004) and the characteristics of the top management team (Reuber and Fischer, 1997, 2002) both affect the firm's internationalisation. Furthermore, the need to augment the management teams of these firms has also been recognised (Loane et al., 2007). If this is the case, it raises the question of what kind of team composition would be optimal in international entrepreneurial firms from the viewpoint of decision-making. Should the team include members who work according to similar logic or would it be better to have people working with both the affordable loss principle and expected returns mechanisms? Future research projects might shed light on these intriguing questions.

The present study is a qualitative study and as such it produces context-specific knowledge that can be applied to different contexts only with caution. Future research will hopefully extend this investigation to different sectors and countries. Moreover, we focused on fairly new international ventures. Although this category of firm has received considerable attention over the last few years, most of the SMEs are not international since inception and they have followed different internationalisation pathways. Therefore, it is also important to understand how such companies make their decisions during their entrepreneurial internationalisation. Finally, this is a longitudinal retrospective study. This type of study suffers from the interviewees' capability to correctly recall events that happened previously, sometimes more than ten years before. We therefore suggest performing real-time longitudinal studies by, for example, observing the internationalisation process at various points by revisiting the company from time to time and by personally pointing out the differences.

Note

1. *Mental accounting is a set of cognitive operations used by individuals and households to organise, evaluate and keep track of financial activities* (Thaler, 1999).

References

Aharoni, Y. (1966). *The Foreign Direct Investment Decision Process*, Boston: Harvard Business School.

Aharoni, Y., Tihanyi, L. and Connelly, B.L. (2011). 'Managerial decision-making in international business: A forty-five-year retrospective', *Journal of World Business*, 46(2), 135–142.

Andersson, S. (2004). 'Internationalization in different industrial contexts', *Journal of Business Venturing*, 19(6), 851–875.

Bains, W. (2006). 'What you give is what you get: Investment in European biotechnology', *Journal of Commercial Biotechnology*, 12(4), 274–283.

Brännback, M., Carsrud, A. and Renko, M. (2007). 'Exploring the born global concept in the biotechnology context', *Journal of Enterprising Culture*, 15(1), 79–100.

Brännback, M., Hyvönen, P., Raunio, H., Renko, M. and Sutinen, R. (2001). *Finnish Pharma Cluster – Vision 2010*, Helsinki.

Burns, L.R. (2005). *The Business of Healthcare Innovation*, Cambridge: Cambridge University Press.

Butterfield, L.D., Borgen, W.A., Amundsen, N.E. and Maglio, A.-S.T. (2005). 'Fifty years of the critical incident technique: 1954–2004 and beyond', *Qualitative Research*, 5(4), 475–497.

Choi, Y.R. and Shepherd, D.A. (2004). 'Entrepreneurs' decisions to exploit opportunities', *Journal of Management*, 30(3), 377–395.

Dew, N., Read, S., Sarasvathy, S.D. and Wiltbank, R. (2008). 'Outlines of a behavioral theory of the entrepreneurial firm', *Journal of Economic Behavior & Organization*, 66(1), 37–59.

—— (2009a). 'Effectual versus predictive logics in entrepreneurial decision-making: Differences between experts and novices', *Journal of Business Venturing*, 24(4), 287–309.

—— (2009b). 'Affordable loss: Behavioral economic aspects of plunge decision', *Strategic Entrepreneurship Journal*, 3(2), 105–126.

Eisenhardt, K.M. (1989). 'Building theories from case study research', *Academy of Management Review*, 14(4), 532–550.

Eisenhardt, K.M. and Graebner, M.E. (2007). 'Theory building from cases: Opportunities and challenges', *Academy of Management Journal*, 50(1), 25–32.

Ellis, P.D. (2011). 'Social ties and international entrepreneurship: Opportunities and constraints affecting firm internationalization', *Journal of International Business Studies*, 42(1), 99–127.

Eselius, L., Nimmagadda, M., Kambil, A., Hisey, R.T. and Rhodes, J. (2008). 'Managing pathways to convergence in the life sciences industry', *Journal of Business Strategy*, 29(2), 31–42.

EuropaBio (2015). 'EuropaBio'. Available at: http://www.europabio.org/ [accessed 26 January 2015].

Flick, U., Von Kardoff, E. and Steinke, I. (2004). 'What is qualitative research? An introduction to the field'. In U. Flick, E. von Kardoff, and I. Steinke (eds), *A Companion to Qualitative Research*, London: Sage Publications.

Ghauri, P.N. (2004). 'Designing and conducting case studies in international business'. In R. Marchan-Piekkari and C. Welch (eds), *Handbook of Qualitative Research Methods for International Business*, Cheltenham: Edward Elgar Publishing.

Hermans, R., Kulvik, M. and Yla-Anttila, P. (2005). 'International mega-trends and growth prospects of the Finnish biotechnology industry: Recent economic research and policy implications', *Journal of Commercial Biotechnology*, 11(2), 134–145.

Hine, D. and Kapeleris, J. (2006). *Innovation and Entrepreneurship in Biotechnology, An International Perspective – Concepts, Theories and Cases*, Cheltenham: Edward Elgar Publishing.

Kalinic, I., Sarasvathy, S.D. and Forza, C. (2014). 'Expect the unexpected: Implications of effectual logic on the internationalization process', *International Business Review*, 23(3), 635–647.

Loane, S., Bell, J.D. and McNaughton, R. (2007). 'A cross-national study on the impact of management teams on the rapid internationalization of small firms', *Journal of World Business*, 42(4), 489–504.

Mainela, T., Puhakka, V. and Servais, P. (2014). 'The concept of international opportunity in international entrepreneurship: A review and a research agenda', *International Journal of Management Reviews*, 16(1), 105–129.

Mathews, J.A. and Zander, I. (2007). 'The international entrepreneurial dynamics of accelerated internationalisation', *Journal of International Business Studies*, 38(3), 387–403.

Nummela, N., Saarenketo, S. and Puumalainen, K. (2004). 'Global mindset – a prerequisite for successful internationalisation?', *Canadian Journal of Administrative Sciences*, 21(1), 51–64.

OECD (2014). *OECD Biotechnology Statistics*. Available at: http://www.oecd.org/sti/biotech/statisticaldefinitionofbiotechnology.htm [accessed 15 December 2014].

Perry, J.T., Chandler, G.N. and Markova, G. (2011). 'Entrepreneurial effectuation: A review and suggestions for future research', *Entrepreneurship Theory and Practice*, 36(4), 837–861.

Pisano, G.P. (2006). 'Can science be a business? Lessons from biotech', *Harvard Business Review*, 84(10), 114–125.

Read, S., Dew, N., Sarasvathy, S.D., Song, M. and Wiltbank, R. (2009). 'Marketing under uncertainty: The logic of an effectual approach', *Journal of Marketing*, 73(3), 1–18.

Reuber, A.R. and Fischer, E. (1997). 'The influence of the management team's international experience on the internationalization behaviors of SMEs', *Journal of International Business Studies*, 28(4), 807–825.

—— (2002). 'Foreign sales and small firm growth: The moderating role of the management team', *Entrepreneurship Theory and Practice*, 27(1), 29–45.

Sarasvathy, S.D. (2001). 'Causation and effectuation: Toward a theoretical shift from economic inevitability to entrepreneurial contingency', *Academy of Management Review*, 26(2), 243–263.

—— (2008). *Effectuation: Elements of Entrepreneurial Expertise*, Cheltenham: Edward Elgar Publishing.

Sarasvathy, S.D., Kumar, K., York, J.G. and Bhagavatula, S. (2014). 'An effectual approach to international entrepreneurship: Overlaps, challenges, and provocative possibilities', *Entrepreneurship Theory and Practice*, 38(1), 71–93.

Sarasvathy, S.D., Simon, H.A. and Lave, L. (1998). 'Perceiving and managing business risks: Differences between entrepreneurs and bankers', *Journal of Economic Behavior & Organization*, 33(2), 207–225.

Shane, S. and Venkataraman, S. (2000). 'The promise of entrepreneurship as a field of research', *Academy of Management Review*, 25(1), 217–226.

Smith, N.C. (1991). 'The case study: A vital yet misunderstood research method for management'. In N.C. Smith and P. Dainty (eds), *The Management Research Handbook*, London: Routledge.

Stake, R.E. (1995). *The Art of Case Study Research*, Thousand Oaks, CA: Sage Publications.

Thaler, R.H. (1999). 'Mental accounting matters', *Journal of Behavioral Decision Making*, 12(3), 183–206.

Weintraub, A. (2008). 'Big Pharma: What safe haven?', *Business Week*.

Wiltbank, R., Dew, N., Read, S. and Sarasvathy, S.D. (2006). 'What to do next? The case for non-predictive strategy', *Strategic Management Journal*, 27(10), 981–998.

Yin, R.K. (1994). *Case Study Research: Design and Methods*, Newbury Park, CA: Sage Publications.

—— (2009). *Case Study Research, Design and Methods*, Thousand Oaks, CA: Sage Publications.

6
Business Strategies in Internationalisation Outcomes among SMEs

Lasse Torkkeli, Sami Saarenketo, Olli Kuivalainen and Kaisu Puumalainen

Introduction

In this chapter, we investigate the influence of business strategies upon the internationalisation of SMEs. In particular, we investigate the effect of strategic aim for unique products development and quality focus, the two business strategies suggested to be linked to the international performance of rapidly internationalising firms by Knight and Cavusgil (2004). These firms have been defined as *'born-globals'* (Rennie, 1993; Knight and Cavusgil, 1996; Madsen and Servais, 1997), and in Knight and Cavusgil's (2004) article (see also Cavusgil and Knight, 2015), these business strategies, along with leveraging organisational competences, were suggested as acting as main intermediators of strategic orientation towards their increased performance.

In this chapter, we suggest that the result is both interesting and in need of further elaboration for several reasons. First, much of the scholarly research on born-globals has been conducted in the field of international entrepreneurship, or 'the discovery, enactment, evaluation, and exploitation of opportunities – across national borders – to create future goods and services' (Oviatt and McDougall, 2005, p. 540), where the discussion of business strategies has tended to concentrate on managerial decision-making related to internationalisation and entry-mode decisions (Spence, 2003; Levesque and Shepherd, 2004; Gleason and Wiggenhorn, 2007; Tuppura et al., 2008) rather than product, service and customer strategies as such. Thus, the role of strategic frameworks such as global marketing strategies (Zou and Cavusgil, 2002) and export marketing strategies (Cavusgil and Zou, 1994) has received less attention in the literature on born-globals and on international entrepreneurship in general.

Second, while the argument can be made that smaller firms may, in general, have less formalised and pre-planned strategies for internationalisation, Knight and Cavusgil (2004) found that certain strategic focuses may be relevant even for the most rapidly internationalising firms. This implies that studying business strategies in a more formal sense may also be called for in the context of smaller internationalising firms as well.

Third, more elaboration is called for in terms of different types of internationalising firms, particularly SMEs. Born-globals have been defined in various ways (see Gabrielsson et al., 2008). The review of international entrepreneurship studies by Jones et al. (2011) concludes that the term 'born-global' is generally considered to encompass firms that internationalise early and rapidly, with Knight and Cavusgil (2004, p. 124) defining born-globals as *business organizations that, from or near their founding, seek superior international business performance from the application of knowledge-based resources to the sale of outputs in multiple countries.* While this definition does not restrict born-globals by the size of the firm, other studies have denoted them as small knowledge-intensive firms (Knight, 1996; Moen, 2002; Gabrielsson et al., 2008), which they often tend to be, particularly in small open economies with limited domestic markets and the prevalence of niche-oriented high-technology start-ups. Thus, they can be contrasted to non-born-globals, that is, internationalising SMEs that do not fit the definition of a born-global.

This contrasting may be relevant in order to elaborate on the internationalisation business strategies of different types of small firms, particularly as an earlier exploratory study by Bell et al. (2004) found differences between business strategies and internationalisation of firms from knowledge-intensive and more traditional manufacturing fields. This implies that the dynamics of business strategies may vary between born-globals and other types of internationalising small firms.

For these reasons we consider it relevant to continue the investigation by Knight and Cavusgil (2004) and examine the relevance of the business strategies of SMEs to their internationalisation. In doing so we aim to investigate whether the relevance of the business strategy varies between born-globals and other types of internationalising SMEs, whether strategic focus is linked to more rapid foreign expansion in SMEs overall, and whether the positive influence of the product development and quality-focused strategies on international performance of born-globals (Knight and Cavusgil, 2004) are also generalisable to SMEs as a whole.

This chapter is constructed as follows: the next section discusses the theoretical background and the extant literature on the topic of business strategies and internationalisation of SMEs, and consequently presents our hypotheses derived from the literature review. The third section explicates the empirical data and the research methods used, with the fourth section presenting the results of the empirical analysis. The fifth section discusses the policy and practical implications of the results, and we conclude in section six by assessing the limitations of this study and potential future research avenues.

Literature review

Born-globals are the type of firms that by nature seek to internationalise earlier and more intensely than more traditional types of SMEs. In doing so, their emergence has challenged the traditional models of internationalisation, such as the 'Uppsala Model' (Johanson and Wiedersheim-Paul, 1975; Johanson and Vahlne, 1977, 2003, 2009) that have tended to present internationalisation in the SME context as a gradual learning process. The emergence of new knowledge-intensive industry sectors such as the software industry (Bell, 1995) has, in particular, often presented scholars with a host of small firms that tend to leap-frog some of the stages in the internationalisation process suggested by the traditional models. Accordingly, various typologies and definitions of these firms have risen in the field of international entrepreneurship (see Jones et al., 2011).

In this study we concentrate on the difference between born-globals and other types of SMEs. With the former we adhere to the definition by Knight and Cavusgil (1996) and Knight et al. (2004, p. 649) which 'is consistent with those used to operationalise other studies on born-global firms', where born-globals are those firms that have: (1) begun internationalising within three years of firm foundation and (2) generate at least a quarter of their total sales from abroad. Similarly, when discussing SMEs we refer to firms employing less than 500 people (OECD, 2005; Knight, 1996).

Overall, organisational emergence is said to occur through the actions taken by the organisation rather than its characteristics, that is, through achieving strategic rather than conforming legitimacy (Tornikoski and Newbert, 2007). In the context of internationalisation, a seminal study by Knight and Cavusgil (2004) found that international strategic orientations in born-global firms come to determine their business strategies, two of which are related to leveraging the organisational competences and the competences of foreign distributors for the firm. There are also two main strategies related to the products of the firm: those related to unique products development and quality focus. These are strategies that in turn lead to increased performance in international markets. In particular, unique products development 'reflects the creation of distinctive products, and is akin to differentiation strategy, which involves creating customer loyalty by uniquely meeting a particular need' (Knight and Cavusgil, 2004, p. 131). Accordingly, quality focus 'reflects efforts to develop products that meet or exceed customer expectations with respect to features and performance' (ibid., p. 131). These definitions, taken together with the results of the study, imply that for born-globals a strategy focused on delivering innovative products that respond to the needs of, and meet the expectations of, the customers of the firm will result in increased success in global markets. On the other hand, strategy formation of SMEs has been suggested to occur through opportunistic behaviour (Crick and Spence, 2005) and their internationalisation process through serendipity (Merrilees et al., 1998; Meyer and Skak, 2002).

Consequently, we could assume that the beneficial effects of such strategies are more clearly seen in born-globals, compared to internationalising SMEs in general. For one, enterprises that internationalise early tend to apply strategies appropriate to their unique characteristics, such as age and size (Cavusgil and Knight, 2015). Market response to the internationalisation of born-globals can be distinctly positive (Gleason and Wiggenhorn, 2007), and globalisation tends to facilitate conduction of born-global strategies (Andersson and Wictor, 2003). As born-global–type firms tend to be in abundance, particularly in innovative high-technology sectors, it is therefore not surprising that innovative product development and focus upon quality is linked to increased success among these firms.

However, the internationalisation process and the accompanying strategies may be different in more traditional manufacturing firms (see Bell et al., 2004). Thus, we might expect not only that these business strategies are linked to performance among born-globals (as suggested by Knight and Cavusgil, 2004), but also that other types of internationalising SMEs might not benefit from these strategies in equal measure. This would imply that SMEs with more focused business strategies would tend to be born-globals, rather than non-bornglobals:

Hypothesis 1: The higher the focus of an SME on unique products development, the more likely it is a born-global.

Hypothesis 2: The higher the quality focus of an SME, the more likely it is a born-global.

Similarly, once an SME enters its first foreign market, and thus turns from a domestic into an international operator, we could expect its product development and quality-focused business strategies to lead to increased growth. This would be in line with the definition of born-globals as firms that not only internationalise early, but also do so intensely, acquiring a large share of their turnover from abroad within a few years of starting their internationalisation process (e.g. Rennie, 1993; Knight and Cavusgil, 1996; Chetty and Campbell-Hunt, 2004). If born-globals in particular tend to benefit from such strategic focus, we might posit that the more focused SMEs are in their business strategies, the more rapidly they are able to grow abroad:

Hypothesis 3: The higher the focus of an SME on unique products development, the more rapid its growth in international markets.

Hypothesis 4: The higher the quality focus of an SME, the more rapid its growth in international markets.

Finally, Knight and Cavusgil (2004) explicitly linked these business strategies to the increased international performance of born-globals. In doing so they applied a measure based on managerial assessment of the extent of performance related to the prior expectations of the managers, as well as of the extent of success with products and compared to the main competitors of the respondents. We refer to this performance as 'subjective international performance' (as opposed to, for example, degree of internationalisation calculated directly from the absolute amount of foreign sales or the number of countries in which the firm operates), and posit that this applies to internationalising SMEs in general:

Hypothesis 5: The higher the unique products development of an SME, the better its subjective international performance.

Hypothesis 6: The higher the quality focus of an SME, the better its subjective international performance.

Research methodology

Data collection

The empirical data to test the hypotheses was collected in Finland via an online survey during the first half of 2008 (February–July). We considered the country context relevant due to much of the extant research on born-globals, having found the phenomenon particularly prevalent in small open economies such as that of Finland (e.g. Autio et al., 2000; Jantunen et al., 2008; Kuivalainen et al., 2007; Laanti et al., 2007; Tuppura et al., 2008). Moreover, a cross-sectional sample of SMEs was sought that would include both knowledge-intensive and less knowledge-intensive firms across several industry sectors, as knowledge-intensiveness has been noted as a major factor distinguishing between born-globals and other types of SMEs (Bell et al., 2004; Kuivalainen et al., 2007; Cavusgil and Knight, 2015), with the former leveraging their knowledge-based resources when aiming for rapid internationalisation (Knight and Cavusgil, 2004). Thus, a sample covering five industry sectors was sought: metal, furniture and food industry firms were selected to present the more traditional manufacturing industries, with the software industry and knowledge-intensive business services industries selected to present the more knowledge-intensive group. Moreover, by applying the definition of SMEs suggested by OECD (2005) and Knight (2001), we limited the search to those firms employing less than 500 people.

The Amadeus online database was used to draw up the initial sample. By using the limitations discussed above, 1,147 SMEs were found. These firms were then contacted by phone and asked to participate in the study. To those who agreed to take part, an email was sent with a link to the online survey. The survey itself was prepared with the online questionnaire tool Webropol, back-translated with the help of a professional translator and pre-tested with managers from two different fields. The prospective respondents were offered a printed questionnaire as an alternative, but no respondent took the offer; all preferred to respond online.

To those firms that had promised to participate in the survey, reminder emails were sent one week apart, up to four times each. When the data collection was concluded in July 2008, 298 SMEs had responded to the questionnaire, giving a response rate of 26 per cent. A total of 119 firms were listed as having foreign operations, and thus comprise the final sample in this study. At the time of the data collection, these internationally operating SMEs were, on average, 23 years old, employed an average of 77 people, and had an average turnover of 9.3 million euros. The respondent managers could identify as a *'managing director'*, *'owner'*, or *'other key person'*. Among the international firms the vast majority (81) were managing directors, with 15 identifying themselves as owners and 18 as 'other key person'. Consequently, we conducted ANOVA tests among the key variables in order to ensure that the respondent type did not significantly influence the given responses. No statistically significant differences at the 5 per cent risk level were found, and thus all the responses in the sample were deemed adequate for the analysis. We also checked for non-response bias, following the suggestions by Armstrong and Overton (1977), and found no problems with the data.

Measure development

The measures for the strategy focuses were adapted from Knight and Cavusgil's (2004) born-global study. We included both the items describing unique products development and the items describing quality focus into a primary component factor analysis using varimax rotation, and when necessary dropped an item due to a poor fit to a factor (i.e. one exhibiting a low commonality or cross-loading on several factors). The resulting two-factor solution captured 61 per cent of the total variation. Consequently, a five-item scale for unique products development focus with adequate reliability (Cronbach's alpha = 0.80) was developed:

- Our primary product/service caters to a specialised need that is difficult for our competitors to match.
- In our industry, our products/services represent a new, innovative approach to addressing the customer's basic need.

- Compared with our main competitors' offerings, our products/services are unique with respect to design.
- Compared with our main competitors' offerings, our products/services are unique with respect to technology.
- Compared with our main competitors' offerings, our products/services are unique with respect to performance.

The items for the quality focus factor also exhibited sufficient reliability as a scale (alpha = 0.72) and were as follows:

- Emphasising quality customer service is important to our firm's strategy in this market.
- Emphasising product/service quality is important to our firm's strategy in this market.
- For us, success in this market is driven by truly satisfying the needs of our customers there.

Subjective international performance was measured via a set of 7-point Likert scale items which were designed to inquire about the extent of success of international operations of the firm from the point of view of the management. Thus, the scale essentially measured the international performance of the firm subjectively, similarly to Knight and Cavusgil's (2004) study. The items formed a one-factor solution capturing 77 per cent of the total variation and exhibiting high reliability (alpha = 0.95). While such a high Cronbach's alpha may in theory suggest potential redundancy between the individual items in the scale, the threshold itself is debatable (see e.g. Clark and Watson, 1995), and the inter-correlations between the items remained at a feasible range. Thus, the final scale used included items as follows:

- Generally speaking, we are satisfied with our success in the international markets.
- We have achieved the turnover objectives we set for internationalisation.
- We have achieved the market-share objectives we set for internationalisation.
- Internationalisation has had a positive effect on our company's profitability.
- Internationalisation has had a positive effect on our company's image.
- Internationalisation has had a positive effect on the development of our company's expertise.
- The investments we have made in internationalisation have paid themselves back well.

We operationalised the difference between born-globals and other SMEs by dividing the sample firms into two groups according to the definition of born-globals by Knight and Cavusgil (1996). As a result, a dichotomous variable was created distinguishing between born-globals (1) and other types of SMEs (0). The rapidity of foreign market expansion was measured by the share of turnover the firm derived from foreign markets three years after the first entry. The three-year threshold has been suggested repeatedly in the context of born-global definitions (Knight et al., 2004; Knight and Cavusgil, 2005; Jones et al., 2011). Since born-globals have been suggested to be distinguishable from other types of firms by their level of knowledge-intensity, we also controlled for the knowledge-intensity of the sample firms. We created a dichotomous variable denoting knowledge-intensive firms (1), that is, the sample firms from software industry and knowledge-intensive business services, and the other types of more traditional manufacturing SMEs (0), that is, sample firms from metal, food and furniture industries. Finally, in our analysis we also controlled for firm size (as measured by number of employees) and age. The descriptive statistics and intercorrelations between the variables can be seen in Table 6.1.

Results and discussion

First, we conducted binary logistic regression analysis in order to test for H1 and H2, that is, if the strategic focus of SMEs would determine whether they had become born-globals or not. The results, as shown in Table 6.2, provide support for H1. The model with the control variables was non-significant (Chi-square = 4.68, p>0.05), with neither of the two control variable coefficients statistically significant. We included the main explanatory variables to the second regression model, and this model was significant at the 5 per cent risk level (Chi-square = 13.31, p<0.05). In particular, the coefficient for unique products

Table 6.1 Descriptives and intercorrelations of the variables used in hypotheses testing

	Mean	Std. dev.	1	2	3	4	5	6	7	8
1 Unique Prod. Devel.	4.70	1.05	1							
2 Quality Focus	6.11	0.78	0.19*	1						
3 Foreign Share of Turnover	35.63	31.79	0.22	−0.06	1					
4 Firm type	0.55	0.50	0.27*	−0.10	0.76**	1				
5 Subjective Int. Perform.	4.33	1.74	0.19	0.16	0.33*	0.04	1			
6 Firm Age	23.02	19.75	−0.27**	0.13	−0.21	−0.32*	0.06	1		
7 Firm Size	77.30	200.89	−0.18	−0.00	0.34*	0.15	−0.08	0.10	1	
8 Industry Sector	0.33	0.47	−0.08	0.07	−0.23	−0.15	−0.04	−0.23*	−0.05	1

Notes: **p<0.01, *p<0.05.

Table 6.2 Results of testing for H1–H2

Variables	Model 1 (Controls)		Model 2 (All variables)	
	B	Wald	B	Wald
Unique Prod. Develop.			0.85	2.34*
Quality Focus			−0.66	2.23
Firm Size	0.00	0.59	0.01	1.12
Industry Sector	1.05	2.55	0.91	1.57
Model Chi Square		4.68		13.31*
Cox and Snell R^2		0.09		0.23
Nagelke R^2		0.12		0.30
% correctly classified		56		73

Notes: **$p<0.01$, *$p<0.05$. Dependent variable: Firm Type (1=born-global; 0=other).

development was both positive and significant (0.85, $p<0.05$), indicating that the strategy of unique products development determined the likelihood of an SME having become born-global. Interestingly, the strategy of quality focus did not have a similar effect, and the coefficient was in fact negative (−0.66, $p>0.05$). This implies that the non-born-globals in the sample would have been more likely to adhere to the strategy of quality focus, although this result was not remotely significant in the statistical sense.

Next, we applied linear regression models in order to test if the strategic focus of SMEs in general was linked to the intensiveness of their international expansion (H3–H4). Table 6.3 illustrates the result, and while the model including only the control variables (Model 1, Table 6.3) was non-significant (F=2.46, $p>0.05$), model 2 with all the variables included was statistically significant (F=2.79, $p<0.05$), while explaining a fifth of the growth that the SMEs had achieved from foreign markets immediately following their internationalisation (adjusted $R^2 = 0.19$). Notably, the results were similar to Table 6.2 in that higher levels of focus in unique products development were positively related to increased share of turnover from foreign markets ($\beta = 0.35$, $p<0.05$), thus supporting H3.

On the other hand, H4 did not receive support from the analysis, as the coefficient for quality focus was again negative and non-significant ($\beta = -0.22$, $p>0.05$). Interestingly, the industry type was negatively related to foreign market growth ($\beta = -0.36$, $p>0.05$), indicating that the knowledge-intensive SMEs had not been successful in growing rapidly in terms of scale of their international operations. This was a surprising result, as extant research in general has supported the idea of knowledge-intensive firms internationalising rapidly and intensely (Bell, 1995; Bell et al., 2004; Kuivalainen et al., 2007). However, in our sample the knowledge-intensiveness of firms was negatively

Table 6.3   Results of testing for international expansion (H3–H4)

Variables	Model 1 (Controls)		Model 2 (All variables)	
	β	t-value	β	t-value
Unique Prod. Develop.			0.35	2.22*
Quality Focus			−0.22	−1.44
Firm Age	−0.30	−1.84	−0.18	−1.08
Firm Size	0.01	0.09	0.02	0.11
Industry	−0.40	2.46*	−0.35	−2.28*
Adj. R^2	0.10		0.19	
F	2.46		2.79*	

Notes: Significance levels: **$p<0.01$, *$p<0.05$. Dependent variable: Foreign share of turnover 3 years after internationalisation.

correlated with their born-globalness (see Table 6.1), and although the correlation was not significant, we suggest that may have been due to the nature of firms in the knowledge-intensive business services sector not fully aligning with that of the software industry (which is clearly an industry sector where born-globals are prevalent; see Bell, 1995; Boter and Holmquist, 1996; Sharma and Blomstermo, 2003; Freeman et al., 2006).

Finally, we tested for H5 and H6, in order to investigate if the dual strategic focus would be linked to increased international performance in SMEs overall, as they have been linked in born-globals specifically (Knight and Cavusgil, 2004). The results, shown in Table 6.4, provide no support for these hypotheses. First, the controls-only model (Model 1, Table 6.4) was non-significant (F = 0.28, $p>0.05$). Similarly, the model with the strategy variables included (Model 2, Table 6.4) was also non-significant (F = 1.13, $p>0.05$), and neither unique products development (β = 0.19, $p>0.05$) nor quality focus (β = 0.11, $p>0.05$) coefficients were statistically significant. Therefore, no link was found between the strategic focus of SMEs and their international performance, a contrary result in comparison to that found in the born-global context (Knight and Cavusgil, 2004).

In sum, the results suggest that the strategy of unique products development determines whether an SME can successfully realise its born-global status by internationalising within three years of its foundation, while simultaneously growing its foreign share of turnover to more than a quarter of its total turnover. Interestingly, the strategy of quality focus is not a differentiating factor among different types of SMEs. This is a contrary result to that of born-globals (Knight and Cavusgil, 2004) and may suggest that focusing on customer satisfaction in terms of experienced quality may be particularly relevant for born-globals. However, we also note that there are various

Table 6.4 Results of testing for subjective international performance (H5–H6)

Variables	Model 1 (Controls)		Model 2 (All variables)	
	β	t-value	β	t-value
Unique Prod. Develop.			0.19	1.61
Quality Focus			0.11	1.03
Firm Age	0.07	0.61	0.10	0.83
Firm Size	−0.08	−0.71	−0.04	−0.39
Industry	−0.03	−0.26	−0.01	−0.09
Adj. R^2	−0.03		0.01	
F	0.28		1.13	

Notes: Significance levels: **$p<0.01$, *$p<0.05$. Dependent variable: Subjective international performance.

definitions of what constitutes a born-global in extant literature, and the one used in our analysis is merely one of them. Innovativeness in product development, however, proves a significant factor differentiating born-globals from other types of companies, and also predicts faster international growth immediately following the start of internationalisation among the SMEs. This result is in line with Knight and Cavusgil's (2004) study, and thus extends the implications to SMEs in general.

The results further suggest that the dual business strategies may not have an influence on international performance of the SMEs. This result is contrary to the findings of Knight and Cavusgil (2004), and may imply that the beneficial effect of a focused business strategy on product innovativeness or quality may be particularly heightened in born-globals, while the more traditional SMEs may not expect similarly satisfactory results when internationalising with such focus. This may further imply that strategic focus on innovativeness and product quality are competitive advantages unique to born-globals, advantages that enable them to accrue international success, whereas potential customers globally do not value the same product and service characteristics in non-born-global SMEs. It may also be that there is an underlying factor which may explain these differences in more detail. For instance, in certain contexts, social and business networks may mediate a relationship between born-globals and their performance: Zhou et al. (2007) provide such an example in the Chinese context, while several studies (e.g. Rasmussen and Madsen, 2001; Sigfusson and Chetty, 2013) point towards similar implications on the importance of networking in a developed small, open economy context. Individual business relationships (Agndal and Chetty, 2007) as well as social capital (Agndal et al., 2008) may also have a relevant role. In addition, we also consider it possible that the market or institutional environment may moderate such relationships in the general SME context.

Implications and relevance for policy and practice

The results of this study point towards several implications for both managers and for public policymakers. First, they suggest that specific strategic focus towards innovation may enable an SME to internationalise rapidly and intensely, thus enabling it to become a born-global rather than a gradually internationalising company. This is a crucial implication, since born-global as a definition (see Rennie, 1993; Madsen and Servais, 1997; Knight and Cavusgil, 2004) merely distinguishes such firms, rather than providing managers of SMEs the strategic tools to help their company achieve born-global status. By finding that emphasising strategic focus towards unique products development will result in an SME becoming born-global and in rapid foreign market expansion, we suggest that innovativeness may provide unique competitive advantage that helps domestic SMEs to break into foreign markets. This is crucial in particular to SMEs originating from small, open economies such as Finland, that are characterised by small domestic markets and relatively high labour costs, where continued growth of enterprises can generally only be realised through internationalisation.

Second, the results indicate that all strategic focuses are not created equal: emphasising quality may not provide an SME a fast track into foreign markets, particularly in contexts such as ours where competitors tend to favour quality focus as well. This further implies that, in order for an SME to successfully realise rapid and intense internationalisation, it may need to emphasise strategic focus that distinguishes it from its domestic competitors, rather than developing a focus similar to them. For public policymakers, this correspondingly implies that, instead of aiming to help SMEs enhance the strategic strengths prevalent in the industry and in the national context, public institutions should rather concentrate on helping companies develop in areas that are not their main operative strengths: as seen in the results, in the Finnish context this means supporting SMEs in their innovativeness-related, rather than quality-related strategies.

Such a decision in public policy towards supporting SMEs may have far-reaching results, as growth-seeking enterprises have a crucial role in becoming both significant employers as well as payers of substantial corporate tax, thus having a dual impact on national economies. For the managers of internationalisation-seeking companies, the noted difference between unique products development and quality-focused strategies further implies that strategies aimed at product differentiation carry potential for rapid growth through internationalisation, growth that will not necessarily be available through quality-enhancing efforts.

Third, the fact that neither of the strategic focuses were linked to subjective international performance (i.e. strategic success of internationalisation, as measured by managerial assessment) emphasises that internationalisation may be unpredictable, enabling companies to grow rapidly, yet not in a way foreseen by the management when developing overall company strategy for internationalisation. The internationalisation process may therefore be, as Schweizer (2012) has suggested, a 'muddling-through' process, one where rapid foreign market entry and expansion is facilitated by product-related strategies rather than ex-ante internationalisation strategy as such. Managers of internationalisation-seeking SMEs should therefore be wary of developing far-reaching market strategies aimed at specific internationalisation outcomes, and instead concentrate on the product level. Correspondingly, public policy towards SMEs should therefore also be geared towards innovation-seeking, rather than internationalisation-seeking strategic development.

Simultaneously, we note that different market contexts may require different focus: while strategies aimed at optimising quality may not provide unique competitive advantage among SMEs in the Nordic context, other market areas (such as China and other developing markets) may still offer such possibilities for differentiation through quality. However, our study was conducted in the empirical context of Finland, and thus we are confident in its applicability in the context of similar small and open economies (e.g. Denmark, Norway, Sweden or Ireland). Therefore, as SMEs further proceed in expanding the scale and scope of their international operations, we suggest that SMEs may have to reassess their product strategy depending on their subsequent target markets.

Still, for many companies the first foreign market entry proves a major challenge. They need to overcome it rapidly in order to achieve the growth they require to cover sunk costs, for example, those committed to product R&D. The main resulting implication for both public policy and managerial practice therefore remains that focus on innovation, conceptualised here as the strategic focus on unique products development, may present a key to overcome that challenge, and may be crucial to accelerating internationalisation of SMEs, even as the results of that impact do not closely adhere to the formal organisational goals set for the internationalisation process.

Conclusion

The aim of this study was to investigate how the product- and service-related business strategies of SMEs are linked to their internationalisation outcomes. We further conceptualised these outcomes in terms of how rapidly and intensely SMEs were likely to internationalise (i.e. whether it could be defined as born-global or not), whether these business strategies enabled them more rapid international growth (i.e. how rapidly their foreign share of turnover had grown in the years immediately following their internationalisation) and whether the international performance of SMEs in general could be explained through the dual strategies of unique products development and quality focus, as suggested by Knight and Cavusgil (2004) to be the case with born-globals. Such an examination was called for, since the internationalisation strategies of SMEs may differ depending on their knowledge-intensity (Bell et al., 2004), and knowledge-intensity is a main characteristic denoting a born-global firm (Knight, 1996; Moen, 2002; Gabrielsson et al., 2008). In addition, the strategies of internationally operating SMEs have been examined in international entrepreneurship literature mainly through the lens of entry mode and internationalisation path decisions. Thus, providing a view of product- and service-based strategies in this context contributes to an increasingly holistic view into the phenomenon of business strategies conducive to the internationalisation of SMEs.

Our study also contains several limitations. A cross-sectional survey naturally limits the interpretation of causal relationships between the variables to hypothesising based on theory and extant literature. A follow-up study could therefore be called for, in order to establish temporal relationships. We also note that for clarity our investigation did not distinguish firms beyond born-global–type SMEs and other types of SMEs. That is to say that we did not specifically consider firm types such as international new ventures (Oviatt and McDougall, 1994) which can be argued to be distinct from born-globals in general (see Coviello, 2015). As our sample is restricted to SMEs, it does not account for the possibility of larger born-globals.

Due to our sample size, we also were not able to establish direct relationships through for example, structural equation modelling, and thus examining the antecedents of the business strategies (e.g. international strategic orientations; see Knight and Cavusgil, 2004) is left for future research. Accordingly, we suggest that exploring moderation and mediation effects by business networks and networking (see Rasmussen and Madsen, 2001; Zhou et al., 2007; Sigfusson and Harris, 2013) could shed further light on the dynamics between strategic focus and internationalisation outcomes among SMEs. Finally, organisational competencies were not part of our study, and should be included in future analysis. However, by extending the view of the dual business strategies to the SME context in general, the present study contributes to increasing our understanding of their role in determining the differences of business strategy on outcomes of not only born-globals specifically, but SMEs in general. In doing so it provides an extension to the results by Knight and Cavusgil (2004) by investigating the impact of strategic focus on internationalisation outcomes while distinguishing between born-globals and other types of SMEs.

References

Agndal, H. and Chetty, S. (2007). 'The impact of relationships on changes in internationalisation strategies of SMEs', *European Journal of Marketing*, 41(11/12), 1449–1474.

Agndal, H., Chetty, S. and Wilson, H. (2008). 'Social capital dynamics and foreign market entry', *International Business Review*, 17(6), 663–675.

Andersson, S. and Wictor, I. (2003). 'Innovative internationalisation in new firms: Born globals–the Swedish case', *Journal of International Entrepreneurship*, 1(3), 249–275.

Armstrong, S.J and Overton, T.S. (1977). 'Estimating nonresponse bias in mail surveys', *Journal of Marketing Research*, 14(3), 396–402.

Autio, E., Sapienza, H.J. and Almeida, J.G. (2000). 'Effects of age at entry, knowledge intensity, and imitability on international growth', *Academy of Management Journal*, 43(5), 909–924.

Bell, J. (1995). 'The internationalization of small computer software firms: A further challenge to "stage" theories', *European Journal of Marketing*, 29(8), 60–75.

Bell, J., Crick, D. and Young, S. (2004). 'Small firm internationalization and business strategy an exploratory study of "'knowledge-intensive'" and "'traditional'" manufacturing firms in the UK', *International Small Business Journal*, 22(1), 23–56.

Boter, H. and Holmquist, C. (1996). 'Industry characteristics and internationalization processes in small firms', *Journal of Business Venturing*, 11(6), 471–487.

Cavusgil, S.T. and Knight, G. (2015). 'The born global firm: An entrepreneurial and capabilities perspective on early and rapid internationalization', *Journal of International Business Studies*, 46(1), 3–16.

Cavusgil, S.T. and Zou, S. (1994). 'Marketing strategy-performance relationship: An investigation of the empirical link in export market ventures', *The Journal of Marketing*, 58(1), 1–21.

Chetty, S. and Campbell-Hunt, C. (2004). 'A strategic approach to internationalization: A traditional versus a "born-global" approach', *Journal of International Marketing*, 12(1), 57–81.

Clark, L.A. and Watson, D. (1995). 'Constructing validity: Basic issues in objective scale development', *Psychological Assessment*, 7(3), 309–319.

Coviello, N. (2015). 'Re-thinking research on born globals', *Journal of International Business Studies*, 46(1), 17–26.

Crick, D. and Spence, M. (2005). 'The internationalisation of "'high performing'" UK high-tech SMEs: A study of planned and unplanned strategies', *International Business Review*, 14(2), 167–185.

Freeman, S., Edwards, R. and Schroder, B. (2006). 'How smaller born-global firms use networks and alliances to overcome constraints to rapid internationalization', *Journal of International Marketing*, 14(3), 33–63.

Gabrielsson, M., Kirpalani, V.H.M., Dimitratos, P., Solberg, C.A. and Zucchella, A. (2008). 'Born globals: Propositions to help advance the theory', *International Business Review*, 17(4), 385–401.

Gleason, K.C. and Wiggenhorn, J. (2007). 'Born globals, the choice of globalization strategy, and the market's perception of performance', *Journal of World Business*, 42(3), 322–335.

Jantunen, A., Nummela, N., Puumalainen, K. and Saarenketo, S. (2008). 'Strategic orientations of born globals – do they really matter?', *Journal of World Business*, 43(2), 158–170.

Johanson, J. and Vahlne, J.-E. (1977). 'The internationalization process of the firm: A model of knowledge development and increasing foreign market commitments', *Journal of International Business Studies*, 8(1), 23–32.

——— (2003). 'Business relationship learning and commitment in the internationalization process', *Journal of International Entrepreneurship*, 1(1), 83–101.

—— (2009). 'The Uppsala internationalization process model revisited: From liability of foreignness to liability of outsidership', *Journal of International Business Studies*, 40(9), 1411–1431.

Johanson, J. and Wiedersheim-Paul, F. (1975). 'The internationalization of the firm: Four Swedish cases', *Journal of Management Studies*, 12(3), 305–322.

Jones, M.V., Coviello, N. and Tang, Y.K. (2011). 'International entrepreneurship research (1989–2009): A domain ontology and thematic analysis', *Journal of Business Venturing*, 26(6), 632–659.

Knight, G.A. (1996). *Born Global*, Wiley International Encyclopedia of Marketing, 6.

—— (2001). 'Entrepreneurship and strategy in the international SME', *Journal of International Management*, 7(3), 155–171.

Knight, G.A. and Cavusgil, S.T. (1996). *The Born Global Firm: A Challenge to Traditional Internationalization Theory, Advances in International Marketing*, New York: Jai Press, 11–26.

—— (2004). 'Innovation, organizational capabilities, and the born-global firm', *Journal of International Business Studies*, 35(2), 124–141.

—— (2005). 'A taxonomy of born-global firms', *Management International Review*, 45(3), 15–35.

Knight, G.A., Madsen, T.K. and Servais, P. (2004). 'An inquiry into born-global firms in Europe and the USA', *International Marketing Review*, 21(6), 645–665.

Kuivalainen, O., Sundqvist, S.-K. and Servais, P. (2007). 'Firms' degree of born-global-ness, international entrepreneurial orientation and export performance', *Journal of World Business*, 42(3), 253–267.

Laanti, R., Gabrielsson, M. and Gabrielsson, P. (2007). 'The globalization strategies of business-to-business born global firms in the wireless technology industry', *Industrial Marketing Management*, 36(8), 1104–1117.

Lévesque, M. and Shepherd, D.A. (2004). 'Entrepreneurs' choice of entry strategy in emerging and developed markets', *Journal of Business Venturing*, 19(1), 29–54.

Madsen, T.K. and Servais, P. (1997). 'The internationalization of born globals: An evolutionary process?', *International Business Review*, 6(6), 561–583.

Merrilees, B., Miller, D. and Tiessen, J. (1998). 'Serendipity, leverage and the process of entrepreneurial internationalization', *Small Enterprise Research*, 6(2), 3–11.

Meyer, K. and Skak, A. (2002). 'Networks, serendipity and SME entry into Eastern Europe', *European Management Journal*, 20(2), 179–188.

Moen, Ø. (2002). 'The born globals: A new generation of small European exporters', *International Marketing Review*, 19(2), 156–175.

OECD (2005). *OECD SME and Entrepreneurship Outlook: 2005*, OECD Paris, p. 17.

Oviatt, B.M. and McDougall, P.P. (1994). 'Toward a theory of international new ventures', *Journal of International Business Studies*, 25(1), 45–64.

—— (2005). 'Defining international entrepreneurship and modeling the speed of internationalization', *Entrepreneurship Theory and Practice*, 29(5), 537–554.

Rasmussen, E.S. and Madsen, T.K. (2001). 'The founding of the born global company in Denmark and Australia: Sensemaking and networking', *Asia Pacific Journal of Marketing and Logistics*, 13(3), 75–107.

Rennie, M.W. (1993). 'Born global', *McKinsey Quarterly*, 4, 45–52.

Schweizer, R. (2012). 'The internationalization process of SMEs: A muddling-through process', *Journal of Business Research*, 65(6), 745–751.

Sharma, D.D. and Blomstermo, A. (2003). 'The internationalization process of born globals: A network view', *International Business Review*, 12(6), 739–753.

Sigfusson, T. and Chetty, S. (2013). 'Building international entrepreneurial virtual networks in cyberspace', *Journal of World Business*, 48(2), 260–270.

Sigfusson, T. and Harris, S. (2013). 'Domestic market context and international entrepreneurs' relationship portfolios', *International Business Review*, 22(1), 243–258.

Spence, M. (2003). 'International strategy formation in small Canadian high-technology companies–a case study approach', *Journal of International Entrepreneurship*, 1(3), 277–296.

Tornikoski, E.T. and Newbert, S.L. (2007). 'Exploring the determinants of organizational emergence: A legitimacy perspective', *Journal of Business Venturing*, 22(2), 311–335.

Tuppura, A., Saarenketo, S., Puumalainen, K., Jantunen, A. and Kyläheiko, K. (2008). 'Linking knowledge, entry timing and internationalization strategy', *International Business Review*, 17(4), 473–487.

Zhou, L., Wei-Ping, W. and Luo, X. (2007). 'Internationalization and the performance of born-global SMEs: The mediating role of social networks', *Journal of International Business Studies*, 38(4), 673–690.

Zou, S. and Cavusgil, S.T. (2002). 'The GMS: A broad conceptualization of global marketing strategy and its effect on firm performance', *Journal of Marketing*, 66(4), 40–56.

7

Foreign Direct Investment (FDI) and Indigenous Firms' Innovation: The Moderating Effect of Environmental Dynamism

Yoo Jung Ha

Introduction

Strategy, international business and economics literatures have explored whether foreign presence has an impact on innovation and productivity in a host country. A commonly shared argument is that when MNEs conduct FDI, host country firms are exposed to greater technological opportunities, with positive impact (Zhang et al., 2010). These positive externalities are known as FDI spillovers. Recent empirical work has advanced knowledge about FDI spillovers by suggesting various antecedents and moderators, such as strategies of senders (foreign MNE subsidiaries), absorptive capacity of recipients (host country firms), and modes of interaction between MNEs and local industry stakeholders through formal or informal collaborative linkages (Crespo and Fontura, 2007; Smeets, 2008). Despite sophistication of conceptual modelling and fineness of methodology, empirical evidence has delivered mixed results about the impact of foreign presence on a host country (Havranek and Irsova, 2011; Irsova and Havranek, 2013). The lack of consensus in the empirical literature intimates that the impact of foreign presence is subject to a number of unobserved contingency factors (Eapen, 2012).

This study investigates the extent to which the impact of FDI on indigenous firms' innovation is contingent on levels of environmental dynamism in the local market. Environmental dynamism refers to the degree of variation in the market and technological change (Eisenhardt, 1989; Sidhu et al., 2007). High levels of environmental dynamism mean a firm's competitive advantage rapidly becomes obsolete. This will influence a firm's strategy for gaining and protecting maximum returns from innovation. Nevertheless, existing analysis of FDI's impact on indigenous firms has neglected the dynamic aspect of task environments. This research gap prevents understanding of FDI impact in industries marked by dynamic change and hyper-competition, as seen in the case of FDI inflows in the UK pharmaceutical industry.

Our empirical analysis uses firm-level panel data for the South Korean manufacturing sector, drawn from three waves of innovation survey conducted in 2005, 2008 and 2010. We use South Korea as a case which has comparative advantages in both fast-changing and moderately changing industries, with a national innovation system known for its high adaptability to global competition (Dodgson, 2009). To investigate the impact of foreign presence from the perspectives of various industry stakeholders, this chapter divides technology spillovers from FDI into two types – horizontal spillovers on competitors and backward spillovers on upstream suppliers.

This chapter makes several contributions. First, our findings show that FDI at different levels of environmental dynamism has varying effects on the innovation performance of indigenous firms. Previous studies have focused on the moderating effects of static levels of external resources in indigenous firms' task environments, but paid little attention to environmental dynamics. We also conceptualise how levels of environmental dynamism interact with horizontal and backward channels which transfer technology spillovers from foreign MNEs to local competitors and suppliers differently. While previous studies have proposed differential potentials for each channel, few have scrutinised whether the two types of FDI spillover are differently sensitive to contextual factors. Furthermore, our study brings the literature of innovation in a dynamic environment to the new context, and has implications for the likelihood of inter-firm technology spillovers in fast-moving industries in the global context, compared with a single firm–level knowledge management strategy in the domestic context.

The remainder of the chapter is organised as follows. The next section reviews previous literature, conceptualises the moderating effect of environmental dynamism on the impact of FDI on indigenous firms' innovation, and develops hypotheses. The methodology section follows, presenting model specification and estimation strategy. After a discussion of test results and new findings, the chapter ends with conclusions and suggestions for future studies.

Literature review

MNEs operate in multiple foreign locations based on organisational capabilities to create, retain and transfer knowledge through social and technical knowledge management mechanisms across subunits across foreign subsidiaries (Argote et al., 2003; Gupta and Govindarajan, 2000). On that basis, existing studies have postulated that the entry of foreign firms presents local firms with opportunities to observe and learn from advanced benchmark technological and managerial knowledge, known as FDI spillover (Zhang et al., 2010).

FDI spillovers have implications for the innovation performance of indigenous firms. Foreign entry extends the overall set of advanced technology in a host country, as foreign subsidiaries of MNEs have access to superior firm-specific assets from their home country or enjoy greater access to advanced technologies from other overseas sources (Veugelers and Cassiman, 2004). Foreign presence also adds technological heterogeneity in terms of the geographic origin of technology, and increases the scope of technological opportunities for firms in the host country to search, integrate with existing internal technology, and harness new values (Zhang et al., 2010). Therefore, innovation performance in an indigenous firm improves if the intensity of foreign activities increases in the local firm's industry or in industries where its upstream suppliers or downstream customers operate (García et al., 2013; Liu and Buck, 2007; Liu et al., 2009).

The effect of FDI spillovers is not automatic and this means foreign technological opportunities are realised contingent on unobserved factors, such as the characteristics of the task environments where a firm's innovation activities are organised. Indigenous firms' sensitivity to technological opportunities from foreign subsidiaries of MNEs varies depending on different levels of external munificence, competition and catch-up motivation. Current external information and resources in the host country are required for successful acquisition and learning of technologies of foreign origin (Judge and Miller, 1991; Tan and Litschert, 1994). A local firm is more likely to benefit from technology spillovers from FDI if it operates in industries of high technological intensity than otherwise (Buckley et al., 2007; Haskel et al., 2007; Keller and Yeaple, 2009; Sembenelli and Siotis, 2008). The effect of FDI spillovers is also greater in industries where the performance gap between local technology laggards and foreign technology leaders is wide than otherwise (Findlay, 1978; Kokko, 1994). Furthermore, the higher the competitive pressures within the market, the greater FDI spillovers that local rivals enjoy (Hallin and Holmström-Lind, 2012; Kokko, 1994; Perri et al., 2013).

While studies so far have focused on static environmental features as a contingency, existing studies do not inquire into the moderating effects of levels of environmental dynamism. There has been an implicit assumption that the impact of FDI is invariant across levels of environmental dynamism, or that FDI spillovers occur in a stable environment in terms of technological and market changes. However, this is not the case. In recent years an MNE's locational decision tends to be related to the anticipation of a positive cascading effect of the high rate of technological and market change in the host country on its global production network. This means that location advantages for FDI amid dynamic change are determined by the extent to which an MNE can leverage technological opportunities in the host country for rapid renewal of its competitive advantages. Locations such as newly industrialised economies in East Asia with a resilient manufacturing base provide task environments that meet MNEs' demands for adaptability and technological entrepreneurship amid global competition (Dodgson, 2009; McKinsey and Company, 2010). Studies assuming a stable environment cannot fully explain variation in FDI spillovers in a dynamic setting in terms of technological and market changes.

Overall, the moderating effect of environmental dynamism should improve understanding of the impact of FDI on indigenous firms in a host country which has locational advantages in industries undergoing both stable and dynamic changes. Dynamism in a firm's task environments has received less attention in empirical studies of FDI spillovers, although the Strategy and International Business literatures have suggested environmental dynamism as a motivation of innovation and variation in knowledge exchanges through inter-firm linkages in a dynamic environment (Baum and Wally, 2003). The next section develops hypotheses about the moderating effect of environmental dynamism on the impact of FDI on indigenous firms. We consider two types of FDI spillovers, horizontal and backward spillovers.

Hypothesis development

Environmental dynamism and horizontal spillovers from FDI

FDI spillovers horizontally influence indigenous firms competing with foreign MNEs in the same industry. MNEs' globally competitive technology and practices can support local firms' strategies to improve performance through imitation (Haunschild and Miner, 1997). MNE technology and practices are also diffused when workers trained by MNEs move to domestic firms, passing on not only knowledge and know-how, but also norms and values acquired from their MNE training (Lipsey and Sjöholm, 2005; Markusen, 2005). Former MNE employees may establish start-ups as virtual spin-offs from MNEs. Nevertheless, empirical evidence has returned mixed verdicts (Havranek and Irsova, 2011; Irsova and Havranek, 2013) because, depending on the country and industry context, the positive effects of foreign technological opportunities can often be discounted in research by the negative effect of foreign competition and market crowding-out (Aitken and Harrison, 1999). In other words, only under specific contexts might indigenous firms benefit from horizontal spillovers from FDI.

We predict that increased environmental dynamism in a host country will strengthen the positive effect of horizontal FDI spillovers on the innovation of indigenous firms. In a dynamic context, competition is about speedier introduction of new products than that by competitors. It is difficult for managers to predict the consequences of new product and process development or adoption of managerial practices. Increased environmental uncertainty promotes the importance of external benchmarks in a firm's strategy in place of a firm's own private information (Lieberman and Asaba, 2006). Thus, in a dynamic rather than stable environment indigenous firms are likely to benefit from the presence of MNE subsidiaries which act as sources of information about globally competitive products, process technology and managerial practices (Haunschild and Miner, 1997).

Another reason for stronger positive effects from horizontal FDI spillovers in dynamic rather than stable environments is that foreign MNEs are concerned less about the risk of imitation. In a stable environment, the adaptation of new technology from the home country or other centres of excellence may raise for the MNE issues of protection of intangible assets from local competitors (Alcácer and Chung, 2007; de Faria and Sofka, 2010). However, in a dynamic environment the speed at which current technology loses value is greater in a fast-paced industry than in a slow-paced one (D'Aveni et al., 2010). This characteristic of the fast-cycle market reduces threats arising from unwanted leakage of technology to partners, and foreign MNEs are likely to overlook technology spillovers to indigenous firms in the same industry. On that basis, we postulate that environmental dynamism enhances the potential for positive effects of horizontal FDI spillovers on indigenous firms.

Hypothesis 1: The impact of horizontal spillovers from FDI on indigenous firms' innovation increases as levels of environmental dynamism increase.

Environmental dynamism and backward spillovers from FDI

FDI spillovers can be generated through vertical transactional linkages among local suppliers of intermediate inputs and foreign MNE customers (Driffield et al., 2002). While advanced technology is difficult to transfer due to tacitness, complexity and specificity, a diffusion process can be facilitated when two firms share common organisational ground (Spencer, 2008). Transactional linkages foster persistent organisational interactions to facilitate transfer of technology between MNEs and local firms (Liu et al., 2009). Nevertheless, literature also reports opposing evidence. There could be limited use of supplier-assistance programs for foreign MNEs to support local suppliers (Dries and Swinnen, 2004). An MNE may design a global production network to transfer cost-reduction pressures from downstream to upstream external suppliers in the first place, while blocking unwanted technology spillovers (Driffield et al., 2002; Motohashi and Yuan, 2010). In other words, only under specific contexts might indigenous firms benefit from backward spillovers from FDI. .

We predict that high environmental dynamism will strengthen transactional linkages between foreign MNEs and indigenous firms, and thereby result in greater positive effects from backward FDI spillovers (Spencer, 2008).

Unlike in a stable environment, a turbulent environment poses for downstream customers' greater uncertainty and risk of product development arising from increased speed and discontinuity in technological and market changes. In response, there can be strong motivation for more frequent and intimate collaboration between customers and suppliers on production and development in a dynamic environment (Zhao and Cavusgil, 2006). Persistent organisational contacts in a dynamic environment facilitate trust-building between downstream customers and upstream suppliers (Zhao and Cavusgil, 2006), followed by greater commitment and assistance from customers (Vilkamo and Keil, 2003), leading to increased opportunities for suppliers to capture backward technology spillovers from customers (Jones, 2003). On that basis, we postulate that environmental dynamism enhances the potential for positive effects from backward FDI spillovers on indigenous firms.

Hypothesis 2: The impact of backward spillovers from FDI on indigenous firms' innovation increases as levels of environmental dynamism increase.

Methodology

Data

To test our hypotheses, we use data from three waves of the Korean Innovation Survey, provided by Korea's Science and Technology Policy Institute (STEPI). This survey series is equivalent to innovation surveys by other governments, including the EU's Community Innovation Survey, conducted under the direction of the OECD Oslo Manual. Innovation survey data has been employed for various recent publications exploring innovation activities within firms and FDI spillover research (Crescenzi et al., 2015; Ha and Giroud, 2015; Sofka et al., 2014). Across three waves of survey, in 2005, 2008 and 2010, a total of 9,753 firms participated. Our data consists of 5,032 observations of indigenous firms which responded to at least one of the surveys and provided full information for variables of our interest.

Our dataset is pooled cross-sectional rather than panel data. While our data include observations that feature in more than one survey, most are observed only once or twice. This means panel estimation is not possible (Sofka et al., 2014).

Variable specification

Innovation performance

Innovation performance in a firm is measured by counts of product patent application. A patent of a firm indicates the level of new-to-the-market knowledge that is open to the public and contributes to the public knowledge pool in a national innovation system (Furman et al., 2002; Salomon and Shaver,

2005). We consider product count application rather than those that are already granted in order to approximate potential innovation outputs resulting from innovation activities during the period covered by this study (García et al., 2013). We focus on product patents excluding process patents to capture innovation output that leads to significant changes in new products and competence creation, rather than incremental changes in existing products and competence exploitation.

Horizontal and backward spillovers from FDI

As proxy for horizontal spillovers, we use the ratio of MNE subsidiaries in an industry's total R&D expenditures. A firm is classified as an MNE subsidiary if it identifies itself as such. While percentage ratio of foreign ownership is often used as an identifier of a firm's foreignness (Haskel et al., 2007), it does not necessarily show that any single foreign MNE is participating in meaningful governance activities in the local firm. Due to this difficulty, this study depends on a respondent's subjective judgement to determine whether it is a domestic firm or a subsidiary of a foreign MNE. The industry is identified by the two-digit NACE industry classification. We focus on a three-year lagged effect of FDI, that is, an indigenous firm's innovation performance is determined by FDI that took place three years before. This is to reduce endogeneity bias that could be caused by the use of non-lagged FDI effect.

As a proxy for backward spillovers, we compute the weighted sum of foreign R&D expenditure ratios in all downstream industries of a local firm, excluding the firm's own industry. The weighted sum is computed based on backward linkage coefficients from OECD's input–output table (Blalock and Gertler, 2008; Javorcik, 2004).

Environmental dynamism

To measure levels of environmental dynamism each firm faces, we use self-reported responses by firm managers about the number of years the firm's most important product survives in the market before replacement by a new product. Strategists' perception is essential, as ultimately the impact of environments depends on the extent to which managers perceive environmental dynamism (Carillo, 2005; Chen et al., 2010; Duncan, 1972). Previous studies have suggested cut-off points for fast, medium and slow rates of new-product introduction within an industry (Fine, 2000; Nadkarni and Narayanan, 2007). Following their definition, we assign ratings of 5 (product life < 3 years), 4 ($3 \leq$ product life < 10 years), 3 ($10 \leq$ product life < 40 years), 2 (40 years $\leq$ product life) and 1 (Permanent product life). In other words, 5 is the most dynamic environment, while 1 is the least dynamic (most stable). We acknowledge that our measurement is based on a single dominant product rather than all product lines within a firm.

Control variables

We incorporate several other factors into the model as control variables that may influence an indigenous firm's innovation performance. R&D expenditures (with log), R&D capacity measured as the ratio of R&D staff in a firm, and R&D centre as a dummy variable for the presence of permanent or temporary R&D teams in the organisational structure are related to the firm's absorptive capacity to identify, transform and exploit external technology and organisational capabilities for innovation activities. Age (with log) captures the amount of accumulated knowledge through all past learnings. To capture alternative sources of external technologies in the domestic setting, we enter Business group, a dummy variable indicating whether a firm is part of a large business group or not, and External search, another dummy variable, capturing whether a firm has engaged in R&D cooperation with any industry or non-industry partners.

Estimation method

Our model follows the knowledge production function (KPF). As a modified version of the production function, KPF considers innovation, organisational capabilities and commercial success in development as dependent variables (Liu and Buck, 2007; Wang and Yu, 2007), instead of overall performance. Our baseline model regresses a firm's innovation performance (the dependent variable) on proxies for horizontal and backward FDI spillovers and environmental dynamism (key independent variables). Thereby, this research explores the link between FDI spillovers and indigenous firm innovation performance (Salomon and Shaver, 2005) not yet translated into commercial success and overall productivity changes (Motohashi and Yuan, 2010). We estimate the model by the negative binomial model and use robust standard errors to deal with potential heteroscedasticity issues. We also control for time effects and unobserved factors at the industry level by including dummy variables for observations from each year and each industry.

Results

Baseline model

Descriptive and correlation matrices are as reported in Table 7.1. The correlation matrix does not reveal any multicollinearity issues. This is complemented by a mean variance inflation factor (VIF) of 1.23 and a condition number of 15.41.

Table 7.2 shows the result of the negative binomial regression. Model 1 is the baseline model including control variables only. R&D expenditures, R&D capacity, and R&D centre are all positively related to indigenous firms' innovation performance. This is consistent with past studies' predictions based on the importance of a firm's absorptive capacity for innovation performance (Cohen

Table 7.1 Correlation matrices and descriptive statistics

Variables	1	2	3	4	5	6	7	8	9	10
1 Innovation performance	1.000									
2 R&D expenditures	0.102	1.000								
3 R&D capacity	0.103	0.286	1.000							
4 R&D centre	0.130	0.499	0.496	1.000						
5 Age	0.061	0.104	-0.068	0.242	1.000					
6 Business group	0.108	0.065	-0.011	0.135	0.114	1.000				
7 External search	0.073	0.251	0.123	0.253	0.091	0.117	1.000			
8 Horizontal FDI spillovers	0.030	0.117	0.107	0.136	0.016	-0.006	0.076	1.000		
9 Backward FDI spillovers	-0.011	-0.023	-0.085	-0.062	0.055	0.038	-0.019	-0.157	1.000	
10 Environmental dynamism	0.049	0.233	0.222	0.316	0.019	0.001	0.156	0.164	-0.214	1.000
Observations	5032	5032	5032	5032	5032	5032	5032	5032	5032	5032
Mean	3.507	2.634	0.071	0.563	2.733	0.079	0.119	0.021	0.035	2.689
Standard deviation	22.403	2.821	0.114	0.496	0.638	0.270	0.324	0.053	0.059	1.332

Table 7.2   FDI spillovers and the moderating effect of environment velocity

	Model 1	Model 2	Model 3	Model 4	Model 5
<Control variables>					
R&D expenditures	0.177***	0.179***	0.180***	0.179***	0.180***
	(0.0234)	(0.0221)	(0.0220)	(0.0221)	(0.0220)
R&D capacity	3.554***	3.574***	3.563***	3.582***	3.573***
	(0.582)	(0.566)	(0.565)	(0.566)	(0.566)
R&D centre	2.028***	2.074***	2.078***	2.088***	2.089***
	(0.155)	(0.146)	(0.145)	(0.144)	(0.144)
Age	0.436***	0.424***	0.427***	0.437***	0.438***
	(0.0958)	(0.0947)	(0.0947)	(0.0942)	(0.0943)
Business group	0.920***	0.971***	0.942***	0.962***	0.938***
	(0.194)	(0.196)	(0.195)	(0.191)	(0.192)
External search	0.439**	0.433**	0.439**	0.431**	0.436**
	(0.163)	(0.160)	(0.159)	(0.159)	(0.158)
Year effect	Included	Included	Included	Included	Included
Industry effect	Included	Included	Included	Included	Included
<Environmental dynamism, FDI spillovers>					
Environmental dynamism	0.233***	0.214***	0.249***	0.149*	0.189***
	(0.0647)	(0.0594)	(0.0621)	(0.0667)	(0.071)
Horizontal FDI spillovers		−2.265	4.450	−2.046	3.768
		(1.419)	(3.148)	(1.411)	(3.188)
Backward FDI spillovers		−6.778†	−6.345†	−9.263*	−8.537*
		(3.687)	(3.640)	(3.835)	(3.830)
<Moderating effects>					
Horizontal FDI spillovers × Environmental dynamism			−1.873*		−1.628†
			(0.835)		(0.846)
Backward FDI spillovers × Environmental dynamism				1.955*	1.679
				(0.995)	(1.021)
Constant	−4.536***	−4.535***	−4.630***	−4.359***	−4.467***
	(0.527)	(0.524)	(0.526)	(0.536)	(0.542)
Observations	5032	5032	5032	5032	5032
Log likelihood	−6908.462	−6899.227	−6896.121	−6896.300	−6894.009
Chi square	1108.05***	1210.70***	1221.56***	1232.55***	1240.86***

Note: Robust standard errors are in parentheses; † $p<0.10$, * $p<0.05$, ** $p<0.01$, *** $p<0.001$.

and Levinthal, 1989). Age also has a positive effect on a firm's innovation performance, reflecting on the prediction that cumulative firm-level learning from past years matters (Levitt and March, 1988). Also in line with the literature's prediction is the positive effect of Business group and External search, meaning the importance of R&D collaboration, either locally within business groups or widely with external alliance partners (Hagedoorn and Wang, 2012; Mahmood et al., 2011).

Model 2 includes the main effects of two types of FDI spillover and environmental dynamism. The coefficients for both horizontal and backward spillovers are negative and not significant. While this result is not consistent with the theoretical prediction of positive horizontal and forward effects from FDI, empirical literature has reported mixed results. In other words, depending on the contingency of industry- and firm-level context, the impact of FDI on indigenous firms may vary.

The coefficient of environmental dynamism is positive and statistically significant. This means that as environmental dynamism increases, indigenous firms increase innovation activities and innovation performance improves accordingly. This result is in line with theoretical predictions and findings in existing studies (Sidhu et al., 2007).

The moderating effect of environment dynamism

Models 3, 4 and 5 provide regression results to test Hypotheses 1 and 2. The coefficients of the interaction terms between FDI spillovers and environmental dynamism indicate changes in FDI spillover effects as environmental dynamism increases. Furthermore, the regression results are complemented by further graphical scrutiny (Hagedoorn and Wang, 2012). This allows us to examine interaction effects more carefully, as magnitude, statistical significance and the sign of the marginal effect may vary across different levels of environmental dynamism in a non-linear negative binomial model.

Our Hypothesis 1 concerned the positive moderating effect of environmental dynamism on the relationship between horizontal FDI spillovers and the innovation performance of an indigenous firm. In both Models 3 and 5, coefficients of the interaction term Horizontal FDI spillovers x Environmental dynamism are negative and statistically significant. This indicates that in a dynamic environment there are fewer positive horizontal spillovers than in a stable environment. As a further scrutiny of the interaction term, Figure 7.1 represents the marginal effect of horizontal FDI spillovers and innovation performance of indigenous firms at different levels of environmental dynamism. It shows that the marginal effect of horizontal spillovers is positive when environmental dynamism is low, that is, in a relatively stable environment, but the positive effect diminishes as levels of environmental dynamism rise. This means that indigenous firms may experience positive horizontal spillovers, but this is likely to be cancelled out by negative competition effects as the level of environmental dynamism increases. In other words, there is a negative moderating effect of environmental dynamism on the association between horizontal FDI spillovers and innovation performance of indigenous firms. Thus, Hypothesis 1 is not accepted.

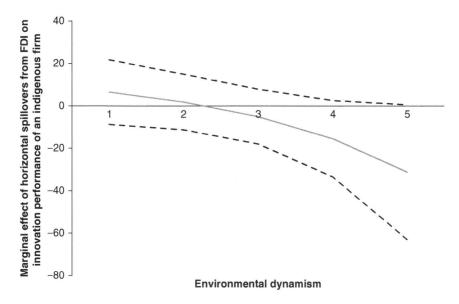

Figure 7.1   The moderating effect of environmental dynamism on the relationship between horizontal spillovers from FDI and innovation performance of indigenous firms
Note: The dotted lines are 95% Confidence Interval.

Our Hypothesis 2 proposed the positive moderating effect of environmental dynamism on the relationship between backward FDI spillovers and the innovation performance of an indigenous firm. The coefficient of the interaction term Backward FDI spillovers x Environmental dynamism is positive and significant in Model 4. However, the positive effect is not significant in Model 5, although the sign is positive consistently. We turn to Figure 7.2 to further examine the marginal effect of backward FDI spillovers and innovation performance of indigenous firms at different levels of environmental dynamism. It shows that the marginal effect of backward spillovers is negative in stable environments. However, the negative marginal effect is replaced by a positive effect as environmental dynamism comes closer to the highest level, that is, the most dynamic environment. This indicates a positive moderating effect of environmental dynamism on the association between backward FDI spillovers and the innovation performance of indigenous firms. Thus, Hypothesis 2 is partially accepted.

Conclusion

Main findings and contributions

This chapter has explored the moderating effect of environmental dynamism on the relationship between horizontal and backward FDI spillovers and

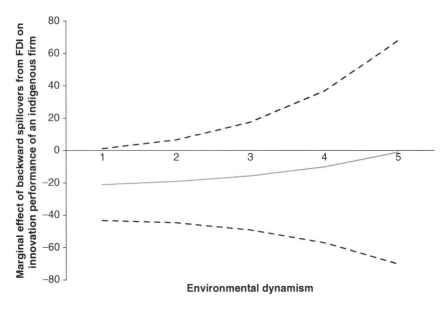

Figure 7.2 The moderating effect of environmental dynamism on the relationship between backward spillovers from FDI and innovation performance of indigenous firms
Note: The dotted lines are 95% Confidence Interval.

the innovation performance of indigenous firms in the host country. Our empirical analysis shows that high environmental dynamism weakens the positive effect of horizontal spillovers from FDI. In a dynamic environment, indigenous firms may benefit from a positive demonstration effect due to foreign presence, but are also likely to experience challenges due to intense competition with foreign MNEs with advantages accruing from HQ's assets and intra-MNE knowledge integration systems. We also find partial evidence for a positive effect that backward FDI spillovers are strengthened in a dynamic environment. This means that upstream suppliers in the host country are likely to capture positive externalities to strengthen their innovation performance when they have transactional linkages with foreign MNEs in a dynamic environment.

This chapter's key contribution is to confirm the moderating effect of environmental dynamism on technology spillovers from FDI. The suggestion of an environmental moderating effect explains a source of mixed evidence on FDI spillovers in past studies. So far, this mixed evidence has often been ascribed to insufficient specification of the external and internal contexts of FDI spillovers (Havranek and Irsova, 2011). Recent studies have partly responded to this call for research by suggesting that the intrinsic availability of information and resources in task environments influences the occurrence of technology spillovers from FDI (Buckley et al., 2007; Haskel et al., 2007; Keller and Yeaple, 2009; Sembenelli and Siotis, 2008). Relatively less attention has been paid to the moderating effect of environmental dynamics of change. To fill this gap, we integrated the literature of environmental dynamism with FDI spillover literature. As a result, our study complements the literature on the moderating factors of FDI spillovers, conceptually and empirically.

Another contribution is to show differences between horizontal and backward FDI spillovers. Past studies have assumed that both types of spillover respond identically to changes in intra-firm or external settings, and any previous studies exploring suitable circumstances for positive effects on horizontal or backward spillovers, if performed, have been isolated from one another. This chapter shows that effects of horizontal and backward spillovers are likely to be maximised at different levels of environmental dynamism.

This research also contributes to the environmental dynamism literature. Strategy scholars have noted the interplay between rates of change at firm and industry levels. Firms' strategy, behaviour and organisational structure have been investigated extensively. However, the concept has been bounded in domestic economies. In reality, more and more firms operate in multiple locations, so that what environmental dynamism influences is not only a firm's strategy, behaviour and structure but also interactions between foreign MNEs and indigenous firms in the host country. Thus, we propose that environmental dynamism is a key contextual dimension explaining technology and knowledge spillovers in international business.

Practical implications

This research has practical implications for both MNE subsidiaries and domestic firms in a dynamic industry. Firms in a host country may access technological opportunities by participating in value chains led by foreign MNEs. High environmental dynamism creates a situation where foreign need to access the fast-changing technologies that a local supply network in a host country provides. Overall, there is a virtuous cycle wherein suppliers and customers of different country origins co-develop in a dynamic market and industry.

A policy implication is that policymakers may have to consider the varying impact of FDI spillovers under different task environments. So far, FDI policy effect is assessed according to the industry classification scheme, where industries are defined as clusters of products. However, this classification assumes common task environments within the product group, while firm-level strategy-making and performance cannot be homogeneous due to heterogeneous task environments within industries (Rumelt, 1991). Therefore, it is proposed that policymakers should pay more attention to the firm-level perspective of external environmental conditions under which foreign and local firms operate.

Research limitations and future research directions

This study has some limitations. First, we measure environmental dynamism based on firm-level responses about a single dimension focusing on a dominant product's life span. Environmental dynamism should have been measured in multiple dimensions and the effect needs to be examined holistically (McCarthy et al., 2010). This research also focuses on environmental dynamism in a host country. Although foreign operations in a host country are in response to local environmental dynamism, subsidiaries can be aligned with MNE strategy, which is a response to global environmental dynamism. Therefore, future research might consider multidimensionality of the original concept in a global context.

Furthermore, this chapter has a few methodological limitations. Our data is pooled cross-sectional data. While this is a decision constrained by inability to construct strong panel data, there are repeated observations remaining in the dataset. This means interpretation of coefficients may take this issue under consideration. Furthermore, our data does not include variables to control for MNE group-level strategy and organisational characteristics. Foreign subsidiaries are part of MNE-level knowledge production systems and this should be taken into account. Building on this chapter's empirical findings, future research may explore factors causing variance of FDI spillover effects at different levels of environmental dynamism, focusing on interaction of strategies between MNEs and indigenous firms.

References

Aitken, B.J. and Harrison, A.E. (1999). 'Do domestic firms benefit from direct foreign investment? Evidence from Venezuela', *American Economic Review*, 89(3), 605–618.

Alcácer, J. and Chung, W. (2007). 'Location strategies and knowledge spillovers', *Management Science*, 53(5), 760–776.

Argote, L., McEvily, B. and Reagans, R. (2003). 'Managing knowledge in organisations: An integrative framework and review of emerging themes', *Management Science*, 49(4), 571–582.

Baum, J.R. and Wally, S. (2003). 'Strategic decision speed and firm performance', *Strategic Management Journal*, 24(11), 1108–1129.

Blalock, G. and Gertler, P.J. (2008). 'Welfare gains from Foreign Direct Investment through technology transfer to local suppliers', *Journal of International Economics*, 74(2), 402–421.

Buckley, P.J., Clegg, J. and Wang, C. (2007). 'Is the relationship between inward FDI and spillover effects linear? An empirical examination of the case of China', *Journal of International Business Studies*, 38(3), 447–459.

Carillo, J.E. (2005). 'Industry clockspeed and the pace of new product development', *Production and Operations Management*, 14(2), 125–141.

Chen, M.-J., Lin, H.-C. and Michel, J.G. (2010). 'Navigating in a hypercompetitive environment: The roles of action aggressiveness and TMT integration', *Strategic Management Journal*, 31(13), 1410–1430.

Cohen, W.M. and Levinthal, D.A. (1989). 'Innovation and learning: The two faces of R&D', *Economic Journal*, 99(397), 569–596.

Crescenzi, R., Gagliardi, L. and Iammarino, S. (2015). 'Foreign multinationals and domestic innovation: Intra-industry effects and firm heterogeneity', *Research Policy*, 44(3), 596–609.

Crespo, M. and Fontura, M.P. (2007). 'Determinant factors of FDI spillovers: What do we really know?', *World Development*, 35(3), 410–425.

D'Aveni, R.A., Dagnino, G.B. and Smith, K.G. (2010). 'The age of temporary advantage', *Strategic Management Journal*, 31(13), 1371–1385.

De Faria, P. and Sofka, W. (2010). 'Knowledge protection strategies of multinational firms: A cross-country comparison', *Research Policy*, 39(7), 956–968.

Dodgson, M. (2009). 'Asia's national innovation systems: Institutional adaptability and rigidity in the face of global innovation challenges', *Asia Pacific Journal of Management*, 26(3), 589–609.

Dries, L. and Swinnen, J.F.M. (2004). 'Foreign direct investment, vertical integration, and local suppliers: Evidence from the Polish dairy sector', *World Development*, 32(9), 1525–1544.

Driffield, N., Munday, M. and Roberts, A. (2002). 'Foreign direct investment, transactions linkages, and the performance of the domestic sector', *International Journal of the Economics of Business*, 9(3), 335–351.

Duncan, R.B. (1972). 'Characteristics of organisational environments and perceived environmental uncertainty', *Administrative Science Quarterly*, 17(3), 313–327.

Eapen, A. (2012). 'Social structure and technology spillovers from foreign to domestic firms', *Journal of International Business Studies*, 43(3), 244–263.

Eisenhardt, K. (1989). 'Making fast strategic decisions in high-velocity environments', *Academy of Management Journal*, 32(3), 543–576.

Findlay, R. (1978). 'Relative backwardness, direct foreign investment, and the transfer of technology: A simple dynamic model', *Quarterly Journal of Economics*, 92(1), 1–16.

Fine, C.H. (2000). 'Clockspeed-based strategies for supply chain design', *Production and Operations Management*, 9(3), 213–221.

Furman, J.L., Porter, M.E. and Stern, S. (2002). 'The determinants of national innovative capacity', *Research Policy*, 31(6), 899–933.

García, F., Jin, B. and Salomon, R. (2013). 'Does inward foreign direct investment improve the innovative performance of local firms?', *Research Policy*, 42(1), 231–244.

Gupta, A.K. and Govindarajan, V. (2000). 'Knowledge flows within multinational corporations', *Strategic Management Journal*, 21(4), 473–496.

Ha, Y.J. and Giroud, A. (2015). 'Competence-creating subsidiaries and FDI technology spillovers', *International Business Review*, 24(4), 605–614.

Hagedoorn, J. and Wang, N. (2012). 'Is there complementarity or substitutability between internal and external R&D strategies?', *Research Policy*, 41(6), 1072–1083.

Hallin, C. and Holmström-Lind, C. (2012). 'Revisiting the external impact of MNCs: An empirical study of the mechanisms behind knowledge spillovers from MNC subsidiaries', *International Business Review*, 21(2), 167–179.

Haskel, J.E., Pereira, S.C. and Slaughter, M.J. (2007). 'Does inward Foreign Direct Investment boost the productivity of domestic firms?', *The Review of Economics and Statistics*, 89(3), 482–496.

Haunschild, P.R. and Miner, A.S. (1997). 'Modes of interorganisational imitation: The effects of outcome salience and uncertainty', *Administrative Science Quarterly*, 42(3), 472–500.

Havranek, T. and Irsova, Z. (2011). 'Estimating vertical spillovers from FDI: Why results vary and what the true effect is', *Journal of International Economics*, 85(2), 234–244.

Irsova, Z. and Havranek, T. (2013). 'Determinants of horizontal spillovers from FDI: Evidence from a large meta-analysis', *World Development*, 42(0), 1–15.

Javorcik, B.S. (2004). 'Does foreign direct investment increase the production of domestic firms? In search of spillovers through backward linkages', *American Economic Review*, 94(3), 605–627.

Jones, N. (2003). 'Competing after radical technological change: The significance of product line management strategy', *Strategic Management Journal*, 24(13), 1265–1287.

Judge, W.Q. and Miller, A. (1991). 'Antecedents and outcomes of decision speed in different environmental contexts', *Academy of Management Journal*, 34(2), 449–463.

Keller, W. and Yeaple, S. (2009). 'Multinational enterprises, international trade, and productivity growth: Firm-level evidence from the United States', *Review of Economics and Statistics*, 91(4), 821–831.

Kokko, A. (1994). 'Technology, market characteristics, and spillovers', *Journal of Development Economics*, 43(2), 279– 293.

Levitt, B. and March, J.G. (1988). 'Organisational learning', *Annual Review of Sociology*, 14, 319–340.

Lieberman, M.B. and Asaba, S. (2006). 'Why do firms imitate each other?', *Academy of Management Review*, 31(2), 366–385.

Lipsey, R.E. and Sjöholm, F. (2005). 'Host country impacts of inward FDI: Why such different answers?', in *The Impact of Foreign Direct Investment on Development: New Measurements, New Outcomes, New Policy Approaches*, eds Blomström, M., Graham, E., and Moran, T., Institute for International Economics, Washington DC, 23–43.

Liu, X. and Buck, T. (2007). 'Innovation performance and channels for international technology spillovers: Evidence from Chinese high-tech industries', *Research Policy*, 36(3), 355–366.

Liu, X., Wang, C. and Wei, Y. (2009). 'Do local manufacturing firms benefit from transactional linkages with multinational enterprises in China?', *Journal of International Business Studies*, 40(7), 1113–1130.

McCarthy, I.P., Lawrence, T.B., Wixted, B. and Gordon, B.R. (2010). 'A multidimensional conceptualisation of environmental velocity', *Academy of Management Review*, 35(4), 604–626.

McKinsey & Company (2010). 'South Korea: Finding its place on the world stage', *McKinsey Quarterly*, April.

Mahmood, I.P., Zhu, H. and Zajac, E.J. (2011). 'Where can capabilities come from? Network ties and capability acquisition in business groups', *Strategic Management Journal*, 32(8), 820–848.

Markusen, J., Thomas F. Rutherford and David Tarr (2005). 'Trade and direct investment in producer services and the domestic market for expertise', *Canadian Journal of Economics*, 38(3), 758–777.

Moran, T.H., Graham, E.M. and Blomström, M. (eds) (2005) *Does Foreign Direct Investment Promote Development?* Washington, DC: Institute for International Economics.

Motohashi, K. and Yuan, Y. (2010). 'Productivity impact of technology spillover from multinationals to local firms: Comparing China's automobile and electronics industries', *Research Policy*, 39(6), 790–798.

Nadkarni, S. and Narayanan, V.K. (2007). 'Strategic schemas, strategic flexibility, and firm performance: The moderating role of industry clockspeed', *Strategic Management Journal*, 28(3), 243–270.

Perri, A., Andersson, U., Nell, P.C. and Santangelo, G.D. (2013). 'Balancing the trade-off between learning prospects and spillover risks: MNC subsidiaries' vertical linkage patterns in developed countries', *Journal of World Business*, 48(4), 503–514.

Rumelt, R.P. (1991). 'How much does industry matter?', *Strategic Management Journal*, 12(4), 167–185.

Salomon, R.M. and Shaver, J.M. (2005). 'Learning by exporting: New insights from examining firm innovation', *Journal of Economics & Management Strategy*, 14(2), 431–460.

Sembenelli, A. and Siotis, G. (2008). 'Foreign Direct Investment and mark-up dynamics: Evidence from Spanish firms', *Journal of International Economics*, 76(1), 107–115.

Sidhu, J.S., Commandeur, H.R. and Volberda, H.W. (2007). 'The multifaceted nature of exploration and exploitation: Value of supply, demand, and spatial search for innovation', *Organization Science*, 18(1), 20–38.

Smeets, R. (2008). 'Collecting the pieces of the FDI knowledge spillovers puzzle', *World Bank Research Observer*, 23(2), 107–138.

Sofka, W., Shehu, E. and de Faria, P. (2014). 'Multinational subsidiary knowledge protection: Do mandates and clusters matter?', *Research Policy*, 43(8), 1320–1333.

Spencer, W.J. (2008). 'The impact of multinational enterprise strategy on indigenous enterprises: Horizontal spillovers and crowding output in developing countries', *Academy of Management Review*, 33(2), 341–361.

Tan, J. and Litschert, R.J. (1994). 'Environment-strategy relationship and its performance implications: An empirical study of the Chinese electronics industry', *Strategic Management Journal*, 15(1), 1–20.

Veugelers, R. and Cassiman, B. (2004). 'Foreign subsidiaries as a channel of international technology diffusion: Some direct firm level evidence from Belgium', *European Economic Review*, 48, 455–476.

Vilkamo, T. and Keil, T. (2003). 'Strategic technology partnering in high-velocity environments: Lessons from a case study', *Technovation*, 23(3), 193–204.

Wang, C. and Yu, L. (2007). 'Do spillover benefits grow with rising foreign direct investment? An empirical examination of the case of China', *Applied Economics*, 39(3), 397–405.

Zhang, Y., Li, H., Li, Y. and Zhou, L.A. (2010). 'FDI spillovers in an emerging market: The role of foreign firms' country origin diversity and domestic firms' absorptive capacity', *Strategic Management Journal*, 31(9), 969–989.

Zhao, Y. and Cavusgil, S.T. (2006). 'The effect of supplier's market orientation on manufacturer's trust', *Industrial Marketing Management* 35(4), 405–414.

Part III

Strategy and Management: Ownership Modes, Networks and People

8
Multilevel Analysis of Ownership Mode Strategy in China

Yi Wang, Jorma Larimo and Huu Le Nguyen

Introduction

Foreign direct investments' (FDIs) entry mode strategy has received considerable attention from researchers in both the international business (IB) and the strategic management field (Zhao et al., 2004; Brouthers and Hennart, 2007; Morschett et al., 2010; Slangen and Hennart, 2015). Ownership mode strategy (OMS) is one of the most important dimensions of FDI entry mode strategy (Endo et al., 2014). Multinational enterprises (MNEs) can choose between wholly owned subsidiaries (WOS) and joint ventures (JVs). The level of ownership is a challenging strategic decision, as it determines the level of resource a firm must commit to foreign markets, the degree of risk a firm must bear in the target country, and the extent of control a firm can excise over its foreign subsidiary (Anderson and Gatignon, 1986; Hill et al., 1990). Furthermore, OMS has important implications for the survival and performance of foreign subsidiaries (Papyrina, 2007; Kim et al., 2010).

Existing studies have considerably analysed the determinants of OMS (Zhao et al., 2004; Brouthers and Hennart, 2007). There are two streams of research in existing ownership mode literature. The first line of studies has analysed the effects of characteristics of investing firms such as R&D/advertising intensity and level of experience (e.g. Erramilli and Rao, 1993; Erramilli, 1996; Padmanabhan and Cho, 1996, 1999; Li and Meyer, 2009; Slangen and Hennart, 2008). The other line of studies has addressed the influence of industrial conditions (Elango and Sambharya, 2004) or country/institutional specific variables (Yiu and Makino, 2002; Meyer and Nguyen, 2005). Thus, existing studies mainly used one level or another to analyse OMS.

As referred by Arregle et al. (2006) and Brouthers and Hennart (2007), OMS is a multilevel phenomenon and it is influenced by variables at various levels: parent, subsidiary, industry and country. Several scholars emphasised the importance of adopting a multilevel analysis in the IB studies (Buckley and Lessard, 2005). Thus, there is a need to develop a more comprehensive framework, analysing OMS at multiple levels. Furthermore, existing studies have provided mixed findings about the impacts of variables on OMS (Zhao et al., 2004; Brouthers and Hennart, 2007). It has been referred that those inconsistent findings can partly be explained by ignored interaction effects (Zhao et al., 2004; Brouthers and Hennart, 2007).

The overall goal of our study is to provide further understanding of OMS of foreign subsidiaries in China. In more detail, our goal is to analyse: (1) the determinants of OMS in China at general level, using three different levels of analysis: firm, industry and country levels and (2) the interaction effects of country (i.e. regional institutional advancement) and firm-specific determinants (i.e. international experience and degree of product diversification). This chapter shows that OMS in China is determined by variables at multi-level. Furthermore, the impacts of the firm-specific variables are contingent on country-specific variables.

This study differs from existing China-based ownership mode studies in three important ways. First, the focus of this study is to analyse the determinants of OMS in China at three different levels: firm, industry, and country. In order to analyse the determinants at multiple levels, this study draws on three theories: transaction cost economics (TCE) (Anderson and Gatignon, 1986; Hennart, 1991), the resource-based (RBV) (Barney, 1991) and the institution-based view (IBV) (Peng, 2002). The choice of those three theories is justified in that they differ in the level of analysis. Second, the present study analyses the interaction effects of country- and firm-specific determinants. In more detail, we are interested in analysing two interaction effects: (1) between regional institutional advancement and international experience and (2) between regional institutional advancement and degree of product diversification. It is expected that the analysis of interaction effects can partly explain mixed findings in existing literature.

Third, most of the existing China-based studies analysed MNEs from the largest economies such as the United States and Japan as well as Asian countries (Luo, 2001; Shi et al., 2001; Chen and Hu, 2002; Chiao et al., 2010). MNEs originating in Small and Open Economies (SMOPECs) such as Nordic countries have received very limited attention. Due to relatively small home market size, MNEs based in SMOPECs are more likely to internationalise than those based in larger economies (Benito et al., 2002; Luostarinen and Gabrielsson, 2006; Laanti et al., 2009). Thus, it is of great interest to analyse the determinants of OMS of MNEs originating in SMOPECs.

This chapter starts with theoretical discussion leading to hypotheses development. Then, methodology and data collection are presented followed by an analysis of study findings. The chapter ends with discussion concerning study limitations, future research avenues and managerial implications.

Literature review and development of hypotheses

Ownership mode literature

MNEs face significant challenges when entering emerging markets. A key challenge for MNEs is to determine the OMS, which refers to the choice between WOS and JVs (Zhao et al., 2004; Brouthers and Hennart, 2007). OMS has been one of the most important research topics in both the IB and the strategic management literature (Zhao et al., 2004; Brouthers and Hennart, 2007; Morschett et al., 2010; Shaver, 2013; Slangen and Hennart, 2015).

There are two streams of research in existing ownership mode literature. In the first line of studies, scholars have mainly explained the OMS from the perspective of MNEs (Hennart, 2009, 2012). The choice between WOS and JVs is a trade-off of different levels of control, resource commitment and dissemination risk (Anderson and Gatignon, 1986; Hill et al., 1990; Padmanabhan and Cho, 1996; Wei et al., 2005). MNEs tend to opt for WOS if their need of control is high, while JVs are preferred if MNEs' need of control is low. In this line of research, scholars have primarily applied TCE as their main theoretical foundation and focused on the effects of characteristics of MNEs such as R&D/advertising intensity and levels of experience on the OMS (for example, Erramilli and Rao, 1993; Erramilli, 1996; Padmanabhan and Cho, 1996, 1999; Li and Meyer, 2009).

The other stream of research has analysed how ownership structure is determined by industry structure (Elango and Sambharya, 2004) and country/institution specific variables (Yiu and Makino, 2002; Meyer and Nguyen, 2005; Yu et al., 2015; Demirbag et al., 2007, 2009). Industry- or country/institution-specific determinants have been referred as significant determinants for entry strategies in emerging markets (Meyer and Peng, 2005; Meyer et al., 2009). Thus, existing studies have mainly used one level (i.e. firm level) or another (i.e. industry/country) to analyse the determinants of OMS. There are so far very limited studies which have included both streams of research into their analysis (Hill et al., 1990; Luo, 2001).

Researchers have analysed OMS in both non-China-based (e.g. Hennart, 1991; Padmanabhan and Cho, 1996; Hennart and Larimo, 1998; Cho and Padmanabhan, 2005; Bai et al., 2013) and China-based studies (Luo, 2001; Chiao et al., 2010; Li and Li, 2010; Duanmu, 2011; Kuo et al., 2012). Those studies have focused their analysis on determinants at firm or industry/country level. It has been referred that OMS is a multilevel phenomenon and there is a need to analyse its determinants at different levels (Arregle et al., 2006; Brouthers and Hennart, 2007). Furthermore, both non-China-based and China-based studies have provided mixed findings as to the impacts of various determinants such as international and host country experience, asset specificity, industry competition and growth as well as cultural distance on OMS

(Zhao et al., 2004; Slangen and Hennart, 2015). Additionally, a limited number of China-based studies have attempted to analyse potential interaction effects on OMS (Chiao et al., 2010; Li and Li, 2010; Duanmu, 2011; Kuo et al., 2012).

The characteristics of the key existing China-based ownership studies are summarised in Table 8.1. Of the reviewed studies, three studies analysed OMS of FDIs made by firms originating in selected Asian regions such as Hong Kong (Shi et al., 2001) and Taiwan (Chiao et al., 2010; Kuo et al., 2012). Other China-based studies have included FDIs made by firms from multiple countries into their analysis (Luo, 2001; Chen and Hu, 2002; Li and Li, 2010; Duanmu, 2011). The smallest sample size included in the analysis was around 200 FDIs (Luo, 2001; Shi et al., 2001), while the largest was several thousands of investments (Duanmu, 2011). The ownership level of JVs and WOS is equally distributed in those China-based studies.

Development of hypotheses

International experience: MNEs with higher levels of international experience have developed general processes and systems for managing their subsidiaries around the globe (Erramilli, 1991; Barkema et al., 1996; Larimo, 2003). Hence, more experienced MNEs are less likely to form JVs to access international market knowledge and practices. The above-mentioned argument implicitly assumes that MNEs are able to effectively transfer their experiential knowledge abroad (Johanson and Vahlne, 1977). This may not hold true for transition economies where the business environment is dynamic and the legal framework is less developed (Li and Meyer, 2009). Furthermore, it has been referred that more experienced firms have developed search routines and screening processes which facilitate finding the right partners (Erramilli, 1991). Thus, it can be expected that international experience increases the preference of JVs over WOS in transition economies. Existing China-based studies have provided mixed findings (Shi et al., 2001; Chiao et al., 2010; Kuo et al., 2012). Nevertheless, we argue that international experience results in preference of JVs over WOS in China, since local partners know how to deal with uncertainties and especially with local authorities in business procedure and legal matters. Thus, we expect that:

> *Hypothesis 1:* International experience is negatively associated with the probability of MNEs choosing WOS over JVs.

Host country experience: Both TCE and RBV studies have considered host country experience as an important determinant of OMS (Brouthers and Hennart, 2007). Knowledge of host country is embedded in the local firms and is costly to access through WOS (Hennart, 2009, 2012). Firms with limited host country experience may prefer to form their subsidiaries jointly with local partners.

Table 8.1 A summary of key China-based ownership mode studies

Study	Home country	Set of choice	Entry modes determinants	MNE type	Time period	Sample size	Methodology	Findings (+ = WOS; − = JVs; n.s. = non-significant)
Luo (2001)	Hong Kong, Taiwan, Singapore, US, Japan, UK, Germany, France and so on.	WOS or JVs	*Independent variables*: government intervention, weak property right systems, environmental uncertainty, industry sales' growth, industry asset intensity, growth of number of firms in each industry, knowledge protection, global integration, host country experience, project orientation, project size and project location. *Interaction terms*: industry asset intensity and risk diversification, industry asset intensity and long-term profit. *Control variables*: cultural distance, risk diversification and long-term profit.	Manufacturing	1993–1996	174	Binary logistic regression	*Independent variables*: government intervention (+), weak property right systems (+), environmental uncertainty (-), industry sales' growth (n.s.), industry asset intensity (n.s.), growth of number of firms in each industry (+), knowledge protection (+), global integration (+), host country experience (+), project orientation (–), project size (n.s.), project location (+). *Interaction terms*: industry asset intensity and risk diversification (–), industry asset intensity and long-term profit (+). *Control variables*: cultural distance (n.s.), risk diversification (–), long-term profit (n.s.)
Shi et al. (2001)	Hong Kong	WOS or JVs	*Independent variables*: export-orientation, market-seeking, firm size, international experience, host country experience, relationship, contractual risk, asset specificity, market potential, production costs, restrictive host government policy and location of investment (SEZs).	SMEs manufacturing	Pre-1996/97	218	Binary logistic regression and interviews	*Independent variables*: export-orientation (+), market-seeking (–), firm size (+), international experience (n.s.), host country experience (–), relationship (–), contractual risk (n.s.), asset specificity (n.s.), market potential (n.s.), production costs (n.s.), restrictive host government policy (–), location of investment (SEZs) (–).

Continued

Table 8.1 Continued

Study	Home country	Set of choice	Entry modes determinants	MNE type	Time period	Sample size	Methodology	Findings (+ = WOS; − = JVs; n.s. = non-significant)
Chiao et al. (2010)	Taiwan	WOS or JVs	*Independent variables*: firm specific assets, complementary assets, R&D capacity, international experience, following customers. *Moderator*: perceived institutional differences. *Control variables*: parent firm size and industry dummies.	Manufacturing	Pre-2001	819	Binary logistic regression	*Independent variables*: firm-specific assets (+), complementary assets (−), R&D capacity (+), international experience (+), following customers (+). *Moderator*: institutional distance and complementary assets (+), institutional distance and international experience (−), other interactions (n.s.).
Li and Li (2010)	61 countries	Majority JV or WOS, minority JV or WOS, minority JV or majority JV and foreign equity share	*Independent variable*: demand volatility. *Moderator*: industry growth potential, irreversibility and competition. *Control variables*: high-tech industry, industry R&D/advertising intensity, foreign presence, country dummies, patent numbers and exchange rate volatility.	Manufacturing	2000–2006	5055	Multinomial logistic regression and Tobit estimation	*Independent variable*: demand volatility (−). *Moderator*: the positive relationship between demand volatility and JVs is stronger for industries with lower level of sales growth and competition. *Control variables*: high-tech industry (+), industry R&D/advertising intensity (n.s.), foreign presence (+), patent numbers (n.s.), exchange rate volatility (n.s.).

Duanmu (2011)	72 countries	WOS or JVs	Manufacturing	1981–2005	9564	Random effects logistic regression	*Independent variables*: Less corrupt countries, corruption distance_1 (less corrupt countries and China), corruption distance_2 (more corrupt countries and China), market orientation. *Interaction terms*: corruption distance_1 and market orientation. *Control variables*: political risk, rule of law, egalitarian distance, cultural distance, geographic distance, resource intensive industry, project size, capital intensity and total foreign capital investment.	*Independent variables*: Less corrupt countries (+), corruption distance_1 (+), corruption distance_2 (n.s.), local market orientation (–). *Interaction term*: corruption distance_1 and market orientation (n.s.). *Control variables*: political risk (n.s.), rule of law (n.s.), egalitarian distance (n.s.), cultural distance (n.s.), geographic distance (n.s.), resource-intensive industry (–), project size (–), capital intensity (–), total foreign capital investment (+).
Kuo et al. (2012)	Taiwan	WOS or JVs	Electronics and computer manufacturing firms	1996–2006	1550	Binary logistic regression	*Independent variables*: international experience breadth and depth.* *Interaction terms*: international experience breadth/depth and family/ non-family firms. *Control variables*: investment size, parent firm size, R&D intensity, debt ratio, industry dummies and location.	*Independent variables*: inexperienced firms (–). *Interaction terms*: inexperienced family firms (–), experienced family firms (+). *Control variables*: investment size (–), parent firm size (–), R&D intensity (+), debt ratio (–), location (East and South) (+).

Note: *International experience breadth refers to the number of countries the firm is active in. International experience depth refers to the total number of foreign subsidiaries prior to the observed investment.

On the other hand, firms with more host country experience have accumulated local knowledge and therefore are less dependent on JV partners. China-based studies have provided mixed results. Luo (2001), Claver and Quer (2005) and Wei et al. (2005) found that host country experience resulted in the preference of WOS as opposed to JVs. However, Shi et al. (2001) and Li and Meyer (2009) found that host country experience is negatively associated with WOS as opposed to JVs. Since China-based studies have provided mixed results, we follow implications of TCE and RBV. Thus, we expect that:

Hypothesis 2: Host country experience is positively associated with the probability of MNEs choosing WOS over JVs.

Degree of product diversification: Both TCE and RBV have considered degree of product diversification as an important determinant of entry strategies (Larimo, 2003; Slangen and Hennart, 2007; Demirbag et al., 2009). More diversified firms may find that they do not possess enough product-specific knowledge in all industries where they operate in (Larimo, 2000). Product-specific knowledge is tacit, and therefore it is costly to replicate such knowledge internally and difficult to purchase it in the market (Hennart and Park, 1993; Slangen and Hennart, 2007). Thus, one would expect that firms operating in multiple product markets may find JVs to be the most appropriate OMS to access product-specific knowledge for local markets. Demirbag et al. (2009) found that degree of product diversification is negatively associated with the preference for Turkish firms to opt for WOS over JVs. So far China-based studies have not specifically addressed the impact of degree of product diversification on the OMS, and therefore, based on TCE and RBV arguments, we expect that:

Hypothesis 3: Degree of product diversification is negatively associated with the probability of MNEs choosing WOS over JVs.

Resource intensive industry: MNEs need to combine their firm-specific resources with complementary assets controlled by local firms to successfully compete in the foreign markets (Meyer et al., 2009). In natural resource industries, local firms, being the first movers in the markets, pre-empt the scarce natural resources. Furthermore, host governments in emerging markets often discourage MNEs from setting up WOS in some strategically important resource-intensive industries (Hennart, 1991). We would expect that MNEs are more likely to form JVs to access complementary local assets in resource-intensive industries. In China-based studies, Duanmu (2011) found that resource-intensive industry increased the probability of choosing JVs over WOS. We follow both theoretical arguments and empirical findings and expect that:

Hypothesis 4: Resource-intensive industry is negatively associated with the probability of MNEs choosing WOS over JVs.

Industry growth in terms of the number of firms: It has been referred that industry growth in terms of the number of firms is positively associated with greater business potential and market opportunities in transition economies like China (Luo, 2001). Thus, MNEs are expected to use WOS to capture more rents when entering industries where the number of firms is growing fast. In China-based studies, Luo (2001) found that industry growth in terms of the number of firms increases the preference of WOS as opposed to JVs. Thus, the authors expect that:

> *Hypothesis 5*: Industry growth in terms of the number of firms is positively associated with the probability of MNEs choosing WOS over JVs.

Industry sales' growth: TCE-based studies have used growth in industry sales as a proxy for external uncertainty (Luo, 2001; Cui and Jiang, 2009). It has been argued that MNEs are less likely to commit large amount of resources when the sales growth in the target industry is unpredictable. Large commitment limits the flexibility of MNEs to withdraw from the host market when the market demands do not reach the desired level of sales (Luo, 2001). On the other hand, when the sales growth in an industry is stable and predictable, MNEs prefer to choose WOS as opposed to JVs to capture more rents (Hennart, 1991). For example, the results by Cui and Jiang (2009) indicated clearly that the impact of industry sales' growth on the choice of WOS is positive. In China-based studies the results have been mixed. Luo (2001) found that the relationship between industry sales' growth and the preference for WOS over JVs was not significant, whereas Chen and Hu (2002) and Li and Li (2010) found that sales' growth increased the probability of choosing WOS as opposed to JVs. Since the existing findings have been mixed, we follow TCE-based arguments and expect that:

> *Hypothesis 6*: Industry growth in terms of sales is positively associated with the probability of MNEs choosing WOS over JVs.

Cultural distance: Cultural distance has been referred in the IB studies as the differences in national culture characteristics of the home and of the host country (Hennart and Larimo, 1998). The relationship of cultural distance and OMS has been analysed in the context of MNEs' need for risk reduction by several past IB studies (Kogut and Singh, 1988; Tihanyi et al., 2005). From this perspective, MNEs operating in culturally distant target countries often require greater flexibility in their strategies as well as operations, which can be achieved by setting up JVs (Tihanyi et al., 2005).

It has also been argued that differences in national cultures result in the preference of WOS as opposed to JVs. This is because the larger the cultural distance between the home and host country, the costlier it is for MNEs to transfer intangible assets such as organisational and managerial practices to their JVs (Slangen and Hennart, 2007). Thus, the arguments for the impact of cultural distance on OMS have been ambiguous. In China-based studies such as those of Luo (2001), Chen and Hu (2002), and Duanmu (2011), cultural distance was found to be non-significantly associated with OMS of MNEs in China.

Hypothesis 7: Cultural distance is positively associated with the probability of MNEs choosing WOS over JVs.

The later stage of institutional transition: An important goal of China's institutional reform was to transit from a centrally planned to a market-oriented economy (Child and Tse, 2001; Peng, 2002; Polsa et al., 2005). The Chinese government has gradually removed FDI restrictions on full ownership and entry barriers (Papyrina, 2007; Yang et al., 2011). Thus it can be expected that Western firms are more likely to establish WOS as opposed to JVs to absorb more rents at the later stage of institutional transition. In their study focusing on entry-mode strategy in the Central and Eastern Europe, Dikova and van Witteloostuijn (2007) found that greater institutional advancement resulted in the preference for JVs as opposed to WOS. They argued that institutional advancement reduced the risk of asset expropriation, and therefore JVs were preferred over WOS. Nevertheless, we argue that as transaction costs and FDI restrictions on WOS have been gradually reduced in China, MNEs are more likely to opt for WOS as opposed to JVs so that they can capture more rent from their subsidiaries.

Hypothesis 8: The later stage of institutional transition is positively associated with the probability of MNEs choosing WOS over JVs.

Regional institutional advancement: One of the key features in transition economies like China is that the level of institutional development differs across provinces. China provides incentives such as tax reduction for MNEs investing in institutional advanced provinces. Furthermore, there is better infrastructure and greater market demand in institutional advance provinces (Wei et al., 2005). Thus, the transaction costs associated with operating in institutional advanced provinces tend to be lower (Yeung et al., 2009). In an existing China-based study, Li and Li (2010) found that MNEs investing in institutional advanced provinces in China are more likely to choose WOS as opposed JVs. Hence, based on both theoretical arguments and existing empirical findings, we expect that:

Hypothesis 9: Regional institutional advancement in China is positively associated with the probability of MNEs choosing WOS over JVs.

Interaction effect of regional institutional advancement and international experience: As discussed earlier, it is expected that international experience results in the preference of JVs as opposed to WOS in China because general IB knowledge is not necessarily applicable to emerging markets (Li and Meyer, 2009). We argue that this relationship becomes stronger for subsidiaries established in regions where institutional framework is more developed, since it is more efficient to transfer firm-specific resources such as organisational and managerial practices to local partners. On the other hand, it is costlier to transfer MNEs' best practices to JVs located in regions where legal institutions such as property right systems and contractual enforcement systems are less developed. Therefore, based on the above theoretical arguments, we expect that:

> *Hypothesis 10a:* The interaction effect of regional institutional advancement and international experience on the probability of MNEs choosing WOS is negative.

Interaction effect of regional institutional advancement and degree of product diversification: The second interaction effect we analysed is regional institutional advancement and degree of product diversification. It is expected that MNEs are more likely to opt for WOS as opposed to JVs for subsidiaries established in regions where institutions are more developed. We argue that this relationship turns out to be weaker when MNEs operate in multiple product markets, as more diversified MNEs need to access product-specific knowledge possessed by local partners (Larimo, 2000). Thus, we expect that:

> *Hypothesis 10b:* The interaction effect of regional institutional advancement and degree of product diversification on the probability of MNEs choosing WOS is negative.

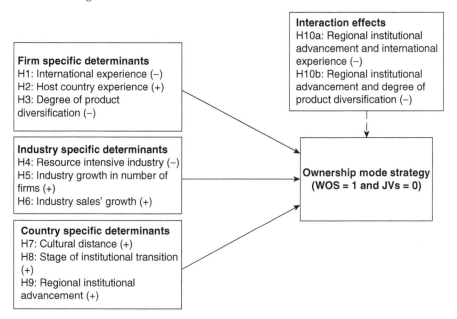

Figure 8.1   Research model of this study

Research methodology

Data, sample and descriptive statistics

The data for this study is a part of a large internal databank at the Department of Marketing, University of Vaasa, focusing on FDIs made by Nordic manufacturing firms in various foreign countries collected over several years. The data were mainly collected from the annual reports and press releases of the investing firms, supplemented with the data gathered from the Thomson One Banker and Orbis databanks and also from direct contact with several of the investing companies. This internal databank includes information from approximately 10,000 FDIs made by Nordic firms. We identified 437 FDIs made by Nordic MNEs in China during the period of 1987–2012. Nordic countries have been referred as SMOPECs (Laanti et al., 2009). Furthermore, Nordic MNEs are of great importance to their home country (Benito et al., 2002). The time period of 1987–2012 was chosen because foreign WOS was permitted by the Chinese government in 1986 (Teng, 2004). Due to missing information, the empirical analysis consists of 402 FDIs, which is 93 per cent of the identified FDIs.

Before running binary logistic regression, a correlation analysis was conducted to diagnose any multicollinearity between various variables (see Table 8.2). The bivariate correlation between international experience and degree of product diversification is above the cut-off point of 0.70, indicating a potential for multicollinearity. Following Pallant (2007), additional multicollinearity diagnostics (variance inflation factor (VIF)) were conducted for the analysis of the dependent variable. The VIF values for different variables used in regression analysis should not exceed 2.50 (Wetherill, 1986). Since the VIF value for international experience was above the cut-off point of 2.50, the potential multicollinearity between international experience and degree of product diversification is expected to influence the results of binary logistic regression. Following Kennedy's (1998) recommendation, the author estimates the models with various combinations.

One way to assess the extent to which the logistic regression model fits the data is to detect its ability to classify the observations. Its ability should be judged against the classification rate that would have been obtained by chance. The classification rate is computed as $a^2 + (1-a)^2$ (Hair et al., 1998), where a is the proportion of WOS. In this study, the base score is 0.50. All the statistical models have higher correct classification rates than those of base rates. Thus it can be said that the logistic regression model fits the data well. Furthermore, most of the statistical models show a highly significant chi-square (x^2), indicating that the explanatory powers of all models are good. The predictive capability of the models is also evident from Nagelkerke R-square values, which are acceptable for all models. Hosmer and Lemeshow's (1989) tests are statistically

Table 8.2 Correlation table

	Mean	S.D.	1	2	3	4	5	6	7	8	9	10	11	12	13
1.	0.48	0.50	1.00												
2.	0.72	0.45	0.12*	1.00											
3.	1.92	0.78	-0.00	0.08	1.00										
4.	0.14	0.35	-0.10	0.05	0.16**	1.00									
5.	40.72	43.60	-0.20**	-0.14**	-0.04	0.20**	1.00								
6.	3.51	4.62	0.01	-0.26**	0.04	0.11*	0.59**	1.00							
7.	8.85	8.18	-0.22**	-0.09	-0.08	0.11*	0.71**	0.27**	1.00						
8.	0.30	0.46	-0.09	-0.09	-0.60**	-0.18**	0.05	0.05	0.12*	1.00					
9.	0.07	0.09	0.11*	-0.02	0.10*	0.03	0.06	0.28**	-0.06	-0.11*	1.00				
10.	0.22	0.21	0.09	0.06	0.09	-0.03	0.03	0.10	-0.02	-0.08	0.40**	1.00			
11.	5.03	0.48	0.07	-0.04	-0.05	0.05**	-0.05	0.07*	-0.09	0.12*	-0.05	0.01	1.00		
12.	2.26	0.76	0.27**	-0.15**	-0.07	-0.03	0.16**	0.43**	-0.07	0.10	0.35**	0.02	-0.11*	1.00	
13.	6.98	2.28	0.32**	-0.12*	0.03	-0.03	0.08**	0.33**	-0.09	-0.05	0.54**	0.17**	-0.21**	0.68**	1.00

Notes: *Correlation is significant at 0.05 level (two-tailed test); **Correlation is significant at 0.01 level (two-tailed test); *Dependent variables*: 1= WOS ownership mode; *Control variables*: 2 = Greenfield establishment mode; 3 = Industry R&D intensity; 4 = Investment restrictions; *Independent variables*: 5 = International experience; 6 = Host country experience; 7 = Degree of product diversification; 8 = Resource-intensive industry; 9 = Industry growth in terms of the number of firms; 10 = Industry sales' growth; 11 = Cultural distance; 12 = The later stage of institutional transition; 13 = Regional institutional advancement.

insignificant in all models, indicating that there is no difference between the observed and predicted values.

Sample characteristics

Of the four countries, FDIs by Danish firms were 94 (23 per cent), by Finnish firms were 124 (31 per cent), by Norwegian firms were 34 (9 per cent), and by Swedish firms were 150 (37 per cent). With regard to the ownership level, 208 (52 per cent) investments were JVs, whereas 194 (48 per cent) FDIs were WOS. Of the total FDIs, 290 (72 per cent) were greenfields and 112 (28 per cent) were acquisitions. The highest level of international experience of Nordic firms was 193 subsidiaries, but on the other hand the sample included 41 first and second FDIs. The maximum host country experience was 20 years and on the other hand 197 first FDIs in China by the sample firms. Furthermore, of the 402 FDIs by Nordic MNEs, 136 (34 per cent) were in low-tech branches, 154 (38 per cent) in medium-high-tech branches, and 112 (28 per cent) in high-tech branches. A detailed analysis shows that 76 (19 per cent) investments were made in the period 1987–1995, 144 (36 per cent) in the period 1996–2001, and 182 (45 per cent) in the period 2002–2012.

Operationalisation of variables

In this study the dependent variable is OMS. It is operationalised with a dummy variable, which takes the value 1 if the firm owned 95 per cent or more of the subsidiary equity and 0 if it owned at least 10 per cent, but no more than 94 per cent (Gatignon and Anderson, 1988; Hennart, 1991). The operationalisation of independent variables is summarised in Table 8.3.

In addition to independent variables, we added three control variables that are also likely to influence OMS. First, the authors included establishment mode strategy as a control variable (Hennart and Larimo, 1998). Establishment mode strategy was measured with a dummy variable, where 1 indicates green-field investments and 0 for acquisitions. The expected sign for establishment mode strategy is positive. Second, we controlled for research and development intensity of investing firms (Larimo, 2003). Third, the authors controlled for investment restrictions, a dummy variable where 1 indicates restricted manufacturing industries and 0 indicates encouraged manufacturing industries (Chang et al., 2012). It is expected that restricted manufacturing industries would increase the probability of choosing JVs over WOS.

Statistical analysis method

Since the dependent variable in this research is binary in nature, this study applies binary logistic regression to examine the impacts of the explanatory variables on the dependent variable. It is worth noting that several scholars

Table 8.3 Operationalisation of independent variables

Variables	Operationalisation
Firm-specific determinants	
International experience	The number of foreign manufacturing investments made by the company before the observed investment (e.g. Padmanabhan & Cho, 1999; Larimo, 2003) (Source: internal database).
Host country experience	The experience in years from the first manufacturing investment of the firm in China (e.g. Hennart & Park, 1993; Padmanabhan & Cho, 1999; Larimo, 2003) (Source: internal database).
Degree of product diversification	The number of 4-digit SIC codes in which the company was operating based on the annual reports and websites of the firms (e.g. Hennart & Larimo, 1998; Vermeulen & Barkema, 2001) (Source: internal database).
Industry-specific determinants	
Resource-intensive industry	A dummy variable which equals 1 if the subsidiary's main products are in a resource-intensive industry such as SIC 20 (food and beverage), 22 (textile), 24 (wood except furniture), 26 (paper and paper-related products), 29 (petroleum), 30 (rubber), 32 (stone and glass) and 33 (primary metals) (e.g. Hennart, 1991) and 0 for the other industries (Source: internal database).
Industry growth in number of firms	Compound growth rate in terms of number of firms over three consecutive years prior to the establishment year (e.g. Luo, 2001) (Source: China Statistical Yearbook).
Industry sales' growth	Compound sales' growth rate over three consecutive years prior to the establishment year (e.g. Luo, 2001) (Source: China Statistical Yearbook).
Country-specific determinants	
Cultural distance	Cultural distance is measured using the methodology developed by Kogut and Singh (1988) based on Hofstede's (1980) six cultural dimensions: power distance, uncertainty avoidance, masculinity/femininity, individualism, long-term orientation, and indulgence/restraint (Hennart & Larimo, 1998) (Source: internal database).
Regional institutional advancement	An index of China's marketisation in provinces (Source: Gang et al., 2011; NERI index of marketisation of China's provinces).
Stage of institutional transition	A dummy variable where 1 stands for investments made from 1982 to 1995, 2 for investments made during the period of 1996–2001 and 3 for investments after 2002 (e.g. Zhang, Zhang & Liu, 2007) (Source: internal database).

have stated that Multi-level Modelling (MLM) is the most appropriate statistical analysis method to address the multilevel phenomenon (Arregle et al., 2006; Peterson et al., 2012). However, it has been referred that the use of non-multilevel method is not likely to be a problem when MNEs engage in one or few investments (Arregle et al., 2006). In our sample, on average the Nordic firms made two FDIs in China. Thus, binary logistic regression is an appropriate statistical method to analyse the OMS. The regression coefficients estimate the impact of various variables on the probability that the investment will be a WOS. In general, the terms of the model can be expressed as: $P(y_i = 1) = 1/(1 + exp\ (-a - X_iB))$,where y_i is the dependent variable, X_i is the vector of the independent variables for the ith observation, a is the intercept parameter and B is the vector of regression coefficients (Amemiya, 1981).

Results

The results are presented in Table 8.4. The coefficient related to greenfield establishment mode is positive and highly significant (p<0.01), suggesting that Nordic MNEs are more likely to choose WOS greenfields. The relationship of R&D intensity and WOS is negative and significant (p<0.05; p<0.10), and hence Nordic firms from high-tech industries are more likely to opt for JVs as opposed to WOS. The coefficients associated with investment restrictions are negative and significant (p<0.05; p<0.10), indicating that Nordic MNEs entering into more restrictive manufacturing industries in China are more likely to use JVs as opposed to WOS.

Of the nine independent variables, seven hypotheses receive empirical support. As expected, the coefficient associated with international experience is negative and significant (p<0.01). Thus, *H1* is strongly supported. The effect of host country experience is not significant, thus *H2* is not supported. Degree of product diversification is negatively and significantly associated with WOS (p<0.01). Hence *H3* is strongly supported. The effect of resource-intensive industries on the choice of WOS is significantly negative (p<0.01; p<0.05), suggesting that MNEs entering into resource-intensive industries are more likely to form JVs as opposed to WOS. Thus, *H4* is strongly supported. Furthermore, the impact of industry growth in terms of number of firms is significantly negative (p<0.05; p<0.10). Thus *H5* is not supported. The coefficients associated with industry sales' growth are positive and significant (p<0.10), suggesting that Nordic MNEs entering into industries with higher degrees of sales growth are more likely to use WOS as opposed to JVs. *H6* is mildly supported.

The coefficients associated with cultural distance are positive and significant (p<0.01; p<0.05), and hence Nordic MNEs from culturally distant

Table 8.4   Results of binary logistic regression (WOS=1, JVs=0)

Variables	Model 1a	Model 1b	Model 2a	Model 2b
Control variables				
Greenfields establishment mode	0.95***	0.90***	0.98***	0.94***
R&D intensity	−0.44**	−0.32*	−0.48**	−0.33*
Investment restrictions	−0.71*	−0.82**	−0.84**	−0.86**
Firm-specific determinants				
International experience	−0.02***			
Host country experience	0.06	0.00	0.06	0.00
Degree of product diversification		−0.05***	−0.02	
Industry-specific determinants				
Resource-intensive industries	−1.10***	−0.85***	−1.12***	−0.84**
Growth in number of firms	−3.96**	−3.26*	−4.06**	−3.48**
Industry sales' growth	1.13*	0.77	1.03	0.77
Country-specific determinants				
Cultural distance	0.66**	0.69***	0.66**	0.69***
Stages of institutional transitions	0.59**	0.55**	0.45*	0.54**
Regional institutional advancement	0.32***	0.28***	0.41***	0.35***
Interaction terms				
Regional institutional advancement × international experience			−0.01***	
Regional institutional advancement × product diversification				−0.01***
Number of FDIs (402)	WOS(194)	WOS(194)	WOS(194)	WOS(194)
Nagelkerke R^2	0.31	0.26	0.30	0.27
Correctly classified (%)	68.5%	68.4%	68.0%	68.9%
Model Chi square (x^2)	97.53***	82.54***	93.61***	83.84***

Notes: Significant level: *** $p<0.01$, ** $p<0.05$, * $p<0.10$ (two-tailed); Model 1a=without product diversification; model 1b=without international experience; model 2a=interaction effect of regional institutional advancement and international experience is included; model 2b=interaction effect of regional institutional advancement and product diversification is included.

countries are more likely to opt for WOS as opposed to JVs in China. Thus *H7* is supported. The effect of stages of institutional transition are significantly positive (p<0.05; p<0.10), suggesting that FDIs made during the later stages of institutional transition increase the preference of Nordic MNEs to opt for WSO over JVs. Thus *H8* is supported. The coefficients associated with regional institutional advancement are positive and highly significant (p<0.01), suggesting that the progress of institutional development at provincial level in China increases the probability of Nordic firms to opt for WOS. Thus *H9* is strongly supported. We additionally found that there are both similarities and differences in the behaviours of firms based in different Nordic countries (see Appendix 8.1).

This study analysed two interaction effects: (1) between regional institutional advancement and international experience and (2) between regional institutional advancement and degree of product diversification. The regression coefficient of the first interaction term is negative and highly significant at level $p<0.01$. This result points out that Nordic firms with higher levels of international experience results in the preference of JVs as opposed to WOS when the regional institutional advancement is more progressed. In other words, less experienced firms are more likely to choose WOS as opposed to JVs in provinces where the progress towards market economy is more advanced. Thus *H10a* is supported.

The coefficient associated with the second interaction effect of regional institutional advancement and degree of product diversification is significantly negative ($p<0.01$). Thus, Nordic firms with higher degrees of product diversification are more likely to opt for JVs when the level of regional institutional advancement is higher. On the other hand, lower degrees of product diversification leads to WOS for subsidiaries established in provinces where the progress towards institutional development is more advanced. The results thus support our *H10b*.

Discussions and conclusion

In this study we addressed (1) the determinants of the OMS in China at multiple levels: firm, industry and country and (2) the interaction effects of country (i.e. regional institutional advancement) and firm-specific (i.e. international experience and degree of product diversification) determinants. The hypotheses were tested on a sample of 402 FDIs made by Nordic MNEs in China during the period of 1987–2012.

Most of our hypotheses were supported. We found that there was a negative relationship between international experience and the probability of choosing WOS. This result contradicted some China-based studies (Chiao et al., 2010; Kuo et al., 2012). First, given the unique socio-culture in China, Nordic managers having more international experience were still unfamiliar with the business environment in China. Second, higher levels of international experience facilitate finding the right partners (Erramilli, 1991). This study also supported the view that degree of product diversification resulted in the preference of JVs over WOS. As expected, we found that resource-intensive industries increased the probability of choosing JVs as opposed to WOS. Furthermore, we found a positive relationship between industry sales' growth and the preference for WOS. In line with our expectation, we found that cultural distance increased the probability of choosing WOS as opposed to JVs. As expected, this study revealed that both the later stage of institutional transition and regional institutional advancement significantly increased the probability of choosing WOS as opposed to JVs.

Against expectations we found that the target country experience was not a significant determinant of the OMS of Nordic firms. This result was in line with the study by Luo (2001), but contradicted the finding by Shi et al. (2001). Additionally, this study found that industry growth in terms of number of firms was negatively associated with the choice of WOS as opposed to JVs. This finding contradicted the finding by Luo (2001). The possible explanation for the inconsistent findings is that the studies by Luo (2001) and Shi et al. (2001) focused on MNEs based in the United States, Japan and Hong Kong, whereas the current study analysed firms originating in SMOPECs.

This study theoretically contributes to existing literature on OMS in emerging markets in two important ways. First, this study analyses the determinants of OMS in China at three levels: firm, industry and country. In order to analyse the determinants at multiple levels, this chapter drew on three theories: transaction cost economics (Andersson and Gatignon, 1986; Hennart, 1991), the resource-based (Barney, 1991) and the institution-based view (Peng, 2002). The combination of TCE and theoretical perspectives such as institutional perspectives provide fruitful research avenues for future foreign entry mode studies (Brouthers, 2013). Second, this study contributes to existing literature by analysing two interaction effects. We found that regional institutional advancement in China moderates the impacts of two firm-specific determinants: international experience and degree of product diversification.

There are empirical contributions as well. First, since this study used a unique sample of Nordic firms, the findings of this study can be generalised to MNEs based in SMOPECs. We found that there are significant differences about the determinants of OMS of MNEs based in Nordic countries and those in larger economies. We found that Nordic firms with higher levels of international experience were more likely to choose JVs as opposed to WOS. This finding was different from studies including those of Shi et al. (2001), Chiao et al. (2010), Li and Li (2010) and Kuo et al. (2012), focusing on FDIs made by MNEs based in the United States, Japan and other Asian countries. This study found that the host country experience was not a significant determinant, whereas Luo (2001) and Shi et al. (2001) found a significant effect. We found that cultural distance increased the probability of choosing WOS as opposed to JVs, whereas

Luo (2001) and Duanmu (2011) found non-significant influence. A second empirical contribution is related to the sample size and observation period. Our sample size is clearly larger than several previous China-based studies, including those of Luo (2001) and Shi et al. (2001) which addressed FDIs made by MNEs from the largest economies such as the United States and Japan. The observation period (26 years) in this study is clearly longer than most of the existing China-based studies.

Managerial and policy implications

This research provides useful implications for the managers of MNEs based in SMOPECs. First, our findings revealed that country-specific variables are the most important determinants of OMS in China. In more detail, the later stage of institutional transition, regional institutional advancement and cultural distance increased the preference of WOS over JVs. Second, this study found that Nordic managers especially consider two industrial variables in their choice of WOS and JVs in China: resource-intensive industry and industry growth in terms of number of firms. Nordic managers tend to opt for JVs as opposed to WOS when entering resource-intensive industries. Industry growth in terms of the number of firms increases the probability of JVs as opposed to WOS. Third, this study found that managers of MNEs based in SMOPECs evaluate two firm-specific variables before making their OMS in China. Both international experience and degree of product diversification increase the probability of choosing JVs as opposed to WOS.

As usual there are several notable limitations in this study. First of all, this research analysed three variables at the country-specific level: cultural distance, the stage of institutional transition, and regional institutional advancement. It should be noted that institution is a multidimensional construct and consists of both formal and informal institution (North, 1990). Future studies are encouraged to address the impacts of both formal and informal institution on OMS in China. In addition, the analysis of the relationship between entry motives and OMS would be of great interest (Chen, 2008). Furthermore, FDI behaviour of service firms may differ from that of manufacturing firms (Brouthers and Brouthers, 2003). The analysis of similarities and dissimilarities between manufacturing and service firms' OMS would be of great interest. Last but not the least, future studies can link the determinants of the OMS to subsidiary survival and performance.

Appendix 8.1 Results of binary logistic regression (country of origin analysis: WOS = 1, JVs = 0)

	Finland		Sweden		Denmark and Norway	
Variables	Model 3a	Model 3b	Model 4a	Model 4b	Model 5a	Model 5b
Control variables						
Greenfields establishment mode	1.30**	1.23**	0.80	0.76	0.76	0.79
R&D intensity	−0.18	−0.23	−0.59	−0.12	−0.76*	−0.83*
Investment restrictions	−0.60	−0.45	−0.66	−0.99**	−1.09	−1.28
Firm-specific determinants						
International experience	−0.02**		−0.02***		−0.02*	
Host country experience	0.06	−0.02	0.09	0.03	0.03	−0.02
Degree of product diversification		−0.06*		−0.04		−0.07**
Industry-specific determinants						
Resource-intensive industries	−0.38	−0.33	−0.76	0.06	−2.49***	−2.52***
Growth in number of firms	−0.85	−0.93	−9.22**	−6.87*	−8.50*	−7.02
Industry sales' growth	0.89	0.95	1.33	0.26	2.94*	2.63*
Country-specific determinants						
Cultural distance						
Stages of institutional transitions	0.46	0.44	0.61	0.94**	0.93**	0.65
Regional institutional advancement	0.27	0.24	0.39**	0.23	0.28*	0.31**
Number of FDIs (402)	124		150		128	
Nagelkerke R^2	0.28	0.24	0.39	0.31	0.38	0.39
Correctly classified (%)	71.1	65.0	73.1	71.0	75.4	76.5
Model Chi square (x^2)	28.33***	23.50***	44.28***	36.53***	38.63***	40.28***

Notes: Significant level: *** $p<0.01$, ** $p<0.05$, * $p<0.10$ (two-tailed).

References

Amemiya, T. (1981). 'Qualitative response models: A survey', *Journal of Economic Literature*, 19(4), 1483–1536.

Anderson, E. and Gatignon, H. (1986). 'Modes of foreign entry: A transaction cost analysis and propositions', *Journal of International Business Studies*, 17(3), 1–26.

Arregle, J.L., Hebert, L. and Beamish, P.W. (2006). 'Mode of international entry: The advantages of multilevel methods', *Management International Review*, 46(5), 597–618.

Bai, T., Jin, Z. and Qi, X. (2013). 'Chinese firms outward FDI entry mode choice: The role of ownership and network', *Journal of Innovation Management*, 1(1), 108–124.

Barkema, H.G., Bell, J.H.J. and Pennings, J.M. (1996). 'Foreign entry, cultural barriers, and learning', *Strategic Management Journal*, 17(2), 151–166.

Barney, J. (1991). 'Firm resources and sustained competitive advantage', *Journal of Management*, 17(1), 99–120.

Benito, G.R.G., Larimo, J., Narula, R. and Pedersen, T. (2002). 'Multinational enterprises from small economies: Internationalisation patterns of large companies from Denmark, Finland, and Norway', *International Studies of Management and Organisation*, 32(1), 57–78.

Brouthers, K.D. (2013). 'A retrospective on: Institutional, cultural, and transaction cost influences on entry mode choice and performance', *Journal of International Business Studies*, 44(1), 14–22.

Brouthers, K.D. and Brouthers, L.E. (2003). 'Why service and manufacturing entry mode choices differ: The influence of transaction cost factors, risk and trust', *Journal of Management Studies*, 40(5), 1179–1204.

Brouthers, K.D. and Hennart, J.F. (2007). 'Boundaries of the firm: Insights from international entry mode research', *Journal of Management*, 33(3), 395–425.

Buckley, P.J. and Lessard, D.R. (2005). 'Regarding the edge of international business research', *Journal of International Business Studies*, 36(6), 595–599.

Chang, Y.C., Kao, M.S., Kuo, A. and Chiu, C.F. (2012). 'How cultural distance influences entry mode choices: The contingent role of host country's governance quality', *Journal of Business Research*, 65(8), 1160–1170.

Chen, H.Y. and Hu, M.Y. (2002). 'An analysis of determinants of entry mode and its impact on performance', *International Business Review*, 11(2), 193–210.

Chen, S.F.S. (2008). 'The motives for international acquisitions: Capability procurements, strategic considerations, and the role of ownership structure', *Journal of International Business Studies*, 39(3), 454–471.

Chiao, Y.C., Lo, F.Y. and Yu, C.M. (2010). 'Choosing between wholly-owned subsidiaries and joint ventures of MNCs from an emerging market', *International Marketing Review*, 27(3), 338 –365.

Child, J. and Tse, D.K. (2001). 'China's transition and its implications for international business', *Journal of International Business Studies*, 32(1), 5–21.

China Statistical Yearbook (1983–2013) Beijing: National Bureau of Statistics of China.

Cho, K.R. and Padmanabhan, P. (2005). 'Revisiting the role of cultural distance in MNCs' foreign ownership mode choice: The moderating effect of experience attributes', *International Business Review*, 14(3), 307–324.

Claver, E. and Quer, D. (2005). 'Choice of market entry mode in China: The influence of firm-specific factors', *Journal of General Management*, 30(3), 51–70.

Cui, L. and Jiang, F. (2009). 'FDI entry mode choice of Chinese firms: A strategic behaviour perspective', *Journal of World Business*, 44(4), 434–444.

Demirbag, M., Glaister, K.W. and Tatoglu, E. (2007). 'Institutional and transaction cost influences on MNEs' ownership strategies of their affiliates: Evidence from an emerging market', *Journal of World Business*, 42(4), 418–434.

Demirbag, M., Tatoglu, E. and Glaister, K.W. (2009). 'Equity-based entry modes of emerging country multinationals: Lessons from Turkey', *Journal of World Business*, 44(4), 445–462.

Dikova, D. and Van Witteloostuijn, A. (2007). 'Foreign direct investment mode choice: Entry and establishment modes in transition economies', *Journal of International Business Studies*, 38(6), 1013–1033.

Duanmu, J.L. (2011). 'The effect of corruption distance and market orientation on the ownership choice of MNEs: Evidence from China', *Journal of International Management*, 17(2), 162–174.

Elango, B. and Sambharya, R.B. (2004). 'The influence of industry structure on the entry mode choice of overseas entrants in manufacturing industries', *Journal of International Management*, 10(1), 107–124.

Endo, N., Ozaki, T. and Ando, N. (2014). 'Firm level factor versus national institutional difference: Ownership structure in a foreign subsidiary of a Japanese logistic firm', *The Asian Journal of Shipping and Logistics*, 30(3), 393–413.

Erramilli, M.K. (1991). 'The experience factor in foreign market entry behaviour of service firms', *Journal of International Business Studies*, 22(3), 479–501.

—— (1996). 'Nationality and subsidiary ownership patterns in multinational corporations', *Journal of International Business Studies*, 27(2), 225–246.

Erramilli, M.K. and Rao, C.P. (1993). 'Service firms international entry mode choice: A modified transaction cost analysis approach', *Journal of Marketing*, 57(3), 19–38.

Gang, F., Wang, X.L. and Zhu, H.P. (2011). *NERI Index of Marketization of China's Provinces*, Beijing: Economic Science Press.

Gatignon, H. and Anderson, E. (1988). 'The multinational corporations' degree of control over foreign subsidiaries: An empirical test of a transaction cost explanation', *Journal of Law, Economics, and Organisation*, 4(2), 305–336.

Hair, J.F., Anderson, R.E., Tatham, R.L. and Black, W. (1998). *Multivariate Data Analysis*, 5th ed. Upper Saddle River, NJ: Prentice Hall.

Hennart, J.F. (1991). 'The transaction costs theory of joint ventures: An empirical study of Japanese subsidiaries in the United States', *Management Science*, 37(4), 483–497.

—— (2009). 'Down with MNE-centric theories! Market entry and expansion as the bundling of MNE and local assets', *Journal of International Business Studies*, 40(9), 1432–1454.

—— (2012). 'Emerging market multinationals and the theory of the multinational enterprise', *Global Strategy Journal*, 2(3), 168–187.

Hennart, J.F. and Larimo, J. (1998). 'The impact of culture on the strategy of multinational enterprises. Does national origin affect ownership decisions?', *Journal of International Business Studies*, 29(3), 515–538.

Hennart, J.F. and Park, Y.R. (1993). 'Greenfield vs. acquisition: The strategy of Japanese investors in the United States', *Management Science*, 39(9), 1054–1070.

Hill, C.L., Hwang, P. and Kim, W.C. (1990). 'An eclectic theory of the choice of international entry mode', *Strategic Management Journal*, 11(2), 117–128.

Hofstede, G. (1980). *Cultures Consequences: Internal Differences in Work-related Values*, Newbury Park, CA: Sage.

Hosmer, D.W. and Lemeshow, S. (1989). *Applied Logistic Regression*, New York: Wiley.

Johanson, J. and Vahlne, J.E. (1977). 'The internationalisation process of the firm. A model of knowledge development and increasing foreign market commitment', *Journal of International Business Studies*, 8(1), 23–32.

Kennedy, P. (1998). *A Guide to Econometrics*, Cambridge, MA: MIT Press.

Kim, T.Y., Delios, A. and Xu, D. (2010). 'Organisational geography, experiential learning and subsidiary exit: Japanese foreign expansions in China, 1979–2001', *Journal of Economic Geography*, 10(4), 579–597.

Kogut, B. and Singh, H. (1988). 'The effect of national culture on the choice of entry mode', *Journal of International Business Studies*, 19(3), 412–432.

Kuo, A., Kao, M.S., Chang, Y.C. and Chiu, C.F. (2012). 'The influence of international experience on entry mode choice: Difference between family and non-family firms', *European Management Journal*, 30(3), 248–263.

Laanti, R., Mcdougall, F. and Baume, G. (2009). 'How well do traditional theories explain the internationalisation of service MNEs from Small and Open Economies? Case: National Telecommunication Companies', *Management International Review*, 49(1), 121–144.

Larimo, J. (2000). 'Choice of organisational structure in foreign markets: The impact of ownership and location specific determinants on foreign direct investment behaviour of Nordic firms', Paper presented at AIB meeting, 17–20 November, Phoenix, AZ.

—— (2003). 'Form of investment by Nordic firms in world markets', *Journal of Business Research*, 56(10), 791–804.

Li, J. and Li, Y. (2010). 'Flexibility versus commitment: MNEs ownership strategy in China', *Journal of International Business Studies*, 41(9), 1550–1571.

Li, P.Y. and Meyer, K.E. (2009). 'Contextualizing experience effects in international business: A study of ownership strategies', *Journal of World Business*, 44(4), 370–382.

Luo, Y.D. (2001). 'Determinants of entry in an emerging economy: A multilevel approach', *Journal of Management Studies*, 38(3), 443–472.

Luostarinen, R. and Gabrielsson, M. (2006). 'Globalization and marketing strategies of born global in SMOPECs', *Thunderbird International Business Review*, 48(6), 773–801.

Meyer, K.E. and Nguyen, H.V. (2005). 'Foreign investment strategies and sub-national institutions in emerging markets: Evidence from Vietnam', *Journal of Management Studies*, 43(1), 63–93.

Meyer, K.E., Estrin, S., Bhaumik, S.K. and Peng, M.W. (2009). 'Institutions, resources, and entry strategies in emerging economies', *Strategic Management Journal*, 30(1), 61–80.

Meyer, K.E. and Peng, M.W. (2005). 'Probing theoretically into Central and Eastern Europe: Transactions, resources, and institutions', *Journal of International Business Studies*, 36(6), 600–621.

Morschett, D., Schramm-Klein, H., and Swoboda, B. (2010). 'Decades of research on market entry modes: What do we really know about external antecedents of entry mode choice?', *Journal of International Management*, 16(1), 60–77.

North, D.C. (1990). *Institutions, Institutional Change and Economic Performance*, Cambridge: Cambridge University Press.

Padmanabhan, P. and Cho, K.R. (1996). 'Ownership strategy for a foreign affiliate: An empirical investigation of Japanese firms', *Management International Review*, 36(1), 45–65.

—— (1999). 'Decision specific experience in foreign ownership and establishment strategies: Evidence from Japanese firms', *Journal of International Business Studies*, 30(1), 25–41.

Pallant, J. (2007). *SPSS Survival Manual: A Step by Step Guide to Data Analysis Using SPSS for Windows*, Buckingham, UK: Open University Press.

Papyrina, V. (2007). 'When, how, and with what success? The joint effect of timing and entry mode on survival of Japanese subsidiaries in China', *Journal of International Marketing*, 15(3), 73–95.

Peng, M.W. (2002). 'Towards an institution-based view of business strategy', *Asia Pacific Journal of Management*, 19(2–3), 251–267.

Peterson, M.F., Arregle, J.L. and Martin, X. (2012). 'Multilevel models in international business research', *Journal of International Business Studies*, 43(5), 451–457.

Polsa, P., So, S.L.M. and Speece, M.W. (2005). 'The People's Republic of China and Hong Kong: Markets within a market'. In A. Pecotich and C.J. Schultz (eds), *Handbook of Markets and Economics: East Asia, Southeast Asia, Australia, New Zealand*, New York: Sharp M.E.

Shaver, J.M. (2013). 'Do we really need more entry mode studies?', *Journal of International Business Studies*, 44(1), 23–27.

Shi, Y.Z., Ho, P.Y. and Siu, W.S. (2001). 'Market entry mode selection: The experience of small Hong Kong firms investing in China', *Asia Pacific Business Review*, 8(1), 19–41.

Slangen, A.H.L.and Hennart, J.F. (2007). 'Greenfield or acquisition entry: A review of the empirical foreign establishment mode literature', *Journal of International Management*, 13(4), 403–429.

———— (2008). 'Do multinationals really prefer to enter culturally distant countries through greenfields rather than through acquisitions? The role of parent experience and subsidiary autonomy', *Journal of International Business Studies*, 39(3), 472–490.

———— (2015). 'Yes, we really do need more entry mode studies! A commentary on Shaver', *Journal of International Business Studies*, 46(1), 114–122.

Tihanyi, L., Griffith, D.A. and Russell, C.J. (2005). 'The effect of cultural distance on entry mode choice, international diversification, and MNE performance: A meta-analysis', *Journal of International Business Studies*, 36(3), 270–283.

Teng, B.S. (2004). 'The WTO and entry modes in China', *Thunderbird International Business Review*, 46(4), 381–400.

Vermeulen, F. and Barkema, H. (2001). 'Learning through acquisitions', *Academy of Management Journal*, 44(3), 457–476.

Wei, Y.Q., Liu, B. and Xia, M.L. (2005). 'Entry modes of foreign direct investment in China: A multinomial logit approach', *Journal of Business Research*, 58(11), 1495–1505.

Wetherill, G.B. (1986). *Regression Analysis with Applications*, London: Chapman and Hall.

Yang, J.Y., Tipton, F.B. and Li, J. (2011). 'A review of foreign business management in China', *Asia Pacific Journal of Management*, 28(3), 627–659.

Yeung, Y.M., Lee, J. and Kee, G. (2009). 'China's special economic zones at 30', *Eurasian Geography and Economies*, 50(2), 222–240.

Yiu, D. and Makino, S. (2002). 'The choice between joint venture and wholly owned subsidiary: An institutional perspective', *Organisation Science*, 13(6), 667–683.

Yu, J., Lee, S.H. and Han, K. (2015). 'FDI motives, market governance, and ownership choice of MNEs: A study of Malaysia and Thailand from an incomplete contracting perspective', *Asia Pacific Journal of Management*, 32(2), 335–362.

Zhang, Y., Zhang, Z.G. and Liu, Z.X. (2007). 'Choice of entry modes in sequential FDI in an emerging economy', *Management Decision*, 45(4), 749–772.

Zhao, H.X., Luo, Y.D. and Suh, T. (2004). 'Transaction cost determinants and ownership-based entry mode choice: A meta-analytical review', *Journal of International Business Studies*, 35(6), 524–544.

9
Creating Value in Cross-Border M&As through Strategic Network
William Y. Degbey and Melanie E. Hassett

Introduction

M&As provide unique opportunities for the acquirer to grow rapidly, to gain new capabilities which an organisation might otherwise find difficult to develop on its own, and to gain access to new markets (e.g. Haspeslagh and Jemison, 1991; Hitt et al., 2001). Recent trends indicate that cross-border mergers and acquisitions (M&As) keep increasing following the double-dip recession (World Investment Report, 2014). While M&As have become increasingly popular as a method of organisational growth and development, the acquisition success rate has remained mediocre at best. Accordingly, M&A success and value creation have been at the heart of M&A research and have been approached from various disciplines (cf. King et al., 2004; Cartwright and Schoenberg, 2006; Schoenberg, 2006; Degbey, 2015). A number of scholars have tried to explain cross-border M&A failure through external issues, such as national cultural differences, but the results have been inconclusive (cf. Teerikangas and Very, 2006; Stahl and Voigt, 2008), and it has been argued that the effect of culture on M&A performance is mediated by the post-acquisition integration strategy, the acquisition experience and integration capabilities of the acquirer, and the level of integration (e.g. Morosini and Singh, 1994; Slangen, 2006; Dikova and Sahib, 2013). However, a growing body of literature on post-acquisition integration has focused on internal issues, that is, the human side, and argues that M&A failure is largely down to socio-cultural challenges such as change resistance, acculturation stress and so forth (e.g. Buono and Bowditch, 1989; Datta, 1991; Cartwright and Cooper, 1993; Very et al., 1996; Birkinshaw et al., 2000; Stahl and Voigt, 2008). In this research we don't focus on M&A failure, but on how to create value through M&As, and argue that M&As can be effective strategic tools in creating value through strategic networks.

Mergers and acquisitions (M&A) research from a strategy perspective focuses mostly on internal dynamics of the merging parties, and assesses how merging firms create value on the basis of synergy potentials, particularly from strategic and process factors in a neo-classical time environment (Cartwright and Schoenberg, 2006). However, the high M&A failure rate (cf. King et al., 2004; Shimizu, 2007) raises concerns that neo-classical management models of value creation in M&A might be underspecified (e.g. Hitt et al., 1998; Schoenberg, 2006). In addition, strategy field scholars in M&A literature usually employ an individual firm perspective mostly when discussing effects of M&A on firm performance (Larsson and Finkelstein, 1999). However, firms are increasingly interrelated with other firms due to the globalised nature of the market (Hatani and McGaughey, 2013), and it has been argued that competitive advantage can be derived from interfirm networks that compete with other networks (Gulati et al., 2000; Moller and Rajala, 2007). Hence, we argue that in order to obtain a better understanding of M&A failure, or success for that matter, it is important to view M&As in their context, that is, the network in which the focal firms are embedded (cf. Anderson et al., 2001).

The network concept has shown to be useful for exploring complex organisational phenomena such as strategic alliances (including M&A), multinational corporations and interorganisational exchange governance (Ferriani et al., 2013; Gulati, 1998; Ghoshal and Bartlett, 1990; Degbey and Pelto, 2013; Borch and Arthur, 1995). Our locus of attention here is on strategic networks, a subset of the network research activity focused on intentionally created interfirm economic exchange. Prior studies suggest that interactions or networks could be an important unit of analysis (Benson, 1975; Hakansson and Snehota, 1989; Ford et al., 2003), even if the analysis is primarily dyadic (Storbacka and Nenonen, 2009). As firms, for example in the European Economic Area (EEA) stainless steel industry, formulate their strategies to enable them take advantage of vital opportunities or deflect/cope with consequential environmental threats, the realisation is dawning that they are embedded in a network of relationships which may enhance or constrain their value creation potential. Such realisations are critical for understanding the network structure and position of actors within the industry in order to determine their likely behaviour and performance (Gulati et al., 2000), that is, their value creation in an M&A context.

Accordingly, this study contributes to both the emerging theory of network management in the field of strategy research, as well as the field of cross-border M&As. In order to illustrate the relevance of networks (Jarillo, 1988) this study is based on an M&A case in the European Steel Industry. This study demonstrates how the network approach provides a deeper and more contextual understanding of highly strategic phenomena such as M&As. While the network approach enhances our understanding of strategic events such as M&As, our study demonstrates how M&As are used as strategic tools to impact the network of the companies involved. For example, the acquirer's ability to influence and change the acquired firm's network position and structure could form a way of strategising and managing in networks (e.g. Harrison and Prenkert, 2009; Golfetto et al., 2007). Moreover, this study addresses the ongoing debate regarding the empirical application of the concept of network/network research to strategy literature, and contributes by addressing the lingering ambiguity of network concepts as compatible and complementary to the field of strategy (cf. McEvily and Marcus, 2005; Jarillo, 1988). Additional contribution may stem from the understanding that a focal firm's network structure construed not only in terms of closure (Coleman, 1988), but most importantly in terms of access to structural holes (Burt, 1992), may improve firm value creation in M&A. For example, a firm that bridges the structural holes created by industry consolidation via M&A may gain superior performance.

The purpose of this research is twofold: *first*, to study a focal firm's network position in the external environment of the industry through its embed-dedness in a network of external relationships with other actors for potential value creation, and *second*, to analyse how the dissolution of acquired firm's customers' network may influence a focal actor's ability to reduce its excess capacity within the industry. Consequently, in this chapter we argue that companies are able to influence their networks through M&As in a way that enables them to improve their value-creation capability. In other words, M&As can be used as a strategic tool to improve the firm's network position and structure. This chapter is organised in the following way. First we present an overview of M&A value creation and strategic networks. Then we present a case study on M&A in the EEA stainless steel industry. Finally we present our findings and main conclusions.

Value creation and strategic networks in M&A: an overview

Strategic networks

Truly changed market conditions (e.g. low competition and low complexity towards more turbulent, complex and demanding operating conditions) present strategic management research with major challenges, including eco-logical concerns, global aspects, social responsibility, and long-term commit-ment and cooperation among firms (Borch and Arthur, 1995). Yet the strategic network view seems to accommodate most of these challenges due to its the-oretical basis that moves beyond the limited, common-sense and intuitive model of management to also include applicability of multidisciplinary, more complex models of strategy research (Borch and Arthur, 1995). Hence, the stra-tegic network perspective may help clarify a fundamental question in strategy research, that is, *why firms differ in their conduct and performance* (Gulati et al., 2000). In this study the strategic network view is employed to illustrate per-formance differential of a focal firm in the European stainless steel industry using its acquired firm's customers' strategic networks to create value following a cross-border M&A.

The differential conduct and performance among firms has been a major focus of strategic management research over the years. There have been many different approaches to explain the performance (and conduct) heterogeneity among firms. For example, Ansoff's (1965) contribution to firms' performance heterogeneity highlights both the internal strengths and weaknesses of the firm, as well as external concerns related to opportunities and threats in the market space. Porter's (1980) work on competitive strategy strives to explain the differences in performance by examining industry structures and the firm's positioning in the industry. The Porterian school of thought implicitly assumes resource homogeneity and resource mobility among rival firms in an industry (Storbacka and Nenonen, 2009). In both Ansoff's (1965) and Porter's (1980) work strategy is viewed as the 'fit' between firm and its environment (competitors and the macro-environment). A third example of an influential work in the strategy literature is that of Barney (1991). His work on the resource-based view (first introduced by Wernerfelt, 1984) assumes that firms' control of relevant strategic resources is heterogeneous, and that resources are imperfectly mobile among firms.

Indeed, in the aforementioned strategy scholars have recognised the firm as an autonomous entity whose competitive advantage may come from the favourability of its external industry environment (Porter, 1980) or from its internally controlled (unique) resources – which are valuable, rare, imperfectly imitable and difficult to substitute by other competing firms (Barney, 1991). In contrast to the 'fit' views of the above-mentioned strategy scholars, it can be said that network researchers see the network of relationships as the 'fit' between the firm and its environment. With notable exceptions (see Jarillo, 1988; Gulati et al., 2000), the interdependent nature of the firm that both enhances and constrains its behaviour and performance has received relatively little attention in prior strategy research. This, however, should not come as a surprise considering the fact that the concept of network was coined outside the strategy field – interorganisational relationships' researchers coined the network concept from the organisational theory tradition (Benson, 1975; Jarillo, 1988; Van de Ven, 1976). Moreover, earlier seminal empirical works on interorganisational relationships were conducted on non-profit organisations. When it comes to profit-oriented organisations, it appears that strategy research scholars have been grappling with how to fit the network concept (e.g. the cooperative behaviour of firms) with the basic paradigm of competitive strategy, especially by way of formal empirical studies (Jarillo, 1988).

Notwithstanding the conceptual challenges, interest in network research has become common and significant among business and management scholars, especially among European industrial marketing, organisation studies and international business, as well as M&A scholars (see, e.g. Araujo and Easton, 1996; Grandori and Soda, 1995; Oliver and Ebers, 1998; Johanson and Mattsson, 1987; Johanson and Vahlne, 2009, 2011; Moller and Rajala, 2007; Turnbull et al., 1996; Oberg et al., 2007; Havila and Salmi, 2000; Degbey and Pelto, 2015). From the world of *market* (structure and process) and *action* (e.g. Ford and Hakansson, 2006) in particular, M&As can be viewed as a strategic phenomenon. However, the world of network view may construe them in terms of *network* and *interaction* (see Ford and Hakansson, 2006; Hakansson and Ford, 2002), where network position and network structure of firms in economic exchange relationships are critical to value creation. In the following sections we briefly define the concepts of network position and network structure.

Network position and network structure

Network position: Network research scholars assert that the concept has emerged simultaneously with the industrial network approach (Nystrom et al., 2008), and the concept is a relative one as no two parties' positions are alike (Hakansson and Snehota, 1989). According to Gadde et al. (2003), each actor (firm) in a network has a unique position with respect to other actors but the various actors in the network perceive the position of an actor differently. Johanson and Mattsson (1992) describe network position on the basis of how the individual actors in the network are related to one another in a network structure, while Thorelli (1986) describes it as a location of power to create and/or influence networks. Nystrom et al. (2008) emphasise that time and commitment are necessary ingredients that shape network positions, and position changes may be difficult or sometimes impossible to achieve. In addition, Nystrom et al. (2008) note that network position depicts a focal actor's relations to other actors and are consequences of earlier activities in the network, determined both by the focal actor and by other actors. In terms of positional benefits, the network perspective suggests that firms occupying preferred network positions may be better able to access information needed to be both creative and innovative (Zaheer and Bell, 2005). Another benefit an actor may derive from occupying an advantageous network position is the control benefits that the actor may generate (Gulati, 1998). According to Burt (1992, p. 78), both benefits are analytically distinct but also overlap, since much of the control benefit can arise from the manipulation of information.

Following this line of reasoning, we can expect that in an M&A context like the vertical integration one we illustrate in this chapter, where a firm acquired a major distributor in the industry and as a consequence cuts off its major competitors' customer network, could be seen as occupying preferred network positions to garner superior value creation with respect to other actors in the industry. Zaheer and Bell (2005, p. 814) defined superior network position to mean '*access to structural holes*'. They argue that a focal firm's access to structural holes may yield several positive influences on its performance, for example, enhanced efficiency, better access to resources, and superior identification of and responses to emerging threats and opportunities (Zaheer and Bell, 2005). Based on all the descriptions and definitions provided above on network position, the chapter adopts the definition provided by Zaheer and Bell (2005) in combination with that of Johanson and Mattsson (1992) to illustrate the strategic relevance of networks for value creation in M&As.

Network structure: Johanson and Mattsson (1992) describe network structure to mean the ways in which the firms are linked to one another and the framework within which business is carried out. Easton (1992) argues that the interdependence rather than independency of firms in an industrial system will provide a network with a structure. Further, he argues that the interdependence introduces constraints on the actions of individual firms which create structure 'in the large' (Easton, 1992, p. 16). According to Ford and Hakansson (2006) the world of market and action usually observe structure as atomistic, defined by products, competitive, competition between independent firms, change stemming from external sources, and based on the actions of single firms. On the other hand, the network perspective recognises structure as particular, defined by the threads between nodes, conflictual and cooperative, relationships between interdependent companies, change emanating from internal as well as external sources but all influencing through relationships and interactions based on the interplay between actors (Ford and Hakansson, 2006).

A strategic network perspective to M&A value creation

Since the early 1990s, value creation has maintained a popular status in M&A performance or success literature (e.g. Seth, 1990a, 1990b; Haspeslagh and Jemison, 1991; Birkinshaw et al., 2000; Kohli and Mann, 2012; Craninckx and Huyghebaert, 2014). Even in a recent meta-analysis by Haleblian et al. (2009), value creation has been reiterated as a major antecedent driving firms to undertake M&As, in addition to three other antecedents: managerial self-interest, environmental factors and firm characteristics. In that spirit, Riviezzo (2013) notes that a growing body of research has focused attention on antecedents that can be used to explain the variance in M&A performance.

From a strategic management perspective, value creation in M&A tends to be justified particularly in terms of *synergies*, and also in terms of competitive advantage (Calipha et al., 2010). Indeed, Larsson and Finkelstein (1999) note that synergy realisation is an important metric for value creation in M&As, and its determination is derived from integrating strategic, organisational and human resource factors. Specifically, Larsson and Finkelstein (1999) state that synergy realisation is a function of combination potential, organisational integration and employee resistance. In short, the synergy-based argument of M&A can be encapsulated as the whole (the merged entities) should exceed the sum of the individual parts. In other words, the profit of the amalgamated entities is expected to exceed the profits of the independent entities through the reduction of average costs or the enhancement of revenues (Shaver, 2006). However, Shaver (2006) posits that M&A actions taken to facilitate synergy capture may lead to both *contagion effect* (i.e. amplified threats from environment or actions by competitors across the integrated and interdependent firms compared to if it had not been integrated) and *capacity effect* (i.e. integration of two businesses may increase the capacity utilisation of underlying resources and thus inhibits firms' ability to respond to positive shocks in the business environment due to capacity constraints). While Shaver's (2006) work is theoretically relevant, it concentrates mainly on the two merging parties and their strategic fit with the business environment.

As important as these strategic management views on M&A value creation are, however, they still focus mostly on the internal dynamics of the merging parties. Indeed, Anderson et al. (2000) note that M&A parties do not always act as actors embedded in a broader network, where all actors are connected and dependent on one another. Besides, Borch and Arthur (1995) argue that increased interdependency makes it critical for a firm to focus on strategic relations to a larger set of actors in the task environment, and to also increase awareness of important contextual variables behind the market scene. According to both scholars, strategic networks are 'investments in cooperative relations among firms in order to exchange or share information or resources' (Borch and Arthur, 1995, p. 420; Anderson et al., 2000). Consistent with this reasoning, Zaheer and Bell (2005) add to the strategic network perspective that firms are embedded in a network of external relationships with other actors (firms) with significant consequences for firm performance. In this chapter we define strategic networks simply as firms' investment to attain preferred network position and network structure for superior value creation. Figure 9.1 below shows the theoretical framework of strategic network and M&A value creation in this study.

Figure 9.1 below illustrates how M&A value creation can be augmented through strategic networks, both by enhancing network position and network structure. The heterogeneity of firms both inside and between units contrasts the homogeneity assumption of some early economic models in strategy research such as the competitive strategy school of thought by Porter (1980). It is argued that the greater the interdependence the clearer the network structure becomes, making the determination of individual firm behaviour more important (Easton, 1992). Again, Easton (1992) notes that network heterogeneity and interdependence are mutually reinforcing, and hence emphasises that interdependence in networks is not only a source of heterogeneity, it is also a result of it. Within the context of this chapter, firms are seen as the key elements of the structure. Generally, having a network view regarding an actor's network position and structure may yield an understanding of possible constraints and opportunities for the actor's operations (Axelsson and Johanson, 1992; Johanson and Vahlne, 1992). Also, positioning within a foreign

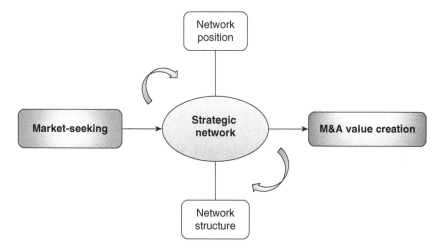

Figure 9.1   Strategic network and M&A value creation

network may create additional opportunities for an actor (firm) to develop rela-tionships that, in turn, can lead to further linkages with other actors (Axelsson and Johanson, 1992).

In sum, we argue that in order to create value in cross-border M&As, acquirers need to consider their strategic network and how the acquisition in question affects their network position and structure. In other words, M&As can be stra-tegic in nature and employed simply to enhance acquirers' network position and structure. In the literature this M&A motive is not stated explicitly but motives such as market-seeking, growth, product-line expansion/extension, business expansion into new geographic markets and following the move of customers all hint towards that direction. In the next section we analyse in depth a case of an M&A taking place in the EEA stainless steel industry. The main results and conclusion are presented following the case description.

Empirical research – an illustrative case study

We adopt a case study approach to analyse the networks among the merging parties and their business counterparts. The case study method is important when a study aims to understand the dynamics present in a particular (single) setting and when the boundaries between the phenomenon and the context are not clearly evident (Eisenhardt, 1989; Yin, 2003). For these reasons the case study approach is often considered as the most appropriate method in studying networks (Halinen and Törnroos, 2005; Easton, 1998; Eisenhardt, 1989). According to Siggelkow (2007), case research may be used for illus-tration as well as an additional, but not sole, justification for one's arguments.

In this chapter we employ the case study approach to illustrate the relevance of strategic networks for firms' value creation in the context of an M&A. Cases may be selected because they represent a critical, extreme or unique case, or they are representative, that is, typical cases (Yin, 2003). In order to obtain a better understanding of strategic networks in the M&A context we decided to choose a typical case. This is in line with the illustrative role of our case study (Siggelkow, 2007). Our case is 'typical' as it represents a cross-border acquisition in the stainless steel industry, which fulfils the definition given in the literature (e.g. Shimizu et al., 2004; Jagersma, 2005). A suitable case needed to fulfil several requirements. The most important criteria, beyond the obvious requirement that the deal had to take place in the stainless steel industry, was the international nature of the acquisition. It also needed to be fairly recent in order to avoid retrospective bias during the interviews, but not too recent so that there is enough data available.

The case selected for the research was a cross-border acquisition within Europe in the stainless steel industry. The acquisition took place in 2008. The acquisition type was vertical and the nature of the deal can be defined as friendly. The acquirer was a multinational corporation headquartered in northern Europe (referred to in the study as Gamma) that acquired a southern European multinational (referred to in the study as Theta). The reported data on the case was collected by semi-structured, face-to-face interviews. There were eight interviews in total, with key decision makers in the M&A process, such as the Vice President, M&A Integration Manager as well as the Director for Legal Affairs and M&A. The interviews took place in 2009 soon after the completion of the deal. In addition to the interview data, the empirical data was complemented with several secondary materials such as annual reports, internal company documents and company websites, as well as newspaper articles.

Based on sales by market area, EEA stainless steel market alone accounts for 75 per cent of Gamma's global sales, making it a relevant empirical setting for the case study. Specifically, the case described here involves a large distributor and its supplier in the stainless steel industry. This industry is heavily affected by economic cycles (e.g. Eurozone crisis), relies mainly on specific metals, experiences frequent fluctuation in the price of raw materials, is fraught with fierce competition and dwindling profit margins, and characterised by speculative investment in the raw material market, industry overcapacity and consolidations. Gamma is one of the key producers/suppliers of products in the industry and Theta is a major distributor with customer and supplier networks in several European countries. The deal's (i.e. M&A) monetary value was EUR 335 million. Indeed, a study of over two thousand European M&A deals from the period 2001–2007 underscores the friendly nature of such transactions, and also highlights a strong increase in the average value of European cross-border M&A deals, as opposed to largely domestic concentration (Moschieri and Campa, 2009). Table 9.1 below demonstrates the acquirer and acquired

Table 9.1 Acquirer and acquired firm description and business/geographical markets operation within EEA

Company	Pre-M&A 2008			Post-M&A 2009–2012		
	Main geographical markets in EEA	Main Business*	Main business divisions	Main product and geographical markets in EEA	Main Business*	Main business divisions
Acquirer (Gamma) – Publicly owned – 8 471 employees (2008)	Italy, Sweden, Finland, the Netherlands and the UK	**Production, sale and distribution of stainless steel products:** cold-rolled, white-hot strip, quarto plate, tubular products, long products, semi-finished products	(i) Production: stock and processing. (ii) Distribution, further processing	Joint expanded networks across EEA plus new production site in Estonia. Other Gamma networks: Austria, Denmark, Norway	(i) Production, sale and distribution of stainless steel products (ii) Metal steel distribution from Theta	General stainless, specialty stainless, and other operations
Target (Theta) – privately owned – 350 employees (2008)	Service Centres: Italy and the UK Stock Operation: Italy, Germany, UK, Turkey,** Ireland, Belgium, Finland, France	(i) **Stainless Steel Service:** Servicing and distribution of cold-rolled, hot-rolled and quarto plate products; (ii) **Metal steel:** stocking and distribution of long products, tubes and fittings	(i) Stainless steel service (ii) Metal steel			

Notes: *Attention more focused on sales and distribution rather than geographical markets of production.
** Not an EU member but has special/bilateral commercial treaties with most EEA members.

Sources: Companies' annual reports and official documents.

firms' main product and geographical markets, main business, and business divisions pre- and post-M&A.

The main products include cold- and hot-rolled stainless steel coil, sheet and plate, quarto plate, thin strip, tubular and long products. They come in different grades and dimensions. Gamma's main customers include distributors, re-rollers and further processors, tube makers as well as end-user and project customers in different industrial segments. In addition, the typical customer industries using stainless steel include architecture, building and construction, chemical, petrochemical and energy, transportation, catering and appliances, process industries and resources.

The main findings

Consolidation within the industry made it quite easy for the actors, or the main players, to know one another fairly well. Gamma already had a business relationship with Theta before the corporate change: the only difference was that it was not Theta's largest supplier before the acquisition. The main strategic rationale behind Gamma's acquisition of Theta was to obtain *proximity to the end-user market* (i.e. *market-seeking*). Indeed, the M&A could be thought of as a mere increase in market share on the part of Gamma's competitors. However, it was one of Gamma's four main strategic priority areas (focus on end-customers) to enhance profit and stability. Figure 9.2 illustrates the pre- and post-acquisition network environment of the focal actors (Gamma and Theta) and Gamma's main competitors. We focus mainly on the focal actors (acquirer and acquired firms) and their connected major actors in the environment. As can be seen in Figure 9.2, Theta had stock operations in nearly ten countries in Europe and service centres in the United Kingdom and Italy. Gamma's headquarters was in Northern Europe while Theta's was in Southern Europe. Gamma had production plants in Finland, Sweden, Britain and the United States. Theta represented the first attempts for Gamma to grow vertically and expand from being merely focused in production to taking a more active role in sales and getting closer to the end-user.

Figure 9.2 shows the strategic network environment at the pre-M&A stage comprising the initial competitive environment of Gamma, Theta and Theta's main supplier (known in the figure as *Gamma's competitor 1*) with their respective network positions and structures. As can be observed from Figure 9.2, the pre-acquisition network environment was mainly dominated by fierce competition among Gamma, Gamma's major competitor (competitor 1) as well as other competitors (known simply as competitor 2) all struggling to sell more to a major wholesale distributor (Theta). Both Gamma and Gamma's competitor 1 had both separate and common (e.g. Theta) direct customer relationships, and both desired the acquisition of each other's separate customer network.

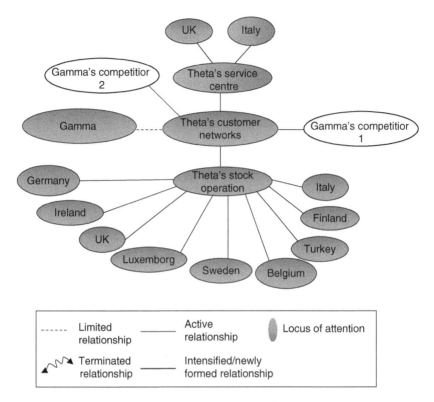

Figure 9.2   Pre-M&A strategic network environment (the grey sections are the locus of attention)

Gamma's strategic priority is to reach and sell directly to end-customers' (e.g. sell directly to Theta's customers all across EEA). Yet achieving that strategic goal successfully would require a change in both its positional and structural networks of external relationship. Acquiring Theta may yield or provide the potential preferred position to access information and other resources as well as bridge the structural holes between itself and Theta's customer networks. Figure 9.3 shows the acquisition of Theta by Gamma in an attempt to bridge the gaps between its disconnected networks (i.e. bring Gamma a step closer to Theta's end-customers).

From the post-M&A strategic network environment, it can be observed that Gamma's initial limited relationship with Theta has turned into an active one, and Theta's relationships with Gamma's competitors have also been terminated. Indeed, the post-acquisition network position changed accordingly, especially in terms of structure (the linkages between the firms and the framework within which the business exchanges take place). As a consequence

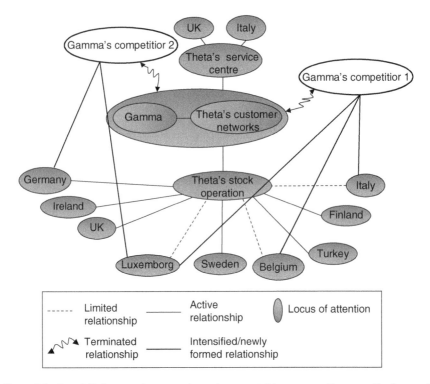

Figure 9.3   Post-M&A strategic network environment (the grey sections are the locus of attention)

of Gamma's competitors' 1 and 2 deficiencies in both network structure and position, they resort to either intensifying or establishing new exchange relationships with some of Theta's customer networks, especially those with existing limited exchange relationship with Theta (see stock operations to Luxembourg, Belgium and Italy in Figure 9.3). These steps by Gamma's competitors have strategic implications for Gamma to create value. One implication is that Gamma could start losing some of Theta's existing customer networks, especially those not so familiar with Gamma or who easily buy into Gamma's competitors' products during the M&A transition period. The acquisition has changed favourably both network structure and position for Gamma but it was a means to an end (e.g. superior value creation/performance), and not an end in itself. Thus, it is now incumbent upon Gamma to work in close collaboration with Theta in order *to maintain* the existing network of external relationships in order to preserve its value creation potential, and also *assist/enhance* Theta's customer networks in their own firms' value creation. The latter point is critical because the acquisition of Theta does not automatically mean the acquisition of its customers (cf. Anderson et al., 2001). As stated earlier, Gamma must nurture the new customer networks from Theta as well as its own existing networks. Expansion into new geographical markets and also diversifying into other product segments to meet new requirements from a new network of relationships in the EEA is critical to expanding its network structure and maintaining its network position for superior value creation. It is also critical to note that the EEA competition authority's industry M&A activity regulations may also affect the focal actor's ability to achieve its desired network structure and network position for superior value creation.

In addition, prior business relations of Gamma with Theta was found to be empirically relevant as an antecedent for gaining preferred network position with Theta's customer networks, and as a consequence helped improve the overall importance of strategic networks for value creation.

Based on the interviews and secondary data several key factors emerged regarding both network position and network structure. Table 9.2 below shows strategic network factors and the empirical data sample. The key factors related to network position were informational resources, activities and prior business relations. Consequently, the M&A enabled to Gamma to enhance its network position by accessing informational resources (Theta's location in the most competitive and important market), being in the heart of the most active market, and by knowing Theta prior to the deal. And this prior business relationship did help in identifying and selecting the right target firm for acquisition. Since

Table 9.2   Strategic network factors for value creation in M&A

Key Factors	Data Sample
Network position: i. resource (informational) ii. activities (control) iii. prior business relationship	i. '... And northern Italy is potentially the most important market in Europe. It is also the most competitive market; it works as a thermometer too: it shows instantly where the market is heading.' ii. '... What we did was to buy a market share from that competitor. But we knew that Theta relied on the facts that if four million tons of stainless steel were sold in Europe in a year, then two million tons were sold in both Germany and Italy. ...' iii. '... We knew Theta before; it was a sort of customer, although we weren't their biggest supplier. ...'
Network structure: i. actor linkages ii. actor structural hole bridge	i. 'Our largest customer segment includes suppliers and steel wholesalers. They are of course our customers but also partners. The product goes to the end consumers through them.' ii. '... What we did was to buy a market share from that competitor. ...'

prior business relationship serves as antecedent of network position, we can argue that this finding corroborates Zaheer and Bell's (2005) argument about network positions yielding superior identification of emerging opportunities in actors' environment.

Discussion and conclusions

We began by observing that consolidations via M&As have become so pervasive, particularly in certain industries such as the stainless steel industry within the EEA, fraught with fierce competition and dwindling profit margins, industry overcapacity, economic cycles (e.g. Eurozone crisis), reliance on specific metals, price fluctuation and speculation in raw material markets, and a growing number of new stainless steel manufacturers from outside the EEA. Based on these industry dynamics, we highlight through empirical illustration a recasting of research in the field of strategy that avers the firm as embedded in a network of external relationships in order to create value from both the external industry environment (Porter, 1980) and its internally controlled (unique) resources (Barney, 1991). In this chapter, one area was focused on in terms of strategic networks for value creation in M&As, that is, the importance of acquired firm (Theta) customer networks.

The outcome of this study is an empirical illustration (cf. Siggelkow, 2007) designed to bring the relevance of strategic network concepts to bear upon strategy research and practice. Strategic network, as defined in terms of investment in network position and network structure, matters in an industry (e.g. rife with excess capacity, heavily influenced by economic cycles, etc.) where firms continually seek to outperform one another and consolidate in order to strengthen their dyadic/network ties for value creation. Using a strategic network lens, we point out that while competing actors as well as industry regulatory (competition) authorities within the external environment may attempt to derail the intended motive of an M&A agenda, the embeddedness of a focal actor in network of external relationships with other actors may help shape its network position and network structure for superior value creation in its geographic and product markets. For example, the vertical M&A strategy of Gamma redistributed market share from its competitors by improving upon the deficiency in its network structure. This corroborates Burt's (1992) argument that bridging structural holes created between disconnected actors (in this case between Gamma and Theta via the M&A) indeed can improve performance. In addition, prior business relations between acquirer and acquired firm was found as a strong antecedent for gaining preferred network position with acquired firm customer networks.

Further, the dissolution of acquired firm customer networks may impact the acquirer's ability to reduce its excess capacity within the industry. The above points indicate that for an existing firm within the EEA stainless steel industry to create meaningful economic value via consolidation (e.g. M&As), it must endeavour to back its strategic actions with a clear understanding of the industry or environment as networks (both network position and structure) comprising heterogeneous actors in interdependent relationships. As Axelsson and Johanson (1992), and Zaheer and Bell (2005) note, the firm's strategic action should be an attempt to change network position to a preferred one.

Implications

The implications to practitioners and policymakers are important. From the business practitioners' perspective, M&As provide a very useful tool to relatively rapidly achieve the desired network position and structure. However, it is important to note that M&As are highly risky ventures, and their success depends largely on a successful post-acquisition integration phase (cf. Buono and Bowditch, 1989; Cartwright and Cooper, 1993; Birkinshaw et al., 2000; Stahl and Voight, 2008). The level of investment on the post-acquisition integration phase depends obviously on the initial M&A motives, that is, whether the business has been acquired to be integrated and to what extent, or to be terminated. Policymakers have traditionally monitored M&As to ensure that no company in a market and industry segment receives a ruling market share. However, a deeper understanding of the network positions and structures would enable a deeper and more systematic analysis of the competitive situation.

Acknowledgements

The authors wish to warmly thank all the reviewers of earlier versions of this chapter. We also wish to thank the Academy of Finland (VCIG project 26080068), the Foundation for Economic Education and Marcus Wallenberg Foundation for their financial support during this research.

References

Anderson, H., Andersson, P., Havila, V. and Salmi, A. (2000). 'Business network dynamics and M&As: Structural and processual connectedness', Paper presented at the 16th IMP Conference, Bath, UK.
Anderson, H., Havila, V. and Salmi, A. (2001). 'Can you buy a business relationship? – On the importance of customer and supplier relationships in acquisitions', *Industrial Marketing Management*, 30(7), 575–586.
Ansoff, H.I. (1965). *Corporate Strategy*. New York: McGraw-Hill.
Araujo, L. and Easton G. (1996). 'Networks in socio-economic systems: A critical review', in: D. Iacobucci (ed.), *Networks in Marketing*. Newbury Park, CA: Sage.

Axelsson, B. and Johanson, J. (1992). 'Foreign market entry: The textbook vs. the network view', in B. Axelsson and G. Easton (eds), *Industrial Networks: A New View of Reality*. London: Routledge.

Barney, J.B. (1991). 'Firm resources and sustained competitive advantage', *Journal of Management*, 17(1), 99–120.

Benson, J.K. (1975). 'The interorganisational network as a political economy', *Administrative Science Quarterly*, 20(2), 229–249.

Birkinshaw, J., Bresman, H. and Håkanson, L. (2000). 'Managing the post-acquisition integration process: How the human integration and task integration processes interact to foster value creation', *Journal of Management Studies*, 37(3), 395–425.

Borch, O.J. and Arthur, M.B. (1995). 'Strategic networks among small firms: Implications for strategy research methodology', *Journal of Management Studies*, 32(4), 419–441.

Buono, A.F. and Bowditch, James L. (1989). *The Human Side of Mergers and Acquisitions – Managing Collisions between People, Cultures, and Organisations*. Jossey-Bass Inc.: San Francisco.

Burt, R.S. (1992). *Structural Holes: The Social Structure of Competition*. Cambridge, MA: Harvard University Press.

Calipha, R., Tarba, S. and Brock D. (2010). 'Mergers and acquisitions: A review of phases, motives and success factors', in S. Finkelstein and C. Cooper (eds), *Advances in Mergers and Acquisitions*. Bradford, UK: Emerald Group Publishing Ltd.

Cartwright, S. and Schoenberg, R. (2006). 'Thirty years of mergers and acquisitions research: Recent advances and future opportunities', *British Journal of Management*, 17(S1), 1–5.

Cartwright, S. and Cooper, C.L. (1993). 'The role of culture compatibility in successful organisational marriage', *Academy of Management Executive*, 7(2), 57–70.

Coleman, J.S. (1988). 'Social capital in the creation of human capital', *American Journal of Sociology*, 94(1), 95–120.

Craninckx, K. and Huyghebaert, N. (2014). 'Large shareholders and value creation through corporate acquisitions in Europe. The identity of the controlling shareholder matters', *European Management Journal*, forthcoming (in press).

Datta, D.K. (1991). 'Organisational fit and acquisition performance: Effects on post-acquisition integration', *Strategic Management Journal*, 12(4), 281–297.

Degbey, W.Y. (2015). 'Customer retention: A source of value for serial acquirers', *Industrial Marketing Management*, 46(1), 11–23.

Degbey, W.Y. and Pelto, E. (2013). 'Cross-border M&A as a trigger for network change in the Russian bakery industry', *Journal of Business and Industrial Marketing*, 28(3), 178–189.

——— (2015). 'Uncovering different forms of customer network changes in mergers and acquisitions', *Management Research Review*, 38(11), forthcoming.

DePamphilis, D. (2011). *Mergers and M&A Basics: All You Need to Know*. Oxford: Elsevier Inc.

Dikova, D. and Sahib, P.R. (2013). 'Is cultural distance a bane or a boon for cross-border acquisition performance?', *Journal of World Business*, 48(1), 77–86.

Easton, G. (1998). 'Case research as a methodology for industrial networks: A realist apologia', in P. Naude and P.W. Turnbull (eds), *Network Dynamics in International Marketing*, Oxford: Elsevier Science.

——— (1992). 'Industrial networks: A review', in B. Axelsson and G. Easton (eds), *Industrial Networks: A New View of Reality*. London: Routledge.

Eisenhardt, K.M. (1989). 'Building theories from case study research', *Academy of Management Review*, 14(4), 532–550.

European Commission (2008). *General Report on the Activities of the European Union*, Luxembourg. available at: http://europa.eu/generalreport/pdf/rg2008_en.pdf.

Ferriani, S., Fonti, F. and Corrado, R. (2013). 'The social and economic bases of network multiplexity: Exploring the emergence of multiplex ties', *Strategic Organisation*, 11(1), 7–34.

Ford, D. and Håkansson, H. (2006). 'IMP – some things achieved: Much more to do', *European Journal of Marketing*, 40(3/4), 248–258.

Ford, D., Gadde, L.-E., Håkansson, H. and Snehota, I. (2003). *Managing Business Relationships*, 2nd edition. Chichester: Wiley.

Gadde, L.-E., Huemer, L. and Håkansson, H. (2003). 'Strategizing in industrial networks', *Industrial Marketing Management*, (32)5, 357–364.

Ghoshal, S. and Bartlett, C.A. (1990). 'The multinational corporation as an interorganisational network', *The Academy of Management Review*, (15)4, 603–625.

Golfetto, F., Salle, R., Borghini, S. and Rinallo, D. (2007). 'Opening the network: Bridging the IMP tradition and other research perspectives', *Industrial Marketing Management*, 36(7), 844–848.

Gomes, E., Angwin, D.N., Weber, Y. and Tarba, S.Y. (2013). 'Critical success factors through the mergers and acquisitions process: Revealing pre- and post- M&A connections for improved performance', *Thunderbird International Business Review*, 55(1), 13–35.

Grandori, A. and Soda, G. (1995). 'Inter-firm networks: Antecedents, mechanisms and forms', *Organisation Studies*, 16(2), 183–214.

Gulati, R., Nohria, N. and Zaheer, A. (2000). 'Strategic networks', *Strategic Management Journal*, 21(3), 203–215.

——— (1998). 'Alliances and networks', *Strategic Management Journal*, 19(4), 293–317.

Håkansson, H. and Ford, D. (2002). 'How should companies interact in business networks?', *Journal of Business Research*, 55(2), 133–139.

Håkansson, H. and Snehota, I. (1989). 'No business is an island: The network concept of business strategy', *Scandinavian Journal of Management*, 4(3), 187–200.

Haleblian, J., Devers, C.E., McNamara, G., Carpenter, M.A. and Davison, R.B. (2009). 'Taking stock of what we know about mergers and acquisitions: A review and research agenda', *Journal of Management*, 35(3), 469–502.

Halinen, A. and Törnroos, J.Å. (2005). 'Using case methods in the study of contemporary business networks', *Journal of Business Research*, 58(9), 1287–1297.

Harrison, D. and Prenkert, F. (2009). 'Network strategising trajectories within a planned strategy process', *Industrial Marketing Management*, 38(6), 662–670.

Haspeslagh, P.C. and Jemison, D.B. (1991). *Managing Acquisitions: Creating Value through Corporate Renewal*. New York: The Free Press.

Hatani, F. and McGaughey, S.L. (2013). 'Network cohesion in global expansion: An evolutionary view', *Journal of World Business*, 48(4), 455–465.

Havila, V. and Salmi, A. (2000). 'Spread of change in business networks: An empirical study of mergers and acquisitions in the graphic industry', *Journal of Strategic Marketing*, 8(2), 105–119.

Hitt, M.A., Harrison, J.S. and Ireland, R.D. (2001). *Mergers and Acquisitions: A Guide to Creating Value for Stakeholders*. New York: Oxford University Press.

Hitt, M.A., Harrison, J.S., Ireland, R.D. and Best, A. (1998). 'Attributes of successful and unsuccessful acquisitions of US firms', *British Journal of Management*, 9(2), 91–114.

Jagersma, P.K. (2005). 'Cross-border acquisitions of European multinationals', *Journal of General Management*, 30(3), 13–34.

Jarillo, J.C. (1988). 'On Strategic Networks', *Strategic Management Journal*, 9(1), 31–41.

Johanson, J. and Mattsson, L.G. (1987). 'Interorganisational relations in indus-
trial systems: A network approach compared with the transaction-cost approach',
International Studies of Management and Organisation, 17(1), 34–48.
—— (1992). 'Network positions and strategic action – an analytical framework'. In B.
Axelsson and G. Easton (eds), *In Industrial Networks: A New View of Reality.* London:
Routledge.
Johanson, J. and Vahlne, J.-E. (1992) 'Management of Foreign market entry', *Scandinavian
International Business Review,* 1(3), 9–27.
—— (2009). 'The Uppsala internationalisation process model revisited: From liability
of foreignness to liability of outsidership', *Journal of International Business Studies,*
40(9), 1411–1431.
—— (2011). 'Markets as networks: Implications for strategy-making', *Journal of the
Academy of Marketing Science,* 39(4), 484–491.
King, D.R., Dalton, D.R., Daily, C.M. and Covin, J.G. (2004). 'Meta-analyses of post-acquisition performance: Indications of unidentified moderators', *Strategic Management
Journal,* 25(2), 187–200.
Kohli, R. and Mann, B.J.S. (2012). 'Analyzing determinants of value creation in domestic
and cross border acquisitions in India', *International Business Review,* 21(6), 998–1016.
Larsson, R. and Finkelstein, S. (1999). 'Integrating strategic, organisational, and human
resource perspectives on mergers and acquisitions: A case survey of synergy real-
isation', *Organisation Science,* 10(1), 1–26.
McEvily, B. and Marcus, A. (2005). 'Embedded ties and the acquisition of competitive
capabilities', *Strategic Management Journal,* 26(11), 1033–1055.
Möller, K. and Rajala, A. (2007). 'Rise of strategic nets: New modes of value creation',
Industrial Marketing Management, 36(7), 895–908.
Morosini, P. and Singh, H. (1994). 'Post-cross-border acquisitions: Implementing national
culture compatible strategies to improve performance', *European Management Journal,*
12(4), 390–400.
Moschieri, C. and Campa, J.M. (2009). 'The European M&A industry: A market in the
process of construction', *The Academy of Management Perspectives,* 23(4), 71–87.
Nyström, A.G., Ramström, J. and Törnroos, J.Å. (2008). 'Coping with Business Network
Dynamics: Strategizing through Role and Position', *24th Annual IMP Conference,*
Uppsala.
Öberg, C., Henneberg, S.C. and Mouzas, S. (2007). 'Changing network pictures: Evidence
from mergers and acquisitions', *Industrial Marketing Management,* 36(7), 926–940.
Oliver, A.L. and Ebers, M. (1998). 'Networking network studies: An analysis of con-
ceptual configurations in the study of inter-organisational relationships', *Organisation
Studies,* 19(4), 549–583.
Porter, M.E. (1980). *Competitive Strategy: Techniques for Analyzing Industries and Competitors.*
New York: Free Press.
Riviezzo, A. (2013). 'Acquisitions in knowledge-intensive industries: Exploring the dis-
tinctive characteristics of the effective acquirer', *Management Research Review,* 36(2),
183–212.
Schoenberg, R. (2006). 'Measuring the performance of corporate acquisition: An
empirical comparison of alternative metrics', *British Journal of Management,* 17(4),
361–370.
Seth, A. (1990a). 'Value creation in acquisitions: A reexamination of performance issues',
Strategic Management Journal, 11(2), 99–115.
—— (1990b). 'Sources of value creation in acquisitions: An empirical investigation',
Strategic Management Journal, 11(6), 431–446.

Shaver, M.J. (2006). 'A paradox of synergy: Contagion and capacity effects in mergers and acquisitions', *Academy of Management Review*, 31(4), 962–976.

Shimizu, K. (2007). 'Prospect theory, behavioral theory, and the threat-rigidity thesis: Combinative effects on organisational decisions to divest formerly acquired Units', *Academy of Management Review*, 50(6), 1495–1514.

Shimizu, K., Hitt, M.A., Vaidyahath, D. and Pisano, V. (2004). 'Theoretical foundation of cross-border mergers and acquisitions: A review of current research and recommendations for the future'. *Journal of International Management*, 10(3), 307–353.

Siggelkow, N. (2007). 'Persuasion with case studies', *Academy of Management Journal*, 50(1), 20–24.

Slangen, A.H.L. (2006). 'National cultural distance and initial foreign acquisition performance', *Journal of World Business*, 41(2), 161–170.

Stahl, G.K. and Voigt, A. (2008). 'Do cultural differences matter in mergers and acquisitions? A tentative model and examination', *Organisation Science*, 19(1), 160–176.

Storbacka, K. and Nenonen, S. (2009). 'Customer relationships and the heterogeneity of the firm performance', *Journal of Business and Industrial Marketing*, 24(5/6), 360–372.

Teerikangas, S. and Very, P. (2006). 'The culture-performance relationship in M&A: From yes/no to how', *British Journal of Management*, 17(1), 31–48.

Thorelli, H.B. (1986). 'Networks: Between markets and hierarchies', *Strategic Management Journal*, 7(1), 37–51.

Turnbull, P., Ford, D. and Cunningham, M. (1996). 'Interaction, relationships and networks in business markets: An evolving perspective', *Journal of Business and Industrial Marketing*, 11(3/4), 44–62.

Van de Ven, A.H. (1976). 'On the nature, formation, and maintenance of relations among organisations', *Academy of Management Review*, 1(4), 24–36.

Very, P., Lubatkin, M. and Calori, R. (1996). 'A cross-national assessment of acculturative stress in recent European mergers', *International Studies of Management and Organisation*, 26(1), 59–86.

Wernerfelt, B. (1984). 'A resource-based view of the firm', *Strategic Management Journal*, 15(22), 171–180.

World Investment Report (2014). *Investing in the SDG's – An Action Plan*. United Nations Publications: Geneva.

Yin, R. (2003). *Case Study Research. Applied Social Research Methods Series*, 3rd ed. Thousands Oak, CA: Sage Publications.

Zaheer, A. and Bell, G.G. (2005). 'Benefiting from network position: Firm capabilities, structural holes and performance', *Strategic Management Journal*, 26(9), 809–825.

10
Single or Hybrid Career Paths of MNC RD&E Employees?
Emmanouil Sofikitis, Dimitris Manolopoulos and Pavlos Dimitratos

Introduction

Recent developments in the career choice literature have shown a clear transition from the traditional view of linear career paths to a multiple career theoretical approach (Feldman and Ng, 2007). During the past decade, researchers have concentrated much more on the inevitability of career change and its benefits than on its infrequency and drawbacks (Feldman, 2002). Thus, traditional perceptions and models that marginalised the multidirectional career view are commonly considered aged and obsolete.

This contemporary view of multiple individual career paths is not without criticism (Guest and Rodrigues, 2014). Recently, Rodrigues et al. (2014) argued that boundaryless careers are associated with losses both for the employers and the employees. McDonald et al. (2005) find that traditional career paths are still present at least in the public sector, and, Inkson et al. (2012) propose that boundary-focused career studies need further development. In the same vein, some authors hold the view that stability and the vertical progression in the organisation can still be conceived as a powerful theoretical basis to facilitate empirical research (e.g. Baruch, 2006; Ituma and Simpson, 2009).

Existing evidence is contradictory and far from conclusive; hence, no dominance of a particular career form appears to exist (Inkson et al., 2012). Our current empirical study does not support one particular approach against the other. Instead, it holds that the choice over a stable or dynamic career path is a matter of individual and contextual factors (Duffy and Dik, 2009; Savickas et al., 2009).

Viewed in this light, we seek to explore the impact of the employee work environment as well as employee-related factors on their intention to choose a single over a hybrid career path (among managerial, technical, entrepreneurial or project-based paths). A single career path reflects the employee intended devotion to a sole career (e.g. technical path), while a hybrid one represents his intended choice to follow multiple alternatives (e.g. a technical path followed by managerial path advancement).

The examination of single versus hybrid career paths contributes to the existing literature in four ways. First, the career literature has largely investigated occupational groups such as accountants and healthcare employees (Ozbilgin et al., 2005), leaving surprising research space for the category of knowledge professionals. This paper particularly focuses on employees in research, development and engineering (RD&E) activities employed in multinational corporations (MNCs); these employees are fundamental contributors to the MNC competitive advantage (Redpath et al., 2009), yet have received substantially less attention (Manolopoulos, 2006). Second, recent studies argue that human behaviour is not only a function of the person but also of the environment (Savickas et al., 2009). This chapter examines individual characteristics and responds also to the calls for input of the work context; specifically, it incorporates the strategic roles of R&D units which, to the best of our knowledge, has not been examined hitherto. Third, it adds evidence to the debate of whether employees stay strictly on one career route or desire the multiple alternative one. Fourth, most of the existing empirical evidence relates to MNCs based in developed economies (mainly in the United States). Our study contributes to the investigation of the phenomenon in under-investigated countries, as it was conducted in Greece. Greece is a European and Monetary Union country that has significant levels of human capital, and although it is currently under conditions of economic recession, it has traditionally drawn the attention of many MNCs to establish R&D units.

Theoretical background: traditional versus boundaryless approaches

Early conceptualisations of careers support the view that 'a career is a succession of related jobs, arranged in a hierarchy of prestige, through which persons move in an ordered, predictable sequence' (Wilensky, 1960, p. 554). The notion of *traditional careers* is grounded in hierarchical and rigid structures that resemble the typical public service career structure (Smith, 1993). The traditional career ensures security of tenure and linear promotion based on seniority and length of service. It is primarily defined in terms of an individual relationship to an employer where the latter is in control of the employee career structure. Career changes and mobility are rather infrequent in this respect.

During the last decade, criticism on traditional theoretical approaches rose in response to rapid changes in the work environment, such as corporate restructuring, internationalisation, recession and technological advancements (Kirchmeyer, 2006), as well as changes in the demographic trends, notably increased female employment, dual-career couples, and the rise of part-time employment in response to high pension liabilities and insurance costs (London and Greller, 1991). In addition to the new employment opportunities that emerged (e.g. the Internet as an inexpensive tool to engage in entrepreneurial activity), they have all doubted the durability and validity of the patterns described by the traditional view.

Following the scepticism towards the linear career model, the concept of *boundaryless career* has been coined to offer an alternative in career theories. Made popular by Arthur and Rousseau (1996), the term embraces the belief that careers are independent from traditional organisational arrangements (DeFillipi and Arthur, 1994). It brings forward the idea that individuals are proactive creators of their own career and–among others–includes careers that (a) move across the boundaries of separate employers; (b) break traditional organisational assumptions about hierarchy and career advancement; (c) are affected by personal or family reasons (Arthur and Rousseau, 1996). A common criterion by which a boundaryless career is distinguished from the traditional one is the frequent employee mobility across organisations (Becker and Haunschild, 2003; Lazarova and Taylor, 2009). Other ideas explored in this concept include the borders of employee choices related to occupation, industry and country (Inkson et al., 2012).

The boundaryless career concept has gained extensive credence in career research, providing practical implications for both individuals and organisations (Sullivan and Baruch, 2009; Baruch et al., 2015). Yet, recent contributions highlight the need to reconsider its undisputed dominance. Stevens (2005) in a longitudinal objective data study provides strong support that the frequent career changes apply only to some individuals and contexts. Following Brousseau et al. (1996), Pringle and Mallon (2003) warn of the risk of replacing one normative career form with another. At the same time, Baruch (2006) argues that the traditional career system, while not being the norm, is definitely not abandoned. This may be more applicable to specific workforce categories that have not been extensively investigated (other than management-educated employees, women or other minorities; see Currie et al., 2006).

The career choice question is evidently still open to investigation. Our premise is that both the boundaryless and the boundary-focused career conceptualisations serve as fruitful fields of investigation, and it is rather a matter of *individual* and *contextual* factors what influences the choice between the two valid options (single and hybrid paths).

Empirical research is largely engaged in the investigation of individual characteristics (highlighting cognitive traits, e.g. Dik et al., 2008). Regarding demographics, what we know is their significant presence in the career-shaping procedure (Krieshok, 1998). What we still lack is the clear direction of their effect (Patton and Creed, 2001). Career decision-making scholars now direct their attention to the vocational interests of undergraduate students and leave demographic variables 'loosely specified and unmeasured, creating a black box' (Lawrence, 1997, p. 2; Bowen and Ostroff, 2004).

Further, following the pronounced attention in individual agency that is closely associated with the boundaryless career concept, there are few empirical studies on the examination of the diverse contextual influence (Pringle and Mallon, 2003). Tams and Arthur (2010, p. 638) argue that 'attention to the contexts in which agency is situated is essential to unpack the relationship between people's enactment of agency and its outcomes', and Mayrhofer et al. (2007) support the notion that the contextual influence constrains even the most agentic actors (e.g. information and technology workers found to be constrained by several institutional contexts; Ituma and Simpson, 2009). It emerges as vital that social subsystems and structures are not viewed as independent entities from the employee career decision-making (Ozbilgin et al., 2005).

The stability versus mobility intentions of knowledge professionals are reflected in the dilemma between the traditional and the boundaryless theoretical concepts. Regarding the latter, career scholars attempted to capture the degree of 'boundarylessness' in the past decade using diverse constructs that mainly measure employee job post or organisation mobility (Inkson et al., 2012). In the current study, we focus on the career change component of the boundaryless concept, which has received significantly less attention (Sullivan, 1999).

Research background and hypotheses

Types of R&D units

In the current study, we refer to two types of MNC R&D laboratories which can be *asset exploiting* or *asset augmenting*. The laboratories characterised as asset exploiting fall into the type of 'Support Laboratory' (SL) which is classified as such in the comprehensive typologies of Haug et al. (1983) and Hood and Young (1982). These particular R&D units deal with the effective implementation of well-existing technologies and procedures of the MNC with a view to becoming embodied in the production process of well-established products.

The second type of R&D laboratories refers to the asset augmenting units. The description of those laboratories match that of 'Locally Integrated Laboratories' (LILs) and 'Internationally Interdependent Laboratories' (IILs) which have been incorporated in the studies of Haug et al. (1983) and Hood and Young (1982). LILs seek to operate as a closely integrated part of a subsidiary in order to develop distinctive products. This suggests that LILs have a 'productive' scope and a more empowered role than SLs (Papanastassiou and Pearce, 1999). IILs refer to the provision of basic or applied research inputs into a programme of pre-competitive work undertaken by the MNC. They have a close coordination not only with the subsidiary's functional departments but also with MNC laboratories in other countries, as well as with the parent laboratory (Pearce, 1999).

RD&E employees in asset exploiting laboratories show higher levels of MNC embeddedness and apparently follow closely the mandates of the headquarters (Manolopoulos, 2006).They show low levels of flexibility and autonomy in work-related tasks which is additionally corroborated by the fact that they predominantly choose to seek international assignments only in parent laboratories rather than other MNC subsidiaries or host country R&D facilities (Manolopoulos et al., 2010). These characteristics counter evidence to the free and flexible notion of boundaryless careers and resemble the more rigid structures of traditional patterns.

On the contrary, RD&E professionals employed in asset augmenting laboratories are quite autonomous, and their everyday tasks are largely unstandardised and not so formalised (Pearce and Papanastasiou, 1997). This is because the influence of headquarters in the operations of their R&D units is relatively weak. Given the likely autonomy and flexibility that these employees possess away from parent-firm pressure, one may expect that their behaviour will be in accordance with the significant levels of independence and leeway that other career paths (such as the entrepreneurial) incorporate (Stewart and Roth, 2007). Crossing boundaries may be relatively more intimate to them, and consequently expected to lean towards other paths. Altogether, we posit:

> *Hypothesis 1*: Other things being equal, knowledge professionals employed in asset exploiting laboratories are more likely to prefer a single career path, while knowledge professionals employed in asset augmenting laboratories are more likely to prefer a hybrid career path.

Employee demographic variables

Age. A large-sample survey conducted in the mid-2000s reports that the average job tenure in the United States and Western Europe for employees under 30 years old varies between two and three years while the respective average for employees over 50 ranges between 13 and 20 years, depending on the country (OECD, 2006). Alongside, Warr (1997) postulates that older employees exhibit a higher need for career security, which is further confirmed in the case of RD&E professionals (Igbaria et al., 1999). More recent evidence supports the view that young employees 'may welcome changing career boundaries' (Currie et al., 2006) while older individuals are less likely to prefer a career change (Cheramie et al., 2007).

McCathy and Garavan (2006) report that older employees show low levels of behavioural change. In a related vein, authors investigating behavioural change in the career development field find that older employees are less receptive to making changes (Ryan, Brutus, Greguras and Hakel, 2000). Openness to new experiences (a concept closely tied to the boundaryless mindset construct; see Briscoe et al. 2006) is found to be positively related to young employees (Warr and Birdi, 1998). Taking also into consideration Lyons et al.'s recent (2015) suggestion that job mobility is more common among young employees, we posit that:

Hypothesis 2a: Other things being equal, older knowledge professionals are more likely to prefer a single career path, while younger ones are more likely to choose a hybrid path.

Educational background. Employees with managerial education are mostly expected to either follow managerial posts (Manolopoulos et al., 2011; Igbaria et al., 1991) or be engaged in entrepreneurial activity (Chianglin et al., 2004). Technical-oriented careers are mostly preferred by employees with technical background (Allen and Katz, 1992).

Research on employees with managerial education does not provide evidence for mixed career routes (i.e. managerial and technical). That is, they intend to follow a single managerial route.MBA graduates especially are generally thought to have concrete career directions (Simmering and Wilcox, 1995). Seemingly, they are more focused and display high introspection when formulating career plans, which implies their focus on specific career targets (Beutell and O'Hare, 2006). As Baruch and Peiperl (2000) identify, employees that hold an MBA degree score higher on self-efficacy compared to their colleagues with different educational background. Higher levels of self-efficacy are associated with higher decisiveness in respect to career decision-making (Betz and Voyten, 1997), which entails a single career preference.

Employees that hold a technical degree (which is very likely the case of MNC RD&E knowledge professionals; Wynarczyk and Renner, 2006) are recipients of rather unfavourable perceptions. To illustrate, as Ituma and Simpson (2009) posit, polytechnic graduates are believed to be of lower social status compared to those that hold a university degree. Given that the managerial path is especially associated with higher status quo, prestige, social recognition and higher economic return, technically educated professionals are often expected to shift to this path (Erdoğmus, 2004); that is, they are expected to follow a mixed, hybrid path.

Hypothesis 2b: Other things being equal, knowledge professionals with technical educational background are more likely to prefer a hybrid path, while knowledge professionals with managerial educational background are more likely to prefer a single career path.

Gender. Prior research indicates that women are less inclined to change careers (Sullivan and Arthur, 2006). This is attributed to the barriers women face due to gender discrimination that, in turn, restricts them from developing competencies that would eventually enhance their career mobility (Ituma and Simpson, 2009). Other restrictions relate to more work/family balance (Litzky and Greenhaus, 2007). Forret et al. (2010) contend that a woman's physical mobility is often bounded by her relationships and commitments to others. For instance, they support the idea that women are more likely to be reluctant to travel or be relocated as this would reduce family time and keep them away from elderly relatives who need assistance. Being favoured by societal norms and expectations, men, on the other hand, have a lot more freedom to engage in physical mobility (across firms or industries; Sullivan and Arthur, 2006). Focusing on the change of career (rather than the mobility across organisations), we posit that:

> *Hypothesis 2c*: Other things being equal, male knowledge professionals are more likely to prefer a hybrid career path while female knowledge professional are more likely to choose a single path.

Marital status. Groeneveld (2008), focusing especially on the careers of diplomats, posits that, until recently, spouses had simply been expected to give up their own career and follow a different one if their partner was offered an overseas post. However, he continues that with an increasing number of dual-career couples nowadays, this is not the case. As Reynolds and Bennett (1991) argue, spouses are more and more not willing to give up their careers when they encounter the aforementioned circumstances.

Further, marriage creates an environment of stability and avoidance of behavioural changes. This is why Felmlee (1984) posits that it creates constraints that limit the possibilities of career mobility. Married employees (especially female ones) are not willing to change their career route in the case of a job relocation offer, even for improved job opportunities (Markham and Pleck, 1986; Markham et al., 1983). Thus, they may not be willing to be engaged in a multiple career route. Such behaviour can be attributed to either the involvement and satisfaction or the attachment of the employee to his or her environment. Authors find a negative correlation between the extent to which individuals are linked to other people (Mitchell et al., 2001) and their willingness to leave current job posts (Feldman and Bolino, 1998; Fisher and Shaw, 1994).

Except for the concept of job relocation that has most evidently been researched in the literature, we may extend the argument to all possible cases of occupational changes of spouses. We speculate that:

> *Hypothesis 2d:* Other things being equal, married knowledge professionals are more likely to prefer a single career path, while single knowledge professionals are more likely to prefer a hybrid career path.

Methodology

Data collection

The sample for this study was drawn from the population of MNC subsidiaries based in Greece. The International Capital (ICAP) database was the sampling frame employed. This database is the most comprehensive sampling frame that exists in Greece. In total, 317 subsidiaries of different MNCs were included in this database. The sectors of investigated subsidiaries incorporated automobiles and transport equipment, electronics and information technology, manufacturing, chemicals and pharmaceuticals, food and beverages, textiles and services. Examined MNCs originated primarily from the EU, United States and Japan.

The study was conducted in two stages. The first stage involved a national questionnaire-based postal survey in order to identify MNC subsidiaries that had an R&D department. Questionnaires were posted to subsidiary CEOs to acquire this necessary information. Out of 315 subsidiaries, 133 usable responses were collected (two questionnaires from the original 317 firms were returned undelivered). Consequently, the effective response rate for this first stage is 42 per cent, which is deemed to be perfectly acceptable when compared with similar postal surveys (Harzing, 1997). Among those 133 subsidiaries, 70 had an R&D department.

The second stage of the study involved a survey on career preferences of knowledge professionals of MNC R&D laboratories in Greece. The questionnaire was pre-tested by two academics, two professional consultants, five MNC subsidiary CEOs and ten RD&E professionals. In the 70 R&D laboratories identified from the first stage of the study, all employed RD&E professionals were posted the questionnaire. Out of the 948 initially posted questionnaires and following two reminders, 598 fully usable questionnaires were collected. In addition, a research assistant solicited telephone responses from 323 RD&E employees who did not respond through the post, bringing the total number of responses of full-time professionals to 921. Therefore, the effective response rate of the second stage of the research is a remarkable 97 per cent (921/948). No statistically significant differences among respondents through the post, respondents through the telephone and non-respondents were obtained in relation to the number of R&D employees and years of operations of the laboratories. Consequently, response bias does not appear to constitute a threat to the results.

Measures and method

In order to test the hypotheses, a logistic regression model was run with the career preferences of the RD&E employees. The dependent variable in the regression examination is the RD&E employee intention to follow a single career path or a hybrid one. Respondents were asked to provide information on whether they showed preference on multiple career paths or were determined to select a single career during the period of the coming three to five years (cf. Gardner, 1990). The dependent variable is captured through a dummy variable whereby 1 reflects the knowledge professionals that have reported a desired hybrid path while 0 refers to the knowledge professionals that have shown preference for a single path. Out of 921 respondents in 70 MNC R&D units, 603 professionals (i.e. 65.5 per cent) reported a preference for a single path whereas 318 (i.e. 34.5 per cent) favoured a hybrid route. Measures of the dependent variables incorporated in the model are presented in Figure 10.1.

Findings and discussion

Means, standard deviations and correlation patterns among the variables of current research are reported in Figure 10.2. The strongest positive correlation coefficients were found to be, first, the one between the marital status of the respondent and his/her age; and second, the correlation coefficient between the gender of the employee and his/her age. The correlation between the age of respondent and the desired career path was the strongest negative coefficient. Multicollinearity seemingly is not a source of bias, and therefore does not pose a threat to the regressions results reported in this chapter. The estimation of variance inflation factors for the regression variables resulted in values close to 1, which are significantly lower than the accepted cut-off value of 10. This provides further support that multicollinearity does not constitute a problem to the results reported (cf. Netter et al., 1996).

Figure 10.3 presents the results of the logistic regression model. The eight independent and control variables were regressed on the professional desired career path which forms the dummy dependent variable of the study. The pseudo R^2 value in the regression model is 22 per cent, which is satisfactory taking into consideration the cross-sectional and cross-national nature of the sample. The F ratio is large with corresponding statistically significant levels.

Based on the logistic regression model, the results show that hypotheses 1 and 2d are supported while the remaining are not. In the main, three out of five hypotheses showed strong statistical significance, with the remaining two being weak predictors for single versus hybrid career path preference of RD&E professionals. Specifically, the types of R&D laboratories variable was statistically significant at a level of 0.01 and two out of the four employee-related variables (namely age and marital status) were found to be significant at a level of 0.05. The remaining two variables incorporated in the employee-related category, that is, educational background and gender appear to be significant only at a 0.1 level, suggesting that they are weak predictors of RD&E professionals' career path preference.

As discussed, the literature does not focus on RD&E knowledge professionals, and therefore our conjecture on both employee-related factors that were found

Variables	As appear in the empirical part	Type[1]	Operational definition
			In order to evaluate laboratories' role respondents were asked to grade each of the following roles in terms of the importance in the operations of the R&D lab as being: (i) not part of their role, (ii) main role, (iii) secondary role and (iv) only role:
Types of R& D units			(1) Adaptation of existing products and/or processes to make them more suitable to our markets and conditions; (2) To play a role in the development of new products for our distinctive markets; (3) To carry out basic research (not directly related to the current products) as part of a wider MNE group level research programme
Asset Exploiting	ASSEXP	B/D	Laboratory that adapt existing products and/or processes (4=only role, 3=main role, 2=secondary role, 1=not part of role)
Demographic			
Age of Researcher	AGERES	L/D	According to the date of researchers' birth three categories were created: R&D professionals over 45 years old take the value of 3, professionals between 36–45 take the value of 2, professionals under 36 years old take the value of 1
Educational Background	EDU	B/D	1=Researcher with a technical oriented background, 0=Researcher with a managerial oriented / other educational background
Gender	MALE	B/D	1=Male, 0=Female
Marital Status	MARRIED	B/D	1=Married, 0=Single
Control Variables			
Nationality of the Respondent	NR	B/D	1=Greek, 0=Foreign employee (e.g. Srivastava, Blakely, Andrews, and McKee-Ryan, 2007)
Technological Intensity of the Sector	HIGHTECH	B/D	1=Firm in highly-intensive tech, 0=in medium- or low-technology sector (Pearce, 1994), high-technology sectors included MNC operations in telecommunications, electronics and information technology, chemicals and pharmaceuticals)
Prior Working Experience	PWE		Logarithm of the number of years the RD&E professional has spent in related previous working experience (e.g. Dokko, Wilk, and Rothbard, 2009)

Figure 10.1   Operationalisation of variables

Notes: [1] Binary (B); / Likert - Type (L); / Continuous (C); Discrete (D).

Variable	Rubric	Mean	Std. Deviation	Min	Max	1	2	3	4	5	6	7	8	9
y	HYB	0.34	.108	0	1	1								
x_1	ASEXP	0.78	.654	0	1	-.457**	1							
x_2	AGERES	1.52	.775	1	3	.252	.185	1						
x_3	EDU	2.36	.854	1	3	.274	-.339**	-.181	1					
x_4	NR	0.92	.785	0	1	-.189	.206	-.153	.261	1				
x_5	MALE	.62	.449	0	1	.331**	-.327*	.488***	-.087	-.422**	1			
x_6	MARRIED	.60	.417	0	1	-.415**	.274	.509***	.336**	-.291*	-.368**	1		
x_7	HIGHTECH	.31	.107	0	1	.227	-.388***	-.232	.108	-.115	.177	-.085	1	
x_8	PWE	4.1	2.7	0.301	1.176	-.194	.109	.346**	-.164	-.094	.204	.109	-.216	1

Figure 10.2 Descriptive statistics and correlation

Note: * significant at .10, ** significant at .05, *** significant at .001.

Variables	Regression Results (Ordered Probit)
x_1 – ASEXP	−747***
	(.225)
x_2 – AGERES	.554**
	(.251)
x_3 – EDU	.256*
	(.104)
x_4 – NR	−.624
	(.598)
x_5 – MALE	.385*
	(.164)
x_6 – MARRIED	−.482**
	(.204)
x_7 – HIGHTECH	.754
	(.601)
x_8 – PWE	−.332*
	(.181)
Pseudo R square	0.22
F	5.37***
n = 921	

Figure 10.3   Logistic regression results

Notes: * Significant at .10, ** significant at .05, *** significant at .001. Figure in ( ) is standard error.

weak predictors (i.e. educational background and gender) was not strictly in line with the special needs and preferences of this particular employee category. Thus, the education and gender results may be attributed to this particular lack of RD&E career evidence in the literature hitherto (Manolopoulos et al., 2011).

In line with our expectations in hypothesis 1 are the findings that knowledge professionals working in asset exploiting R&D units prefer a single career path. Their colleagues in asset augmenting laboratories were found to prefer a hybrid one. This is in accordance with previous literature on the RD&E employee profiles (Pearce and Papanastassiou, 1997). Extending this finding, one may imply a positive relationship between employee autonomy and job mobility, which is seemingly contradictory to Igbaria and Siegel's (1992) argument about a negative association of the aforementioned variables.

It is noteworthy that MNC RD&E professionals constitute a special employee category that may be particularly different from other employee groups in respect to the desire for a single career path versus a multiple one (Petroni, 2000). Hence, MNC managers that deal with career advancements (e.g. such as the dual ladder system), should take into consideration the likely intentions employees may have. Professionals employed in asset exploiting units are likely to be quite autonomous and open to change. The evidence suggests that managers should provide them with motives such as challenging tasks and opportunities for learning (Amabile et al., 1996) in order to increase their job satisfaction and limit their intentions for job shift (Amabile et al., 1996; Igbaria and Siegel, 1992).

The age of researcher was found to be a strong predictor (Loughlin and Barling, 2001), albeit not in the direction we have hypothesised. Hypothesis 2a suggested that older knowledge professionals would more likely prefer a single career path whereas younger ones would follow a multiple career route. However, the results indicate the opposite. These findings may support the notion that younger professionals aim at developing expertise in specific areas that they truly enjoy more than older ones (Kim and McLean, 2008). They present higher levels of excitement towards their careers and need to be self-fulfilled through their work (Lewis et al., 1998). Following the same reasoning, older generations place more importance on job security (Kim and McLean, 2008), and thus are more willing to change career route if this is to secure them. Further, career decisiveness is positively related to one's levels of self-efficacy and self-awareness (Dik et al., 2008; Flum and Blustein, 2000). Previous contributions follow the rationale that as age increases, self-efficacy increases (e.g. Luzzo, 1993), and therefore individuals tend to be more career certain. However, the results provided in the current study show that older individuals are less career certain, which may be in accord with Mauer's (2001) argument that self-efficacy reduces with age. Altogether, MNC managers should identify older R&D knowledge professionals' devotion to current post as they are likely to take control of their own career and seek different career paths.

In hypothesis 2d, we suggested that married knowledge professionals would more likely prefer a single career path, whereas non-married ones would more likely follow a hybrid route. The results concur with our speculations and provide further support to the literature. Individuals shape certain value systems which affect their occupational choice and vocational behaviour (Brief et al., 1979). They seek careers that fit their value systems (Brenner et al., 1988). Married employee reluctance to change may be attributed to their tendency towards values such as the sense of belonging, stability and inner harmony (e.g. Sagiv and Schwartz, 2000), especially within the Greek context. Further, the reasoning that relationship constraints within marriage may not allow high levels of behavioural change can again be in line with the idiosyncrasies of the Greek context in which the current study was conducted. Following Eaton and Bailyn (2000), we posit that providing insights to human resource managers requires the examination of the individuals as they are embedded in their family or community and often engaged in primary relationships with other adults. Marriage often guarantees social recognition and acceptance, and consequently affects pivotal decisions such as the career route. The traditional notion holds that individuals are more actively in search of their orientation until they get married and settle down, and this research supports the view that this notion is in line with the traditional linear career pattern when knowledge professionals are examined.

Conclusions

This study sought to explore R&D knowledge professionals' desire to follow either a single or a hybrid career path. It was undertaken on a large-scale sample of 921 employees in R&D laboratories of MNC subsidiaries in Greece and resulted in a series of findings that suggest important implications for both researchers and managers.

The career-related literature has surprisingly scant empirical evidence on the career orientation of this particular employee category. Our study adds light to a significant but neglected research area. To the best of our knowledge, this study is the first to include the types of R&D laboratories as a predictor of the career choice between a single and a hybrid path. The research findings display the importance of the incorporation of the work environment in such a study. In addition, it provides stimulus for further research.

Managerial and policy implications

This research is particularly useful to organisations as it begets several managerial implications. Schein (1982, 1978) viewed employees' careers as stable throughout their duration, supporting the traditional view. On the contrary, Derr (1986) claimed that modifications in career paths exist always with respect to changes in environment, and Arthur and Rousseau (1996) introduced the boundaryless career concept as the alternative to the traditional path. On the debate of employee preferences on a single, stable career or a multiple path, this research provides evidence that both options are possible depending on the circumstances. Therefore, we posit that there is no clear tendency of knowledge professional choice on either a single or hybrid path. This is in accordance with the critical questioning of the inevitability of the boundaryless view and the respective weakening of the traditional pattern (Baruch, 2006; Inkson et al., 2012). We thus posit that in order to detect their employees' intentions, human resource managers should pay attention to both work environment (i.e. types of R&D units) and employee-related characteristics (i.e. mostly age and marital status). This implies that managers should handle each case differently, depending on the variables discussed (see the contingency approach, e.g. Zeffrane, 1994).

Limitations and future study directions

This study faces limitations that can provide suggestions for further research. Three of them are outlined in this section. First, the findings presented in this research may not be generalisable to other countries, as the study draws from MNC subsidiary operations in Greece. Hence, replication of this research in subsidiaries based in other nations with different levels of technological development is essential. Second, this study captures intended career preferences of knowledge professionals, which can be different from what employees actually did. Future research is likely to seek to discover the extent to which intended and realised career routes overlap. Third, further study should take into consideration features of the national context such as the level of technological advancement of a country and MNC subsidiary roles in this country (cf. Manolopoulos et al., 2007, 2010).

References

Allen, T.J. and Katz, R. (1992). 'Age, education and the technical ladder', *IEEE Transactions on Engineering Management,* 39(3), 237–45.

Amabile, T.M., Conti, R., Coon, H., Lazenby, J. and Herron, M. (1996). 'Assessing work environment for creativity', *Academy of Management Journal,* 39(5), 1154–1184.

Arthur, M.B. and Rousseau, D.M. (1996). *The Boundaryless Career: A New Employment Principle for a New Organisational Era,* Oxford: Oxford University Press.

Baruch, Y. (2006). 'Career development in organisations and beyond: Balancing traditional and contemporary viewpoints', *Human Resource Management Review,* 16(2), 125–138.

Baruch, Y. and Peiperl, M. (2000). 'The impact of an MBA on graduate careers', *Human Resource Management Journal,* 10(2), 69–90.

Baruch, Y., Szucs, N. and Gunz, H. (2015). 'Career studies in search of theory: The rise and rise of concepts', *Career Development International,* 20(1), 3–20.

Becker, K.H. and Haunschild, A. (2003). 'The impact of boundaryless careers on organisational decision making: An analysis from the perspective of Luhmann's theory of social systems', *International Journal of Human Resource Management,* 14(5), 713–727.

Betz, N.E. and Voyten, K. (1997). 'Efficacy and outcome expectations influence career exploration and decidedness', *The Career Development Quarterly,* 46(2), 179–189.

Beutell, I.J. and O'Hare, M.M. (2006). 'Career pathfinders: A qualitative study of career development', *Psychological Reports,* 98(2), 517–528.

Bowen, D.E. and Ostroff, C. (2004). 'Understanding HRM-firm performance linkages: The role of "strength" of the HRM system', *Academy of Management Review,* 29(2), 203–221.

Brenner, O.C., Blazinni, A.P. and Greenhaus, J.H. (1988). 'An examination of race and sex differences in managerial work values', *Journal of Vocational Behaviour,* 32(3), 336–344.

Brief, A.P., Van Sell, M. and Aldag, R.J. (1979). 'Vocational decision making among women: Implications for organisational behaviour', *Academy of Management Review,* 4(4), 521–530.

Briscoe, J.P, Hall, D.T, and Frautschy DeMuth, R.L. (2006). 'Protean and boundaryless careers: An empirical exploration', *Journal of Vocational Behavior,* 69(1), 30–47.

Brousseau, K.R., Driver, M.J., Eneroth, K. and Larsson, R. (1996). 'Career pandemonium: Realigning organisations and individuals', *Academy of Management Executive,* 10(1), 52–66.

Cheramie, R.A., Sturman, M.C. and Walsh, K. (2007). 'Executive career management: Switching organisations and the boundaryless career', *Journal of Vocational Behaviour*, 71(3), 359–374.

Chianglin, C.Y., Chen, J.S. and Yu, P.L. (2004). 'Transforming from a researcher into a leader in high-tech industries', *International Journal of Information Technology and Decision Making*, 3(3), 379–393.

Creed, P.A. and Patton, W. (2003). 'Predicting two components of career maturity in school based adolescents', *Journal of Career Development*, 29(4), 277–290.

Currie, G., Tempest, S. and Starkey, K. (2006). 'New careers for old? Organisational and individual responses to changing boundaries', *International Journal of Human Resource Management*, 17(4), 755–774.

Defillipi, R.J. and Arthur, M.B. (1994). 'The boundaryless career: A competency-based perspective', *Journal of Organisational Behaviour*, 15(4), 307–324.

Derr, C.B. (1986). *Managing the New Careerist*, San Francisco: Jossey-Bass.

Dik, B.J., Sargent, A.M. and Steger, M.F. (2008). 'Career development strivings: Assessing goals and motivation in career decision-making and planning', *Journal of Career Development*, 35(1), 23–41.

Dokko, G., Wilk, S.L. and Rothbard, N.P. (2009). 'Unpacking prior experience: How career history affects job performance', *Organisation Science*, 20(1), 51–68.

Duffy, R.D. and Dik, B.J. (2009). 'Beyond the self: External influences in the career development process', *The Career Development Quarterly*, 58(3), 29–43.

Eaton, S. and Bailyn, L. (2000). 'Career as life path'. In M. Peiperl, M.B. Arthur, R. Goffee and T. Morris (eds), *Career Frontiers: New Conceptions of Working*, Oxford: Oxford University Press.

Erdoğmus, N. (2004). 'Career orientations of salaried professionals: The case of Turkey', *Career Development International*, 9(2), 153–175.

Feldman, D.C. (2002). Stability in the midst of change: A developmental perspective on the study of careers. In D.C. Feldman (ed.) *Work Careers: A Developmental Perspective*, San Francisco: Jossey-Bass.

Feldman, D.C. and Bolino, M.C. (1998). 'Moving on out: When are employees willing to follow their organisation during corporate relocation?', *Journal of Organisational Behaviour*, 19(3), 275–288.

Feldman, D.C. and Ng, T.W.H. (2007). 'Careers: Mobility, embeddedness, and success', *Journal of Management*, 33(3), 350–377.

Felmlee, D.H. (1984). 'The dynamics of women's job mobility', *Work and Occupations*, 11(2), 259–281.

Fisher, C.D. and Shaw, J.B. (1994). 'Relocation attitudes and adjustment: A longitudinal study', *Journal of Organisational Behaviour*, 15(3), 209–224.

Flum, H. and Blustein, D.L. (2000). 'Reinvigorating the study of vocational exploration: A framework for research', *Journal of Vocational Behaviour*, 56(3), 380–404.

Forret, M.L., Sullivan, S.E. and Mainiero, L.A. (2010). 'Gender role differences in reactions to unemployment: Exploring psychological mobility and boundaryless careers', *Journal of Organisation Behaviour*, 31(5), 647–666.

Gardner, A.M. (1990). 'Career orientations of software developers in a sample of high tech companies', *R&D Management*, 20(4), 337–352.

Groeneveld, S. (2008). 'Dual careers & diplomacy: The willingness of dual-career couples to accept an international assignment within the Dutch foreign services', *Review of Public Personnel Administration*, 28(1), 20–43.

Guest, D. and Rodrigues, R. (2014), 'Beyond the duality between bounded and boundaryless careers: New avenues for careers research', *Career Development International*, 19(6), ISSN (print) 1362–0436.

Harzing, A.W. (1997). 'Response rates in international mail surveys', *International Business Review*, 6(6), 641–665.

Haug, P., Hood, N. and Young, S. (1983). 'R&D intensity in the affiliates of US-owned electronics companies manufacturing in Scotland', *Regional Studies*, 17(6), 383–392.

Hood, N. and Young, S. (1982). 'US multinational R&D: Corporate strategies and policy implications for the UK', *Multinational Business*, 2(1), 10–23.

Ibgaria, M., Kassicieh, S. and Silver, M. (1999). 'Career orientations and career success among research and development and engineering professionals', *Journal of Engineering and Technology Management*, 16(1), 29–54.

Ibgaria, M., Greenhaus, J.H. and Parasuraman, S. (1991). 'Career orientations of MIS employees: An empirical analysis', *MIS Quarterly*, 15(2), 151–169.

Ibgaria, M. and Siegel, S.R. (1992). 'An examination of the antecedents of the turnover propensity of engineers: An integrated model', *Journal of Engineering and Technology Management*, 9(1), 101–126.

Inkson, K., Gunz, H., Ganesh, S. and Roper, J. (2012). 'Boundaryless careers: Bringing back boundaries', *Organisation Studies*, 33(3), 323–340.

Ituma, A. and Simpson, R. (2009). 'The "boundaryless" career and career boundaries: Applying an institutionalist perspective to ICT workers in the context of Nigeria', *Human Relations*, 62(5), 727–761.

Kanfer, R. and Ackerman, P.L. (2004). 'Aging, adult development, and work motivation'. *Academy of Management Review*, 29(3), 440–458.

Kim, N. and Mclean, G.N. (2008). 'Stability and dominance in career success orientation in South Korean employees', *Human Resource Development International*, 11(1), 19–34.

Kirchmeyer, C. (2006). 'The different effects of family on objective career success across genders: A test of alternative explanations', *Journal of Vocational Behaviour*, 68(2), 323–346.

Krieshok, T.S. (1998). 'An anti-introspectivist view of career decision making', *Career Development Quarterly*, 46(3), 210–229.

Lawrence, B.S. (1997). 'The black box of organisational demography', *Organisation Science*, 8(1), 1–22.

Lazarova, M. and Taylor, S. (2009). 'Boundaryless careers, social capital, and knowledge management: Implications for organisational performance', *Journal of Organisational Behaviour*, 30(1), 119–139.

Lewis, S., Smithson, J., Brannen, J., Guerreiro, M.D., Kugelberg, C. and Nilsen, A. (1998). *Futures on Hold: Young Europeans Talk about Combining Work and Family*. London: Work-Life Research Center.

Litzky, B. and Greenhaus, J. (2007). 'The relationship between gender and aspirations to senior management', *Career Development International*, 12(7), 637–659.

London, M. and Greller, M.M. (1991). 'Demographic trends and vocational behaviour: A twenty-year retrospective and agenda for the 1990s', *Journal of Vocational Behaviour*, 38(2), 125–164.

Loughlin, C. and Barling, J. (2001). 'Young workers' work values, attitudes, and behaviours', *Journal of Occupational and Organisational Psychology*, 74(4), 543–558.

Luzzo, D.A. (1993). Value of career-decision-making self-efficacy in predicting career-decision-making attitudes and skills', *Journal of Counseling Psychology*, 40(1), 194–199.

Lyons, S.T., Schweitzer, L. and Ng, E.S.W. (2015). 'How have careers changed? An investigation of changing career patterns across four generations', *Journal of Managerial Psychology*, 30(1), 8–21.

McArdle, S., Waters, L., Briscoe, J.P. and Hall, D.T. (2007). 'Employability during unemployment: Adaptability, career identity and human and social capital', *Journal of Vocational Behaviour*, 71(2), 247–264.

McCarthy, A. and Garavan, T. (2006). 'Post-feedback development perceptions: Applying the theory of planned behaviour', *Human Resource Development Quarterly*, 17(3), 245–267.

McDonald, P., Brown, K. and Bradley, L. (2005). 'Have traditional career paths given way to protean ones? Evidence from senior managers in the Australian public sector', *Career Development International*, 10(2), 109–129.

Manolopoulos, D. (2006). 'Motivating R&D professionals: Evidence from MNEs' decentralized laboratories in Greece', *International Journal of Human Resource Management*, 17(4), 616–646.

Manolopoulos, D., Dimitratos, P. and Sapouna, P. (2010). 'An investigation into international assignment directions of R&D MNE employees: Evidence from Greece', *International Journal of Human Resource Management*, 22(5), 1093–1108.

Manolopoulos, D., Dimitratos, P. and Sofikitis, E. (2011). 'Predictors of career preferences of MNC knowledge professionals', *Personnel Review*, 40(4), 466–484.

Manolopoulos, D., Papanastassiou, M. and Pearce, R. (2007). 'Knowledge-related competitiveness and the roles of multinationals' R&D in Greece', *Management International Review*, 47(1), 1–21.

Markham, W.T., Macken, P.O., Bonjean, C.M. and Corder, J. (1983). 'A note on sex, geographic mobility, and career advancement', *Social Forces*, 61(4), 1138–1146.

Markham, W.T. and Pleck, J. (1986). 'Sex and willingness to move for occupational advancement: Some national sample results', *Sociological Quarterly*, 27(1), 121–143.

Mauer, T.J. (2001). 'Career-relevant learning and development, worker age and beliefs about self-efficacy for development', *Journal of Management*, 27(2), 123–140.

Mayrhofer, W., Meyer, M. and Steyrer, J. (2007). 'Contextual issues in the study of careers. In H. Gunz and M. Peiperl (eds.), *Handbook of Career Studies*, Thousand Oaks, CA: Sage Publications.

Mitchell, T.R., Holtom, B.C., Lee, T.W., Sablynski, C.J. and Erez, M. (2001). 'Why people stay: Using job embeddedness to predict voluntary turnover', *Academy of Management Journal*, 44(6), 1102–1121.

Narayan, A. and Steele-Johnson, D. (2007). 'Relationships between prior experience of training, gender, goal orientation and training attitudes', *International Journal of Training and Development*, 11(3), 166–180.

Netter, J., Wasserman, W. and Kutner, M. (1996). *Applied Linear Statistical Models*, 4th ed. Homewood, IL: Irwin.

OECD (Organisation for Economic Co-operation and Development) (2006). *Live Longer, Work Longer*, Paris: OECD.

Özbilgin, M., Küskü, F. and Erdogmuş, N. (2005). 'Explaining influences on career "choice": The case of MBA students in comparative perspective', *International Journal of Human Resource Management*, 16(11), 2000–2028.

Papanastassiou, M. and Pearce, R. (1999). *Multinationals, Technology and National Competitiveness*, Cheltenham: Edward Elgar.

Patton, W. and Creed, P.A. (2001). 'Developmental issues in career maturity and career decision status', *The Career Development Quarterly*, 49(4), 336–351.

Pearce, R.D. (1994). 'The internationalisation of research and development by multinational enterprises and the transfer sciences', *Empirica*, 21(3), 297–311.

———— (1999). 'Decentralized R&D and strategic competitiveness: Globalised approaches to generation and use of technology in multinational enterprises', *Research Policy*, 28(2), 157–178.

Pearce, R.D. and Papanastassiou, M. (1997). 'European markets and the strategic roles of multinational enterprise subsidiaries in the UK', *Journal of Common Market Studies*, 35(2), 243–266.

Petroni, A. (2000). 'Career route preferences of design engineers: An empirical research', *Career Development International*, 5(6), 288–294.

Pringle, J.K. and Mallon, M. (2003). 'Challenges for the boundaryless career odyssey', *International Journal of Human Resource Management*, 14 (5), 839–853.

Redpath, L., Hurst, D. and Devine, K. (2009). 'Knowledge workers, managers and contingent employment relationships', *Personnel Review*, 38(1), 74–89.

Reynolds, C. and Bennett, R. (1991). 'The career couple challenge', *Personnel Journal*, 48(4), 46–49.

Rodrigues, R.M., Guest, D.E. and Oliviera, T. (2014). 'Who benefits from the new career? Employees, organisations, or both?', *Academy of Management Proceedings. The Power of Words*, 1–5 August 2014, Philadelphia, U.S.

Ryan, A.M., Brutus, S., Greguras, G.J. and Hakel, M.D. (2000). 'Receptivity to assessment-based feedback for management development', *Journal of Management Development*, 19(2), 252–276.

Sagiv, L., & Schwartz, S. H. (2000). 'A new look at national culture: Illustrative applications to role stress and managerial behavior', in N. N. Ashkanasy, C. Wilderom, & M. F. Peterson (Eds), *The Handbook of Organizational Culture and Climate* (pp. 417–436). Newbury Park, CA: Sage.

Savickas, M.L., Nota, L., Rossier, J., Dauwalder, J.P., Duarte, M.E., Guichard, J., Soresi, S., Esbroeck, R.V., Vianen, V.A.E.M. (2009). 'Life designing: A paradigm for career construction in the 21st century', *Journal of Vocational Behaviour*, 75(3), 239–250.

Schein, E.H. (1978). '*Career Dynamics: Matching Individual Needs and Organisational Needs*, Boston: Addison-Wesley.

——— (1982). *Individuals and Careers* (Contract N00014-80-C0905), Arlington, VA: Office of Naval Research.

Segers, J., Inceoglu, I., Vloeberghs, D., Bartram, D. and Henderickx, E. (2008). 'Protean and boundaryless careers: A study on potential motivators', *Journal of Vocational Behaviour*, 73(2), 212–230.

Simmering, M. and Wilcox, I.B. (1995). 'Career exploration and identity formation in MBA students'. *Journal of Education for Business*, 70(4), 233–237.

Smith, C. (1993). 'A new career service?'. In M. Gardner (ed.), *Human Resource Management and Industrial Relations in the Public Sector*, Australia: Macmillan.

Srivastava, A., Blakely, G.L. and Rews, M.C. and Mckee-Ryan, F.M. (2007). 'Mechanisms linking nationality and subjective well-being in managers in China and the United States', *Journal of Managerial Issues*, 19(4), 494–516.

Stevens, A.H. (2005). 'The more things change, the more they remain the same: Trends in long-term employment in the United States, 1969–2002', Cambridge, MA: National Bureau of Economic Research, Working paper No. 11878.

Stewart, W.H. and Roth, P.L. (2007). 'A meta-analysis of achievement motivation differences between entrepreneurs and managers', *Journal of Small Business Management*, 45(4), 401–421.

Sullivan, S.E. (1999). 'The changing nature of careers: A review and research agenda'. *Journal of Management*, 25(3), 457–484.

Sullivan, S.E. and Arthur, M. (2006). 'The evolution of the boundaryless career concept: Examining physical and psychological mobility', *Journal of Vocational Behaviour*, 69(1), 19–29.

Sullivan, S.E. and Baruch, Y. (2009). 'Advances in career theory and research: A critical review and agenda for future exploration', *Journal of Management*, 35(6), 1542–1571.

Sullivan, S.E., Carden, W.A. and Martin, D.F. (1998). 'Careers in the next millennium: Directions for future research', *Human Resource Management Review*, 8(2), 165–185.

Tams, S. and Arthur, M.B. (2010). 'New directions for boundaryless careers: Agency and interdependence in a changing world', *Journal of Organisational Behaviour,* 31(5), 629–646.

Warr, P.B. (1997). 'Age, work, and mental health'. In K.W. Schaie and C. Schooler (eds.), *The Impact of Work on Older Adults,* New York: Springer.

Warr, P.B. and Birdi, K. (1998). 'Employee age and voluntary development activity', *International Journal of Training and Development,* 2(3), 190–204.

Wilensky, H.L. (1960). 'Work, careers and social integration', *International Social Science Journal,* 12(4), 543–574.

Wynarczyk, P. and Renner, C. (2006). 'The gender gap in the scientific labour market: The case of science, engineering and technology-based SMEs in the UK', *Equal Opportunities International,* 25(8), 660–673.

Zeffrane, R.M. (1994). 'Understanding employee turnover: The need for a contingency approach', *International Journal of Manpower,* 15(9), 22–37.

Part IV

Rigour and Relevance: Some Roadmaps for Internationalisation Research

11
Making Research More Policy Relevant: A Longitudinal Case Study of Engaged Scholarship

Margaret Fletcher, Stephen Young and Pavlos Dimitratos

Introduction

Following calls for more policy-relevant academic research, this paper utilises an engaged scholarship (ES) approach (associated with Van de Ven, 2007) to study an innovative evaluation and research (E&R) study of the Scottish Enterprise (SE) Global Companies Development Programme (GCDP).[1] The latter was a public policy initiative to support the internationalisation of small and medium-sized enterprises (SMEs) in Scotland, UK. The E&R study was undertaken by academics and included a combined formal evaluation and research study; a follow-up workshop and group interviews; and policymaker reflections. The chapter demonstrates the value of a longitudinal approach to evidence-based policy analysis that engages stakeholders through continuous dialogue, and presents lessons from this evaluation and research project for implementing an effective ES methodology.

There has been debate on the need for more relevance in academic research for a number of years, with increasing pleas for greater engagement between researchers and practitioners in a learning community (e.g. Pettigrew, 1997; Rynes et al., 2001; Starkey and Madan, 2001; Thorpe et al., 2011; Van de Ven, 2007). In this research we adopt Van de Ven's (2007, p. 9) definition that ES is 'a participative form of research for obtaining the different perspectives of key stakeholders ... in studying complex problems', and thereby 'produce knowledge that is more penetrating and insightful than when scholars or practitioners work on the problems alone'. It appears that the learning community 'jointly produces knowledge that can both advance the scientific enterprise and enlighten a community of practitioners' (Van de Ven, 2007, p. 7). This E&R project was a purposefully selected information-rich 'extreme' case (Patton, 2002, p. 230). It enabled the study of a successful collaboration between the academic researchers and Scottish Enterprise, the main policy-making organisation in Scotland. The E&R was a new approach to evaluation funded by SE. A feature of the study from the outset was the high and sustained levels of engagement between and among the participating stakeholders – specifically a three-person academic team, GCDP-participating firms and Scottish Enterprise policymakers. We respond to pleas for empirical investigations into how useful academic knowledge can be produced and provide insights into how knowledge transfer works (Jarzabkowski et al., 2010).

The remainder of the chapter is structured as follows: the following section reviews the ES literature; section three provides the background to the GCDP within an engaged scholarship context; and the fourth section summarises the findings from the GCDP. The final discussion and conclusions sections reflect on the implications of this research for engaged scholarship theory and public policy, and suggest future research directions.

Engaged scholarship and academic-practitioner engagement

Calls from the academic community for greater engagement between researchers and practitioners include leading proponents such as Pettigrew (1997) in the United Kingdom and Van de Ven (2007) in the United States. Specifically, in the United Kingdom there is a growing interest in the provision of policy-relevant academic research (Atherton, 2008). There has been debate in the field of management research as to the apparent marginality of business school academics in the production of management knowledge, and the lack of engagement by academics in developing and conducting research with practitioners and communicating the results to this audience. This has been identified as a rigour-relevance gap (Fincham and Clark, 2009).

In an early review of the literature on the use of organisational research, Beyer and Trice (1982) concluded that researchers and practitioners belong to separate communities with different values and ideologies. More recently, Keiser and Leiner (2009) posit that these communities operate according to completely separate institutional logics, with the consequence that communication of knowledge cannot be absorbed from one to the other and collaboration is futile. Starkey et al. (2009) suggest that as a result of the proliferation of different modes of enquiry, there is a range of versions of science, but that management research has sought rigour over relevance. Hence, in order to improve knowledge creation and dissemination, academia needs to better reflect user interests (Starkey and Madan, 2001).

In contrast, other researchers argue that there are examples of successful collaborations that have resulted in superior research and outputs which provide high-quality scholarship and social usefulness, while not compromising the needs of academics and practitioners (Hodgkinson and Rousseau,

2009). In addition, Paton et al. (2013, p. 1) argue that by pursuing advanced-level scholarship, academics can make a contribution to practice by presenting 'counterintuitive perspectives' that challenge conventional business wisdom. Bridging the gap between the two groups may lead to cross-fertilisation and richer understanding of organisations. By obtaining different perspectives of stakeholders regarding complex problems, ES has the potential to 'produce knowledge that is more penetrating and insightful' (Van de Ven, 2007, p. 265). In order for this to happen, Hodgkinson and Rousseau (2009) highlight the need for appropriate training in theory and research methods, and deep partnership between academics and practitioners. Authors such as Rynes et al. (2001) and Schein (2001) posit that this requires good social relations and setting the research agenda with practitioner involvement. Although there are difficulties in creating successful collaborative research teams, Amabile et al. (2001) find that success can be influenced by the team, environment and process characteristics. Designing an academic-practitioner team includes careful selection of team members, clarification of roles, regular communication, development of trust and setting time to reflect on the process and relationship conflicts. Van de Ven (2007) argues for the necessity of reconciling the different viewpoints, negotiating the relationship, reflecting about the researcher role and spend time at research sites.

Forms of ES research

In his book, Van de Ven (2007) posits that ES addresses complex problems and surpasses the relevance and rigour issue as it studies problems with and for practitioners and other stakeholders. It is based on a critical realism philosophy. Recognising that there are many ways of practising ES, the author presents four alternative forms:

1. *Informed basic research with stakeholder advice;*
2. *Co-produced knowledge with collaborators;*
3. *Design and evaluation studies for professional practice;*
4. *Action research for a client.*

He suggests the specific approach will depend on the purpose of the study and the degree to which a researcher performs an 'extension' role as a detached, external observer, or an 'intension' role as attached, internal participants. Informed basic research and evaluation forms are extension approaches, whereas collaborative and action research are viewed as intension roles.

According to Van de Ven (2007), *informed basic research* involves reflective practitioners, whereby informants and stakeholders are generally advisory only. Researchers are viewed as friendly outsiders. The research is grounded in reality and informed by stakeholders. *Collaborative basic research* comprises insiders and outsiders, whereby the complementary skills of research teams support a collective learning experience through repeated meetings and jointly sharing in activities, for example, towards developing the research question(s). A potential problem concerns the sharing of proprietary findings. *Evaluation research* involves an outsider perspective but with engagement roles for stakeholders which provide the opportunity to participate in study decisions concerning problem formulation, research design and problem-solving, meaning that informed consent is needed. Following Lewin (1945), Van de Ven (2007) views *action research* as problem-focused, (clinical) research undertaken for a client, but with the researcher having an attached insider role. It involves high researcher involvement with client-initiated research, where participants are motivated to reveal more information and so depth and validity can be improved (Schein, 2001). The participants study and solve their problems in an informal data-gathering process (Patton, 2002). Van de Ven (2007, p. 283) admits that 'in practice, there are many variations and overlap' in his four-dimensional model of ES, and that one form may transition into another. The ES model of Van de Ven (2007) is based on the question of how scholarship that is engaged *with* practitioners can advance knowledge rather than focus on the relevance of academic research *for* practice. This presents challenges which require researchers to reconcile different viewpoints, establish and maintain relationships, be reflexive about their role, and spend time in the research field.

Van de Ven's (2007) approach portrays different forms of ES involving academia and practice. It represents to a significant extent a rather phenomenological type of study. While significant, it is largely lacking in the portrayal of what behavioural and relational processes influence effective ES. Such a limitation potentially obstructs the development of the ES literature and cultivation of effective ES relations.

Global companies' development programme

The context of this study concerns the significance of the internationalisation of SMEs in the economic performance of developed nations which is evident in the lengthy history of public policy support directed at export promotion and internationalisation more generally, supported by a rapidly growing academic literature (e.g. Oviatt and McDougall, 1994; Bell et al., 2003; Johanson and Vahlne, 2009; Jones et al., 2011). Evaluation of internationalisation support programmes is essential to ensure effectiveness and value for money, and in the United Kingdom and Scotland the approach increasingly taken is to evaluate the need for export assistance in terms of 'market failure'.

The GCDP was designed to address a broad range of market failures that inhibit the internationalisation of Scottish SMEs, including (i) facilitating access to information, (ii) enhancing the scale and pace of international activity, (iii) improving access to public goods (especially R&D), and (iii) stimulating positive externalities (particularly learning benefits). It was a firm-specific, six-month programme with follow-up aftercare, directed at the CEO and the senior management of the business, during which time there was a total input from external consultants of 20 working days per company. The aims were: (a) to build the management capability of the firm in the context of developing a shared vision and international business strategy; and, (b) to achieve outputs in respect of agreement by management on global vision, globalisation strategy, scenario planning and action plans, with ongoing SE network support for the implementation of these. This ambitious and high-profile public policy initiative was an outcome of the findings of an earlier research enquiry that highlighted the limited extent of 'globalisation' of indigenous enterprises (including SMEs) (Scottish Enterprise, 1999a; Scottish Enterprise, 1999b).

Specifically, the GCDP was launched in 2000 by Scottish Enterprise with the aim of enabling firms that are controlled from Scotland to achieve a significant international presence (Scottish Enterprise, 2003) and to accelerate the learning processes required for globalisation (Raines and Brown, 2001). From its launch, the objective was to recruit a 'cohort' of between 15 and 20 firms per year to the programme, and seminars, workshops and peer group (networking) events were held regularly to stimulate information exchange and learning among participating firms. There were a range of criteria for the selection of participating firms, namely that they should: (i) have international business development aspirations; (ii) have the necessary business funding in place; (iii) possess an appropriate management team, with an open management style which encourages change; (iv) be strategically controlled from Scotland; (v) have annual sales in the range of £5–20m; and (vi) have aggressive growth targets.

The GCDP research and evaluation project had four constituents:

- *Programme evaluation.* The study was designed to provide a longitudinal evaluation of the GCDP, a new approach to evaluation within Scottish Enterprise. It was based on the premise that programme effects on SME internationalisation were longer-term in nature than could be identified by cross-sectional research.
- *Academic research.* Undertaken in parallel with the evaluation, the academic (doctoral) research was forward-looking, investigating key issues of knowledge acquisition and learning in the internationalisation process which had been proposed by previous academic study as a major constraint on firms' international performance.
- *Action research workshop and focus groups.* E&R results were presented to stakeholders in the finalisation stages of the project in an action research

workshop. Focus group discussions were also undertaken to test the findings from the research on knowledge and learning processes. Together these activities facilitated integration between the evaluation and academic research constituents of the programme.

- *Reflections on engaged scholarship.* Three years after the conclusion of the E&R, in-depth interviews were conducted with Scottish Enterprise executives to reflect on the contributions and challenges of the project within an engaged scholarship framework.

A summary of the major features of the research methodology are presented in Appendix 11.1.

GCDP evaluation and research initiation

The E&R study of the GCDP programme was undertaken by a three-person academic team (the chapter authors). The project was initiated by an approach from the lead GCDP executive at SE to the authors as a follow-up to earlier collaboration on cognate research. The client-researcher relationship was interactive and engaged from the outset since this was a new approach to evaluation for SE, reflecting the objectives of the GCDP which were concerned with longer-term and sustainable internationalisation development. A high level of engagement was pursued throughout the project at different levels and involving a range of stakeholders. An early outcome of engagement between policymakers and the research team was that the evaluation should be longitudinal in nature so as to be able to understand and respond to the strategic changes introduced by participating SMEs. The initial client-researcher discussions also focused upon the need to investigate potential new innovations in the SME support provided by the GCDP, and the sponsorship of a doctoral research study running parallel to the evaluation was approved. Scottish Enterprise funded both the evaluation and research studies on a direct-cost basis rather than as a consultancy project.

Evaluation and research objectives

The first project objective was to evaluate the impact of the GCDP on internationalising SMEs, with a specific focus upon longitudinal evaluation and qualitative impacts. The second objective was to explore the learning processes employed by internationalising SMEs as they implement an international entry and development strategy. The underlying rationale for the E&R was that certain of the impacts of the GCDP would be long-term and qualitative in nature, and that these could not be captured through a conventional static evaluation methodology. Thus the approach agreed collaboratively with Scottish Enterprise was predominantly qualitative and inductive, which enabled key issues to emerge from the data, and, combined with the longitudinal, case study approach, deep and new insights were pursued, and complex and dynamic processes were captured.

Stakeholders in the E&R and engagement process

Stakeholders comprised: (i) three academics (1 full-time for four years, including doctoral study); (ii) participant GCDP firms; (iii) GCDP external consultants; and (iv) Scottish Enterprise policymakers, represented by (a) the lead GCDP executive who had primary responsibility for the E&R; (b) two GCDP executives responsible for managing the programme; (c) a member of the SE appraisal and evaluation team project; and (d) managers from the regional (within Scotland) company account teams who were responsible for facilitating the implementation of external consultants' recommendations.

Nature and forms of engagement

(i) Programme evaluation. The academic team engaged with all the stakeholders with the exception of the consultants. From the beginning there were regular monthly, then quarterly, meetings with the lead GCDP executive[2] and regular meetings with other SE executives and evaluation team at Scottish Enterprise to ensure that ideas and feedback formed part of an ongoing development process. The longitudinal approach required a succession of in-depth interviews with GCDP firms and involved regional Scottish Enterprise account team managers. These company interviews were formal, and engagement per se was limited to ensure factual objectivity. In addition, there was favourable response from firms from what they perceived as these 'annual reviews', and there was further ad hoc interface between the researchers and firms at the 'peer events' which were sponsored by Scottish Enterprise to promote networking. Close engagement between the lead Scottish Enterprise executive, the evaluation expert for the E&R and the research team was particularly crucial to the successful co-production of knowledge (Van de Ven, 2007) pertaining to the project's dual objectives of both policy evaluation and academic research.

The researchers had access to the CEOs and Scottish Enterprise data of firms participating in the GCDP. One of the conditions of acceptance into the programme was that CEOs agreed to participate in evaluations and provide relevant financial and non-financial information (Smallbone and Baldock, 2002). CEOs were the prime focus of attention as the case study key informants since they were the main decision-makers with responsibility for the firms' internationalisation. Other key informants in four firms were interviewed to enhance validity where they were involved in roles involving the firms' internationalisation. Pre-interview access to Scottish Enterprise records, pilot-study evaluation reports and telephone interviews with firms' regional Scottish Enterprise account managers assisted the interviewers to develop trust, probe and confirm responses, and reduce the problem of interviewee recall (Easterby-Smith et al., 1991). This process assisted in enhancing the engagement with Scottish Enterprise stakeholders, in respect to the implementation of consultant recommendations.

Cohort 1 CEOs were interviewed annually during 2003, 2004 and 2005. Cohort 2 CEOs were interviewed during 2004 and 2005. Sixty-four CEO interviews were undertaken over three years. In addition, the researchers had access to GCDP executives within Scottish Enterprise, programme archival data on the firms and internal policy evaluation documentation.[3]

The E&R involved regular meetings with the GCDP executives and evaluation teams at Scottish Enterprise to ensure that ideas and feedback formed part of the development of the evaluation and programme. This supports the ES objective of co-production of knowledge between research and policy-makers (Van de Ven, 2007), and ensured that findings were based on credible evidence which the stakeholders (Scottish Enterprise and the firms) perceived as trustworthy and relevant (Donaldson et al., 2009).

(ii) Academic research. This ran concurrently with the evaluation phase of the project from 2002–2007, focusing upon organisational learning (Huber, 1991) and absorptive capacity (Cohen and Levinthal, 1990; Zahra and George, 2002). Twelve case studies from Cohort 1 were selected for the research study, and the learning theme was incorporated into the final year of the CEO interviews in 2005. Questions on the role of the GCDP in improving knowledge, learning and the capabilities and skills of staff informed the *evaluation*. The academic output from the research was a PhD thesis, conference presentations, books chapters and academic journal articles in the field of international entrepreneurship and internationalisation process.

(iii) Action research workshop and focus groups After the main evaluation period, a workshop and two focus groups, comprising the researchers, firms and Scottish Enterprise policy makers and executives, were held to provide feedback on the evaluation and research findings, and explore in further depth issues that emerged from the case studies. This was supported by an ESRC-funded post-doctoral research. This project adopted an action research paradigm to support ES (Van de Ven, 2007). Although action research has been a widely used policy (e.g. Koshy et al., 2011; Miles and Keenan, 2002), this was a new approach to evaluation by Scottish Enterprise. In this study, action research complemented the other research methods, representing a deeper form of engagement and providing a holistic picture (see Eden and Huxham, 2002; Huxham, 2002; Patton, 2002).

The aims of the workshop were: first, to provide feedback to the GCDP firms and policy makers on the evaluation and research findings; second, to gain further insights into the evaluation and research by collecting research data alongside the intervention (Huxham, 2002); and, third, to provide a forum for engagement which would feed into the GCDP programme and influence the firms' internationalisation behaviour. It was attended by CEOs, Scottish Enterprise programme executives and evaluation staff, as well as invited academics to provide expert outsider perspectives, and was led by interactive presentations from the three-member research team.

In addition to the workshop, two focus group interviews were undertaken with the aim of gaining additional insights into firms' learning processes and the implications of the research findings for policy (Huxham, 2002). Participants in these focus groups comprised six CEOs of GCDP firms, three policymakers/GCDP executives and seven researchers (including the study team).

(iv) Reflections on engaged scholarship. Three years after the formal end of the E&R project, interviews were carried out with the four key SE policymakers to reflect on the contributions and challenges of the study within an ES framework, as well as semi-structured interviews in which the (now former) lead Scottish Enterprise E&R executive, two GCDP executives (independently interviewed) and a member of the Scottish Enterprise Appraisal and Evaluation team were interviewed by two members of the research team. Interview guides were provided in advance of the meetings and were adapted to encompass new information obtained after each interview. The results from these novel reflections form part of the Discussion section of the chapter.

Findings from the evaluation of the GCDP

While the emphasis of this chapter concerns engaged scholarship, the GCDP evaluation findings are highly relevant to the significant public policy implications of the study for SME internationalisation. The overall conclusion was that the programme and SE support played an important role in assisting firms to access knowledge, experience, resources and support to expand internationally. Findings suggested that the GCDP impacted positively on the management of the business and improved management processes in the areas of international strategy, enterprise management, and market entry and development. Thus, a key impact is that the GCDP addressed organisational and motivational barriers facing participating firms.

Regarding the effects of different programme components on internationalisation, the findings showed the most highly rated items were i) the consultant's strategic review, ii) the implementation of action plans, and iii) the development of strategy. The longer-term nature of these impacts was commonly stressed. For example, for some firms the expansion in their overseas activities did not result in increases in revenues immediately. It was considered too early to see the results, although increases in sales were expected in future years.

An important finding was the continuing positive impact of the programme over time, with highest ratings being attributed to improvements in knowledge, learning and the capabilities and skills of employees.

The impacts of the GCDP were positive, and both wide-ranging and longer-term in their influence. Particularly important impacts that were identified in the CEO interviews and questionnaires concerned:

- Improvements in knowledge, learning and the capabilities of staff;
- Enhancement of business scale;
- Understanding of planning processes and the development of strategies and action plans, particularly for international markets;
- Improved management processes in strategy, human resource development and marketing;
- Access to advice from GCDP advisors and greater confidence in using other sources of advice and support, including the private sector.

These are all important for the successful long-term development of firms, albeit intangible and difficult to quantify. Estimates of financial additionality were deemed to be substantial. The case study approach to evaluation enabled fine-grained analysis of the financial, employment and internationalisation impact of each firm.

Discussion: project review and reflections on engaged scholarship

The overall assessment by the SE interviewees was that the project was 'ground-breaking', 'high quality' and 'very cost effective'. Furthermore, an important outcome of the E&R project was that the principle of 'how' changes took place as well as 'what changes' have occurred has been recognised across Scottish Enterprise.

A number of issues of particular significance were identified. First, it was confirmed that the E&R was sponsored by Scottish Enterprise to encourage new thinking, innovation and experimentation through the evaluation methodology and the parallel research study of the newly launched GCDP. Using a longitudinal case study approach to evaluation with action research, the researchers worked closely with Scottish Enterprise to share ideas and insights, and thereby enable the evaluation to be an integral part of an approach to improve policy and service delivery (Papaconstantinou and Polt, 1997; Potter and Storey, 2007). The lead Scottish Enterprise E&R executive observed that the longitudinal element of the methodology was critical: it was instituted because the outputs were long-term and feedback learning during the GCDP programme required ongoing adaptation. It was considered that the delivery of policy had to be 'outcome-based' rather than 'activity-based' in order to assess the impact of programme changes being implemented. The longitudinal evaluation was in-depth, focusing upon 'what was changing in the firms and how long it took'. It represented an 'ongoing business tool' and 'way of running the business' for the participating firms. The longitudinal evaluation was certainly facilitated greatly by high levels of engagement. The continued support of firms was a reflection of their recognition of the benefits from the ongoing feedback from Scottish Enterprise and the annual reviews, plus their rapport with the researchers that developed over time.

Interestingly, there have been no further longitudinal evaluations within SE. This was partly associated within internal changes within Scottish Enterprise: the GCDP was one of a package of company-support programmes, and the individual programmes are no longer evaluated separately.[4] Rather the total package of support (termed 'bespoke' support) provided to companies is evaluated.

Second, although the E&R project was funded by Scottish Enterprise, it was considered essential that the researchers were independent in order to establish the credibility of the study. For example, firms were assured that their responses were confidential. Scottish Enterprise's main role in data collection was to assist with access to the firms and to archival records, and SE did not influence the analysis or the substantive content of the final report. No contentious issues arose in respect of proprietary know-how among the collaborators. Demarcation lines were clear: the reports prepared for Scottish Enterprise contained company-specific information and were confidential, whereas in academic papers emerging from the project, company case material was anonymised, and SE had an interest in promoting its role as a learning organisation and in sharing best practices externally. If the study had been undertaken by a consulting firm, not only would the costs have been substantial, but it might have been difficult to get continued engagement and commitment. This is clearly an issue for ES projects, and relates to the wider debate concerning the role and performance of academic advisers versus consultants (Bouwmeester, 2010).

Third, there were human resource and relationship challenges associated with engaged scholarship in this study. Van de Ven's (2007) ES framework was not designed to incorporate the challenges of engagement, but relationship issues are by definition a critical issue for success. The core personnel involved in an ES project are central to its effectiveness. 'Project champions' with boundary-spanning capabilities (Williams, 2010) are needed at both academic and policy levels. The practitioner project champion in the E&R performed a number of roles, notably: (a) collaborative leadership in evaluation design (along with an Evaluation team executive) and contribution to academic research in the SME internationalisation area; (b) policy intermediation, a role referred to as knowledge broker (Pettigrew, 2011) involving promoting and interpreting the E&R for Scottish Enterprise colleagues, most critically with the firms' regional Scottish

Enterprise account managers, and (c) policy-making through the production and presentation of board papers to justify continued funding for the GCDP.

From the perspective of SE colleagues with client-facing functions (that is, working with GCDP-supported) companies, role (b) appeared to be particularly challenging. Such executives considered the approach pursued by the GCDP and also the E&R somewhat 'theoretical' in their early stages, requiring greater focus upon specific client needs. In part this was due to the fact that historically operational managers were not concerned with evaluation and didn't see its benefits. A related observation which emerged was the need to facilitate understanding and overcome some resistance to 'academic speak' as a means of gaining the respect of SE colleagues.

Overall, it appears that in the E&R *collaborative research* (in which knowledge is co-produced with collaborators) was a prime form of ES, principally involving the research team and the lead GCDP executive, but also through the regular meetings with other GCDP executives and evaluation team at Scottish Enterprise. However, *action/intervention research* for the client was also in evidence since the design and implementation of the project were adapted as experience was gained, and indeed implemented, elsewhere in the client organisation (public policy benefits), and both the ongoing discussions with firms and the emerging findings of the doctoral research on knowledge acquisition and learning induced change at the firm level (business strategy and operations benefits). Supporting this perspective is the *'intension'* role played by one of the project researchers in particular as an 'attached insider' (Van de Ven, 2007), although in undertaking doctoral study this researcher also had an *'extension'* role as a 'detached outsider', hence suggesting an additional form of ES, namely, *basic science with stakeholder advice*. This suggests some limitations of Van de Ven's framework, and certainly there are significant gaps, especially concerning the relationships between and among stakeholders, which are of vital importance to the success of ES.

Other authors have proposed alternative frameworks which are closer to the approach in the E&R (Schein, 2001; Patton, 2002). For example, Schein (2001) identified eight forms of clinical research, distinguishing between four levels (high–low) of researcher-initiated and four levels (again ranging from high–low) of subject/client-initiated research. It is assumed that both the researcher and practitioner will be involved in the problem-solving process and data investigation will become a joint responsibility. The E&R approach is nearer to the client-initiated form since both evaluation and research were proposed by the client, although the academics had a significant role in the design of both dimensions of the project and especially in developing the academic research questions. While the extensive interview programme was undertaken by the academics, the excellent access to companies was facilitated by Scottish Enterprise and archival company-specific data was supplied by SE.

Conclusions

This research has important implications for theory and policy practice. With regard to research, the study addresses previous calls from the academic community for enhanced engagement between academia and practitioners (Pettigrew, 1997; Van de Ven, 2007). Especially in his 2007 work, Van de Ven posits that scholarship addresses complex problems and surpasses the relevance and rigour issue since it examines problems that both academics and practitioners encounter. In the current study, which adopted an inductive approach capturing a complex and dynamic process, we show that there is significant value in a longitudinal processual approach to evidence-based policy analysis that engages stakeholders through continuous dialogue and present lessons from this evaluation and research project for implementing an ES methodology. In particular, the findings attest to the benefits from involvement-oriented, long-term, trustworthy and performance-enhancement collaboration between researchers and policymakers.

In a related vein, when implementing an ES approach, the findings suggest that academia probably needs to move the greater distance and better reflect user interests over a long-run horizon to overcome the rigour–relevance gap (Starkey and Madan, 2001). The view that academics and users belong to separate communities with different values (Beyer and Trice, 1982) did not hold true in this study as the academics had worked in or with private/public sector organisations previously, including Scottish Enterprise. Still, there is a real challenge associated with the lack of experience of many academics in working on policy issues.

Even so, it seems that improved communications and organisational learning are required by participating policymakers to ensure a grounded understanding of the meaning of and contributions from engagement, and to ensure buy-in from different groupings. This implies that the product champion on the practitioner side has a demanding role, encompassing not only relationships with the researchers but also with internal participating teams. Even more important, the policy engagement should occur over a long-term horizon whereby issues of common interest appear to academic and practitioner stakeholders. It is during such a longitudinal process that long-term benefits to the participating parties can accrue.

There is, however, debate concerning the methodological issues associated with qualitative (longitudinal) versus quantitative (cross-sectional) evaluation (Curran and Storey, 2002; Wilson et al., 2008). Longitudinal evaluation exacerbates the design and implementation challenges associated with engaged scholarship. For example, stakeholder engagement cannot be taken for granted and continued efforts had to be made to sustain interest among participating companies over time. In addition, organisational and associated personnel changes among the various internal Scottish Enterprise stakeholder groups meant that new executives may have lacked an understanding of and empathy with the philosophy and objectives underlying the E&R. Nevertheless, the longitudinal approach produced additional insights to those derived from cross-sectional evaluations, especially in revealing the long-term benefits of the GCDP programme for SMEs, the changing managerial challenges over time, and the interrelationships between domestic and international activities that have tended to be viewed in isolation in management research (Karafyllia, 2009). Based on the findings of this study, it seems that cross-sectional evaluations will underestimate both the level and the diversity of the benefits from this type of management-support programme. However, qualitative and quantitative evaluations were basically complementary in the present study. Thus Scottish Enterprise also commissioned a 'conventional' cross-sectional evaluation following the completion of the present project. It was undertaken for a different purpose (i.e. summative), namely to meet Scottish Enterprise audit requirements and justify the programme to the Board to ensure continued funding.

A wider lesson for engaged scholarship is that engagement may be promoted in different ways from the success of an initial project (Thorpe et al., 2011). Following this study, three further collaborative research projects (two of which involved doctoral research funding) have been undertaken with universities, with the participation of one of the SE executives engaged in the GCDP E&R. This addresses the need to enhance awareness of impact in doctoral education (Pettigrew, 2011).

In respect to implications for public policy, there are still gaps in provision, for example, in the development of management capabilities for international business (Autio et al., 2000; Sapienza et al., 2006; Zahra and George, 2002). The GCDP is focused upon such management capabilities and knowledge acquisition, helping, therefore, to address a market failure. However, the doctoral research indicated that the programme assisted not only with the acquisition of specific *foreign* market knowledge, but also with more *general* internationalisation related and technological knowledge (Fletcher and Harris, 2012; Fletcher, et al., 2013). This begins to ask questions about the design of a specifically international programme like the GCDP. Although there are very obvious international knowledge management requirements, firms also have both *general* knowledge needs and *firm-specific* knowledge requirements involving targeted provision tailored to individual company circumstances. The firm-specific approach applied by the GCDP may be difficult and costly for a public sector programme to provide; an alternative is to focus support on improving all SME knowledge acquisition and learning skills and developing absorptive capacity. However the firm-specific, internationalisation focus of the GCDP was an important feature encouraging firm participation. Thus, a challenge facing policy is to design a generic programme which is attractive to firms.

Considering future research, one case of successful engagement was examined, and so further study would benefit from the existence of a 'control group' in which the outcomes of cooperation were not so effective. Essentially the examined E&R on firms' internationalisation represents a best-case scenario against which results from a less effective collaboration could be compared. In addition, the Scottish public-policy setting of this study may restrict the generalisability of the findings to other developed and developing economy contexts where ES activities occur. Future research can investigate ES relationships in other national settings also.

Appendix 11.1: Evaluation & Research Project Design and Methodology

The research methodology followed state-of-the-art principles associated with the project design which comprised:

(a) *Longitudinal case study design*. The research methodology for longitudinal case study design drew upon Huxham (2002); Leonard-Barton (1990); Pettigrew (1992); Van de Ven (1992, 2007); Yin (2003) [2009]. This longitudinal approach that involved close and prolonged engagement with policymakers matched the goals of the study to investigate the dynamic internationalisation process of SMEs and the impact of support (Yin, 2003 [2009]). Time was captured in the study through a combination of retrospective and regular real-time data (Leonard-Barton, 1990; Pettigrew, 1992).

(b) *Qualitative evaluation and interrelated case study data collection, analysis and feedback*. Combined with longitudinal design, the qualitative approach offered a more radical and creative approach to evaluation and a closer, focused analysis of policy and deeper understanding of processes leading to impacts (Curran et al., 1999; Curran and Storey, 2002; Wilson et al., 2008). The evaluation involved case studies of the first two cohorts of firms participating in the programme, comprising 27 firms.

(c) *Data collection and analysis* was an interrelated process that involved multiple phases: first, interviews with CEOs and collection of relevant data from firms participating in the GCDP. Second, access to data from GCDP executives, including collection of programme archival data on firms and internal policy evaluation documentation. Third, after the main evaluation period, a workshop and two focus groups were held to provide feedback on the evaluation and research findings. Fourth, four interviews were undertaken as part of the E&R review and reflection on engaged scholarship. Fifth, extensive data collection took place as part of the doctoral research phase of the E&R project which focused upon organisational learning and absorptive capacity. Sixth and finally, four interviews were undertaken as part of the E&R review and reflection on engaged scholarship.

(d) Methods for establishing trustworthiness and rigour in qualitative research utilised Kaufmann and Denk (2011); Lincoln and Guba (1985); Miles and Huberman (1994); Sharpe (2004); Sinkovics et al. (2008); and Yin (2009).

Notes

1. The GCDP Evaluation and Research Project (E&RP) was not formally designed as an engaged scholarship project. Indeed there was limited awareness of the notion when the project was initiated by Scottish Enterprise (SE), although engaged scholarship projects had begun to proliferate with numerous university-based initiatives, especially in the United States by this time. However, a feature of the project from the outset was the high and sustained levels of engagement between and among the participating stakeholders – specifically the three-person academic team, GCDP-participating companies and Scottish Enterprise policymakers. The project thus provided an excellent setting to explore engaged scholarship in the context of the internationalisation of SMEs.
2. The lead Scottish Enterprise executive for the E&R became an Honorary Research Fellow at the University, and gave lectures and participated in research workshops.
3. Evaluation reports were presented to Scottish Enterprise after each of five phases of data collection (the CEO interviews, questionnaire responses to Likert scales and quantitative financial performance) and a final summary report.
4. There were management and resource challenges associated with the reorganisation, as the GCDP became one of a suite of programmes available to companies.

References

Amabile, T.M., Patterson, C., Mueller, J., Wojcik, T., Odomirok, P.W., Marsh, M. and Kramer, S. J. (2001). 'Academic-practitioner collaboration in management research: A case of cross-profession collaboration', *Academy of Management Journal*, 44(2), 418–443.

Atherton, A. (2008). 'Making enterprise research more policy relevant? A process approach to policy research'. Plenary Session, Institute for Small Business & Entrepreneurship Conference, Belfast, 5–7 November.

Autio, E., Sapienza, H. and Almeida, J. (2000) 'Effects of age at entry, knowledge intensity, and imitability on international growth', *Academy of Management Journal*, 43(5), 909–924.

Bell, J., McNaughton, R., Young, S. and Crick, D. (2003). 'Towards an integrative model of small firm internationalisation', *Journal of International Entrepreneurship*, 1(4), 339–362.

Beyer, J.M. and Trice, H.M. (1982). 'The utilization process: A conceptual framework and synthesis of empirical findings', *Administrative Science Quarterly*, 27, 591–622.

Bouwmeester, O. (2010). *Economic Advice and Rhetoric. Why Do Consultants Perform Better Than Economic Advisers?* Cheltenham, UK: Edward Elgar.

Cohen, W. and Levinthal, D. (1990). 'Absorptive capacity: A new perspective on learning and innovation', *Administrative Science Quarterly*, 35(1), 128–152.

Curran, J., Berney, R. and Kuusisto, J. (1999). *A Critical Evaluation of Industry SME Support Policies in the United Kingdom and the Republic of Ireland*. Stage One Report: 'An introduction to SME support policies and their evaluation', Helsinki: Ministry of Trade and Industry.

Curran, J. and Storey, D.J. (2002). 'Small business policy in the United Kingdom: The inheritance of the small business service and implications for its future effectiveness', *Environment and Planning C: Government Policy*, 20, 163–177.

Donaldson, S.I. (2009). 'A practitioner's guide for gathering credible evidence in the evidence-based global society'. In S.I. Donaldson, C.A. Christie and M.M. Mark (eds), *What Counts as Credible Evidence in Applied and Evaluation Practice?* London: Sage.

Easterby-Smith, M., Thorpe, R. and Lowe, A. (1991). *Management Research: An Introduction.* London: Sage.

Eden, C. and Huxham, C. (2002). 'Action research for the study of organisations'. In S. Clegg, C. Hardy, & W. Nord (eds) *Handbook of Organisation Studies.* London and Thousand Oaks: Sage Publications.

Fincham, R. and Clark, T. (2009). 'Introduction: Can we bridge the rigour-relevance gap?' *Journal of Management Studies*, 46(3), 510–515.

Fletcher, M. and Harris, S. (2012). 'Knowledge acquisition for the internationalization of the smaller firm: Content and sources', *International Business Review*, 21(4), 631–647.

Fletcher, M., Harris, S. and Richey, G. (2013). 'Internationalization knowledge: What, why, where and when?', *Journal of International Marketing*, 21(3), 47–71 (Accepted subject to minor revisions for final submission).

Hodgkinson, G.P. and Rousseau, D.M. (2009). 'Bridging the rigour-relevance gap in management research: It is already happening!' *Journal of Management Studies*, 46, 534–546.

Huber, G.P. (1991). 'Organizational learning. The contributing processes and the literatures', *Organizational Science*, 2(1) 88–115.

Huxham, C. (2002). 'The new public management. An action research proposal'. In K. McLaughlin, S.P. Osborne and Ferlie, E. (eds), *The New Public Management.* London: Routledge.

Jarzabkowski, P., Mohrman, S.A. and Scherer, A.G. (2010). 'Organization studies as applied science: The generation and use of academic knowledge about organizations. Introduction to the special issue', *Organization Studies*, 31(9–10), 1189–1207.

Johanson, J. and Vahlne, J.-E. (2009). 'The Uppsala internationalisation process model revisited: From liability of foreignness to liability of outsidership', *Journal of International Business Studies*, 40(9), 1411–1431.

Jones, M.V., Coviello, N. and Tang, Y.K. (2011). 'International entrepreneurship research (1989–2009): A domain ontology and thematic analysis', *Journal of Business Venturing*, 26(6), 632–659.

Karafyllia, M. (2009). 'Perspectives on the interrelationships between domestic and international markets for the smaller firm'. In M.V. Jones, P. Dimitratos, M. Fletcher and S. Young (eds), *Internationalization, Entrepreneurship and the Smaller Firm: Evidence from around the World.* Cheltenham, UK: Edward Elgar, 53–72.

Kaufmann, L., and Denk, M. (2011). 'How to demonstrate rigour when presenting grounded theory in the supply chain management literature', *Journal of Supply Chain Management*, 46(4), 64–72.

Keiser, A. and Leiner, L. (2009). 'Why the rigour-relevance gap in management research is unbridgeable', *Journal of Management Studies*, (46), 516–533.

Koshy, E., Koshy, V. and Waterman, H. (2011). *Action Research in Healthcare*. London: Sage.

Leonard-Barton, D. (1990). 'A dual methodology for case studies: Synergistic use of a longitudinal single site with replicated multiple sites', *Organization Science*, 1(3), 248–266.

Lewin, K. (1945). 'The research centre for group dynamics at Massachusetts Institute of Technology', *Sociometry*, 8, 126–135.

Lincoln, Y.S. and Guba, E.G. (1985). *Naturalistic Inquiry*. Newbury Park, CA: Sage Publications.

Miles, I.D. and Keenan, M.P. (2002). *Practical Guide to Regional Foresight in the United Kingdom*. Brussels: European Commission.

Miles, M.B. and Huberman, A.M. (1994). *Qualitative Data Analysis*. Thousand Oaks, CA: Sage.

Oviatt, B.M. and McDougall, P.P. (1994). 'Toward a theory of international new ventures', *Journal of International Business Studies*, 25(1), 45–68.

Papaconstantinou, G. and Polt, W. (1997). 'Policy evaluation in innovation and technology: An overview', In *OECD Proceedings, Policy Evaluation in Innovation and Technology – Towards Best Practices*. Paris: OECD.

Paton, S., Chia, R. and Burt, G. (2013). 'Relevance or "relevate"? How university business schools can add value through reflexively learning from strategic partnerships with business'. *Journal of Management Studies*, online publication, 21 March, 1–22.

Patton, M.Q. (2002). *Qualitative Research and Evaluation Methods*, 3rd ed. Thousand Oaks, CA: Sage.

Pettigrew, A.M. (1992). 'The character and significance of strategy process research', *Strategic Management Review*, 13, Special issue, Winter, 5–16.

Pettigrew, A.P. (1997). 'The double hurdles of management research'. In T. Clarke (ed.), *Advancement in Organisational Behaviour: Essays in Honour of D.S. Pugh*. London: Dartmouth Press, 277–296.

——— (2011). 'Scholarship with impact', *British Journal of Management*, 22, 347–354.

Pettigrew, A.P., Woodman, R.W. and Cameron, K.S. (2001). 'Studying organizational change and development for future research', *The Academy of Management Journal*, 44(4), 697–713.

Potter, J. and Storey, D. (2007). *OECD Framework for the Evaluation of SME and Entrepreneurship Policies and Programmes*. Paris: OECD.

Raines, P. and Brown, R. (2001). 'From "international" to global: The Scottish Enterprise global companies strategy and new approaches to overseas expansion', *Regional Studies*, 35(7), 657–668.

Rynes, S.L., Bartunek, J.M. and Daft, D.L. (2001). 'Across the great divide: Knowledge creation and transfer between practitioners and academics', *Academy of Management Journal*, 44(2), 340–355.

Sapienza, H.J., Autio, E., George, G. and Zahra, S.A. (2006). 'A capabilities perspective on the effects of early internationalization on firm growth and survival', *Academy of Management Review*, 31, 914–933.

Schein, E.H. (2001). 'Clinical inquiry/research'. In P. Reason and H. Brandbury (eds), *Handbook of Action Research*. London: Sage.

Scottish Enterprise (1999a). *Global Companies Enquiry Research Findings*. Glasgow: Scottish Enterprise.

——— (1999b). *Global Companies – A Strategy for Scotland*. Glasgow: Scottish Enterprise.

——— (2003). *Global Companies Development Programme*. Glasgow: Scottish Enterprise.

Sharpe, D.R. (2004). 'The relevance of ethnography for international business research'. In R. Marschan-Piekkari and C. Welch (eds), *Handbook of Qualitative Research Methods for International Business*. Cheltenham: Edward Elgar, 306–323.

Sinkovics, R.R., Penz, E. and Ghauri, P.N. (2008). 'Enhancing trustworthiness of qualitative research in international business', *Management International Review*, 48(6), 689–714.

Smallbone, D. and Baldock, R. (2002). 'Policy support for high growth start-ups: The recent English Experience', Rent XVII Conference, Lodz, Poland, 20–21 November.

Starkey, K., Hatchuel, A. and Tempest, S. (2009). 'Management research and the new logics of discovery and engagement', *Journal of Management Studies*, 46, 547–558.

Starkey, K. and Madan, P. (2001). 'Bridging the relevance gap: Aligning stakeholders in the future of management research', *British Journal of Management*, 12, 358–373.

Storey, D.J. (1994). *Understanding the Small Business Sector*. London: International Thompson Business Press.

Thorpe, R., Eden, C., Bessant, J. and Ellwood, P. (2011). 'Rigour, relevance and reward: Introducing the knowledge translation value-chain', *British Journal of Management*, 22(30), 420–431.

Van de Ven, A.H. (1992). 'Strategies for studying strategic process: A research note', *Strategic Management Journal*, 13, Special Issue, Summer, 169–188.

—— (2007). *Engaged Scholarship: A Guide for Organizational and Social Research*. Oxford: Oxford University Press.

Williams, P. (2010). 'Special agents: The nature and role of boundary spanners'. ESRC Research Seminar Series. *Collaborative Futures: New Insights from Intra- and Inter-Sectoral Collaboration*. University of Birmingham, February.

Wilson, N., Hart, M. and Kitching, J. (2008). 'It's the evidence, stupid: Doing and legitimising policy–funder research', Institute for Small Business and Entrepreneurship Conference Proceedings, 5–7 November, Belfast.

Yin, R.K. (2009). *Case Study Research Design and Methods*, 4th ed. Thousand Oaks, CA: Sage.

Zahra, S.A. and George, G. (2002). 'Absorptive capacity: A review, reconceptualization, and extension', *Academy of Management Review*, 27(2), 185–203.

Zhao, Z.J. and Anand, J. (2013). 'Beyond boundary spanners: The "collective bridge" as an efficient inter-unit structure for transferring collective knowledge', *Strategic Management Journal*, 34, 1513–1530.

12
SME Internationalisation and Its Impact on Firm Performance
Qi Cao, Paola Criscuolo and Erkko Autio

Introduction

The past decade has witnessed a growing interest in research on the internationalisation of small and medium-sized enterprises (SMEs). After two decades of development in international SME literature, both business practitioners and researchers in the field of international business and entrepreneurship are starting to consider whether and how multinationalisation impacts the performance of small and medium-sized firms. Lu and Beamish (2001) state that research in this field should 'examine the effects of an international aspect of an entrepreneurial strategy'. In this context, internationalisation is a strategic choice and the focus will be on the consequences of such entrepreneurial activity. McDougall and Oviatt (1996) point out that the impact of multinationalisation on firm performance is one of the most significant concerns in the field. This topic is critical for both business managers who need to take strategic decisions as to whether or not to go global, and for researchers who are trying to unveil the real effects of internationalisation on firm survival and growth.

The majority of the existing literature on SME internationalisation focuses on what sort of firms become international. Few studies examine the consequences of the market entry strategy. The lack of empirical evidence is overshadowed by the incoherent theoretical lenses employed to explain SME internationalisation process. Although a number of studies have tested the relationship between SME internationalisation and firm performance, both empirically and theoretically, research has so far proved inconclusive (Westhead et al., 2004). A 'positive', 'negative' or non-linear relationship does not mean necessarily that individual firms will follow 'positive', 'negative' or non-linear performance trajectories. Within the scope of international business literatures, studies on MNEs' degree of internationalisation (DOI) performance gave a loose conclusion that internationalisation has a positive effect on firm performance (Pangarkar, 2008).

However, SMEs may experience a more complicated situation while going global. A typical anticipation of the relationship between SME multinationalisation and firm performance is a 'U-curve' which indicates a deteriorate performance at the beginning of internationalisation due to the shock of foreignness and resource constraint. In the long term, however, a pickup could happen when the benefit of new opportunity overcomes the negative impact (Orser et al., 2000; Shrader et al., 2000). However, as the authors point out, for SMEs, empirical studies have provided contradictory results as to whether there is a positive or negative relationship between multinationalisation and performance.

Building on the review of relevant literatures, this chapter aims to define the frontier of current research by identifying and grouping the most prevalent mechanisms and factors influencing SME performance outcome during the process of internationalisation. The main research focuses are whether and how different mechanisms transfer the changes of internationalisation to firm performance. Instead of distinguishing different types of SMEs, we rely on firm-level theoretical frameworks that have been employed previously in SME internationalisation studies. Indeed, there are differences in internationalisation of international new ventures (INVs), born-globals and well established international SMEs. As Autio et al. (2000) point out, the age of initial internationalisation could shift the growth strategy, international identity, learning process and many aspects of the firms. That aside, start-ups and INVs are all SMEs in an early stage of establishment.

Among a few significant areas of study, we argue that the following three aspects of SME internationalisation and performance study make research in this area critical. First, abundant literature has focused on the relationship between the degree of international and financial performance of MNEs (Sullivan, 1994), but much less has explored the relationship between the internationalisation and firm performance of SMEs. Second, existing literature on the performance and internationalisation of SMEs (Autio et al., 2000; Zahra et al., 2000; Lu and Beamish, 2001; Qian, 2002; Westhead et al., 2004; Pangarkar, 2008) tries to find empirical evidence for a positive relationship between SME multinationalisation and financial performance. However, the mechanism of whether and how internationalisation impacts firm performance is still unclear (Lu and Beamish, 2001). Last but not least, the literature on entrepreneurship has focused on explaining and legitimating international new venture (INV) multinationalisation. The theoretical methods, however, are derived from international business literature and strategic management theories. Resource-based theory (RBV) (Barney, 1991) and knowledge-based analysis (KBV) (Gilbert et al., 2008) are the most commonly employed methods. RBV and KBV, however, are based on research on large companies. As SMEs are not 'smaller versions of MNEs' (Shuman and Seeger, 1986), a theoretical framework has not been established for the impact of multinationalisation on the performance of resource-constrained, routine absent small and medium-sized businesses.

Theoretical background

In traditional international business (IB) literature, SMEs are not the main object of study. Sullivan (1994) reviewed the literature on DOI performance research from 1970 to 1990. No empirical study employs SMEs as a research sample. On the contrary, companies described as 'the largest U.S. MNCs' (Geringer et al., 1989) and 'Fortune 500' (Vernon, 1971) constitute the whole empirical sample in studies of firm internationalisation. The observation of large companies' trajectories of foreign market entry revealed that mature companies take a few steps to realise the great potential of both downstream market places and upstream resources from foreign countries. This was concluded as process international theory (PIT), which is based on the assumption that incremental changes are made through a path-dependent progress of business patterns (Johanson and Vahlne, 1977; Welch and Luostarinen, 1988). According to PIT, only at certain development levels do companies start to go to the global stage (Johanson and Vahlne, 1990; Autio, 2005). PIT legitimated the internationalisation process of large companies by assuming that companies pursue long-term profitability and keep away from business activities with high uncertainty (Johanson and Vahlne, 1977). Considering SMEs that face resource constraints, uncertain market environments and limited business routines, internationalisation should be avoided. This diverges widely from the reality of SME multinationalisation, therefore a new focus was established by the last decade of the 20th century which began with the observation of the international activities of SMEs and new ventures (Oviatt and McDougall, 2005).

Oviatt and McDougall's 1994 paper is considered the inception of the study of new venture internationalisation (Autio, 2005). The authors argue that the developments in the international business environment since the late 1980s have increased the exposure of SMEs to international activities. The improvements include easier cross-national communication and transportation technology, increased homogeneity of market characters in different countries, more entrepreneurs with multinational operating experience, and flourishing cross-border financial resources (Oviatt and McDougall, 1994). PIT cannot explain the emerging phenomenon of SMEs going global. The exiguous resource availability of SMEs also challenged the traditional RBV theory of resource possession and allocation (Barney, 1991). If an established company's internationalisation is a strategic have-to (considering both resources and market position), the multinationalisation of SMEs is more like a strategic option, or is more in the nature of an opportunistic incentive.

The consequence of research on international SMEs is significant; a new research field, international entrepreneuiship (IE), has been established and is considered a critically distinguished field of international business study (Autio, 2005). The definition of IE has been continuously evolving through the past two decades, from the early focus on the international activities of new ventures (McDougall et al., 1994) to the recent research on entrepreneurial internationalisation (Autio et al., 2010; Keupp and Gassmann, 2009). The trend reflects the shift in research focus from company size and age to an emphasis on entrepreneurial activities. The relationship between IE study and international business literature has been discussed intensively (Oviatt and McDougall, 1994, 2005). Lu and Beamish (2001) argue that IE study is bonded with SME internationalisation literature in that the 'internationalisation of an established yet small firm' is an emerging significant stream of IE research beside the original focus on start-ups and INVs. Indeed, start-ups and INVs are also SMEs in an early stage of establishment. For example, as discussed above, the incentive of a new venture's internationalisation has been explored from demographical, resource-based and strategic aspects. Gilbert et al. (2008) summarise that entrepreneur characteristics, resources, geographic location, strategy, industry context, as well as organisational structure and systems, are critical factors that shape the success or failure of SME internationalisation.

A large percentage of the literature of SME internationalisation and performance focuses on the moderating effects of a single variable, for example organisational learning, or of a couple of correlated variables, such as organisational learning, prior knowledge stock and company absorptive capacity (McDougall and Oviatt, 2000; Teece et al., 1997; Autio et al., 2000; Zahra et al., 2000; Sapienza et al., 2006; Jantunen et al., 2005; Rasheed, 2005; Gray, 2006; Avlonities and Salavou, 2007; Frishammar and Andersson, 2009). These studies have a few inherent disadvantages: the causal links between dependent and independent variables are controversial; correlation between variables can lead to biased empirical results; and the boundary of the control group is unclear. The correlation of a large number of factors leads to empirical results that are too narrowly focused and do not hold when different data are employed. Since there is no conclusion from past literatures as to which factors significantly influence SME internationalisation and performance process, it is necessary to explore all the factors which appear in the literature. Dozens of factors that influence SME performance and the multinationalisation process have been employed in theoretical and empirical studies. Some proxies of these mechanisms have been proposed in the literature. Examples include R&D intensity (Teece et al., 1997; Autio et al., 2000; Bausch and Krist, 2007; Muscio, 2007; Teece, 2007; Hsu and Pereira, 2008; Shimizutani and Todo, 2008; Frenz and Gillies, 2009), prior knowledge stock (Zahra et al., 2000; Gray, 2006; Muscio, 2007, Teece, 2007; Hsu and Pereira, 2008; Bingham, 2009) and product diversification (Geringer et al., 1989; Teece et al., 1997; Zahra et al., 2000; Bausch and Krist, 2007; Gaur and Kumar, 2009). The theoretical gap lies in the fact that the effects of the firm's resource base, growth strategy and strategic position on SME internationalisation and consequent firm performance have not been sufficiently explored.

In general there are three major types of mechanism, namely organisational capabilities, resource endowments and strategic orientations. Regarding organisational capabilities, following the organisational capability approach of Autio et al. (2010), Zahra et al. (2000) and Zahra and George (2002), a company's ability to achieve growth and better performance depends on its substantive capabilities and change capabilities. In a nutshell, change capabilities include factors that improve a company's ability to achieve success when change happens, while substantive capabilities help a company improve the capability of its routines and daily production. The second major category is resource endowments, which includes organisational endowment, environmental endowment and resource optimisation. This approach focuses on a firm's inherent properties and resource-based advantages (Penrose, 1959; Rumelt, 1984; Barney, 1991). MNE internationalisation studies based on international business literature largely rely on resource endowment analysis (Dunning, 1988; Sullivan, 1994; Contractor, 2007; Li, 2007). The third major category is strategic legitimacy. SME internationalisation studies based on strategic management and international entrepreneurship research pay more attention to individual and organisational strategic orientations and their impact on firm performance (Dimitratos et al., 2004; Firshammar and Andersson, 2009). On an individual level, demographic characteristics of the management team focuses on a manager's personal experience in multinationalisation and the managerial team's diversity of knowledge. Many studies have proved that an entrepreneurial team's experience and knowledge stock have significant impact on internationalisation implications (Jantunen et al., 2005; Avlonities and Salavou, 2007). On an organisational level, company strategic orientation includes a firm's strategy preference towards multinationalisation, company risk tolerance level, market entry model and willingness to bring change to the business. Strategic legitimacy also concerns the credibility change after multinationalisation activities. These factors are traditionally highlighted in the internationalisation and performance study of MNEs, and are worth digging into in the study of SMEs as well.

Based on the above review, we propose a research model for the performance consequences of SME internationalisation which uses a series of mechanisms to deliver the changes brought by multinationalisation to performance. These mechanisms include change capabilities, substantive capabilities, organisational endowment, environmental endowment, resource optimisation, demographic characteristics of the management team and strategic legitimacy (Table 12.1).

Table 12.1   Mechanisms and factors employed in SME internationalisation impact studies

Mechanisms	Factors
Organisational capabilities	
Change capabilities	Dynamic capability
	Organisational learning
	Absorptive capacity
Substantive capabilities	R&D intensity
	Prior knowledge stock
	Product/Market diversity
Resource endowments	
Organisational endowment	Firm age
	Firm size
Environmental endowment	Location, network and cultural distance
	Industry dynamics
Resource access and optimisation	Resource position
	Resource fungibility
Strategic orientations	
Demographic characteristics	Manager's business/ intl. experience
	Managerial team diversity
Strategic legitimacy	Firm strategy
	Risk tolerance
	Market entry model
	Strategic change

Change capabilities cover a few factors which help businesses improve performance in the dynamic process of change. Dynamic capability, organisational learning and absorptive capacity are the three most prevalent factors in this domain. Substantive capabilities include R&D intensity, prior knowledge stock, product diversity and the routines and patterns of a firm. These factors facilitate daily operations and performance of the business. Organisational endowment mainly focuses on firm properties like firm age, firm size and so on. Environmental endowment includes external factors like economy of scale, cultural distance, social network and industry dynamics. Resource access and optimisation focuses on factors related to resource-based perspective, including resource position and resource fungibility. The eight factors in the category of resource endowment could be seen as properties of a firm which describe the firm's development stage and define its resource position in the marketplace. Demographic characteristics of the management team focuses on the individual-level capability of the management group which includes the manager's business experience and managerial team diversity. Strategic legitimacy offers a credibility perspective on the firm's ability to deal with changes. The firm's strategy making, risk tolerance level, market entry model and willingness to bring change to the organisation are all factors which measure credibility.

Conceptual framework and proposition-developing

Change capabilities

As argued earlier, internationalisation is a process of bringing change to a company. How well SMEs adapt to the changing internal structure and external environment during the internationalisation process could determine whether or not the companies survive the initial impact of foreignness. Teece et al. (1997) propose that a company's ability to employ both internal and external resources to adapt to a rapidly changing environment may be considered its dynamic capability. The internationalisation of SMEs impacts firm performance by introducing changes and new opportunities. As discussed above, these changes influence both the internal and external structure of the firm. Compared with established multinational companies, SMEs face severe resource and knowledge-stock constraints. However, this does not mean SMEs are in an inferior position in the internationalisation process compared to MNEs. From the dynamic capability perspective, abundant knowledge or technology stock and access to scarce resources are not essential to secure a competitive advantage. It is the ability to respond swiftly to market and technology changes that enables a firm to achieve success.

In the internationalisation context, market change is largely due to entry to new markets when SMEs go global. Past literature on learning capability and knowledge transfer has pointed out the inertness of replicating the successful practice of doing business from the home market to the host country (Kogut and Zander, 1992; Teece, 1986; Cohen and Levinthal, 1990). Before replicating the original practice to a new market, a firm needs to understand its patterns of doing business. Routines and patterns developed by the company are highly path-dependent and not easy to codify and replicate (Kogut and Zander, 1992). Since successful practice and tacit knowledge are the results of learning-by-doing (Malerba and Orsenigo, 1993), the transfer of knowledge and practice from domestic market to foreign market could be improved by prior experience of market expansion. SMEs learn from their experience and accumulate the routines and patterns of replicating and transferring business practice and knowledge.

> *Proposition 1(a)* SMEs with previous experience of entering new markets have obtained relevant capability for geographic expansion, which facilitates performance in the host market.

Coff (1999) argues that a firm is not a unitary role but is constituted by many stakeholders with different interests; therefore, a firm can be seen as a nexus of contracts. Since a firm consists of individuals, small working groups, teams and departments which all have different interests, focuses and knowledge stocks, the exploitation of knowledge stock within the firm is difficult. Similarly, the transfer of technology within the firm also faces obstacles (Teece, 1986). Szulanski (1996) describes these impediments within a firm as 'internal stickiness' which originates from the causal ambiguity of knowledge itself, lack of perceived reliability of sources, lack of absorptive capacity of the recipient and the arduous relationship within the organisational context. In the multi-nationalisation context, in most cases SMEs expand their operating branches as well as employee numbers when entering a new market. The expansion leads to a more complicated organisational structure and greater distances between individuals and working units. We argue that it is difficult for SMEs to exploit existing knowledge stock when an organisation expands over national borders (Contractor, 2007). This leads to the following proposition:

Proposition 1(b) Internationalisation of SMEs increases the complexity of the organisational structure which hinders the exploitation of knowledge within the firm and eventually offsets the benefits of cross-border market expansion.

Absorptive capacity and learning effects in SMEs

Absorptive capacity has been widely accepted as a theoretical framework that offers a distinctive perspective alongside the resource-based view (RBV) (Barney, 1991), knowledge-based analysis (KBV) (Kogut and Zander, 1992), technology and industry change (Dosi, 1982; Malerba and Orsenigo, 1993; Audretsch, 1997) and the dynamic capability perspective (Teece, 2007; Cohen and Levinthal, 1990) on firm internationalisation and performance studies. Cohen and Levinthal (1990, p. 447) define absorptive capability (AC) as a firm's ability to 'recognize and assimilate external information and apply it to commercial ends'. There are three fundamental aspects to this approach: (1) identify the new external knowledge; (2) assimilate the information and knowledge from the new environment; and (3) apply the external knowledge to enhance the firm's own competitiveness. These three aspects are progressively related to one another (Figure 12.1). The first step concerns identifying new technology and recognising opportunities, which is a fundamental requirement for companies exploring new technological opportunities. The second step of assimilating external knowledge focuses on the learning process whereby a firm recodes new knowledge into a common language which can be understood, communicated and replicated within the boundary of the organisation. In the third step the knowledge is applied to firm practice, which emphasises the organisational ability to exploit inner knowledge stock and apply ideas to production. Cohen and Levinthal (1990) proposed that organisational absorptive capacity is a function of prior knowledge stock. Similarly, Kogut and Zander (1992) argue that organisational learning capability cannot be separated from what the firm already knows, that is, the knowledge stock of the company. Their rationale lies in the view that what the company did in the past shapes what they can do in the future. Although in many cases the knowledge stock may not be particularly useful for future development, a rich knowledge stock and operational experience are considered solid ground for better organisational learning capability in the future. Therefore, SMEs with better prior knowledge stock and experience of pattern and routines will have more chance to improve performance.

> *Proposition 1(c)* SMEs with abundant prior knowledge stock explore host market knowledge and information more efficiently, which leads to superior performance.

Oviatt and McDougall (1994) argue that to achieve sustainable growth SMEs have to rely on local (host country) knowledge assimilation and capability development. Exploration of local knowledge and acquisition of host country R&D capabilities therefore is vital to (1) survive in foreign market and (2) achieve profitability in the long term. The adoption of local intangible resources and knowledge-based capacity could improve overall firm performance. Smaller firms have small organisation, fewer power levels and are more homogenous in many aspects in the internationalisation process. MNEs, however, have different departments, lots of subsidiaries and complicated power structure. As a single small company, learning effects, knowledge assimilation and international experience provide more visible impacts compared with MNEs. Although learning effects happen in both SMEs and MNEs, we argue it is more

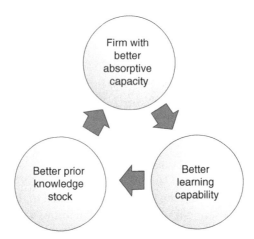

Figure 12.1 Self-enhancing relationship between absorptive capacity, learning capability and knowledge stock

visible in SMEs. Also, SMEs rely more on host country resources and knowledge to achieve success.

> *Proposition 1 (d)* SMEs rely on host market knowledge exploration to achieve sustainable growth.

Substantive capabilities

Substantive capabilities enable firms' daily business operation to run smoothly and efficiently (Autio et al., 2010; Zahra et al., 2000). Autio et al. (2010) argues that substantive capabilities improve routine business practice by 'minimiz[ing] variance and maximize operational efficiency'. Firms' substantive capabilities are widely discussed and considered vital factors in MNE internationalisation studies. A specific focus is on firms' incremental innovation capabilities. R&D intensity, firm prior knowledge stock and product/market diversity are the most significant components in substantive capabilities catalogue.

Firm R&D intensity has been considered a critical indicator of firm innovative capability and major measurement of firm's intangible knowledge level (Frenz and Gillies, 2009). Teece et al. (1997) state that R&D intensity has been employed in resource-based analysis as a threshold preventing outsiders entering the market. R&D activities at the same time are considered the major resource of incremental and radical technology improvements from a product life-cycle perspective. R&D intensity is firmly connected with company prior knowledge stock. Higher R&D intensity builds up in-house technology stock and enables a company to identify and assimilate external knowledge. Abundant firm knowledge stock at the same time could provide solid ground for in-house R&D activities. A positive mutual relationship between R&D intensity and prior knowledge stock has been widely accepted (Muscio, 2007; Hsu and Pereira, 2008).

> *Proposition 2 (a)* R&D intensity, indicating firm technological capabilities and intangible knowledge level, is positively related to SME performance in domestic environment.

Early 'degree of internationalisation' literatures employ foreign sales to total sales ratio (FSTS) or foreign assets to total assets ratio (FATA) as common measurements of firm multinationalisation level; the international diversification performance (IDP) literature however argues that DOI is not sufficient. The major argument is that firms operating in a few foreign markets with diverse culture and market environment could gain more business opportunities compared with firms operating in specific foreign markets (Hsu and Pereira, 2008). The empirical result, similar to performance implication research, is inconclusive. From a dynamic capability perspective, we believe that learning and assimilating of new market knowledge leads to complicated organisational structure and higher managerial costs. Entering a new business environment is always risky for SMEs; at least in the short term new market entry will negatively influence firm performance. Host markets with diverse cultural, political and market backgrounds are a challenging environment for SMEs. It is advisable then to enter market clusters with similarity and geographical proximity.

> *Proposition 2 (b)* Market diversification requires sufficient time for SME adapt to new environment; a negative impact will be induced by market diversification on firm performance in the short term.

Organisational Endowment

Organisational endowment is simply composed of two company properties, firm age and size. Although it is explicitly defined, these two factors have been widely addressed in firm internationalisation studies. The first element, firm age, is an important indicator of a company's business experience and existing knowledge stock. At the same time, business experience and knowledge stock are is the essential part for business routines' and patterns' development (Orser et al., 2000; Sapienza et al., 2006). According to process internationalisation theory, these patterns and routines are critical during the process of multi-nationalisation (Johanson and Vahlne, 1977, 1990; Welch and Luostarinen, 1988).

Following Oviatt and McDougall's (1994) argument, Sapienza et al. (2006) state that earlier internationalisation is not only possible but also provides significant advantage for companies in that the 'imprint effect' of dynamic capabilities will be more efficient as a firm multinationalises at an earlier stage of its development. Autio et al. (2010) state that well-established companies accumulate abundant substantive capabilities through years of operation. We propose that firm age facilitates company daily operations, which as Sapienza et al. (2006) point out may hinder future international profitability. We therefore propose that firm age has a positive relationship with company substantive capabilities. Change capabilities at the same time are not dependent on firm age or firm size but organisational experience of change.

> *Proposition 3* SMEs gain substantive capabilities through daily operation, firm age and size and this therefore has a positive relationship with domestic and substantive knowledge stock.

Network, environment and industry dynamics

The above organisational endowment mechanism focuses on firms' internal characteristics while environmental endowment focuses on companies' external environment. Apart from location choice and cultural distance which have been intensively studied in international business literatures, there are two major factors in this section attracting our attention: network perspectives and industry dynamics.

Dana (2001) points out that SMEs have established networks on all aspects of business activities. On individual level, entrepreneurs and business managers rely on an interpersonal network to exploit business opportunities and information. Ethnic groups, industrial associations and other forms of groups provide business owners a platform to exchange information and knowledge and achieve growth together. On firm level, SMEs not only participate in small business networks but also form alliances with large companies, acting as supplier, outsourcer or buyer. Wright et al. (2007, p. 1021) conclude that from a resource-based perspective, networking provides SMEs the opportunity of utilising 'external tangible and intangible assets' that complement limited internal fungible resources. This is critical for SMEs in the process of market entry. Dimitratos et al. (2012, p. 711) state that network perspective in internationalisation context focuses on 'the extent to which the firm obtains resources from the external environment though alliance creation and social embeddedness in order to use in its activities in markets abroad'. Social networking therefore is an approach of knowledge and opportunity exploration in the foreign market place. Since international SMEs rely on host country knowledge and opportunities to overcome the effects of foreignness, network plays a critical role that determines the outcome of SME market entry activities.

Proposition 4 (a) Social networking facilitates SME performance in internationalisation process.

On the firm level, networking between organisations enables SMEs to act as part of a symbiotic group of firms, cooperating with one another in the markets (Dana, 2001). Similar to social networks, business networks, e.g. business alliances, local partner companies and joint ventures, provide a platform for SMEs to explore external resources and opportunities. Business alliances not only share resources, but also share the risks and shocks of foreignness in the internationalisation process. SMEs could form different business networks with various kinds of companies. Wright et al. (2007, p. 1022) argue that SMEs could be 'pulled into foreign market by large network partners' and 'borrow size and resources' from the companies. Large firms in a business network could facilitate smaller firms' market entering activities. In the meantime, smaller firms have to synchronise their progress with the large network partner to survive the new environment. Alliances with host country firms could also reduce the risks associated with market entry activities and allocate resources more efficiently between local and market exploring firms (Laufs and Schwens, 2014).

Although SME internationalisation strategies are diverse, networks facilitate market entry process by providing resources and opportunities.

Proposition 4 (b) Business alliances facilitate SME performance in internationalisation process.

Environmental factors like company industrial position's impact on SME internationalisation process has been mentioned in many literatures. Zahra and George (2002), for example, argue that environmental elements, that is, industries firms engaged in, could have great impact on firm internationalisation. Similarly, Fernhaber et al. (2007) propose that firms engaged in fast-growing industry, knowledge-intensive industry, highly integrated industry and highly venture capital reliance industry have more likelihood of going global. They point out the linkage between industry endowment of firms and internationalisation, as well as the performance after going global is yet to be explored. Firms engaged in different industrial environments may have great divergence in prior development route before going global. High-tech new ventures, for example, may have a high expectation of globalisation at early stage of establishment and enhance their change capabilities deliberately.

Proposition 4 (c) SMEs engaged in fast-growing, knowledge-intensive, highly integrated, and/or highly venture capital reliance industry have high expectation of globalisation which enables these companies to achieve better performance compared with other companies in different industry.

Resource access and optimisation

Resource position perspective derives from the resource-based theory of firm competitive advantage (Barney, 1991). It has been long established and well developed in international business literatures. The basic assumption is that access to specific non-imitable resources enables firms to outperform competitors (Barney, 1991). Hsu and Pereira (2008) propose a positively related model between company resource position and firm performance after market entry by dividing the process into two stages. First, according to resource-based view, abundant resource offers product advantage (tangible resource) and knowledge enables firms to expand over country borders (intangible resource). Second, three aspects of organisational learning were introduced: social learning, technological learning and market learning which are positively related to firm performance in host markets. A basic assumption is that resource possession has a positive relation with firm performance. Sapienza et al. (2006) define resource fungibility as resource's attribute of whether it could be used in wide range of business functions or focused on certain business operations. Sapienza et al. propose that higher resource fungibility level could reduce the cost of utilising resources which in turn reduces the risks of failure during SMEs' multinationalisation process. Following Penrose's (1959) resource dependence theory, George (2005) argues that it is fungible resources, instead of resource stock as past RBV literature suggests, that facilitate company strategic activities. We therefore propose:

> *Proposition 5* Deploying fungible resources efficiently and effectively could positively influence the outcome of SME market entry activities.

Demographic characteristics of the management team

Management team demographic characteristics, for example manager's demographical background, management team experience, managerial diversity and so on, are important factors influencing SME internationalisation and performance outcomes. Oviatt and McDougall (2005) state that international entrepreneurship (IE) is a behaviour-based that study focuses on proactive actions managers conduct to add new value to company in the context of multinational market entry. The major concern, as Shane and Venkataraman (2000) argue, is on how to find business opportunities and personnel's role in this value-adding adventure. Two factors are critical in this opportunity-identifying process: manager's business experience and managerial team diversity. The first factor, entrepreneur experience, is significant in that entrepreneurs' personal international experience influence the decision-making of time of entry, partnership forming, information collecting, learning capabilities and many other aspects of multinationalisation process (Bingham, 2009; Frishammar and Andersson, 2009). For SMEs, the significance of entrepreneur's role in multinationalisation is more vital compared with established companies. MNEs have a complicated decision-making process which ensures business action follows the right route and looks at the most efficient methods. SMEs often have a less sophisticated management system which means the decision-making relies on individual managers or a few people in the managerial team. The presence of an individual who has in-depth understanding of the external business environment and internal organisation will be vital for SMEs going global. Daily et al. argue that managers with international experience or host country knowledge are favourable when changes happen. SMEs with experienced entrepreneurs and diverse background managerial team members are more likely to achieve efficient and proper decision-making during multinationalisation.

> *Proposition 6* Individual business experience and managerial team diversity have a positive impact on firm performance in the context of internationalisation.

Strategic legitimacy

Strategic legitimacy offers a credibility perspective on the firm's ability to deal with changes. In other words, we look at organisations' attributes on multinationalisation legitimacy. Firms' strategy-making, risk-tolerance level, market entry model and willingness to bring change to the organisation are all factors which measure this credibility. Firm strategy emphasises whether or not the changes have been considered in firm development. SME internationalisation is a strategic decision and business expansion that needs overall consideration. However, in some cases, for example at the initial stage of exporting, the company may have limited strategic orientation on the cross-national boundary activities. The exporting will stay on as a sales or marketing activity without shifting the whole organisational structure (Lu and Beamish, 2001; Shrader et al., 2000). Companies with prior expectation of going global are more likely to put globalisation and consequent impact on organisation into firm strategy. Prior planning and strategy-making enable firms to adapt themselves more quickly to new business models and new marketplace.

Proposition 7 (a) Firms with strategic consideration of internationalisation could more quickly adapt themself to new market and outperform competitors.

The second factor is risk tolerance perspective during market expansion process. Risk tolerance level measures organisation's capability of dealing with risks that come along with internationalisation. There are two kinds of risks in the context of multinationalisation: first, the host country risk, which includes information asymmetry, market unfamiliarity, culture distance and many other concerns conclude as 'freshness cost'; second, the organisational risk, which includes discontinuity of financial support, distance of management, increasing complexity of organisation and other concerns sourced from within the organisation (Shrader et al., 2000). Rasheed (2005) combines two factors, risk tolerance and market entry model, together and proposes that different host market risk level calls for corresponding entry strategy. When the host market risk level is high, non-equity entry may bring down the cost. Frishammar and Andersson (2009) echo Rasheed's proposition and argue that risk-taking in host market has a positive relation with firm's commitment level.

Proposition 7 (b) SMEs with low commitment levels in host country bear lower host market and financial risk exposure.

The last but not least factor is strategic change. Strategic change focuses on firm's change adaptive capability on the strategic level. Strategic change focuses on firm's capability of dealing with change on a strategic level. McDougall and Oviatt (1996) argue that internationalisation brings environmental and organisational changes to a company; these changes should be echoed in firm strategy level otherwise the management efficiency will be in doubt. Environmental contingency theory also supports the view that firm strategy must adapt to external environment to achieve managerial harmony (Westhead et al., 2004). More importantly, strategic change is easier and more effective during the early stage of company development (Teece et al., 1997). Although McDougall and Oviatt (1996) empirically tested the relationship between younger and older firms' strategic change difference, a theoretical framework was only established when Autio et al. (2010) argued that young firms have less well-developed substantive and change capabilities which enable the firm to develop a better change capability when entering foreign markets.

Proposition 7 (c) Firms involved in early strategic change achieve higher management efficiency which in turn leads to better host market performance.

Conclusions and future research directions

Although increasing numbers of studies explore the SME internationalisation, process and consequences, a review of the current status of research is absent. This chapter summarises the prominent theoretical frameworks and empirical evidences of SME internationalisation's impact on firm performance. It defines the frontier of current research by identifying the most prevalent mechanisms and factors that draw on different research perspectives. The significant difference of internationalisation process of SMEs and MNEs has been emphasised. Organisational capability theories, change capabilities and substantive capabilities are the most intensively employed theoretical framework in SME internationalisation analysis. This study includes seven salient mechanisms and 18 factors that are intensively employed in past literatures of SME internationalisation studies: substantive capabilities, for example firm R&D intensity, knowledge stock and business diversity; change capabilities, for example firm dynamic capability, learning capability and absorptive capacity; strategic management and entrepreneurial demographic characteristics; business manager's personal experience and/or managerial team diversity's impact on SME internationalisation process; market entry model's role in SME internationalisation process; resource-based perspective; and resource position's impact on SME internationalisation process. In a nutshell, this chapter develops a framework of how changes produced by internationalisation activities transfer by different mechanisms to firm performance. Aside from the major findings we mentioned above, the literature review also draws a roadmap of future research areas for the exploration of the mechanisms that influence the SME internationalisation process and subsequent firm performance.

In terms of empirical testing, we propose the following three directions that need to be addressed base on this study. First, resource-dependent perspective has been articulated theoretically in SME internationalisation literatures. The empirical test results of its facilitating effects on SME market expansion activities however are inconclusive and limited. Second, KBV and firm dynamic capability theories argue that SMEs rely on the redeployment of knowledge-based resources to overcome the shock of foreignness. Oviatt and McDougall (1994) argue that knowledge is the most outstanding fungible asset that could be explored, accumulated and transferred at low costs. Empirical evidence of such facilitating effects, however, is missing. The difference between knowledge-intensive assets and organisational slacks should be emphasised. Third, as Wright et al. (2007) conclude, performance effects of SME internationalisation literatures are prone to methodological problems. This is partly due to the nature of the empirical data available for testing the SME internationalisation effects. Since a randomly assigned market entry scenario is hardly achievable, all past literature rely on archived data to test the hypotheses.

Managerial and policy-making implications

This study provides invaluable managerial and policy-making implications to both business practitioners and policymakers. Market expansion activities of SMEs are strategic actions business owners or managers deploy to pursue higher margins and achieve sustainable growth. Unlike MNEs and established companies, SME managers enjoy more discretion on the decision-making process of such ventures. Our findings, therefore, could offer a series of useful implications to SME business managers in their strategy-making process.

First, internationalisation as a firm strategy and entrepreneurial activity could indeed improve firm growth. Business managers, especially SME managers, should consider internationalisation as a path to achieve sustainable growth. SMEs with weaker resource position than domestic competitors should take more proactive measures towards market diversification activities. Secondly, SME managers should understand that the underlying logic of a successful internationalisation is not relying on market entry activities per se, but the dynamic learning and capability building process that are associated with the market expansion process. Business managers that plan to explore foreign markets should attach importance to organisational capability building in early stages. Without relevant skills and capabilities, firms could get trapped in the initial stage of hardship and end the action in failure. Thirdly, since resource scarcity is the major source of adversity in the short term, resource allocation and distribution should be planned ahead of action. Fourthly, SME managers should avoid complicated governance structure and adopt alternative resource ownership and flat power structure.

For policymakers, SMEs are an important economic sector that employs a large percentage of the workforce, creates enormous growth and social values, and accounts for many R&D and innovation outputs. For policymakers that aim to promote SME internationalisation, it is critical to understand the process and consequences of such strategic activities. First, it is essential to reduce potential institutional costs for cross-border business activities. This could relieve the initial stage resource drain faced by SMEs when entering foreign markets. Second, encouraging high-tech SMEs to enter the global competition at an early stage could help foster the world's leading technology firms and improve industrial competitiveness in the domestic market. Third, both individual level and regional level networks improve business performance during the internationalisation process. Government should encourage the formation of local industrial clusters and business owner networks. Last but not least, entrepreneurs' knowledge, background and international experience have profound impact on SME internationalisation process. Tolerance of different cultures, positive attitudes towards foreign investment and easy access to modern information and communication technology could provide the essential ground of successful international SMEs.

References

Audretsch, D. (1997). 'Technological regimes, industrial demography and the evolution of industrial structures', *Industrial and Corporate Change*, 6(1), 49–82.

Autio, E. (2005). 'Creative tension: The significance of Ben Oviatt's and Patricia McDougall's article "Toward a theory of international new ventures"', *Journal of International Business Studies*, 36(1), 9–19.

Autio, E., Bruneel, J. and Clarysse, B. (2010). 'Constraint or catalyst? Organisational capabilities and entrepreneurial internationalisation', Imperial College working paper No. 201022.

Autio, E., Sapienza, H.J. and Almeida, J.G. (2000). 'Effects of age at entry, knowledge intensity, and imitability on international growth', *Academic Management Journal*, 43(5), 909–924.

Avlonitis, G.J. and Salavou, H.E. (2007). 'Entrepreneurial orientation of SMEs, product innovativeness, and performance', *Journal of Business Research*, 60(1), 566–575.

Barney, J. (1991). 'Integrating organizational behavior and strategy formulation research: A resource based analysis', *Advances in Strategic Management*, 8(1), 39–61.

Bausch, A. and Krist, M. (2007). 'The effect of context-related moderators on the internationalisation-performance relationship: Evidence from meta-analysis', *Management Science*, 47(3), 319–347.

Bingham, C. (2009). 'Oscillating improvisation: How entrepreneurial firms create success in foreign market entries over time', *Strategic Entrepreneurship Journal*, 3(4), 321–345.

Coff, R.W. (1999). 'When competitive advantage doesn't lead to performance: The resource-based view and stakeholder bargaining power', *Organization Science*, 10(2), 119–213.

Cohen, W.M. and Levinthal, D.A. (1990). 'Absorptive capacity: A new perspective on learning and innovation', *Administrative Science Quarterly*, 35(1), 128–152.

Contractor, F.J. (2007). 'Is international business good for companies? The evolutionary or multi-stage theory of internationalisation vs. the transaction cost perspective', *Management International Review*, 47(3), 453–475.

Dana, L.P. (2001). 'Introduction: Networks, internationalisation, and policy', *Small Business Economics*, 16(2), 57–62.

Dimitratos, P., Lioukas, S. and Carter, S. (2004). 'The relationship between entrepreneurship and international performance: The importance of domestic environment', *International Business Review*, 13(1), 19–41.

Dimitratos, P., Voudouris, I., Plakoyiannaki, E. and Nakos, G. (2012). 'International entrepreneurial culture: Toward a comprehensive opportunity-based operationalization of international entrepreneurship', *International Business Review*, 21(4), 708–721.

Dosi, G. (1982). 'Technological paradigms and technological trajectories', *Research Policy*, 11(3), 147–162.

Dunning, J. (1988). 'The eclectic paradigm of international production: A restatement and some possible extensions', *Journal of International Business Studies*, 19(1), 1–31.

Fernhaber, S.A., McDougall, P.P. and Oviatt, B.M. (2007). 'Exploring the role of industry structure in new venture internationalisation', *Entrepreneurship Theory and Practice*, 31(4), 517–542.

Frenz, M. and Gillies, G. (2009). 'The impact on innovation performance of different sources of knowledge: Evidence from the UK Community Innovation Survey', *Research Policy*, 38(1), 1125–1135.

Frishammar, J. and Andersson, S. (2009). 'The overestimated role of strategic orientations for international performance in smaller firms', *Journal of International Entrepreneurship*, 7(1), 57–77.

Gaur, A.S. and Kumar, V. (2009). 'International diversification, business group affiliation and firm performance: Empirical evidence from India', *British Journal of Management*, 20(2), 172–186.

George, G. (2005). 'Slack resources and the performance of privately held firms', *Academy of Management Journal*, 48(4), 661–675.

Geringer, J.M., Beamish, P.W. and Dacosta, R.C. (1989). 'Diversification strategy and internationalisation: Implications for MNE performance', *Strategic Management Journal*, 10(2), 109–119.

Gilbert, B.A., McDougall, P. and Audretsch, D.B. (2008). 'Knowledge spillovers and new venture performance: An empirical examination', *Journal of Business Venturing*, 23(4), 405–422.

Gray, C. (2006). 'Absorptive capacity, knowledge management and innovation in entrepreneurial small firms', *International Journal of Entrepreneurial Behaviour and Research*, 12(6), 345–360.

Hsu, C. and Pereira, A. (2008). 'Internationalisation and performance: The moderating effects of organisational learning', *The International Journal of Management Science*, 36(2), 188–205.

Jantunen, A., Puumalainen, K., Saarenketo, S. and Kylaheiko, K. (2005). 'Entrepreneurial orientation, dynamic capabilities and international performance', *Journal of International Entrepreneurship*, 3(3), 223–243.

Johanson, J. and Vahlne, J.E. (1977). 'The internationalisation process of the firm: A model of knowledge development and increasing foreign market commitments', *Journal of International Business Studies*, 8(1), 23–32.

—— (1990). 'The mechanism of internationalisation', *International Marketing Review*, 7(4), 11–25.

Keupp, M.M. and Gassmann, O. (2009). 'The competitive advantage of early and rapidly internationalising SMEs in the biotechnology industry: A knowledge based view', *Journal of Management*, 42(3), 350–366.

Kogut, B. and Zander, U. (1992). 'Knowledge of the firm, combinative capabilities, and the replication of technology', *Organization Science*, 3(3), 383–397.

Laufs, K. and Schwens, C. (2014). 'Foreign market entry mode choice of small and medium-sized enterprises: A systematic review and future research agenda', *International Business Review*, 23(6), 1109–1126.

Li, L. (2007). 'Multinationality and performance: A synthetic review and research agenda', *International Journal of Management Reviews*, 9(2), 117–139.

Lu, J.W. and Beamish, P.W. (2001). 'The internationalisation and performance of SMEs', *Strategic Management Journal*, 22(6/7), 565–586.

Malerba, F. and Orsenigo, L. (1993). 'Technological regimes and firm behavior', *Industrial and Corporate Change*, 2(1), 45–71.

McDougall, P.P. and Oviatt, B.M. (1996). 'New venture internationalisation, strategic change, and performance: A follow-up study'. *Journal of Business Venturing*, 11(1), 23–40.

——— (2000). 'International entrepreneurship: The intersection of two research paths', *Academy of Management Journal*, 43(1), 902–906.

McDougall, P.P., Shane, S. and Oviatt, B.M. (1994). 'Explaining the formation of international new ventures: The limits of theories from international-business research', *Journal of Business Venturing* 9(6), 469–487.

Muscio, A. (2007). 'The impact of absorptive capacity on SMEs' collaboration', *Economics of Innovation and New Technology*, 16(8), 653–668.

Orser, B.J., Hogarth-Scott, S. and Riding, A.L. (2000). Performance, firm size, and management problem solving', *Journal of Small Business Management*, 38(4), 42–59.

Oviatt, B.M. and McDougall, P.P. (1994). 'Toward a theory of international new ventures', *Journal of International Business Studies*, 25(1), 45–64.

——— (2005). 'Defining international entrepreneurship and modeling the speed of internationalisation', *Entrepreneurship Theory and Practice*, 29(5), 537–553.

Pangarkar, N. (2008). 'Internationalisation and performance of small- and medium-sized enterprises', *Journal of World Business*, 43(4), 475–485.

Penrose, E.T. (1959). *The Theory of the Growth of the Firm*. New York: John Wiley.

Qian, G. (2002). 'Multinationality, product-diversification, and profitability of emerging US small and medium-sized enterprises', *Journal of Business Venturing*, 17(1), 611–633.

Rasheed, H.S. (2005). 'Foreign entry mode and performance: The moderating effects of environment', *Journal of Small Business Management*, 43(1), 41–54.

Rugman, A.M. and Verbeke, A. (1992). 'A note on the transnational solution and the transaction cost theory of multinational strategic management', *Journal of International Business Studies*, 23(4), 761–771.

Rumelt, R.P. (1984). *Towards a Strategic Theory of the Firm: Competitive Strategy*. Englewood Cliffs, NJ: Prentice Hall.

Sapienza, H.J., Autio, E., George, G. and Zahra, S.A. (2006). 'A capabilities perspective on the effects of early internationalisation on new venture survival and growth', *Academy of Management Review*, 31(4), 914–930.

Shane, S. and Venkataraman, S. (2000). 'The promise of entrepreneurship as a field of research', *Academy of Management Review*, 25(1), 217–226.

Shimizutani, S. and Todo, Y. (2008). 'What determines overseas R&D activities? The case of Japanese multinational firms', *Research Policy*, 37(1), 530–544.

Shrader, R.C., Oviatt, B.M. and McDougall, P.P. (2000). 'How new ventures exploit trade-offs among international risk factors: Lessons for the accelerated internationalisation of the 21st century', *Academy of Management Journal*, 43(6), 1227–1247.

Shuman, J. and Seeger, J. (1986). 'The theory and practice of strategic management in smaller rapid growth firms', *American Journal of Small Business*, 11(1), 7–18.

Sullivan, D. (1994). 'Measuring the degree of internationalisation of a firm', *Journal of International Business Studies*, 25(2), 325–342.

Szulanski, G. (1996). 'Exploring internal stickiness: Impediments to the transfer of best practice within the firm', *Strategic Management Journal*, 17(S2), 27–43.

Teece, D.J. (1986). 'Profiting from technological innovation: Implications for integration, collaboration, licensing and public policy', *Research Policy*, 15(6), 285–305.

—— (2007). 'Explicating dynamic capabilities: The nature and microfoundations of sustainable enterprise performance', *Strategic Management Journal*, 28(13), 1319–1350.

Teece, D.J., Pisano, G. and Shuen, A. (1997). 'Dynamic capabilities and strategic management', *Strategic Management Journal*, 18(7), 509–533.

Vernon, R. (1971). 'Sovereignty at bay: The multinational spread of U.S. enterprises', *Thunderbird International Business Review*, 13(4), 1–3.

Welch, L.S. and Luostarinen, R. (1988). *Internationalisation: Evolution of a Concept: The Internationalisation of the Firm*. London: Thomson.

Westhead, P., Wright, M. and Ucbasaran, D. (2004). 'Internationalisation of private firms: Environmental turbulence and organizational strategies and resources', *Entrepreneurship and Regional Development*, 16(6), 501–522.

Wright, M., Westhead, P. and Ucbasaran, D. (2007). 'Internationalisation of small and medium-sized enterprises (SMEs) and international entrepreneurship: A critique and policy implications', *Regional Studies*, 41(7), 1013–1030.

Zahra, S.A., Ireland, R.D. and Hitt, M.A. (2000). 'International expansion by new venture firms: International diversity, mode of market entry, technological learning, and performance', *Academy of Management Journal*, 43(5), 925–950.

Zahra, S.A. and George, G. (2002). 'Absorptive capacity: A review, reconceptualization, and extension', *Academy of Management Review*, 27(2), 185–203.

Zahra, S.A., Sapienza, H. and Davidsson, P. (2006). 'Entrepreneurship and dynamic capabilities: A review, model and research agenda', *Journal of Management Studies*, 43(4), 917–955.

13

Understanding Internationalisation through the Lens of Social Network Analysis

Yusuf Kurt and Mo Yamin

Introduction

The notion of 'networks' has been applied by a growing number of researchers in different business and management sub-disciplines including organisational studies (Salancik, 1995; Uzzi, 1996; Zaheer and Bell, 2005; Kilduff and Brass, 2010; Tichy et al., 1979), knowledge management (Cross and Parker, 2004; Reagans and McEvily, 2003), innovation (Freeman, 1991; Ahuja, 2000; Dhanaraj and Parkhe, 2006) and international business and marketing (Coviello and Munro, 1997, 1995; Ellis, 2000, 2011; Johanson and Vahlne, 2009; Zhou et al., 2007; Sharma and Blomstermo, 2003; Tikkanen, 1998; Mattsson, 1997; Johanson and Mattsson, 1985). However, while the notion of networks has been a potent idea in the social sciences (Borgatti et al., 2009), most application of the network concept has been criticised for being 'merely descriptive' (ibid.) and not going beyond loose metaphorical narratives.

The advent of Social Network Analysis (SNA) in visualising relationships through mapping social interconnections (sociograms) has enabled a significant shift from loose metaphorical narratives on network relationships to more precise outputs on web of invisible ties among social actors (Knox et al., 2006). SNA can reveal interdependence between social actors and its consequences through employing SNA-specific measurements such as centrality, density and size. The significance of SNA resides in its reference to the importance of social structures, which has been ignored under methodologically individualistic approaches in social science research that has overlooked the interdependence of all social actors through networks (Borgatti and Li, 2009) and thus the potential of social network analysis still remains widely untapped.

In international business and particularly in the literature on firm internationalisation there has been a move away from focusing on firms as

241

'atomistic agents' and towards considering the importance of network linkage and dependence, most sharply demonstrated by the significant revision in the Uppsala model of firm internationalisation (Johanson and Vahlne, 1977, 2009). More broadly, the role of networking and network dependency has been extensively focused in the international business (IB) and internationalisation literatures (Coviello, 2006). However, the key shortcoming has been that the systematic utilisation of social network theories and along with that the application of SNA as an analytical tool to investigate network dimensions (e.g. network density, centrality, reciprocity, frequency, network size and so forth) has been rare. To sum up, even though the SNA hold a great potential, the level of its application as an analytical and methodological tool in internationalisation research is far behind from its potential.

This study aims to highlight the potential value of SNA for the IB research, particularly in the context of firm internationalisation. The arguments are developed with reference to the revised Uppsala model in which internationalisation is regarded as overcoming liability of outsidership and building insidership in the relevant networks. The intended contribution of the present study is to demonstrate the potential of SNA, as an analytical tool, in providing better understanding of network insidership and outsidership in internationalisation research. We specifically argue that:

(a) investigating how the liability of outsidership can effectively be overcome requires a bifocal perspective, namely one that focuses on the firm that seeks an insider position in a relevant network (the 'outside-in') and also one that considers the perspective of an insider considering to 'open doors' for the outsider (the 'insider-out')

(b) both the 'outsider-in' and the 'insider-out' perspectives are strongly shaped by the structural and positioning features of social networks. This then leads to considering the SNA as a descriptive tool re structural and positional attributes of networks that inform the analysis of the relationship between network attributes and the overcoming of the liability of outsidership.

The remainder of the chapter is structured as follows. Section 2 will provide an overview on the application of network approaches in various studies in the IB literature. Section 3 provides a synopsis of SNA, emphasising the key constructs and measures that constitute the core tools of the analysis and also what internationalisation implications may be generated from the application of these tools. Section 4 will be devoted to understanding internationalisation process from LOO perspective and bringing SNA into the research context. In the last section, concluding remarks will be given with implications for practice and directions for future SNA-applied internationalisation research.

Network perspectives in IB research

The debate on whether firms' internal resources and capabilities or external resources constitute firms' competitive advantages, which is seen as a prerequisite of success in international operations, has a long history in the literature (Barney, 1991; Gulati, 1999; Gulati et al., 2000). Whereas the Resource-Based View (RBV) has exclusively focused on internal resources and capabilities of firms, the network literature has highlighted 'the importance of external resources available to the firm through its networks' (Zaheer and Bell, 2005, p. 809). Scholars' interest in network approach has gradually increased over time, and has extended and enriched the RBV approach (e.g. Luo, 2003; Lavie, 2006; Chetty and Agndal, 2007; Kiss and Danis, 2008; Zhou, Wu and Luo, 2007).

The network concept has also been influential via the 'market-as-networks' (MAN) approach (Johanson and Mattsson, 1992; Mattsson, 1997; McLoughlin and Horan, 2002; Johanson and Vahlne, 2011). As highlighted by Johanson and Mattson (1992), markets are understood as systems of networks of relationships among social and economic actors who are highly interdependent (Johanson and Mattsson, 1988, 1994; McLoughlin and Horan, 2002). Johanson and Vahlne (2011, p. 485) proposed that markets are networks of business relationships and importantly regard internationalisation as a process of building insidership position in the relevant network of the targeted market, overcoming the liability of outsidership.

While the network concept has influenced internationalisation research via the network extension of the RBV and the MAN approaches, the influence of another important network approach, namely social network theory and the SNA, has, by comparison, been very rare. This is illustrated by Table 13.1 below which provides overviews of a representative number of recent studies of internationalisation where the network concept has been a key element.

Even though the majority of internationalisation studies have not explicitly considered the relevance of social network theories and the SNA, their relevance has nevertheless been acknowledged by key authors (Coviello, 2006; Johansson and Vahlne, 2009; Vahlne and Johanson, 2013) who have indicated that networks are dynamic and thus revealing structural and interactional dynamics of networks is quite important to understanding their effect on internationalisation (Coviello, 2006). Vahlne and Johansson (2013), while upholding the MAN perspective, acknowledge that inter-firm relationships display different structural patterns of interconnections. Building insidership positions in the relevant network provides several advantages for firms, such as improving dynamic capabilities, learning, internationalising and accessing resources (ibid.). However, structures of the network in which firms build their insidership position affect the value of insidership for the firm. Thus, while the

Table 13.1 Selected studies applying network approach

Study/Journal	Motivation for applying network approach	Analytical lens	Application of SNA
Johanson and Vahlne (2009, *Journal of International Business Studies*)	'[M]arkets are networks of relationships in which firms are linked to each other in various, complex and, to a considerable extent, invisible patterns . . . our original model needs to be developed further in light of such clear evidence of the importance of networks in the internationalization of firms.' (p. 1411)	*Markets-as-Networks View* 'Our core argument is based on business network research...markets are networks of relationships in which firms are linked to each other in various, complex and, to a considerable extent, invisible patterns.' (p. 1411)	Not Applied
Coviello and Munro (1995, *European Journal of Marketing*)	'In particular, the research focuses on their use of network relationships to pursue foreign market opportunities and conduct international marketing activities. This research article endeavours to offer new insights into the international market development activities...the objective of this article is to examine the impact of network relationships on: (1) international market development, and (2) marketing-related activities within international markets.' (pp. 49–51)	*Markets-as-Networks View* 'In network theory, markets are depicted as a system of relationships among a number of players including customers, suppliers, competitors and private and public support agencies.' (p. 50)	Not Applied
Coviello (2006, *Journal of International Business Studies*)	'[T]he purpose of this study is to assess the network dynamics of INVs. Our focus is on INV networks rather than the INV per se, and the network is positioned as the "dependent variable."' (p. 714)	*Structural/Positional Approach* '...the general question guiding this research: what are the network dynamics of INVs in terms of the structural and interactional patterns at various stages of evolution?' (p. 717)	Partially Applied
Loane and Bell (2006, *International Marketing Review*)	'[T]he focus...is on networking dimensions of rapid internationalisation; namely, on how decision-makers acquire, develop, maintain and exploit networks, on the nature of such networks in terms of "strong" or "weak" ties and on their specific impact upon internationalisation activities.' (p. 471)	*Extension of Resource-Based View* 'Following a synthesis of the extant international networking literature and the integration of resource- and knowledge based views (RBV and KBV) of internationalisation, we describe the research approach adopted in the present enquiry.' (p. 468)	Not Applied

Elg, Ghauri and Tarnovskaya (2008, *International Marketing Review*)	'We argue that the position achieved by a firm as it establishes itself on an emerging market will depend on whether it is able to perform efficient matching and networking activities on that market or not....This study sets out to augment our understanding of the role of a retailer's stakeholder relationships on different levels during market entry by applying a network approach.' (pp. 676–677)	*Markets-as-Networks View* 'It is therefore important to look into the role of relationships with different types of socio-political actors in the process of entering an emerging market.' (p. 675)	Not Applied
Kontinen and Ojala (2011, *International Business Review*)	'The aim of this study was to understand how the network ties of family SMEs function in recognizing opportunities to enter foreign markets.' (p. 441)	*Markets-as-Networks View* 'Internationalization is related to the development of network ties with other firms belonging to a network in a foreign market. These ties between firms in different markets act as bridges facilitating foreign market entry.' (p. 441)	Not Applied
Zhou, Wu and Luo (2007, *Journal of International Business Studies*)	'We draw on the social network theories and explain the performance implications of internationalization in SMEs. In line with the theorization of internationalization of SMEs as a process of social dynamics through networking strategies...we postulate a mediating mechanism of social networks underlying the relationship between internationalization orientations and performance outcomes.' (p. 675)	*Extension of Resource-based View* 'We explain that internationally oriented SMEs deploy home-based social networks as an efficient means of obtaining information resources....The central foundation of social network theories is the transmission of knowledge or useful information through interpersonal ties and social contacts with individuals.' (p. 676)	Not Applied
Sharma and Blomstermo (2003; *International Business Review*)	'The purpose of this paper is to contribute to the development of theory by explaining the internationalization process of Born Globals. We propose that models emphasising knowledge and (network) ties are suitable for this purpose. This is appropriate because the ties that firms have may help them to go international by supplying information about clients and markets.' (p. 740)	*Extension of Resource-based View* 'Network research emphasizes the importance of inter-firm ties in accumulating and utilizing knowledge....Firms' ties provide channels for sharing knowledge as well as the motivation to do so.' (p. 744)	Not Applied

Continued

Table 13.1 Continued

Study/Journal	Motivation for applying network approach	Analytical lens	Application of SNA
Coviello (2005, *Qualitative Market Research: An International Journal*)	'…a method enabling empirical assessment of both the structure of the network and the nature of the interactions/relationships between network actors is required. What then, is the appropriate method by which to conduct such an analysis? To address this question, we turn to a discussion of how to assess network structure and interactions over time by applying a bifocal analytic lens to the research method.' (p. 42)	*Structural/Positional Approach* 'Network research is multi-dimensional in that it can involve analysis of network size and structure, the interactional processes by which network structures are created…empirical assessment of both the structure of the network and the nature of the interactions/relationships between network actors is required.' (pp. 39–42)	Partially Applied
Hilmersson and Jansson (2012, *Internal Business Review*)	'[W]e address two core aspects associated with the business network entry process…we assess how the SME initiates and develops relationships when plugging into the new business network.… Our theory is centred on four core constructs developed from literature: network structures and positions, entry nodes and processes. It is a synthesis of established theories and constructs relevant for examining how SMEs establish insidership positions in institutionally different business networks.' (pp. 683–685)	*Structural/Positional Approach* 'We address the entire network evolvement process in the local foreign market by studying how the entrant firm's network position develops over time as it moves from outsidership to insidership.' (p. 683)	Not Applied
Yli-Renko, Autio and Tontti (2002, *International Business Review*)	'In this study, we attempt to capture both the "network structural" and "relational" aspects of social capital and to look at the exchange and assimilation of both tacit and explicit information.…The model aims at explaining the role of intra- and inter-organizational relationships in building the firm's distinctive knowledge base and in achieving international growth.' (p. 282)	*Extension of Resource-based View* 'We will lay out our arguments on how firms can leverage social capital in their external relationships to facilitate knowledge acquisition and experiential learning…social networks provided entrepreneurs with access to external information and advice, as well as other resources.' (pp. 284–285)	Not Applied

Source	Description	View	
Chetty and Agndal (2007, *Journal of International Marketing*)	'Using the network approach, the authors develop three categories of social capital and discuss their role in influencing mode change.... We contribute to the change in internationalization mode literature by using the network approach as a framework...we focus on the resources that a firm acquires through its network, which is referred to as social capital, and how this influences the change in internationalization mode.' (pp. 1–6)	*Extension of Resource-based View* 'One of the major constraints for small and medium-sized enterprises (SMEs) as they go through the internationalization process is that they lack resources...a way to overcome this limitation is for firms to acquire these resources through their business networks.' (p. 2)	Not Applied
Ojala (2009, *International Business Review*)	'[T]his study is aimed to analyze firms' activities in developing network relationships, their focal network relationships, and the impact of these relationships to the market and entry mode choice of knowledge-intensive SMEs when they enter a physically distant market for their products...contributes to the network theory in the context of internationalization of knowledge-intensive SMEs by analyzing market entries in settings where firms are entering an attractive but physically distant market for their products.' (p. 51)	*Markets-as- Networks View* 'Firms' network relationships have been seen as the major initiators in the internationalization process where firms are following their networks to foreign markets...network relationships can act as a bridge to foreign markets.' (p. 50)	Not Applied

MAN perspective can potentially inform the internationalisation process (e.g. Ojala, 2009; Elg et al., 2008), the full realisation of this potential may require revealing the structures of networks where firms build their insidership position. In a similar vein Johanson and Vahlne (2009, p. 1413) have observed that 'the research that has been done to date generally has studied the ways in which networks influence internationalisation, without discussing how those networks have been created, and without considering the network structure in the country or countries firms entered'.

We conclude that a key motivation for applying social network theory and hence the SNA is the observation that network resources are differentially available to firms. As noted by Ter Wal and Boschma (2009, p. 741), 'it is a rule rather than an exception that networks will be unevenly distributed among firms'. The type of opportunities available to firms is dependent on the characteristics of their relationships and network structure (Andersson et al., 2005). In other words, finding and exploiting opportunities is contingent on firms' network structure and relationships. There is no objective opportunity which is evenly distributed to all firms in a network. Different network structures and actor positions generate different advantages. Therefore, through employing a robust social network methodology built on social network theory, the system of resource dissemination can be revealed more systematically by mapping the relationships.

What is social network analysis?

In their seminal book, Wasserman and Faust (1994, p. 20) defined social network as 'a finite set or sets of actors and the relation or relations defined on them'. Different level and type of social units (e.g. individuals, firms, organisations, and non-human agents) are regarded as actors in social network analysis (Borgatti and Li, 2009; Contractor et al., 2006). Network-based research aims to find out how actors are connected to one another and thus influence one another's behaviour (connectionist view), or how their interactions are affected by the structure of overall network (structuralist view) (Hennig et al., 2013). SNA holds an advantage of providing visual descriptions of relationships through using mathematical and graphical techniques (Hanneman and Riddle, 2005). Employing SNA, which allows sophisticated analysis and comparisons of network characteristics, will enable the researcher to 'trace the deeper aspects of the network in its social context; address the organisation system or network as a whole; capture important dynamic dimensions of the network' (Coviello, 2005, p. 43). As network perspectives enable better representation and explanation for complex dependencies which would not be captured in population samples, more and more phenomena are being conceptualised under network paradigms (Hennig et al., 2013). In methodological application of SNA, there are two main constructs: network structure and positioning.

Actors in a network are not equally positioned; while some actors are centrally positioned and occupy critical positions, others are located in less strategic positions. An actor's position can affect the level of potential resources that can be exploited by the actor and its control power within the network. For instance, centrally positioned actors that have higher number of direct ties have advantage in terms of accessing more network assets and less chance of missing vital resources such as information and knowledge (Bell, 2005). Likewise different network structural attributes also create distinctive outcomes such as different level of information, opportunity, and strategic resources. SNA offers some measurements through which an actor's centrality or their number of direct ties can be revealed. The measurements for detecting actor positioning include degree centrality, betweenness centrality and structural holes, whereas measurements for network structures include density, cohesiveness and core-periphery (Giuliani and Pietrobelli, 2011). Even though a wide variety of measurements are available in SNA, whole-network measures are grouped into two as cohesion and shape measures (Borgatti et al., 2013). In order to clarify measurement understandings, some widely used measurements are explained in Table 13.2.

Internationalisation from liability of outsidership perspective

In the original Uppsala Model, internationalisation was defined as a gradual and incremental process though which firms increase their foreign market commitment starting from the markets that have lower physical distance (Johanson and Vahlne, 1977). In the revisited models overcoming liability of foreignness to relevant foreign markets was replaced by overcoming liability of outsidership to the relevant networks through importing business network approach into their research (Johanson and Vahlne, 2003, 2009). The importance of networks in internationalisation was strongly emphasised by indicating that 'internationalisation process is pursued in a network' by Johanson and Vahlne (2009, p. 1424). Liability of outsidership was proposed as the fundamental barrier for internationalisation and opportunity recognition in foreign markets. Outsidership is regarded as the source of uncertainty for internationalising firms and it is stated that 'outsidership, in relation to the relevant network...is the root of uncertainty' (ibid., p. 1411). As markets comprise a complex and invisible web of relationships, being an insider in a relevant network decreases uncertainty and risk perception about foreign markets, and hence facilitate internationalisation process. A firm which is well positioned in the relevant network is defined as an 'insider'. On the other hand, a firm which does not have a well-established position in the relevant network which may

Table 13.2 Structural and positioning measurements of SNA

SNA measurements	Illustration	Description	Implications for internationalisation
Degree Centrality *(Actor Positioning Construct)*		It indicates an actor's number of direct ties in the network. Node A has higher degree centrality with high number of direct ties to other nodes. An actor's degree centrality can be calculated without getting network data of the whole network in which the actor is embedded.	Connection a nodal partner (A) with high degree centrality in the relevant network provides better access to market information, knowledge and resources for the focal company. Higher centrality leads accessing more network resources and information. The nodal partner has more flexibility in having willingness and ability to 'open the doors' for the focal firm to become an insider, as it is not restricted by dense network structure.
Eigenvector Centrality *(Actor Positioning Construct)*		Nodes that are tied to well-connected nodes have higher eigenvector centrality. Even though node A and B have same degree of centrality, node A has higher score as it is connected to a central node. Each actor's 'centrality is proportional to sum of centralities of the nodes it is adjacent to....' (Borgatti et al., 2013, p. 168)	Connecting to a nodal partner (B) that has high degree centrality in the targeted network can increase the focal firms' access to more market information and knowledge requiring for internationalisation. The nodal partner has more flexibility in having willingness and ability to 'open the doors' for the focal firm to become an insider, as it is not restricted by dense network structure.
Structural Holes *(Actor Positioning Construct)*		Structural holes position refers to brokering relationships between otherwise disconnected groups in the network. Node A in the figure occupies a bridging/ structural holes position. Structural holes	Connecting an insider that occupies a structural holes position (A) in the relevant network can generate more novel non-redundant information and opportunities from various actors for the

	create competitive advantages for those whose relationships span across the holes.	focal company. The nodal partner has more flexibility in having willingness and ability to 'open the doors' for the focal firm to become an insider, as it is not restricted by dense network structure.
Core-Periphery (*Network Structure Construct*)	'A core/periphery network structure is characterised by a cohesive subgroup of core actors and a set of peripheral actors that are loosely connected to the core' (Cattani and Ferriani, 2008, p. 826). Central actors are much better and densely connected than peripheral actors.	Forming networks with actors that occupy positions in dense structures (core actors) provides advantages in access tacit and sensitive information and strategic resources easily and fast compared to actors in periphery. The nodal partner's willingness and ability to 'open the doors' for the focal firm to become an insider can be restricted by dense network structure.
Clique (*Network Structure Construct*)	As a subset of whole network, all actors in a clique are connected directly through intense, direct and reciprocal ties to one another.	Building a network position with actors in a clique in the relevant networks can provide advantages such as high level of trust, cooperation, flow of resources and monitoring within the clique for the focal firm. The nodal partner's willingness and ability to 'open the doors' for the focal firm to become an insider can be restricted by dense network structure.

Source: Adapted from Giuliani and Pietrobelli (2011).

be an outcome of liability of foreignness is known as 'outsider' (Johanson and Vahlne, 2009). Firms suffer from liability of outsidership when they have no network position in the targeted foreign market networks. Although 'insidership' was offered as crucial to the internationalisation process, how this status is gained is not considered in sufficient detail. The authors implied that the process through which 'outsidership ' is overcome may be due to happenstance: when a potential partner in a relevant network starts doing business with the focal firm through an ad hoc order, or firms can intentionally seek a network to build insidership position.

The process of overcoming the liability of outsidership

In order to better understand the process through which outsidership is overcome we need to address two main issues: (a) is the process a passive one or is it an active one where firms deliberately take steps to compensate for their outsidership through strategically building insider positions; (b) how is the process of building insidership affected by key structural attributes of the 'targeted' networks and positional attributes of connected actors.

The question of whether firms actively and deliberately seek networks to overcome liability of outsidership or are an autonomous evolutionary process needs to be clarified (Johanson and Vahlne, 2009; Schweizer, 2013). The formation of relationships with actors from targeted networks can be either an active or passive process. In their buyer–seller activeness–passiveness comparison, Johanson and Mattsson (1988) addressed that in active networking initiatives are taken proactively by sellers, whereas in passive networking sellers reactively respond to the initiations taken by buyers. Building on Johanson and Vahlne's (2009) active networking refers to a systematic search of an outsider for relevant networks and actors, yet passive networking happens as a result of ad hoc events between insider and outsider, such as unsolicited orders (Johanson and Vahlne, 2006; Kontinen and Ojala, 2011). There are two related –perspectives: social network and resource-based view which discuss whether overcoming the liability of outsidership and network creation is a passive or active process. Social network view argues that firms are relatively passive and the liability of outsidership is overcome through developing previously existing networks as an evolutionary process over time. This perspective argues that relationships evolve organically though existing relationships and circumstances (Chetty and Patterson, 2002). On the other hand, the other perspective, based on RBV view, argues that firms seek and form new relationships depending on their lack of resources, and thus they compensate their competitive disadvantages (Ahuja, 2000; Schweizer, 2013). Therefore, firms consciously build relationships and become insiders in a strategically chosen network in order to acquire complementary resources necessary for internationalisation. Even though both perspectives bring some important points onto the stage, resource-based view, which emphasises a more conscious and active firm behaviour in network seeking, has come to prominence in many studies (e.g. Hite and Hesterly, 2001; Larson and Star, 1993; Crick and Spence, 2005; Gilmore et al., 2006; Loane and Bell, 2006; Ojala, 2009). The relevance of active network-seeking in knowledge acquisition and foreign market expansion has been emphasised in several studies (Loane and Bell, 2006; Gabrielsson et al., 2008; Ojala, 2009). Similarly, from SNA point of view, we build our arguments that firms taking deliberate internationalisation decisions actively seek their target networks. So, internationalisation and overcoming the liability of outsidership can be seen as an outcome of deliberate actions. Otherwise, if a firm only responds to the opportunities emerging coincidentally, it means the firm does not really have a deliberate intention to internationalise; thus it may end up in a market serendipitously. Hence, revealing or knowing network structures and attributes provide no benefit to them. Besides, these two perspectives are not mutually exclusive. Building an insidership position is an ongoing process, hence firms can both follow their existing relationships for further network formation and actively seek networks based on the resources they lack or need. For instance, firms can initially learn about the targeted networks through existing relationships, which are not necessarily with the actors from the target market. This process eventually enables firms to become more familiar with the targeted network, and then build strategic insidership positions.

Network dependency of overcoming liability of outsidership

Overcoming the liability of outsidership (LOO) is a bilateral engagement and requires motivation and commitment of both insider and outsider. Therefore, it is necessary to take structural and positional attributes of networks in which outsider seeks for building insidership position. So, a broader lens that covers both 'outside-in' and 'inside-out' perspectives is required. However, this process accommodates both benefits and risks. As indicated by Johanson and Vahlne, (2001, p. 19), 'to enter a network from outside requires that other actors have to be motivated to engage in interaction, something which is resource demanding, and which may require several firms to make adaptations in their ways of performing business'. Building an insidership in the targeted networks requires not only outsider's motivation and initiatives but also insider's motivation to open the doors for the outsider which is resource demanding. Moreover, insiders' behaviours are network dependent, as they are dependent on one another's resource and sanction. Thus, network structure and actor positioning are important determinants of insider's behaviours for accepting the outsider into the network. In the extant literature, network-based models have been mainly argued through two structural perspectives: structural holes and network closure. Basically these two arguments are grounded in the social capital phenomena. Social capital is defined as 'the sum of the actual and potential resources embedded within, available through, and derived from the network of relationships possessed by an individual or social unit' (Nahapiet and Ghoshal, 1998, p. 243). Even though there have been various definitions of social capital by many scholars (e.g. Coleman, 1988; Burt, 1992; Lin, 1999), '...they agree on a social-capital metaphor in which social structure is a kind of capital that can create for certain individuals or groups a competitive advantage in pursuing their ends' (Burt, 2008, p. 32). Although social capital arguments admit that actors doing better are those who are better connected, disagreements are based in different perspectives on the meaning of *'better connected'* (ibid.). Network closure approach advocates that social capital is generated in dense network structures. On the other hand, structural holes argument asserts that brokering otherwise connected networks creates social capital. From internationalisation and LOO perspectives, rather than building a one-way argument on whether network closure or structural holes are more beneficial, it is necessary to conceptualise in what conditions and for which outcomes denser or sparser networks can generate better return. A more beneficial return of insidership position can be achieved when the type of network structure matches with the type of necessary market knowledge. Previous studies (Hansen, 1999; Uzzi, 1996; Reagans and McEvily, 2003; Granovetter, 1985) indicated that strong ties and network closure promote the flow of complex tacit knowledge, whereas structural holes and weak ties enable tapping into simple information in a timely manner. Tacitness can be defined as 'the degree to which knowledge is difficult to codify (e.g. in writing) and articulate' (Reagans and McEvily, 2003, p. 245). So strong networks and cohesive network structures can work more efficiently when the outsider is seeking tacit knowledge. On the contrary, weak ties or open network can promote the flow of market-related information and codifiable knowledge, which is the case when the physical distance is low. Hence, network structure does not only affect the motivations of insider and outsider to interact but also their ability to exchange resources. So, it is initially necessary to build a comprehensive understanding of network structure under Coleman's (1988) and Burt's (1992) social capital arguments, before bringing SNA to the stage as a network structure–revealing tool.

Network closure – cohesion

One of the mainstream network-based social capital perspectives is network closure which emphasises the positive impact of dense network structures on developing trust and cooperative exchanges (Gargiulo and Benassi, 2000). Based on the question of how certain groups can generate more or less social capital, Coleman (1994) have extensively focused on network closure as a source of social capital. Basically, Coleman's (1988, 1994) view of social capital asserts that networks with closure, in which all actors are connected, generate more social capital. According to Coleman (1994) network closure creates network properties such as norms, trust and sanctions which curb opportunism, foster mobilisation of network resources among and generation of social capital for group members. Cooperative behaviours and trust among actors can be enhanced within closely connected network structures. As highlighted by Gargiulo and Benassi (2000) network closure surrounding an actor determines the level social capital available to him/her. Network closure facilitates information and knowledge flows among network members, especially tacit type of knowledge (Reagans and McEvily, 2003). On the other hand, building relationships in densely connected regions of the network requires relatively higher level of resource investment in order to maintain strong relations, compared to building weak ties. Willingness and motivation of actors to deal with these costs can be stimulated with certain values provided by dense networks such as effective diffusion of tacit knowledge, supporting relations, building legitimacy in the network and so on.

Network closure can provide strong support and sponsorship for becoming legitimate players in the market. Adler and Kwon (2002, p. 25) indicated that 'closure provides social capital's cohesiveness benefits within an organisation or community; structural holes in the focal actor's external linkages provide cost-effective resources for competitive action'. Network closure increases trust and decreases the competitive and motivational impediments, and thus facilitates flow of knowledge and information (Reagans and McEvily, 2003). Insiders can be more cooperative in sharing knowledge and information when strong third party ties surround a relationship, and cooperative norms and trust are created (Reagans and McEvily, 2003). Social cohesion can increase the motivation and willingness of insiders to devote resources and time to assist network members (ibid.). However, since network members are highly interdependent it could be hard to create space for a newcomer which can serve as a drawback of network cohesion in the targeted network.

Network range – structural holes

Alternatively, open networks are proposed as the potential sources of generating social capital (Burt, 1992). It was indicated that bridging positions between densely connected regions generates more social capital as an outcome of brokerage function (Walker et al., 1997). The actors whose relationships span over the holes in social structure, otherwise unconnected regions, have an advantage of accessing and controlling the flow of non-redundant resources and information. Burt's perspective argues that open networks provide more flexibility for actors whereas closed networks reduce actors' independence (Walker et al., 1997). Not only flexibility, occupying a bridging position across structural holes also provides advantages such as accessing higher volume of novel and non-redundant information from separate groups and controlling flow of information in a timely manner. By contrast with these assets, open networks cannot provide the same benefit of curbing opportunistic actions as closed networks (Ahuja, 2000). Sparse networks maximise information benefits through exploiting structural holes and exchanging information between various actors from different social, organisation and institutional boundaries (Reagans and McEvily, 2003; Hilmersson and Jansson, 2012). Closed networks are more efficient in diffusion of tacit and market-specific information, while open networks provide the advantage of accessing explicit knowledge and novel information. However, closed networks require a relatively higher level of investment into the networks. Hence, a trade-off exists for actors while building insidership position in closed or open networks.

Network-dependent insider and outsider motivations to overcome LOO

Structural attributes of targeted networks affect both the network value for outsider and also insider's motivation to facilitate network entry of outsider. 'Network value for outsider' refers to the outsider's evaluation about the value of forming relationships to achieve an insidership position. If an outsider believes that the value of building insidership is high, the motivation for investing more resources will also be higher. The outsider's value assessment might be based on cost–benefit analysis. For instance, building an insidership in a dense targeted network requires high level of time and resource investment, which involves extra cost. However, if the targeted network is in a highly physical distant market, in which the outsider needs tacit market information, support and legitimacy, the benefits of the insidership can balance the cost. On the other hand, 'insider's motivation to facilitate network entry' represents how eager the insider is to create a space for the outsider, which is affected by the value evaluation of the insider, and constraints arise from the structure of the insider's network. For instance, insiders who are strongly embedded in cohesive networks cannot have enough flexibility and autonomy to create new space for an outsider without getting sanctions from the others. Even though network cohesion facilitates cooperation, safety and creation of social capital, they may also impede network actors from entering into or promoting new cooperative relationships with actors from the outside of its network (Gargiulo and Benassi, 2000). The rigidity of cohesive networks can be seen as the 'dark side' which eventually affects the flexibility of the insider actors. Since these two network attributes are not mutually exclusive, insiders in cohesive dense networks might want to build relationships in order to balance their cohesiveness benefits with structural holes' opportunities through bridging to an outsider. As indicated by Reagans, Zuckerman and McEvily (2004), most productive teams are those which can combine internal cohesive structure with external networks with structural holes. So it can be said that optimal network needs to combine elements of both cohesion and range depending of the type of necessary knowledge for internationalisation (Reagans and McEvily, 2003).

Understanding LOO from SNA lenses

Social network analysis enables examining how different attributes of network structures affect the resource exchange (Haythornthwaite, 1996). Since building insidership position is a way of accessing necessary market-related information and resources, SNA can help to reveal how different network structures affect the value of the insidership. The value of different network structures – cohesion or range – can vary in different contexts, depending on what actors look for and seek to achieve (Stam et al., 2014). Hence, internationalising firms should decide which type of network structure and position would be better to build an insidership depending on their requirements. Even though both closure and sparse networks can generate benefits, from the liability of outsidership perspective, the value of these networks depends on various other circumstances, such as other sources of social capital, type of information and degree of liability of foreignness. From liability of outsidership perspective, the value of network closure or structural holes can vary depending on physical distance between markets in which insider's and outsider's networks are embedded. Overcoming the liability of outsidership may not enable the overcoming liability of foreignness to the same extent. The value of insidership position changes in relation to the physical distance and thus the liability of foreignness. Building insidership position in sparse networks can be effective when physical distance is low. However, if the physical distance is high then it is more efficient to build insidership position in closure network structures in order to access tacit and market-specific knowledge. For instance, when the uncertainty is high and there is less commonality between the environments of the insider and outsider – including institutional commonalities – it could be beneficial to build an insidership position into densely connected networks. Value of insidership positions can be better understood through revealing network structures and actor positioning which can be revealed with analytical techniques provided by SNA (Haythornthwaite, 1996). Table 13.3 will be evaluated in the light of two phenomena: physical distance and type of necessary knowledge.

Here, a few SNA-related network measurements help us to understand how different network structure can affect insidership position of an actor from social capital and structural holes perspectives. Insidership position is created through connecting the target network, however the benefits may vary based on different network structures, actor positioning and to whom the actor is connected. Not only actor's own positioning but also the position of the connected actor (insider) in the targeted network is crucial. The

Table 13.3 Value of insidership positions with social capital/structural holes perspectives

SNA measurements	Value of insidership position	Illustration	Social capital/structural holes perspectives
Betweenness Centrality	If a firm builds its insidership position through connecting an actor with high betweenness centrality in the targeted network, this may increase the level of opportunities and resources accessed through insidership position as the connected actor's position generates abundant resources, information and control power. Hence, the more information and resources can be obtained, the liability of foreignness can be decreased.		From Burt's (1992) structural holes point of view, building an insidership position through connecting an actor with high betweenness centrality shows the presence of structural holes in an open network provides cost-effective resources and information, as actor A has control power over the flow of information and resources within the sparse network. This insidership position can work efficiently when the liability of foreignness of outsider is not very high. It could be easier to build insidership compared to dense networks.
Structural Holes	If the firm builds its insidership position through connecting with an actor occupying bridging position in the targeted network, this may enhance the level of novel information and resources the firm can access through this click. Besides, if connecting a foreign network makes the firm a bridge between its own network and the targeted network this insidership position may also generate more resources compared to non-bridging positions.		Connecting an actor that occupies a bridging position can enable the outsider to build insidership position through accessing cost-effective resource and information, as in Burt's (1992) structural holes argument. Structural holes position does not provide the benefits of dense networks, so this may not work effectively with a network from markets with high physical distance, as decreasing the liability of foreignness requires more tacit information about markets.
Core Periphery	Since core actors mostly occupy advantageous positions which enable them to access more information and resources, building an insidership position through connecting core actors in targeted network (network tie A) can increase the level of resources and information obtained. Connecting peripheral actors (Network Tie B) may generate low level of information about the foreign market which does not decrease the liability of foreignness.		From Coleman's (1988) perspective; building insidership through connecting to the central actors which are densely connected can provide cohesiveness benefits of social capital. Under more effective norms and trust, the more tacit social capital is generated in densely connected structural areas of the network. It could be harder to form networks with densely connected actors compared to the peripheral actors which are not restricted with dense connections.

level of benefits insidership position generates depends highly on the level of resources that the connected actors can access. Therefore, the level of insidership also should be assessed through taking the connected actor's position into account. Along with its measurements on actor positioning and network structures such as centrality, structural holes and core-periphery, SNA can work as a significant tool to investigate the value of insidership for both outsider and insider.

Firms' network positions determine whether they are outsider or insider of the targeted foreign network structures. Not only firm position but also structure of networks (e.g. open versus closed networks) in foreign market networks is also given as an important determinant of insidership position. Regarding network structures, plugging into an open network can benefit through providing information from various weak ties and reducing the degree of insidership of the information network (Hilmersson and Jansson, 2012). On the other hand, connecting to a closed network with strong ties, which mostly forms the core of the targeted local business network, enables achieving insidership. Hence, both firms' network positioning and structures of foreign market network determine the status of insidership and the degree of insidership. Hilmersson and Jansson (2012, p. 686) asserted the degree of insidership as the critical aspect of networks. They indicated that the degree of insidership is related to the degree of coupling of the local network, the control of network and competitive position. Therefore, it can be concluded that degree of insidership is one of the key network determinants which influence firm internationalisation. The questions at this point should be how we can accurately measure a firm's degree of insidership for understanding network outcomes on internationalisation. It requires a systematic analytical research tool which provides specific measurement constructs through which the degree of insidership can be determined. Moreover, the evolutionary process of business networks while a firm is shifting from an outsider position to insider position was given in three stages: exposure network, formation network and sustenance network in the study of Hilmersson and Jansson (2012).

Conclusion and applications

This research brings SNA into the internationalisation research context as an innovative and comprehensive methodological tool in parallel with the call 'networks need to be investigated with appropriate methodologies' (Zucchella et al., 2007, p. 277) in the IB literature. In today's world economy, 'quite literally, networks are reshaping the global business architecture' (Parkhe et al., 2006, p. 560). This status quo of the global marketplace increases the necessity for applying a broader lens which takes network relationships into account while investigating drivers and outcomes of firm behaviours. Similarly, internationalisation behaviours and performance of firms can be better understood in their network contexts. This was highlighted by (Gulati et al., 2000, p. 203) as 'the conduct and performance of firms can be more fully understood by examining the network of relationships in which they are embedded'. Therefore, the IB field requires innovative methodologies that could add the missing invisible component to the broad picture in a systematic way and make significant advances in our knowledge, as the traditional research tools fail to provide a robust analysis on network interdependencies.

On the other hand, firm internationalisation has been one of the main research themes of the IB literature and has been widely studied in different research contexts. Network view taken in recent studies in the IB literature could not go beyond a descriptive approach. However, as a systematic research tool borrowed from sociology, SNA provides various structural and positional dimensions through which the effect of networks on firm internationalisation can be better understood. Similarly, this study also shows how different network attributes facilitate or impede the overcoming the LOO through benefiting from SNA. The impact of network attributes in overcoming LOO is focused from both outside-in and inside-out perspectives. Revealing structural and positional attributes of networks through employing SNA-based measurements demonstrates how structures of networks and actors' position affect overcoming liability of outsidership in internationalisation process. The impact of structural and positional attributes of networks is discussed in relevance to physical distance phenomenon, which affects the type of knowledge an internationalisation firm requires.

As discussed, overcoming liability of outsidership and being an insider in a targeted network is seen as a prerequisite for internationalisation. However, forming and sustaining relationships are resource-demanding which creates a burden especially for small firms which experience lack of resources. In that manner, firms should actively and deliberately seek certain network structures within their targeted foreign markets, depending on the type of knowledge and support they require. For instance, building insidership in an open network in a market with close physical distance, which requires relatively lower investment, can work effectively for internationalising firm. Yet this requires a systematic analysis to reveal the network dynamics and structures. Therefore, SNA also provides practical implications for firms and managers, as they can benefit from this systematic analytical tool for revealing network structures and hence developing their strategies in building insidership positions in foreign markets. Future research should benefit from SNA in internationalisation research, especially through applying a longitudinal approach which can demonstrate evolution of structural and positional attributes of network at different stages of internationalisation.

References

Adler, P.S. and Kwon, S.W. (2002). 'Social capital: Prospects for a new concept', *Academy of Management Review*, 27(1), 17–40.

Ahuja, G. (2000). 'Collaboration networks, structural holes, and innovation: A longitudinal study', *Administrative Science Quarterly*, 45(3), 425–455.

Andersson, U., Holm, D.B. and Johanson, M. (2005). 'Opportunities, relational embeddedness and network structure'. In A. Hadjikhani, P. Ghauri, and J. Johanson (eds), *Managing Opportunity Development in Business Networks*. Basingstoke, UK: Palgrave Macmillan.

Barney, J. (1991). 'Firm resources and sustained competitive advantage', *Journal of Management*, 17(1), 99–120.

Bell, G.G. (2005). 'Clusters, networks, and firm innovativeness', *Strategic Management Journal*, 26(3), 287–295.

Borgatti, S.P., Everett, M.G. and Johnson, J.C. (2013). *Analyzing Social Networks*. New York: Sage Publications.

Borgatti, S.P. and Li, X. (2009). 'On social network analysis in a supply chain context', *Journal of Supply Chain Management*, 45(2), 5–22.

Borgatti, S.P., Mehra, A., Brass, D.J. and Labianca, G. (2009). 'Network analysis in the social sciences', *Science*, 323(5916), 892–895.

Burt, R.S. (1992). 'The social structure of competition', In N. Nohria, and R. Eccles (eds), *Networks and Organisations: Structure, Form, and Action*. New York: Harvard Business School Press.

——— (2008). 'Structural holes versus network closure as social capital'. In N. Lin, K. Cook, and R.S. Burt (eds), *Social Capital: Theory and Research*. New Brunswick, NJ: Transaction Publishers.

Cattani, G. and Ferriani, S. (2008). 'A core/periphery perspective on individual creative performance: Social networks and cinematic achievements in the Hollywood film industry', *Organization Science*, 19(6), 824–844.

Chetty, S. and Agndal, H. (2007). 'Social capital and its influence on changes in internationalisation mode among small and medium-sized enterprises', *Journal of International Marketing*, 15(1), 1–29.

Chetty, S. and Patterson, A. (2002). 'Developing internationalisation capability through industry groups: The experience of a telecommunications joint action group', *Journal of Strategic Marketing*, 10(1), 69–89.

Coleman, J.S. (1988). 'Social capital in the creation of human capital', *American Journal of Sociology*, 94(1), 95–120.

——— (1994). *Foundations of Social Theory*. Cambridge, MA: Harvard University Press.

Contractor, N.S., Wasserman, S. and Faust, K. (2006). 'Testing multitheoretical, multi-level hypotheses about organisational networks: An analytic framework and empirical example', *Academy of Management Review*, 31(3), 681–703.

Coviello, N.E. (2005). 'Integrating qualitative and quantitative techniques in network analysis', *Qualitative Market Research: An International Journal*, 8(1), 39–60.

——— (2006). 'The network dynamics of international new ventures', *Journal of International Business Studies*, 37(5), 713–731.

Coviello, N.E. and Munro, H.J. (1995). 'Growing the entrepreneurial firm: Networking for international market development', *European Journal of Marketing*, 29(7), 49–61.

Coviello, N.E. and Munro, H. (1997). 'Network relationships and the internationalisation process of small software firms', *International Business Review*, 6(4), 361–386.

Crick, D. and Spence, M. (2005). 'The internationalisation of "high performing" UK high-tech SMEs: A study of planned and unplanned strategies', *International Business Review*, 14(2), 167–185.

Cross, R.L. and Parker, A. (2004). *The Hidden Power of Social Networks: Understanding How Work Really Gets Done in Organisations*. New York: Harvard Business Press.

Dhanaraj, C. and Parkhe, A. (2006). 'Orchestrating innovation networks', *Academy of Management Review*, 31(3), 659–669.

Elg, U., Ghauri, P.N. and Tarnovskaya, V. (2008). 'The role of networks and matching in market entry to emerging retail markets', *International Marketing Review*, 25(6), 674–699.

Ellis, P. (2000). 'Social ties and foreign market entry', *Journal of International Business Studies*, 31(3), 443–469.

——— (2011). 'Social ties and international entrepreneurship: Opportunities and constraints affecting firm internationalisation', *Journal of International Business Studies*, 42(1), 99–127.

Freeman, C. (1991). 'Networks of innovators: A synthesis of research issues', *Research Policy*, 20(5), 499–514.

Gabrielsson, M., Kirpalani, V., Dimitratos, P., Solberg, C.A. and Zucchella, A. (2008). 'Born globals: Propositions to help advance the theory', *International Business Review*, 17(4), 385–401.

Gargiulo, M. and Benassi, M. (2000). 'Trapped in your own net? Network cohesion, structural holes, and the adaptation of social capital', *Organisation Science*, 11(2), 183–196.

Gilmore, A., Carson, D. and Rocks, S. (2006). 'Networking in SMEs: Evaluating its contribution to marketing activity', *International Business Review*, 15(3), 278–293.

Giuliani, E. and Pietrobelli, C. (2011). 'Social network analysis methodologies for the evaluation of cluster development programs', *Inter-American Development Bank*, 1–46.

Granovetter, M. (1985). 'Economic action and social structure: The problem of embeddedness', *American Journal of Sociology*, 91(3), 481–510.

Gulati, R. (1999). 'Network location and learning: The influence of network resources and firm capabilities on alliance formation', *Strategic Management Journal*, 20(5), 397–420.

Gulati, R., Nohria, N. and Zaheer, A. (2000). 'Guest editors' introduction to the special issue: Strategic networks', *Strategic Management Journal*, 21(3), 199–201.

Hanneman, R.A. and Riddle, M. (2005). *Introduction to Social Network Methods*. Riverside, CA: University of California, Riverside (online textbook).

Hansen, M.T. (1999). 'The search-transfer problem: The role of weak ties in sharing knowledge across organisation subunits', *Administrative Science Quarterly*, 44(1), 82–111.

Haythornthwaite, C. (1996). 'Social network analysis: An approach and technique for the study of information exchange', *Library and Information Science Research*, 18(4), 323–342.

Hennig, M., Brandes, U., Pfeffer, J. and Mergel, I. (2013). *Studying Social Networks: A Guide to Empirical Research*. Chicago: Campus Verlag/University of Chicago Press.

Hilmersson, M. and Jansson, H. (2012). 'International network extension processes to institutionally different markets: Entry nodes and processes of exporting SMEs', *International Business Review*, 21(4), 682–693.

Hite, J.M. and Hesterly, W.S. (2001). 'The evolution of firm networks: From emergence to early growth of the firm', *Strategic Management Journal*, 22(3), 275–286.

Johanson, J. and Mattsson, L.G. (1985). 'Marketing investments and market investments in industrial networks', *International Journal of Research in Marketing*, 2(3), 185–195.

—— (1988). 'Internationalisation in industrial systems: A network approach'. In N. Hood, and J. Vahlne (eds), *Strategies in Global Competition*. New York: Routledge.

—— (1992). *Network Positions and Strategic Action: An Analytical Framework*. London: Routledge.

—— (1994). *The Markets-as-Networks Tradition in Sweden*. London: Springer.

Johanson, J. and Vahlne, J.E. (1977). 'The internationalisation process of the firm: A model of knowledge development and increasing foreign market commitments', *Journal of International Business Studies*, 8(1), 23–32.

—— (2001). 'The mechanism of internationalisation', *International Marketing Review*, 7(4), 11–24.

—— (2003). 'Business relationship learning and commitment in the internationalisation process', *Journal of International Entrepreneurship*, 1(1), 83–101.

—— (2006). 'Commitment and opportunity development in the internationalization process: A note on the Uppsala internationalization process model', *Management International Review*, 46(2), 165–178.

—— (2009). 'The Uppsala internationalisation process model revisited: From liability of foreignness to liability of outsidership', *Journal of International Business Studies*, 40(9), 1411–1431.

—— (2011). 'Markets as networks: Implications for strategy-making', *Journal of the Academy of Marketing Science*, 39(4), 484–491.

Kilduff, M. and Brass, D.J. (2010). 'Job design: A social network perspective', *Journal of Organisational Behavior*, 31(2–3), 309–318.

Kiss, A.N. and Danis, W.M. (2008). 'Country institutional context, social networks, and new venture internationalisation speed', *European Management Journal*, 26(6), 388–399.

Knox, H., Savage, M. and Harvey, P. (2006). 'Social networks and the study of relations: Networks as method, metaphor and form', *Economy and Society*, 35(1), 113–140.

Kontinen, T. and Ojala, A. (2011). 'Network ties in the international opportunity recognition of family SMEs', *International Business Review*, 20(4), 440–453.

Larson, A. and Starr, J. A. (1993). 'A network model of organization formation', *Entrepreneurship Theory and Practice*, 17, 5–5.

Lavie, D. (2006). 'The Competitive Advantage of Interconnected Firms: An Extension of the Resource-Based View', *Academy of Management Review*, 31(3), 638–658.

Lin, N. (1999). 'Building a network theory of social capital', *Connections*, 22(1), 28–51.

Loane, S. and Bell, J. (2006). 'Rapid internationalisation among entrepreneurial firms in Australia, Canada, Ireland and New Zealand: An extension to the network approach', *International Marketing rejview*, 23(5), 467–485.

Luo, Y. (2003). 'Industrial dynamics and managerial networking in an emerging market: The case of China', *Strategic Management Journal*, 24(13), 1315–1327.

Mattsson, L.G. (1997). '"Relationship marketing" and the "markets-as-networks approach": A comparative analysis of two evolving streams of research', *Journal of Marketing Management*, 13(5), 447–461.

McLoughlin, D. and Horan, C. (2002). 'Markets-as-networks: Notes on a unique understanding', *Journal of Business Research*, 55(7), 535–543.

Nahapiet, J. and Ghoshal, S. (1998). 'Social capital, intellectual capital, and the organisational advantage', *Academy of Management Review*, 23(2), 242–266.

Ojala, A. (2009). 'Internationalisation of knowledge-intensive SMEs: The role of network relationships in the entry to a psychically distant market', *International Business Review*, 18(1), 50–59.

Parkhe, A., Wasserman, S. and Ralston, D.A. (2006). 'New frontiers in network theory development', *Academy of Management Review*, 31(3), 560–568.

Reagans, R. and McEvily, B. (2003). 'Network structure and knowledge transfer: The effects of cohesion and range', *Administrative Science Quarterly*, 48(2), 240–267.

Reagans, R., Zuckerman, E. and McEvily, B. (2004). 'How to make the team: Social networks vs. demography as criteria for designing effective teams', *Administrative Science Quarterly*, 49(1), 101–133.

Salancik, G.R. (1995). 'Wanted: A good network theory of organisation', *Administrative Science Quarterly*, 40(2), 345–349.

Schweizer, R. (2013). 'SMEs and networks: Overcoming the liability of outsidership', *Journal of International Entrepreneurship*, 11(1), 80–103.

Sharma, D.D. and Blomstermo, A. (2003). 'The internationalisation process of Born Globals: A network view', *International Business Review*, 12(6), 739–753.

Stam, W., Arzlanian, S. and Elfring, T. (2014). 'Social capital of entrepreneurs and small firm performance: A meta-analysis of contextual and methodological moderators', *Journal of Business Venturing*, 29(1), 152–173.

Ter Wal, A. and Boschma, R.A. (2009). 'Applying social network analysis in economic geography: Framing some key analytic issues', *The Annals of Regional Science*, 43(3), 739–756.

Tichy, N.M., Tushman, M.L. and Fombrun, C. (1979). 'Social network analysis for organisations', *Academy of Management Review*, 4(4), 507–519.

Tikkanen, H. (1998). 'The network approach in analyzing international marketing and purchasing operations: A case study of a European SME's focal net 1992–95', *Journal of Business and Industrial Marketing*, 13(2), 109–131.

Uzzi, B. (1996). 'The sources and consequences of embeddedness for the economic performance of organisations: The network effect', *American Sociological Review*, 61(4), 674–698.

Vahlne, J.E. and Johanson, J. (2013). 'The Uppsala model on evolution of the multinational business enterprise: From internalisation to coordination of networks', *International Marketing Review*, 30(3), 189–210.

Walker, G., Kogut, B. and Shan, W. (1997). 'Social capital, structural holes and the formation of an industry network', *Organisation Science*, 8(2), 109–125.

Wasserman, S. and Faust, K. (1994). *Social Network Analysis: Methods and Applications* (vol. 8). Cambridge: Cambridge University Press.

Yli-Renko, H., Autio, E. and Tontti, V. (2002). 'Social capital, knowledge, and the international growth of technology-based new firms', *International Business Review*, 11(3), 279–304.

Zaheer, A. and Bell, G.G. (2005). 'Benefiting from network position: Firm capabilities, structural holes, and performance', *Strategic Management Journal*, 26(9), 809–825.

Zhou, L., Wu, W. and Luo, X. (2007). 'Internationalisation and the performance of born-global SMEs: The mediating role of social networks', *Journal of International Business Studies*, 38(4), 673–690.

Zucchella, A., Palamara, G. and Denicolai, S. (2007). 'The drivers of the early internationalisation of the firm', *Journal of World Business*, 42(3), 268–280.

Index

Printed and bound by CPI Group (UK) Ltd, Croydon, CR0 4YY